KT-162-429

How to
SELL

hamlyn

How to
SELL

IMPROVE YOUR TECHNIQUE AND MAXIMIZE YOUR SALES

Robert Ashton

**This book is dedicated to my friend Jon Bates,
the man who in 1979 taught me How to Sell**

First published in Great Britain in 2004 by
Hamlyn, an imprint of Octopus Publishing Group Ltd
2-4 Heron Quays, London E14 4JP

ISBN 0 600 61032 2

A CIP catalogue record for this book is available
from the British Library

Printed and bound in China

10 9 8 7 6 5 4 3 2 1

CONTENTS

INTRODUCTION

If you can sell, you can succeed in almost any business role. Selling is about persuading other people to accept your ideas, after they have shared with you the barriers they perceive to what you are proposing. Clearly, anyone who has a job that brings them face to face with a customer has the greatest need for good selling skills, but other people, too, will benefit from becoming more persuasive.

The world of business has changed dramatically since the standard texts on sales technique were written. Towards the end of the last century selling was too often regarded as commercial combat, with the salesperson determined to win at all costs. No prisoners would be taken, and aggressive tactics were used to such an extent that in some sectors legislation was introduced to protect the public from coercion.

The dawn of the new century has seen a dramatic shift in the way business is done. The Internet now plays a major role in the sales process, with prospects – potential customers – able in seconds to identify and explore alternative suppliers from around the globe. Information abounds, and there are few secrets. Geography is no longer a barrier to trade, and your customer is no longer likely to be content to stay with you because you both work in the same city.

There has also been social change. We are more tolerant of diversity, and people care more about the way in which the goods and services they buy have been produced and prepared. Low prices resulting from the exploitation of workers, poor farming practices or the use of components of dubious provenance are no longer acceptable to even the least sophisticated consumer. Information, opinion and propaganda abound in the public arena.

All this means that to sell you have to know why you are the best – being the cheapest will rarely win you lasting success. The buying process is more complex than ever before. Buyers are more knowledgeable, competitors are more visible and everyone is trying to be fair as well as firm.

This book takes you through every step of the sales process. It describes how to find people to approach, how to identify their needs and how to influence their perception, win their commitment and keep in touch with them after the sale has been made.

You may be an experienced sales manager seeking to refresh your skills and pass them on to the team you manage, or you may be someone for whom selling is a new skill you need to understand and embrace.

Whoever you are and whatever your role, you will find no difficult jargon, no patronizing rhetoric and out-of-date techniques. Reading *How to Sell* will develop your understanding of how selling is carried out in our caring and technological age.

This book will take you through every step of the sales process. Whatever your role, you'll find out how to do it better.

1 GETTING ORGANIZED

Unless you are already doing it, selling can be seen as something of a black art. In reality, there is no mystery. It's simply the skill of making it easy for people to buy your product, service or idea.

Sales is another of those experiences best enjoyed by two consenting adults.

GOOD SALESPEOPLE

- **Like helping other people**
- **Have good self-esteem**
- **Are knowledgeable and confident**
- **Can empathize and see other people's views**
- **Are enthusiastic about what they are selling**

What is selling?

Selling is the process by which one person helps another to make the decision to buy something. If you are doing the selling, it is the moment when all your hard work pays off and someone becomes your customer.

Your product or service will already have been defined and a marketing campaign will have made people aware of what it is you are selling. These people are your **prospects**, and sometimes they will have been sufficiently aroused by your marketing efforts to make themselves known to you. At other times you will seek out people who closely match your typical customer profile and approach them 'cold', but more on this later.

What makes a good salesperson?

Someone who can readily establish an emotional empathic link with their prospects should be good at sales. They will be able to focus and direct a conversation that helps their prospect make the decision to buy. Forget the clichéd stories of someone sticking their foot in the door or outstaying their welcome as they attempt to get you to sign up on the spot. Good salespeople are welcomed because they help to resolve indecision, although, of course, the indecision has been partly created by the salesperson doing their job effectively.

To be good at selling, you have to like people and be able to relate to those who may have different values from your own. In fact, you should relish this exposure to new thinking, because if you resent it, you can easily appear arrogant. It's also best to sell products and services you have some interest in. This will stimulate your enthusiasm and thus increase your success rate.

Selling and the overall business process

Selling stands apart from all other commercial activities in that it involves direct, one-to-one contact with potential customers.

Selling vs. marketing

Marketing, with which selling is often confused, is the process by which your product or service is defined and gains brand values and personality. Marketing also embraces the processes of advertising, direct mail and other awareness-raising techniques. As a salesperson, you need to recognize the valuable role marketing activity can play in creating a welcoming climate in your marketplace.

Selling vs. negotiating

The process of negotiation is also sometimes confused with selling. Negotiating uses many of the sales techniques that are described in this book, but it differs in that it is a far more complex process. A negotiator is constantly trading concessions with the other person, working towards a solution that ideally meets the needs of both – sometimes several – parties. Selling skills are needed by negotiators to focus their interactions and gain commitment as each stage of the deal is concluded successfully.

Selling should be fun

Some common fears and phobias can haunt any salesperson's early days in the job. Later, you will find out how to deal with them. Remember, though, that you must be enthusiastic about your product or service and confident in your organization's ability to deliver what you are selling.

SELLING, MARKETING AND NEGOTIATING

SELLING

- Requires one-to-one contact with potential customers
- Is a process for gaining commitment
- Provides valuable market feedback

MARKETING

- Defines products and services
- Develops branding and personality
- Raises awareness in the marketplace

NEGOTIATING

- Can involve complex trading relationship
- Involves the agreed exchange of concessions
- Uses selling techniques along the way

In reality, people do not buy products or services. They buy the things that those products or services can do for them.

FEATURES AND BENEFITS

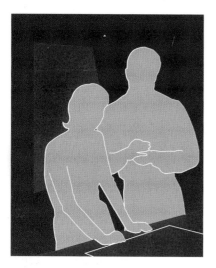

Suppose for a moment you left home at six o'clock in the morning to drive to your first meeting of the day, a two-hour drive from where you live. You've made good time and are within a short distance of your destination. Your tummy rumbles and you pull in to a roadside restaurant. What greets you as you walk in the door is the inviting smell of cooked food. The chances are, even if you planned to have nothing more than a cup of coffee and a Danish pastry, you will be tempted to buy something more substantial.

Stop for a moment and think about what you are interested in when you place your order. Do you really mind where the food came from and whether it is GM free and organically farmed? Probably not. Your mouth

FEATURES VS. BENEFITS

Features define a product or service	Benefits are what appeals about a product or service
What shape is it?	> It will fit in my living room
What colour is it?	> It will match my other saucepans
How much will it pay if I die?	> My children need financial help while they are at university
It has a six-speaker CD sound system	> I love listening to music in my car

is watering and your body craves the satisfaction that has been promised by the smell of the cooked food that greeted you as you walked in.

Features define the product

The waitress comes to take your order but immediately begins to tell you all about the ingredients – the local farm, the regular deliveries that guarantee that everything is fresh every morning. Her eyes glow as she shares with you feature after feature. You glance at your watch. Time is slipping away, and reality kicks in, so you interrupt her: 'I'm sorry, but I only have time for coffee.' She has not only lost a sale but - worse from her point of view - you are now spending a quarter of what you intended as you sat down.

So what went wrong? She was describing the features of the breakfast and all you wanted was the benefit of eating it. Features are the attributes of your product or service that define it – in this instance the thickness of the rasher of bacon, the part of the pig it came from, the way it was smoked (or not) and the way it is cooked.

Benefits appeal more

The benefits, on the other hand, are the aspects of a product or service that make it appealing to you, the buyer. In our example it is the smell, the sound of the food sizzling in the pan, the anticipation of the flavour that set you salivating as you walk in the door.

Suppose for a moment that the waitress had handled things differently. If she had noticed you looking towards the kitchen as she led you to your table, all she had to say was: 'We have some delicious bacon this morning, sir, straight from the farm. Have you time to enjoy the special cooked breakfast?' You'd have said 'Yes, please' straight away. The benefit was quite simply that, from the smell – you felt it would be delicious.

TANGIBLE VS. INTANGIBLE

The features and benefits table opposite deliberately mixes tangible products, such as furniture and saucepans, with an intangible product, insurance. Insurance is intangible because you cannot see, feel or touch it.

TANGIBLE

Physical things you can see, hear or touch e.g., a red sports car

How those physical features will improve your life/work – e.g., the sports car makes you feel really good

INTANGIBLE

Abstract things you can perceive – e.g., an Internet service

How those abstract features will improve your life/work – e.g., you will always receive your e-mails quickly and without viruses

Pricing is always a sensitive issue. The price people will pay for things need not relate to what it has cost you to provide. It is vital that you are asking enough before you start selling.

PRICE AND VALUE

You should never try to be the cheapest.

It's all too easy to work out your selling price on the basis of the cost to you plus a profit margin. If you're anything of an economist you'll know that any business needs a certain level of sales turnover to generate the cash to cover its overhead costs. It is also true that the cost per unit generally falls the more you sell. For example, if you were selling seats on aeroplanes you would expect that, once most of the seats were full, any revenue generated from the last few, otherwise empty seats is virtually all profit. Organizations such as airlines, hotels, theatres, training providers and tourist attractions have time-critical products, which is why they often discount their prices for last-minute bookings or offer the capacity they don't expect to fill to a specialist broker to sell it for them.

What do things really cost?

Take a look at your business as a whole. Even if you simply buy and sell goods you have to consider your transport and administration costs and allow for the time you are not working. The mark-up you put on the stock you sell is not all profit. Even if your job gives you no input into the pricing process, it is important to understand the basics. If nothing else, it will help you defend your pricing structure.

What are things really worth?

Your customer will determine what your offer is worth by assessing the value the purchase brings to them. For example, a book collector seeking the final volume of a set will pay more because the set increases in value when it is complete. A vital valve that enables an oil rig to return to operation is worth more than that same valve sold to repair a farm irrigation system. Marketers exploit these opportunities by creating different brands, product names and packaging for different markets.

The danger of discounting

If you give away too much in the form of discount, you will destroy your profitability. Imagine for a moment that you are running a fast-food van near a park on a summer's afternoon. If you were to sell each hot-dog at 100 units but they cost you 60 units to buy, you are making a profit of 40 units on each sale. In response to competition from a rival you reduce your selling price to 80 units, thereby halving your profit margin, so you now need to sell twice as many hot-dogs to make the same profit. The trouble is, your van only holds a limited amount of stock and the number of visitors to the park is finite, too. Following the same arithmetic, if you can increase your price, you need to carry and sell less stock to make the same amount of profit.

ESTIMATING VALUE TO YOUR CUSTOMERS

Product benefit		Value to customer
Reflective coating on glass reduces heat loss	>	What is their annual fuel bill and how little must be saved to pay for the coating?
Individually wrapped butter portions	>	Preferred by hotel guests and means less butter thrown away; total spend on butter falls, even though wrapped portions cost more (and are more profitable)
Branded coffee with free promotional materials	>	More customers stop at the café because they recognize and are reassured by the coffee brand, which makes more profit than the premium you charge

It is vital to give your prospect plenty of reasons to buy from you today. If they put off the decision, you risk never getting an order at all.

CREATING A SENSE OF URGENCY

TOP WAYS TO INSTIL URGENCY

- **Make your offer seasonal or time specific**
- **Introduce an element of scarcity**
- **Create special offers that do not erode your profit**

Human nature being what it is, we all tend to put things off rather than doing them straightaway. Selling, however, is all about creating urgency and demand. You will make it easier for yourself if you make it easy for people to appreciate why what you are selling needs their urgent attention.

In Chapter 4 we will look at techniques for overcoming your prospects' indecision and for closing sales. First, however, it is important to include in your offer features that will create a sense of urgency, which encourages people to place their orders right now. Achieving this gives you two clear advantages:

- You have greater control over your flow of orders and can better schedule the production and delivery.
- As soon as you have secured the order, you have prevented a rival from grabbing the business while your prospect considers and decides; prospects are vulnerable to approaches from competitors during the decision-making process.

There are three main ways in which you can instil a sense of urgency into the process.

Seasonality
Seasonality can be both a real and a perceived factor in stimulating a sense of urgency. Some businesses build seasonality into their products and create campaigns for each season of the year. This is particularly true of

the clothing industry, and store buyers know that their customers want to buy winter clothes in autumn and not the spring. Chocolate makers create products for different times of the year – eggs for Easter, for example, and prettily packaged items for Christmas.

Limiting supply

Creating scarcity is always a good way to create urgency and also, incidentally, to maintain pricing levels. Scarcity and rarity almost always add value, as can be seen in the art world, where limited edition, numbered prints sell for more than the unnumbered equivalents. If the products are imported, your customers have to order what is on the next ship or perhaps wait for months until the next one arrives.

Even your own time can be a limiting factor, particularly in a technical area where you work with the customer to define their exact needs. Always make good use of the weeks before you take a holiday and make sure that people know that they should order now or leave it to much later (by which time the price might have increased).

Special offers

Salespeople always want something new to talk about. This can be useful for opening conversation, but, as we have already noted (see page 13), discounting alone is rarely a good idea. Special offers should wrap your product or service with something extra, but that something should cost you little (if anything) yet have a real value to your customer. Free delivery on orders above a certain value can be useful if you own your own transport fleet and it is currently under-utilized. Special offers are also a great way to introduce additional lines to existing customers – for example, if they buy two cans of paint, they can try one of your new paint brushes at half price.

You might even try linking with someone who doesn't compete with you. You could offer your customers an introductory offer for his or her product. In return, they could offer a deal on yours. This is called cross-selling and is a good way to widen your customer base.

WHEN PLANNING YOUR STRATEGY

DO

- **Tell prospects who else has already bought your product**
- **Link your offer to a current craze**
- **Focus on value**

DON'T

- **Reveal customer confidences**
- **Stimulate sales you can't deliver**
- **Focus on cost**

You need to make an effective connection between you and your marketplace. Choosing the right route, or combination of routes is key to your success.

ROUTES TO MARKET

Understanding your position in the market pecking order will help you to appreciate which features and benfits apply to the people you sell to.

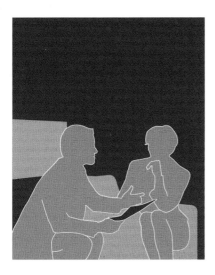

Sometimes you can choose, or at least challenge, your route to market. It is important to be aware that all prospects are subject to the same internal factors when it comes to making their decision to buy. It doesn't matter if someone is buying for themselves, for their home or for their organization – their thought processes will be the same. The offer has to appeal to them as individuals and the benefit/value arguments must add up. The final decision is emotional, however. The prospects must like and want what you are offering and be able to visualize the benefits in purely self-centred terms. There are three main routes to market, and each has a dynamic of its own.

Direct to the consumer

This is the kind of selling we all experience. It is where an experienced salesperson is selling to an inexperienced buyer. If you sell direct, you are probably selling to people in their homes. You may also, however, be selling in a showroom, at an exhibition or in a street market. Direct selling is perhaps the most vibrant work environment for salespeople. Your prospect is spending their hard-earned money on your product or service. It is also the easiest way to sell because the distribution chain is short.

Through distributors

Distributors buy from producers and sell to users. Your local food store buys products from manufacturers and growers and sells them to the people who visit the store. The advantage that chains of stores offer the producer is access to thousands of customers who pick your product off the shelf. The disadvantage, however, is that the store will want a sizeable share of your profit margin. Remember that when you reduce your profit, you need to increase the volume to stand still. Distributors, therefore, tend to be used mainly by people who have large volumes of products or services. Other examples of distributors are travel agents, insurance brokers and builders' merchants.

Business to business

Sometimes your product or service is purchased by an experienced buyer and funded from their own organization's resources. Price, therefore, tends to be a less critical issue, if only because the cost of most business purchases can be offset against tax. The business buyer does, however, have to make a profit themselves and driving your price down, while maintaining their own market pricing level, serves to boost their bottom line at the expense of your own. There are also distributors in the business-to-business world, but their behaviour is similar to that of the business consumer.

TIP

Many businesses successfully combine routes to market. For example, a small furniture maker will sell to showroom outlets and also direct to consumers. As you can imagine, combining routes to market can confuse consumers and alienate distributors. In most situations it is wise to refer retail enquiries on to one of your distributors, even though you are sacrificing margin.

IDENTIFYING ROUTES TO MARKET

Route	Characteristics
Business to consumer	> Inexperienced buyers
Purchasers buying for own use	> Highest margin
Many small orders	> Via distributors
Experienced buyers	> Purchasers buying to sell on
Margin shared	> Fewer large orders
Business to business	> Experienced buyers
Purchasers buying to use to generate profit	> Margin often linked to order size

You may be a salesperson negotiating your pay or a business owner recruiting sales people. Whatever your role, it is vital that the salesperson's income is linked to the profits that they generate.

REWARDING SALESPEOPLE

THE REWARDS SPECTRUM

SALARY

Long-term customer relationships

Complex, team-gained sales

Selling to governments

Salespeople stay a long time

COMMISSION

One-off sales

Individuals compete within teams

Selling to consumers

High turnover of salespeople

Selling is all about making life better for your customer. But how will your efforts be rewarded? If you are in a sales role or if you recruit or manage salespeople, it is important to appreciate the different ways that sales performance can be influenced by earnings.

Of all the jobs you could choose, selling is the one in which an individual's performance is most visible. Many people relish the competitive nature of a career in sales and enjoy watching their position in the company league table rise. However, it is important to remember, particularly if there is a team of salespeople, each with their own list of prospects, that some lists will be more fruitful than others. It will, for example, be far easier to sell consumer goods in an affluent area than in one where many people are out of work.

There is a fine balance to be struck when linking pay to performance. Placing too much onus on performance can encourage bad practice and the acquisition of customers who do not make repeat purchases. If there is too little encouragement, a salesperson may find it hard to motivate themselves to do more than they can get away with. Much depends on the individuals concerned, of course, but managing performance through pay is crucial to an organization's success.

Salary only

Payment by salary only is the usual system for people in quite complex sales structures, where an order can take months to negotiate and many members of a team contribute directly to winning it. An example is a building company that tenders for work in the public sector. The salesperson manages to get the company placed on the list of those invited to tender, but many different people work on the winning tender document.

Basic plus commission

Commission or bonuses that top up a basic salary are perhaps the most common rewards package for salespeople. The size of the basic salary should ideally enable the recipient to cover their basic living expenses, while the commission or bonus payments are linked to an agreed sales performance. It is always best to link commission payments to the profit contribution each deal delivers rather than simply giving a percentage of the gross sales value. Remember the dangers of discounting (see page 13).

Commission rates can also vary according to the product mix the company wants to achieve. Bonuses and incentives can be added to encourage the rapid sale of outdated or obsolete stock. Most businesses have a few 'bargain hunter' customers who only buy distressed stock.

Commission only

This type of pay is almost only ever seen in business-to-consumer markets. For the employer, it links the cost of generating the sale directly to the sale itself, and because the commission is built into the retail price, it is naturally a popular choice for employers.

The drawbacks of the arrangement include the need for the salesperson to win orders in order to earn anything, and in practice commitment can waver.

For businesses involved in direct selling the commission paid to salespeople often broadly equates to the margin given to distributors or retailers. People who sell home-improvement products are often paid on a commission-only basis.

Incentives

Whichever structure you choose, there will be times when it is sensible to introduce short-term specific sales incentives. Incentives focus the salesperson on things they might otherwise not sell.

SALES INCENTIVES

Short-term campaigns that offer salespeople rewards such as travel vouchers can be used to:

- Encourage the opening of new accounts
- Move old stock
- Remind salespeople to sell new products to existing customers

2 PROSPECTING

Before you can start selling you need to find your prospects. These are the people your market research, instinct or experience tells you are most likely to become customers. Time and effort invested in developing lists of quality prospect will be handsomely repaid when you find them receptive to your sales presentation.

10 PLACES TO FIND SALES PROSPECTS

1 **Trade directories**

2 **Membership lists**

3 **Mailing houses**

4 **Exhibition catalogues**

5 **Electoral registers**

6 **Internet**

7 **Neighbours or customers**

8 **Customer supply chains**

9 **Friends of friends**

10 **Newspaper articles**

Selecting and qualifying prospects

Every salesperson wants to find people undiscovered by their competitors, and the world is full of people who like to keep themselves busy by meeting salespeople. Unfortunately, however, many of them will not become the good customers you are seeking.

So how do you identify your prospects? Your plan will depend on your marketplace and what you are selling. If, for example, you sell agricultural fertilizers, it's pretty obvious that only farmers are likely to buy from you. You can easily obtain lists of farmers that tell you who they are, where they are and how much land they farm. The information has usually been supplied by the prospects themselves as part of the process of registering for controlled-circulation trade journals.

If, however, you are selling window blinds direct to the public, offering a range of made-to-measure products, it is much harder to know how to find the best prospects because every house has windows and every householder has the potential to be a customer. In these circumstances you may be wise to focus on more affluent neighbourhoods, on people who have just moved to a new house and on those whose houses front busy thoroughfares and who may be worried about being overlooked.

The people you choose to approach must have the potential to buy, have the cash and authority to buy and be aware of your organization or product.

Potential to buy

It can take as long to sell a single PC as a complete networked system. In fact, you will often find that the larger buyer is more rational and actually much easier to sell to than the buyer who rarely makes a purchase of any size. No matter what your product or service, always look for those with the greatest potential to place frequent, large orders. Remember, too, that large organizations will often try out new suppliers, and a trial order from a big prospect can often end up being larger than a seemingly more significant purchase by a small customer.

Cash and authority to buy

It's surprising how often salespeople forget to ask the simple, and fundamental question: 'Can you say yes to this yourself, or do you have to check with someone else in your organization?' Only ever sell to those who have the authority to buy. You also need to be aware of any budgetary constraints that can prevent an order being placed.

Awareness of your organization

An awareness of your organization by your prospects can work wonders. Some people will be so impressed by your firm's advertising or public relations that they will contact you. Most, however, will simply be reassured by the fact they have heard of the organization and have formed a positive impression of what you're all about. People will also hear about you from your existing customers and, as we see in Chapter 3, getting referrals from existing customers is one of the best ways to build your customer base.

It is often useful for sales, marketing and production teams to collaborate closely to create sales campaigns. Quite simply, this means that the marketers are raising awareness of what production are able to make and you are ready to sell. You'd be suprised how many businesses get this wrong. Typically, this happens where seasonal products are manufactured for stock ahead of market demand. Effective teamwork can help you get this right.

THE BEST PROSPECTS HAVE

- A use for your product or service
- The authority and cash to buy
- The ability to introduce you to other prospects

One of the tricks of the selling business is to confirm that what you are trying to do is achievable. This means planning how much time it will realistically take you to deliver the sales results you are seeking.

BACKWARD PLANNING

It may be obvious, but it needs saying nevertheless: the smaller each order is, the more orders you need to reach your target. It is crucial to understand this premise because it will enable you to focus your effort on those prospects you have identified as having the potential to give you the biggest orders. A 500-bedroom conference hotel will buy more soap than a five-bedroom guest house at the seaside. Many new salespeople tend to find the big buyers rather daunting, and they prefer to spend their time talking to smaller business buyers. In reality, it is often easier to sell to the larger buyers because they are less emotionally attached to the budget they are spending. What's more, the Pareto principle, or 80:20 rule, applies to selling as much as it does to any other activity: up to 80 per cent of your business will come from 20 per cent of your customers. The art, therefore, is to avoid spending too much time with small fry and to concentrate instead on the big fish in your particular market pool. Consequently, measuring performance is vital if you are to succeed. You need to consider not only the average order size but also the activity needed to win an order.

Average order size

Although it is true that a large hotel will buy more soap than a small guest house in terms of volume, don't forget that smaller buyers usually pay higher prices, thus contributing more profit. Some businesses, particularly those where production capacity (or cash flow) makes it difficult to compete on price, will focus on the smaller customer where higher prices often mean better margins. Such companies usually offer an exceptional level and quality of service. So, for your business, you need to determine what the best customer looks like and work out your targets on the size and value of order they will typically place.

Effort needed to win order

You need to go through a number of stages before you can expect to win an order. Each of these takes time, and at each stage some of your prospects will evaporate. Imagine that you have asked 100 people you know to take part in a sponsored charity run. Of that number, 80 might make an excuse and not be interested, but the remaining 20 join you at the starting line, wearing their running clothes and trainers. After 30 minutes, you all stop for a drink and a rest, and half your runners decide to give up and catch the bus home. The rest of you set off again, but two sprain their ankles or get blisters and drop out, two more get tired and give up and one takes a wrong turning and gets lost. You now have five runners who make it with you over the finishing tape. Selling is a bit like that: you need to start with enough runners to be sure of getting a small number over the finish line to reach your target.

Realism boosts morale

If you set out with the expectation that most of your prospects will fall by the wayside, you will not be too disappointed when they do just that. This realism will help you overcome one of the biggest hazards we all face in selling: the pain of rejection. Remember, however, that the rejection is not directed at you and should not be taken personally. You need to manage your performance ratios and even cherish the fact that every 'no' takes you closer to a 'yes'. This process is called **backward planning**.

Multiply the number of orders by your typical order value and you can quickly calculate how many people you need to approach – in this example, 20 – to get each order. The techniques that follow in this book will help you to improve your performance at each stage of this process.

THE BACKWARD PLAN

100 PROSPECTS
(the people you approach to seek an appointment)
GENERATE

20 APPOINTMENTS
(people interested enough to see you)
GENERATE

10 PROPOSALS
(where you identify a need and suggest a solution)
GENERATE

5 ORDERS
(where you actually win the business)

If you ask successful salespeople how they find new customers, you'll be surprised by what they say. Often the best business results from what might appear to be a chance introduction.

READING AND REFERRALS

We have seen how important it is that you reduce the amount of time and effort you waste by converting a greater proportion of prospects into customers.

The ease with which people who have the potential to buy from you can be identified will depend largely on the industry you are in. If you sell passenger aircraft, for example, it is obvious that only airlines will be interested in buying from you. If, however, you sell home improvements, office equipment or mobile phones, there will be far more potential customers than you can ever hope to approach.

Identifying the best people to approach is an art in itself. Experience will, in time, be your best guide, and you will come to target those people who are most like your customers rather than those who are completely different. However, there are three ways you can accelerate that process and improve your own sales performance ratios.

Reading the right journals

You will be amazed how revealing some news stories are. All you need to do is read the same publications that your customers and prospects read. These could be newspapers, industry and professional journals and magazines, and even web-based newsletters and magazines. Job advertisements can tell you when a buyer has moved on. New appointment columns can give you an idea of who is new and who may be looking to make those inevitable changes to suppliers that new people use to assert their authority in a new situation. Product advertising clearly tells you the key benefits that prospects are claiming, which gives you the opportunity to enhance their performance by becoming their supplier.

Disaster stories, on the other hand, can highlight a need to re-stock a fire-damaged store, while redundancy announcements can indicate a renewed interest in outsourcing. Most of your competitors will not follow up leads from the media in this way. Treat it as your opportunity to gain the 'inside track'.

Referrals from customers

Most recently appointed salespeople regard being given the order as their cue to say 'thank you' and to beat a hasty retreat in case the customer changes their mind. In reality, this is unlikely to happen unless (in your excitement) you raise an issue that did not feature in the preceding exchanges and conversations. After checking that you have the details correctly noted, you should ask for a referral. Remember that the customer has just made the decision to buy from you and never again will be feeling as positive and relaxed. Try using the suggestions from the panel above right.

Referrals from non-customers

There will usually be a genuine reason why an order has not been placed. This does not mean that your prospect is impressed with your ability to sell or, more importantly, with the value and integrity of your product or service, but spare them the guilty feelings that can accompany the rejection of your offer and ask who they know that might be in the market right now for what it is you have to offer. You will be surprised at how good a source of referrals non-customers can be.

More opprtunities

It is perhaps obvious, but the people you have yet to identify as prospects will usually move in the same circles as your customers. For example, they may belong to the same professional institute or trade association. Getting involved with these networks will allow you to build relationships with people you might otherwise never meet.

ASKING FOR A REFERRAL

FROM A CUSTOMER

'Who do you know that might also benefit from this?'

'Most of my customers are happy to recommend me to others. Who do you think would most welcome a call from me tomorrow?'

'Who else do you know faces the same challenge we've just overcome together?'

FROM A NON-CUSTOMER

'OK, so it's not for you, but which of your friends might find it just what they need?'

'You're clearly impressed but not in the market right now. Who can you introduce me to who is?'

'I can quite understand why you're not going ahead. But tell me, who in this city would be most likely to say yes?'

Time, as they say, waits for no man. This is particularly true when applied to a sales job. You'll be surprised as how little time you can actually spend talking to customers.

MANAGING YOUR TIME

FIVE WAYS TO SAVE TIME

1 Phone the day before your sales appointment to make sure they've remembered.

2 Use mapping software to locate your destination before you set off.

3 Make sure you know where the nearest car parks are sited.

4 Index your prospects in a way that means you can identify those near to your planned appointments. It's ok to say: 'I'll be close by, can I visit?'

5 Keep time aside to process and follow up so that your firm delivers what you've just promised.

Lack of time is likely to be your biggest barrier to success. You need to plan your days to give you the maximum possible time in front of prospects. That way, you can focus on what you do and are going to do best: the job of selling.

When you've been courting a prospective customer for a while and you get agreement to an interview, it's all too easy to agree to meeting at almost any time. This can play havoc with your travel plans and also make you appear to have time on your hands. Neither will help you manage your time. Of course, it could be that your diary is empty for the week in question and this is your first appointment, but even so there is an advantage in tempering your enthusiasm with discipline. Here are three ways you can manage your time effectively.

Reduce your travelling time

Clearly, the bigger your trading territory, the more time you will spend travelling, but when you are seeking business in the far-flung corners of your business empire, you do need to be mindful of the cost of servicing a customer who is a long way away. Could you make a greater margin getting the same deal closer to home?

For a traditional field sales role, however, it is always best to divide your territory into four sectors, each equally accessible from your base and each logically constructed around the road network. Make your appointments so that you always visit each sector on the same day each week. This means that as you make appointments in the future, you stand a better chance of filling each day before you set off. It enables you to visit more people in a day and reduces the time you spend sitting in your car. On the fifth day, perhaps every Friday, you could spend time effectively on the phone arranging the next week's calls, handling any administrative tasks and carrying out 'emergency calls' anywhere on your patch.

Qualify your appointments

Sometimes you will call a prospect to suggest an appointment and the prospect will agree, not because they have a burning interest in your product or service but merely because they want to bolster their ego and status by having a visitor. Alternatively, they may be genuinely interested in your product or service but not have the budget to spend before next year. They may be curious, but not in a position to buy. This is why it is always best to qualify your appointments – that is, determine how serious the prospect is before you agree to the meeting. Some qualifying questions you can ask are listed in the panel above right.

Plan, plan, plan

Although a creative streak can help your selling style, discipline in the way you plan your time is just as important. We have already seen how dividing up a sales territory can reduce travelling time, but this may not be possible for everyone. You might, for example, sell in a showroom environment where you have to wait for your prospects to be drawn through the door by marketing campaigns or simply by chance. Planning in this context is all about being prepared to spend your time usefully when you are not selling. Researching potential customers to direct mail, reading the material put out by your competitors or even reading this book are all preferable to doing the crossword in your daily paper during those quiet parts of the day. It is also always a good idea to have some work with you when you are out on the road in case an unforeseen change of appointment leaves you spare with an hour or so, which you can then fill effectively.

QUESTIONS QUALIFYING AN APPOINTMENT

- 'If our meeting goes well, will you be able to place an order on the day?'

- 'Tell me, what in particular would you like to discuss when we meet?'

- 'Have you any colleagues who would benefit from joining our meeting?'

To enable your prospectiuve customer to fully consider your proposition you both need to set aside time to talk together. Strangely, most sales interviews will last for about an hour.

MAKING APPOINTMENTS

FIVE GOOD ICE-BREAKERS

1 'What attracts you most about ... ?'

2 'You look to me like someone who ...'

3 'I'm looking for people who are dissatisfied with their ... supplier. Can you help me?'

4 'Excuse me, could you tell me the time?'

5 'When did you last check what you are paying for ... ?'

One of the joys of selling is that you are constantly meeting new people. However, you need their commitment as well as their attention, and making appointments is vital if you are going to meet your targets.

Not appropriate for many markets but the only way for some, face-to-face prospecting is perhaps the hardest and most daunting way to make sales appointments. These techniques are most suitable where everybody has the potential to become a customer, and usually the conversion ratio from cold prospect to warm lead is horribly high. That's not to say there's anything wrong with products offered in this way. Many home-improvement companies, credit card providers and even charities seeking donations trawl the streets to net sufficient interested people to deliver their new business goals.

Of the many ways there are to make sales appointments, the three described here are in order of challenge, with the easiest being dealt with first.

Visitors to a showroom

If you are working from a showroom or perhaps a display stand in a shopping mall, the people you speak to will already have shown some interest in what you are offering. Make sure that they see you approaching them and take an interest in their interest. Find out what it is that has caught their eye. Find out their reasons and explore them through questions (see page 44). Listening to them will give you plenty of clues about their level of interest and, perhaps, their potential as customers. Always encourage them to ask you questions, because this will seem less threatening and will help to put them at ease. Your conversation should soon give you a sense if an appointment is likely to follow or if you need to move politely on and talk to someone else.

Street prospecting

In most towns and cities and in the majority of shopping malls you need permission before canvassing people in the street. This is an advantage, because the people you approach will always know that some authority has approved your activity so will assume it to be of some merit.

Remember to look smart and professional. Eye contact is everything. Follow it up with a welcoming smile when your eyes meet. Next, break the ice with a simple question, ideally one that will put your prospect at ease. It should be an open question – that is, a question that requires an answer other than yes or no – and listening to the answer is vital. Visual aids can help tremendously in this situation, from the logo on your shirt to the collecting tin in your hand. The more obvious your mission, the less frightening you will become.

Taking regular breaks and having a buddy with you doing the same task helps enormously. It is easy to become blasé and 'street fatigued', and this will not help you succeed.

Door to door

This is the most challenging way to prospect because you are intruding on people's personal space and privacy by knocking on their door. However, many people would not respond to any other form of marketing, and many products are traditionally sold as a result of knocking on door after door.

Basic points to remember are to close the gate behind you and not to drop litter, such as cigarette ends, on the prospect's garden path. It does happen! More relevant to your situation perhaps are the techniques in the panel on the right, which will make your unexpected knock more acceptable.

COLD CALLING DOOR-TO-DOOR

- **Step back from the door before it is opened so that you can step forward to greet the prospect when the door opens**

- **Dress in a way that shows you are not a detective bearing bad news**

- **Smile and greet the person by name if you know it**

- **Compliment them as soon as possible – for example, admire their car, garden or home**

- **Never, never step over the threshold unless clearly invited**

Your call will come as less of a surprise if you write to your prospect before phoning. What's more, it provides an opportunity to outline your offer, perhaps even to enclose a sample.

PRE-APPROACH LETTERS

An effective way of introducing yourself to prospective customers is to write to them. Letters are usually better than e-mails for this purpose because they create more impact and are harder to ignore.

We all receive a lot of unsolicited mail. Indeed, your own firm's marketing department might use direct mail to generate leads. The pre-approach letter is different. It is your personal invitation to your prospect to agree

ADDRESSING YOUR PROSPECT

How you address your prospect depends on a number of factors, summarized in the box below.

Factors		What you should do
They are elderly or old people	>	Use formal salutations, such as 'Dear Mr and Mrs Smith'
They are young	>	Use their first name and drop the Mr, Mrs or Ms
You know their address but no name	>	Use salutations linked to your offer – for example, 'Dear Fellow Gardener' (you're selling grass cutters) or 'Dear Borrower' (you're selling re-mortgages)
You only know their company name	>	Use salutations linked to your offer – for example, 'Dear fellow salesperson' (you're selling this book) or 'Dear tenant' (you're selling office space)

to a meeting with you. Of course, you will need to follow it up by phone – hence the term **pre-approach** – but it does eliminate the element of surprise and gives your prospect time to form opinions that you can challenge and influence when you call.

Writing to suggest an appointment can say a lot about your company. You need to consider how you should address your prospect, what type of action you want them to take and whether a gimmick would be appropriate.

How you sign off your letter is also important. Always type your name in full – John Smith – under your signature (and personally sign each letter). If your first name is unusual or ambiguous, add your sex as a suffix – Jo Brown (Mr), for example.

The action you want

The prime role of the pre-approach letter is to prepare the recipient to receive your phone call asking for an appointment. You need to make this clear in the letter. You also need to state clearly why you feel the reader should be interested in your offer. The body of the letter should contain the information listed to the right.

WHAT TO INCLUDE

Product message
Gives the reader information on which they can form their own opinion

Overview (not detail)
You want to meet to discuss the detail

How to contact you
They may be so keen they'd rather not wait for your call

Pass on if recipient is not for you
If they're not the buyer, ask the addressee to give the letter to the relevant person, and when you phone, they'll transfer you

GIMMICKS – YES OR NO

Some gimmicks work really well, but others simply fall flat. However, you want your letter to be remembered, and sometimes enclosures and other gimmicks can make all the difference. Here are some ideas to get you thinking.

You sell explosives	>	Enclose a balloon and pin – 'We give you bigger bangs'
You save customers' money	>	Enclose a calculator and invite them in the letter to work out the potential saving for themselves
You're following up a customer referral	>	Enclose a letter of endorsement from the customer
You sell cars	>	Enclose a key fob with a logo
You sell print	>	Enclose a few samples of your work

Networking is the process that enables people in different groups to get to know each other. It is also the process by which you get to meet new people.

NETWORKING

'Good to meet you. Tell me, what work do you do?'

One of the most productive and cost-effective forms of personal marketing, networking can introduce you to people to sell to no matter what business you're in. In some of the professions, such as law and accountancy, it is the most effective way of meeting new clients.

People are social animals, and we tend to define ourselves by the company we keep. Clubs, associations, and communities of all kinds allow us to mix with small groups of people who share some of our views and values. If you think about your own personal circle of contacts you will see how they fall into separate groups.

Social networking

We all engage in social networking to some extent, widening our circle of friends and contacts by meeting others who share our interests. If you sell to consumers or to small businesses within a relatively small geographical area, investing time in social networking can deliver you handsome dividends. Every small town has its local 'mafia', a group of professionals who seem to have all the business opportunities sewn up among themseves. The lawyer, bank manager, accountant, builder, architect and school teacher will get together regularly, perhaps at Rotary Club meetings, and discuss and swap business opportunities. It makes sense to join these networks if you want to access this group.

Conferences and events

Joining trade associations and attending the same conferences and events your customers attend is bound to pay off. Referrals can be readily obtained joining a group of which an existing customer is part. They will naturally introduce you to the other people. You will probably be able to work out from the conference delegate pack where those people are from, and you can follow up by phone after they've returned home.

Most conferences also produce a delegate list, which will enable you to select and list the people you most want to meet. Delegates usually wear name badges, making it easy for you to introduce yourself to the people you most want to meet.

Networking clubs

Networking can become a habit. In fact, it can become habit forming, and sometimes members of business networking clubs (of which there are many) continue to roll out of bed at dawn every Friday morning to meet the same old faces long after the flow of business introductions and opportunities have dried up. Never be afraid to cut loose from worked-out networks to join fresh ones. What's more, you will find that as your career develops and unfolds you outgrow your old networks and must either find better ones or risk becoming stale.

Virtual networks

Do not discount the many internet based business networks. These are often hosted by providers of business services and make finding and talking with potential customers simple. However, you may need to concentrate on people who live near enough for you to be able to provide a consistent level of service.

FIVE GOOD NETWORKING TRICKS

1 If you're wearing a name badge, emphasize your name with a highlighter pen. It'll catch people's eye and make it easier for you to start conversations.

2 Wear memorable clothes. Brightly coloured scarves and ties – even your socks – will help you stand out from the crowd.

3 If you're chatting but want to move on to grab someone more interesting nearby, touch the person's arm as you make your excuse and leave them. For some reason, the physical contact makes them less likely to feel as if you've simply dumped them.

4 Eat before you go, even if there's a buffet at the event. Eating stops conversations, and you'll cover more ground if you mingle with just a glass in your hand.

5 Take plenty of business cards and do not put the cards you're given in the same pocket. It's all too easy to give away the wrong card!

The telephone is the salesperson's most powerful tool. It enables you to convert raw prospects into qualified appointments. The way you use the phone is therefore crucial to your success.

THE PHONE CALL

Although phone calls can be hard to make, they can also be intensely rewarding as your diary fills with freshly made sales appointments.

You've identified the prospect and perhaps written to introduce yourself. Now it's time to pick up the phone and arrange an appointment. For most of us, this is the hardest part of selling. It's also the point at which your prospect can reject your advances.

After your brain, the telephone is the most powerful tool in your sales armoury. It overcomes geographical barriers, and when it is used correctly it can make the most impossible target seem achievable. However, using the phone as a selling tool is very different from using it for social exchanges.

Phone techniques

You are using the phone to make an appointment and that means your call has to be focused and not too long because you want to avoid presenting your whole argument until you meet face to face. You also want to get through to the person you've perhaps pre-approached by letter. This means getting past a number of so-called **gatekeepers**. Gatekeepers are people whose role is to protect decision-makers from calls that might waste his or her time. They include switchboard operators who are instructed not to put through cold calls and secretaries who may feel empowered to reject your approach on behalf of their boss. Techniques that will make you more successful are:

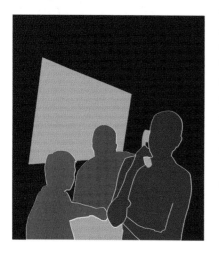

- Make important calls standing up, rather than slouched in a comfortable chair. This will help you sound professional, crisp and not too relaxed and laid back.

- Have a mirror in front of your phone so you can watch your expression change. If you are smiling, you will sound more friendly – and that's good.
- Do not rest the handset on your chin. This can muffle the sound of your voice.
- Beware of 'hands free' phones. They may be convenient for you, but they can make you sound as if you're phoning from inside a submarine.

Phone phrases

The words you use can make all the difference. You have to aim to be familiar enough to gain acceptance without causing offence. This depends a lot on your natural personality, of course, but also on who you're calling. Practise your usual phraseology on a colleague, friend or partner to make sure you've pitched it at the right level. You need to be yourself or the call will sound contrived and your message false. Always try to:

- Introduce yourself by name to whoever picks up the phone.
- Ask for your prospect by first name and family name – for example, ask to speak to Ashok Patel, not Mr Patel. This implies that you know him even if you do not.
- Be honest but persuasive. Do not say, 'I'm returning his call', if you're not. It is ok to say that you're calling at the suggestion of someone you are sure that both of you know. This gets you past gatekeepers.
- When you do get through to your prospect, cut to the chase and make your point clearly and politely. Waffle smacks of insincerity and will not win you appointments.

PHONE PITFALLS

- Be firm and avoid explaining your offer over the phone. It is better to ask for 10 minutes of face-to-face time than to spend ages trying to sell there and then.

- Do not be tempted to sell to the PA. They will not do the job as well as you.

- Do not fill the silence. If you've asked a question – give your prospect time to reflect and then to answer.

- Don't leave voicemail messages. It's always better to call back when they're there. If you've already left a message it looks as if you're chasing them.

- Don't call them on their mobile. The reception may be poor, they may be driving – and it's unlikely that their diary is conveniently to hand.

'Good morning, my name is Jon Bates from ABC Direct. I'm calling to ask what you thought of our latest catalogue that I posted to you last week.'

Focused phone calls are in effect mini sales interviews. However, don't expect to convert every call. If your prospect genuinely isn't interested, visiting them will be a waste of time.

THE PHONE INTERVIEW

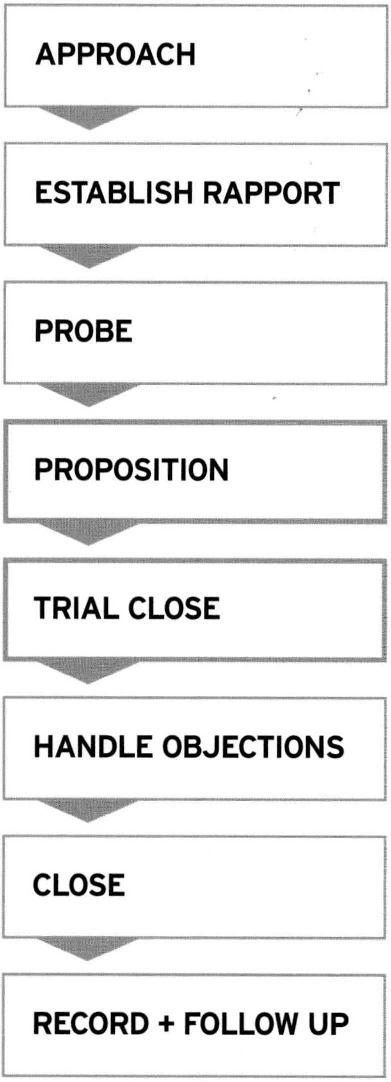

APPROACH

ESTABLISH RAPPORT

PROBE

PROPOSITION

TRIAL CLOSE

HANDLE OBJECTIONS

CLOSE

RECORD + FOLLOW UP

The purpose of your phone call is to get commitment to a face-to-face meeting because it is almost always easier to sell face to face than over the phone. However, phoning to make an appointment is a sales interview all the same and needs to be structured.

Assume that you've written a pre-approach letter to a prospective new customer. Also assume that you're selling ride-on lawnmowers and that your prospect has clipped a coupon from an advertisement. Each stage of your conversation needs to be clearly defined, although it will, of course, flow as a natural conversation should.

Approach

This is how you get talking. You make the call, and you need to introduce yourself and make sure that you are talking to the right person. It is always polite to ask if now is a convenient time to talk, particularly if you are ringing people at home out of office hours. They might, for example, be about to eat. If it's a bad time, agree a time to call back and do it.

Establish rapport

This is where the other person actually decides if they like you. Ask, for example, if they received your letter and if they looked at the brochure you enclosed. Move as quickly as seems respectable on to the next stage.

Probe

At this point you are seeking to qualify their interest. It is important that you only make appointments with people who need your product. Ask a qualifying question such as: 'How much grass do you have to cut?' This will also help you decide which models might be more suitable.

Proposition

This is the point at which you outline your proposition. Perhaps you will suggest that a test-drive would be a good way to try out your product. It is important to suggest something that means you have to meet. Even if it's not to show the product, it might be to discuss product performance or to view together some material that you have only one copy of and cannot send in the post. You usually need to meet to secure an order.

Trial close

Now it is time to pop the question that will lead to a meeting being arranged. You need to make it easy for your prospect to agree, and this means structuring your question so that 'no' is not an easy reply to give. You do need to give choice, so you might ask if next week or the week after would be more convenient.

Handle objections

It's almost inevitable that your prospect will not agree straight away to a meeting. For one thing, they may not want to waste your time, perhaps feeling that you usually spend your time with bigger or better customers than them. Not all objections are genuine, and you need to turn them to your advantage firmly and politely. Reassure the prospect that you do not expect an order just because they've tried the product out – although this might well happen!

Close

Having dealt with their objection to the meeting it's time to take them back to your diary. Repeat your closing question and work on getting a date in the diary that suits you both. Remember the importance of planning your days when you are on the road and make sure you agree a date and time that fits with your own plans.

TIP

It's all too easy to work through a list of calls, fill your diary with appointments and forget to confirm them with the prospects. Send a short letter, which can be of standard format and adapted for each appointment, confirming what you've agreed.

Sometimes you cannot, or do not need to phone for an appointment, for example, when the prospect has just walked into your showroom. Others quite simply cannot be reached by phone.

MORE WAYS TO ARRANGE INTERVIEWS

The structure of your conversation when seeking a sales appointment should always follow that described for use on the telephone. However, you may need to adapt your technique.

E-mail

The biggest advantage of e-mail is that it can get you through to people that may otherwise be impossible to reach. In other words, it can get you past the gatekeepers to speak to your prospect.

When you are e-mailing to suggest a meeting, you need to:

- Research your prospect to find what they are most likely to consider important.
- Make the e-mail short, to the point and spell out the reasons you want to meet in terms of the benefits to your prospect.
- Use the subject line to summarize your message. Make this interesting!
- Add hyperlinks to relevant sections of websites that reinforce your point.
- Give them time to respond before e-mailing again. It's easy to forget how recently you e-mailed when you're eagerly awaiting a response.

In a showroom

You can usually tell if someone's making a return visit or is particularly interested in something on their first visit. Take your diary with you, greet them and follow the same procedure as for a telephone call. It's often good to make an appointment, even if it is for them to return to the showroom for the sales interview. If your product or service is complex or has a high price, you will want to make sure you are free from distraction and have enough of your prospect's time set aside to complete the sale.

Via intermediaries

Intermediaries could be your distributors, a trade organization or fellow professionals. Ask them to arrange surgery sessions at their premises so that you can meet a large number of prospects in one day. They will have promoted you as a specialist or expert, and this will enable you to identify in a cost-effective way who you need to spend more time with. The arrangement will also bolster your relationship with the intermediary.

MAKING APPOINTMENTS ON THE PHONE

DO

- Call back later
- Get gatekeepers on your side
- Stand up and smile
- Do remember that every call is a new opportunity
- Tell them you're having a great day
- Have good reasons for needing to meet
- Take advantage of the relatively informal style of e-mail to get noticed

DON'T

- Leave voicemail messages
- Be short with or rude to gatekeepers
- Slouch in your chair when phoning
- Take rejection personally
- Complain to your prospect
- Get talked into selling on the phone
- Overlook e-mail as a way of reaching otherwise impossible prospects

Looking like a successful salesperson will make you feel like a successful salesperson. It will also reassure your prospect and help them form the opinion that you're a good person to buy from.

LOOKING THE PART

Most things in moderation will be acceptable to your prospects.

Like it or not, people judge us by the way we look, and a poor first impression can jeopardize your chances of success. That's not to say you shouldn't be an individual, with your own style that reflects your tastes, interests and ethnicity. Too many salespeople look the same. Grey suits, for both men and women, seem to dominate the business world. With a little thought you can match your appearance to your business sector and feel more comfortable, too.

You must appreciate that different customers will have different standards of appearance themselves, and if you sell to a wide range of people – from pop stars to politicians – you cannot dress to please them all. There are, however, some basic rules that should stand you in good stead no matter where you go.

How you look

The basics are that you have to look clean, alert and awake. This is easier than it sounds if, for example, you have a young baby who keeps you up all night. The other golden rule is that most things in moderation will be acceptable to your prospects, but too much of anything may put some off. For example:

- Hair should be neat and not too shockingly styled or coloured.
- Facial hair is best avoided unless demanded by religious belief. In body language terms it hides the face and hints of insincerity.
- Tattoos and body piercings should not distract (or revolt).

- Jewellery for men should be simple, perhaps only a wedding ring.
- Jewellery for women should be subtle and appropriate.
- Make-up should be worn to a sensible degree, and by women only.

What you wear

How you dress will largely be dictated by the business you work in. Retail outlets, for example, often ask sales staff to wear a uniform because this makes it easier for customers to tell who is staff and who is not. If you run a sales organization it can be a good idea to introduce uniforms, which will enable you to convey strong visual brand-reinforcing images.

Wherever possible, avoid extremes and recognize that you are meeting people who may not share your personal standards; in other words, do not reveal more of yourself than you feel is appropriate.

Accessories

The biggest accessory most salespeople have is their car. Often, if you have a field sales role, you will drive a company car. Increasingly, though, people are buying their own cars and claiming running costs from their business. Your car should be clean, tidy and not cluttered with empty takeaway containers. Make sure that any damage is promptly repaired. Remember, many buyers look at the car before they even meet you. You want them to form a positive impression.

It is always sensible to make notes during a sales meeting, and many successful salespeople invest in a good-quality pen. This, together with a neat notebook or personal organizer, helps to demonstrate that you mean business. The cheap ballpoint pen you've chewed while working out your pitch should not be seen at any sales meeting!

Finally, it is always good to look in a mirror before going into a meeting. This means you can check your hair. It is also important to check your nose as well, particularly if you have a cold. If you are a smoker, you might consider using a breath freshener.

PROFESSIONAL SALESPEOPLE

DO LOOK

- Well groomed
- Contemporary and appropriate
- Relaxed and focused
- Clean and tidy
- Successful but not wildly so

DO NOT LOOK

- Dishevelled
- Over the top
- Tired and harassed
- Nicotine stained
- Poverty struck

3 QUESTIONING

You may be nervous, anxious and desperately in need of the order to make your target for the month – but this must not be apparent to your prospects. Although it's important that you don't appear to be acting, there are a number of ways in which you can improve that vital first impression you make.

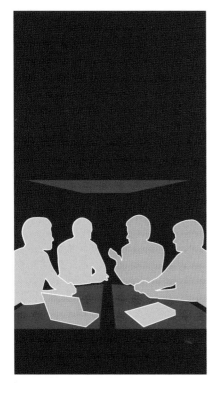

First impressions

The importance of correctly meeting and greeting your prospects may seem obvious to you, but if you are new to sales there are a few 'tricks of the trade' that will help you. Perhaps not surprisingly, they can also make you come over as more assured and confident in a social context, too.

Meeting

You have arranged this meeting so you must look pleased to see your prospect. This is easier if:

- You are not engrossed in a magazine you picked up in their reception area.
- You stand up when they come towards you, even if the meeting is taking place where you are.
- You walk purposefully and do not appear hesitant.

Greeting

It might be a good idea, even at this early stage, to remind your prospect why you're there. This should reassure them and set their mind at ease. It also prepares them for what is to follow.

Remember that business customs vary around the world. Always do some research about how things are done before embarking on sales visits overseas or, just as importantly, before greeting overseas buyers to your own organization.

The three keys to a successful greeting are:

Eye contact

Always look your prospect in the eye as you meet them.

Handshake

Always shake their hand firmly (but do not crush it).

The hello

Greet them with enthusiasm and using appropriate words.

How you start the sales meeting will make a big difference to the result. First impressions are made in the first 30 seconds.

Sitting down

Of course, you will often be invited to sit in a particular chair or at a table when your host settles you in for the conversation that will follow. However, if you are given the choice, you should always try to avoid:

- Sitting on a lower chair than your prospect because this tends to put them in control of the meeting.
- Facing them across their desk. Again, this is about dominance, but what's more, their desk will be distracting, because the phone may ring and e-mails 'ping', taking attention away from what you are saying.

Instead, always try to:

- Sit at the same level as your prospect, which is more conducive to adult-to-adult conversation.
- Sit next to or at right angles to them if you are sitting at a table.
- Sit between them if there are two or more buyers so that you can maintain good contact with everyone in the room. This is particularly important if you are selling to couples in their home (see pages 58–9).

TIP

Use the time you spend waiting for your host to arrive observing and learning what you can about the organization you are visiting.

Receptionists are sometimes happy to chat and can unwittingly share useful information.

The questions you ask in a sales interview can enable you to gather information and seek commitment.

OPEN AND CLOSED QUESTIONS

OPEN VS. CLOSED QUESTIONS

OPEN

Solicits information

Often begins with what, why, how, where, when, who

Encourages your prospect to speak

CLOSED

Checks understanding

Demands a short answer, often yes or no

Encourages your prospect to think

There are essentially only two types of question you ask in a sales meeting. These are **open questions** and **closed questions**. Using them in the right sequence is second nature to the seasoned salesperson.

Now read this piece of dialogue.
A: *'Tell me, how many pigs do you fatten each year?'*
B: *'Oh, I'd say around 5,000.'*
A: *'And what feeding system do you use?'*
B: *'We keep our pigs outside, so buy pelleted feed in bulk. It's easier.'*
A: *'Why is it easier?'*
B: *'Well, we tried mixing our own feed, but there was too much wastage when we fed it out of doors. The weather was the main problem.'*
A: *'That's interesting. What do you do with the grain you used to feed your pigs?'*
B: *'We sell it to the feed mill that we use to provide our pelleted feed.'*

You will have guessed that A is the salesperson and B the prospective customer. All the questions asked have been open questions because A wants to find out what potential B has to buy his animal feed. A knows enough to calculate the annual tonnage of feed purchased. This is important because the potential, or value of the customer, will influence how the interview will progress. Even if this information has already been gathered as part of the prospecting process, it's always wise to ask when face to face with the prospect. Circumstances might have changed.

Now read what happened next.

A: *'So let me see if I've got this right. You prefer pelleted feed because there's less wastage?'*

B: *'Yes, we tried home mix and went back to pellets.'*

A now knows that the move away from pellets was an experiment. Understanding the reason for the initial move away from pellets will reveal some of the thinking behind the decision. Knowing why helps you to determine how to tailor your offer to be most acceptable to your prospect.

A: *'So what made you decide to try home mixed feed?'*

B: *'Well, it seemed daft to sell our grain at a low price for you guys to sell it back to me in expensive pig feed pellets. I wanted to reduce my feed costs.'*

Not surprisingly, B, is concerned about price. Not just the price he pays for his feed, but the price he gets for his grain. This also illustrates another key point. It is rare for there to be only one reason a buyer makes his decision. The factors that influence them will be interlinked. Asking lots of open and closed questions will help you to to find which are important to your prospect.

WHY PEOPLE BUY

Remember that most people buy for a combination of the following reasons:

Security	>	Is it safe?
Performance	>	What does it do?
Appearance	>	Do I like the look?
Convenience	>	Is it simple?
Economy	>	Value for money?
Durability	>	How long will it last?

Questions are both the tiller and the compass of the sales voyage. They guide and steer the sales conversation.

The old adage is true. You have two ears and one mouth and should always use them in proportion. Listening is actually more important than speaking in the sales interview.

LISTENING

Asking questions is only half the story: you also need to listen to the answers. This can be harder than it seems at first because you will also be trying to think of the next question, but it is all too easy to forget to listen and so lose your way.

As someone who has been communicating since early childhood, you may find it strange to be asked to think about how you listen. In fact, every stage of the sales process takes things we have all done for years without thinking and puts them into a fresh context. Remember that your prospect probably doesn't know you too well and needs to be reassured that you are paying attention to what they are saying. There are a number of ways you can do this.

Keeping quiet

When you have asked a question it is vital to give the other person time to answer it. It is always better to ask questions that are sufficiently specific to prompt a fairly short answer, because this gives you the chance to direct the conversation with your subsequent questions. It is also fair to note that your prospect will know that you are selling to them and may take a while to answer your specific question while they consider the implications of what they are saying. Few people are brave enough to admit to being foolish, so a reasoned answer will always seem preferable. But reasoned answers take time.

If you really must break the silence, do it by asking your question again in a slightly different way or by breaking it down and asking some simpler questions that will lead to the answers you want.

Body language

Much of our communication is non-verbal. In fact, research has shown that as much as 50 per cent of what we are trying to say is communicated in non-verbal ways, through our body language and appearance, while 40 per cent is communicated by our tone of voice and only 10 per cent through the words we use (see also pages 54–5).

Reflecting key words

This technique is best illustrated by asking you to imagine two elderly women sitting on a park bench. One of them is doing all the talking and the other all the listening. It always seems to be like that. Their conversation might go something like this.

C: *'It's been really cold recently.'*
D: *'Cold.'*
C: *'Yes. I had to turn up my heating last weekend and order more fuel.'*
D: *'Fuel.'*

What D is doing, probably without even thinking about it, is reflecting back to her friend just one key word each time. Hearing this, C knows she still has the attention of D and keeps going.

In a sales meeting you can use this reflecting technique to encourage and steer your prospect. You do this by picking up and reflecting the words that are of most interest to you. In our example above heating and fuel are key words, and the one that is reflected will tend to focus the other person one way or the other. Reflecting encourages the speaker to keep going and is a good way to elicit more detail when an open question is being answered. Using a closed question, however, will enable you to check that you have understood.

Keeping control

Many people fear that by listening rather than speaking they will start to lose control of the interview. If your prospect does try to turn the tables, use closed questions to regain control.

Many people fear that by listening rather than speaking they will lose control of the interview.

LOOKING INTERESTED

Our posture reveals a lot about what's going on in our minds. People will say more when they think they're being listened to and taken seriously. Good ways to show that you are paying attention are to:

- **Lean forward towards the other person**

- **Nod your head in agreement**

- **Take notes (where appropriate)**

Sometimes it is good to hint at the answer you want your prospect to give in response to your question. Rather like clues in a crossword, they should not be too obvious.

LEADING QUESTIONS

You are getting along nicely and finding out lots about the potential for business. As you move through the stage of building rapport and gleaning information, you need to become more directive because your specific objective is to sell, and you will want to lead your prospect gently to the ground you want to cover. The time has come to get specific.

Leading open questions

Remember that open questions are those that encourage your prospect to open up and give you information. Assume for a moment that you are selling cars and want to find out exactly what the visitor to your showroom thinks about the car they have chosen to sit in. You are a competent salesperson and will already have made a mental note of the car they pulled up in. Now you want to focus the prospect on the features of your car that you know are better than their current model. You might say: 'Tell me, what do like best about the dashboard layout?' This is more specific than simply asking what they think about the car. Leading your prospect in this way will help them to answer because you have chosen the specific area you want to discuss.

Leading closed questions

Closed questions are those that demand a short answer, often yes or no. You could, therefore, ask: 'Do you like the new dashboard layout on this model?' If they say yes, you know that this particular feature will not be a barrier to getting a sale. If they say no, you can ask them why and their answer will give you a specific objection to the product you can explore and get around. (See pages 52–3 for more about objections.)

You can see how, if you constantly choose the topic of the answer you are seeking, your prospect will, unless totally besotted with the product anyway, soon grow weary. When you are asking questions, therefore, use leading questions simply to narrow down the scope of the answer. Having got the information you want, you can then move on to ask a more general open question to give your prospect some freedom to set the route you are both going to follow conversationally.

Leading and following

Sometimes your prospect will be really enthusiastic about your product or service and want to find answers to all their questions. When this happens you can hand control of the flow of exchanges to the prospect, who may ask you questions that, as the salesperson, you should be able to answer. You can encourage your prospect and build their confidence in your product by asking a **following question**, which is opposite to a leading one.

If we return to the car showroom, your prospect is standing beside you having just told you that they are pretty impressed with the overall look and feel of the car. A following question might go something like this: 'You are clearly impressed with this new car. Tell me, what else would you like to know about it?' Asking following questions gives you a valuable insight into the prospect's mind. However, if you only ask following questions, you will appear to be unassertive and not much help. As with every aspect of the selling process, it's all a matter of balance.

If they are used too liberally, leading questions can make you appear forceful and uninterested in what your prospect has to say.

You need to be alert and responsive in the sales interview and it makes sense to jot down the key points.

TAKING NOTES

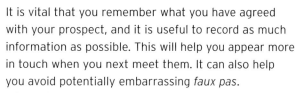

Writing down what your customer says shows that you value them.

It is vital that you remember what you have agreed with your prospect, and it is useful to record as much information as possible. This will help you appear more in touch when you next meet them. It can also help you avoid potentially embarrassing *faux pas*.

Sometimes, however, when people see that you are writing down what they say they become suspicious and less likely to share information, thoughts and feelings with you. The key to successful note-taking is to manage your prospects' expectations and allow them to see why recording your meeting in this way is beneficial to you both.

Note-taking also helps you plan and appear more professional. Of course, you can simply jot down the things you feel are important as you go through your meeting, but you can do much, much more.

Before the meeting

It is always a good idea to make a note of the things you want to be sure you will cover during your meeting. These could include:

- Key questions you want to ask
- Reminders of areas of interest your prospect has already mentioned
- Special offers and deals you want to mention if appropriate

If you prefer to take notes with a pen and pad, write your pre-meeting notes in pencil so they will not be legible to your prospect. This means that as you glance down to write, you can also read your notes. A more creative way to take notes in meetings is to use a piece of plain paper and outline different aspects of the areas you plan to cover on different sectors of the page. You can do this by either creating a series of boxes or clouds or by drawing a spider, with the legs extending and branching to form your notes. Once you have got used to it, a non-linear method of note-taking actually gives you more flexibility.

During the meeting

You should unpack your paper and pen at the start of the meeting. Depending on the circumstances, you might also like to ask your prospect if it's ok to take notes. Explain that they are to help you both.

Taking notes in a sales meeting can provide invaluable opportunities to:

- Remember key points
- List needs and read them back to confirm agreement
- Calculate prices
- List objections and cross them out as they are dealt with

Before you forget

Some successful salespeople leave a photocopy of their notes before leaving the meeting. This is particularly useful if you do not have a formal order pad on which to record what has been agreed. Asking your new customer to sign beside the order details will reinforce their commitment. Of course, when you return to base you can transfer the information you need to customer tracking software. Many of these packages will prompt you when the customer is due for a call back.

It is always good to keep your notes from sales meetings. For one thing, they provide an accurate record of what was discussed. For another they can help you when you return to secure further orders. Should a dispute arise, your notes will support your case and help you to resolve the matter swiftly.

GOOD NOTE-TAKING HABITS

- **Plan your meeting in pencil before arriving**
- **Develop a page layout that lets you move about**
- **Use coloured pens to record different types of information**
- **Leave a copy of your notes with the prospect**
- **Always date and keep notes in case you need to refer back**

You need to know what your prospect is unsure about; otherwise you will not be able to satisfy them that a purchase is the right thing to do.

HANDLING OBJECTIONS

HANDLING OBJECTIONS

DO

- Respect your prospect's view
- Ensure you understand the exact issue
- Check understanding by asking a closed question
- Use samples, pictures, even your company website to illustrate your point

X

DO NOT

- Dismiss their concern
- Assume everyone will object to the same things
- Forget to ask if there are any other concerns
- Talk too quickly

When you are questioning your prospect and ask, quite sensibly, for an order, they will usually object. This does not mean they are not interested but rather that they are not yet convinced.

Your job is to make sure that you identify and remove as many barriers as possible to the order being placed. By raising an objection – usually prefaced by a word such as 'but' – your prospect is highlighting an area of real concern. Objections are valuable and should be welcomed. (See also pages 68–9.)

Why objections are raised

There are two kinds of objection, **sincere and insincere objections**.

Sincere objections arise when the reason for dissatisfaction is genuine. They suggest that:

- **Your prospect likes much of the product you are offering**
- **They have thought in sufficient depth to decide what worries them**
- **You are being given a chance to address and deal with the problem**

Insincere objections occur when the reason expressed is actually a cover for something deeper.

Both types of objection are dealt with in the same way, but if your prospect has an underlying concern that they are choosing not to share – for example, they are not authorized by their firm to place the order – you will meet objection after objection as your prospect digs a bigger and bigger hole. Insincere objections, no matter how much you do to overcome them, often result in your prospect terminating the interview. Sometimes, however, they simply won't tell you what the problem is.

Overcoming objections

Overcoming an objection removes a barrier to purchase. What your prospect is really saying is: 'I would buy from you but for ...' These are the ways you can overcome an objection:

- Paraphrase the objection to make sure you have heard properly. Use a closed question to check that you have grasped the issue and properly understood what it at stake. A good way to do this is to make your sentence begin with, 'So what you want to know is ...'
- Provide information that allays the concern, wherever possible illustrating your point with an additional benefit.
- Use a closed question to check if your prospect is now comfortable and prepared to move closer to an order.

Dealing with an objection

Prospect: *'But the seats are covered with light fabric and will quickly become stained.'*
Salesperson: *'So what you want to know is how does this light-coloured fabric stand up to wear and tear?'*
Prospect: *'Exactly. I don't want to fit out my hotel lounge with your furniture only to have it looking grubby and worn within weeks. We get a lot of people through here.'*
Salesperson: *'Look at this label on the sample. It confirms that all our fabrics are treated with "Octoguard". This means it resists staining, and any spills can be wiped off with a damp cloth.'*
Prospect: *'So it will still look good then, despite being light coloured.'*
Salesperson: *'Yes, it should look good for years. Have you any other concerns?'*

How well you handle objections will dictate how successful you are at securing orders.

TIP

Always be careful about using jargon. It can:

- Demonstrate sector knowledge
- Alienate those not in the know

Your posture and manner is an accurate reflection of your confidence and mood. We all instinctively react to how those around us look and behave.

BODY LANGUAGE

CONFIDENCE

CONFIDENT PEOPLE

Smile a lot

Readily make and hold eye contact

Move about a lot

PEOPLE WHO LACK CONFIDENCE

Smile rarely

Avoid eye contact

Adopt a defensive posture

As we noted on page 47, posture and expression say much more about you than what you say. This is true of both the salesperson and the prospect. Being aware of, and responding to, changes in your prospect's body language, while also being aware of your own, will make you more in tune with your prospect and therefore more successful.

We all communicate non-verbally – that is, through our body language – and one of the joys of non-verbal communication is that it takes place in parallel with your sales conversation. Your prospect may be unaware that they are communicating in this way. Of course, medical conditions and personal quirks can influence body language, and that's why we talk as well.

Reading body language

There are two aspects to reading and interpreting the body language of your prospect. First, there is the insight it gives you into their personal confidence. For example:

Adapt your selling style to put less pressure on people who lack confidence and to give them more opportunity to build rapport through asking open questions.

Second, your prospect's posture and movements will tell you what they are thinking. For example:

Being aware of the significance of these signals allows you to adapt your conversation to take account of what your prospect is subconsciously telling you.

Your body language

Even if your prospect has never studied body language, they will respond to it, and you can speed the sales process by giving out positive, encouraging body language yourself. However, do not become obsessed by this, or you will appear unnatural and false. Here are a few tips:

Non-verbal dialogue

It is possible, with practice, to start to engage your prospect in non-verbal dialogue that they will probably not even notice. Rather like the low, supporting notes played by an organist with their range of foot-operated pipes, non-verbal dialogue should enhance and improve, and never dominate. There are two basic techniques, **mirroring** and **challenging**.

Mirroring is when you start to copy the body language of your prospect, and this will give them the message that you are in agreement with them. Conversely, when your prospect mirrors your body language it is a sure sign they're in agreement with you.

Challenging is when your body language says the opposite. It is a gentle way of saying to the prospect: 'I'm sorry, but I really do not think that is relevant.' Non-verbal challenging is less abrasive than verbal challenging.

Non-verbal dialogue happens spontaneously in any conversation. Watch some people talking and see how their body language changes, mirrors, challenges and supports what they are feeling.

ACTION		MEANS
Smiling/nodding **Leaning forward in their chair**	>	I like what you are saying
Not smiling/arms folded	>	I do not agree
Touching their face	>	I'm thinking about that
Touching/covering their mouth when speaking	>	I'm not telling you everything
Leaning back/hands behind head	>	I've decided to go for it

People buy from people and it makes sense to get recently satisfied customers to help you get the message across. Customers are usually unbiased and therefore more believable.

TESTIMONIALS

EXAMPLES OF TESTIMONIALS

A piece of testimonial is really nothing more than a quote that might be supported by some data. Here are some examples:

- 'Since my new boiler was fitted last winter, my fuel bills have dropped by 20 per cent.'

- 'Now I have replaced my filter set-up with an espresso machine, I've found I'm busier throughout the day, not just at lunchtime.'

- 'I have a bad back and found my old car uncomfortable. The new model is really good and I feel no pain at all, even on long journeys.'

- 'It's true what you say – your paints really do go further. Although they're more expensive per litre, they actually work out cheaper to use.'

People always want to hear how others have fared with the product or service you are selling, and they will be reassured by the experiences of those they admire and respect. However, few people will volunteer positive comments, so you need to ask for feedback you can share.

Testimonials are important no matter what you are selling. They can form a useful part of your marketing armoury as well as making it easier to demonstrate the benefits to your prospect in the sales interview. The best testimonials:

- Are provided by people who are willing to be named
- Quantify the value added
- Mean something to your prospects

Gathering testimonials

Silly as it sounds, all you have to do is ask someone you've already convinced if you can mention their opinion to other people. However, because many salespeople are afraid that asking the question will in some way offend the new customer, or worse, cause them to revisit the decision to purchase, most neglect to gather testimonials.

You need to remember that most people like to be seen as innovative leaders in their business field or community. Listen to your friends talking over a drink and you'll almost always find someone describing their latest purchase. By asking for a testimonial, you are giving your customer the opportunity to demonstrate publicly their wisdom and common sense. It's actually a favour to them.

The time to ask for a testimonial is immediately the decision has been made to buy or not to buy. A person's reasons for saying no can be useful if the information is going to be shared with prospects with clearly different circumstances, and this is particularly true of aspirational products, such as cars or golf club membership. When asking, include phrases such as:

- 'Others would benefit from understanding your motive for buying our health insurance plan. What words would you use to describe your decision and may I quote you to other people I meet?'
- 'I know you are going to measure the cost savings this machine delivers to your company. If I call you in three months time, would you share the figures and may I use them to help other people see how much they might save, too?'

Using testimonials

A testimonial is often best used as written material – for example, a letter from a satisfied customer that can be shown to your prospect. In this form it appears to be more impartial than if you simply read it out or mentioned it in your conversation. This holds true even if you actually helped your customer to write the letter!

If you have quantified testimonial it is always good to show these as percentages for business customers and as figures for consumers. This is because your business prospect will tend to apply the percentage to their circumstances to estimate the value to them, but consumers tend to focus on cash, either saved or spent, so giving the figures makes it easier for them to work out exactly how something will affect them.

Press testimonials

If your product has been positively reviewed by a journalist, it is always worth distributing copies of the feature to your prospects. Testimonial provided by the media is always valuable. Often the publication will reprint the piece for you, which makes it look far more independent than is you simply sent a photocopy.

MARKETING WITH TESTIMONIALS

Here are five ways you can use testimonials to support lead generation:

- **Put customers' quotes on your website with pop-up links to their sites**
- **Picture customers in your advertising alongside their words**
- **Have customers speak to prospects at seminars**
- **Video your product at work with the customer describing the value**
- **Saying that someone famous is a customer but wishes to remain anonymous can sometimes be a powerful tool because it fuels your prospect's imagination**

Sometimes the buying decision is going to be shared. In these situations, it often makes sense to meet and talk with all of those who need to agree to the purchase.

SELLING TO MORE THAN ONE PERSON

FIND OUT WHO YOU'RE TALKING TO

AVOID SURPRISES

CONTROL THE SEATING

WATCH THE BODY LANGUAGE

CONTROL THE CONVERSATION

BRING THEM BACK

SUMMARIZE FREQUENTLY

USE THE TOILET

WATCH THE TIME

A sales interview with more than one prospect can be different from selling to just one person. Usually, the people have more in common than a simple interest in what you are offering. They may be married, colleagues in a business, or manager and subordinate.

Many salespeople make the mistake of focusing only on the person who appears to take the lead and dominate the meeting. If you are selling to a couple, for example, bear in mind that even if a wife greets you with a cup of coffee and leaves you with her husband to 'talk business', she will certainly be influencing your success. Here are ten ways that will help you manage.

Find out who you're talking to

Always ask your hosts to introduce themselves and explain their particular interest or role in the meeting. This makes sure that everyone feels involved and helps you to plan the meeting. Remember, that quiet chap in the corner might even be a competitor!

Avoid surprises

Find out at the outset if anyone has any commitments that might disturb your meeting. Structure the meeting so that the event does not disrupt you.

Control the seating

If you can, take control of the seating. You want to be able to look both of your prospects in the eye and do not want to be sitting higher or lower than anyone else. Sit between your prospects so that you are equidistant from both. This will keep them both feeling involved.

Watch the body language

Particularly when you are meeting long-married couples, there will be lots of non-verbal communication between the two. You need to be aware of this and attempt where possible to respond to it. Do not respond directly – the exchanges are not intended for you – but react as if you have intuitively picked up a hint.

Control the conversation

You need to direct the proceedings and make sure that you ask questions of both people. If one agrees with a point you make, ask the other to comment. They are less likely to challenge their partner than challenge you. Help them sell to each other.

Bring them back

When you are selling in someone's home, it is not unusual for one partner to have to leave the room to answer the phone or put the children to bed. If you feel they've been gone too long for comfort, suggest that they be invited back to see, hear or comment.

Summarize frequently

Different people think in different ways and, inevitably, your prospects will be moving at different speeds. By summarizing at every step of the way, you will keep both prospects moving at the same pace.

Use the toilet

There will be occasions when your instinct tells you that your prospects want to talk between themselves to realign their thinking. Ask if you can use the toilet and use the time to reflect on the meeting thus far. When you return, ask the dominant partner to summarize any thoughts they've had while you've been gone. This brings control back to you.

Watch the time

The more people you are selling to, the longer the meeting will take. Be sure to use all the techniques at your disposal to make firm and steady progress towards your goal.

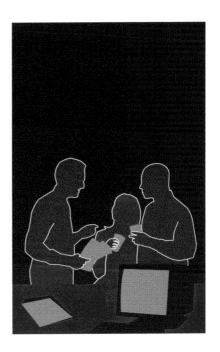

GOOD GUY/ BAD GUY

In a corporate setting, the colleagues you are selling to may well have a routine of adopting opposing styles. Do not be fooled into thinking the one being nice to you is really on your side. Remember that there are almost as many buying techniques as there are selling.

You should never try to be anything other than yourself.
Accept that you will not get on with everyone and be yourself.
Let aspects of your dress or personality make you memorable.

DEVELOPING YOUR STYLE

Two decades ago, sales training was delivered to a formula and recruits followed scripts to guide them. Today, people buy from people they can relate to. How can you balance your organizational and personal styles?

In some situations, such as company showrooms or exhibition stands, or if you are one of many selling in the street or shopping mall, conformity to a corporate style is vital. Even then, however, your personality should be allowed to influence your behaviour. This will help you succeed. For the rest of us, no matter what our marketplace, here are some points for you to consider.

Age matters

Your selling style will be influenced not only by your age but also by the age of your customer. See the panel at the top of page 61 for some examples.

Most of us spend most of our time with people of our own age. This is because we have more in common with them in terms of experience and values. When you are selling to people your own age it is easy to be yourself and bond with your prospect. When there is a marked age difference, however, you should acknowledge this and adapt your behaviour and style so that you feel comfortable and so does your prospect.

Be remembered

Think about your favourite TV entertainer. Do they have a catchphrase or perhaps a physical trademark, such as a funny hat or big glasses? Imagine them now in the aisles of your local supermarket, without the trademark garment or words. Would you still recognize them? Probably not.

PROSPECT	YOUNG SALESPERSON	OLD SALESPERSON
Young	Informal/casual Spontaneous Use 'youth vernacular'	Inhibit urge to 'parent' Understand but don't use 'youth vernacular'
Old	Show respect Be tolerant and listen Allow more time than you think you need Do not rush the prospect	Formal Structured Work hard to establish rapport through identifying shared interests or concerns

Would it help people to remember and recommend you if you also stand out from the crowd?

Not everyone's personality is suited to developing a trademark, but for the more outgoing it's an excellent way to make sure you are remembered.

Match your market

Just as in your questioning you will mirror your prospect's posture to show you are with them – and, more importantly, they will mirror yours – your style needs to match your market. Most people sell in a marketplace they have some empathy with, and so this will happen naturally, but be aware of how styles differ between marketplaces. Dress is an obvious example – few people would visit a farm wearing a suit. See the panel below for some other points to consider.

MARKET PLACE		POSSIBLE STYLES
Food	>	Carry lots of product samples for prospects to taste
Insurance	>	Remember client birthdays and send a card
Cars	>	Dress to mirror your target audience's style

4 GETTING COMMITMENT

Selling is all about getting orders, and closing is the technique that is used to encourage the prospect to make the commitment you are seeking.

ASSERTIVENESS VS. PUSHINESS

ASSERTIVE

Being firm and polite

Acknowledging barriers and working around them

Knowing when to stop trying and move on

Remaining receptive to feedback

PUSHY

Being emotional and rude

Belittling barriers and pushing them over

Outstaying your welcome

Ignoring feedback

How to close

Although books on selling skills may list many ways to close the deal, there are in reality only three ways to close a deal with any degree of sensitivity – the **command close**, the **assumptive close** and the **alternative close**. Before we look at each of these, it is important to recognize that although you need to be assertive when asking for the business, it is vital that you do not push too hard.

Command close

This is where you simply ask for the order, then shut up and wait for your prospect to either agree or object. The silence that ensues as your prospect wrestles with the dilemma can become tense. Asking for the order in such a direct way causes your prospect rapidly to review their thoughts on your offer and the conversation you have had and to reach a decision. Typical command close phrases include:

- 'So we've worked out that you'll need two loads a week delivered, on a Monday and Wednesday. We'll send the first one next Monday then ...'
- 'You're happy with the cost savings, have chosen a colour and we've discussed finance. I'll have our team of fitters here tomorrow to start work ...'

Your prospect will either simply agree or preface their objection with phrases such as 'wait a minute ...' or 'but what about ... ?'

Salesperson: *'Ok, we've talked a lot about your current supplier and the aspects of service you'd like to see improved. Would you want all your staff to be able to order online?'*
Prospect: *'Yes.'*
Salesperson: *'Would you want some paper catalogues as well, for off-line reference?'*
Prospect: *'I guess that would be useful.'*
Salesperson: *'Our system produces a detailed statement of purchases made, showing who has ordered what. This is e-mailed as a spreadsheet. How often would you find that useful?'*
Prospect: *'H-m-m-m – monthly, I guess.'*
Salesperson: *'So all I need now to set up your account is your bank details. Do you have those handy?'*
Prospect: *'Yes, here they are.'*

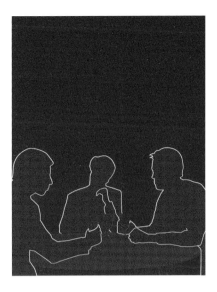

Assumptive close

The assumptive close is a more subtle technique and one that is well suited to complex sales. As you go through the process of defining the specification that best matches your prospect's needs, you effectively build up a pattern of agreement about the order that might be placed. Then you casually ask your prospect to confirm it. Above is an example where the product being sold is office stationery.

By asking for and receiving the bank details, you have the commitment you need to set the whole process in motion.

Alternative close

This is the usual way of asking for an order. By giving an alternative, you avoid the option of 'no'. Examples include:
• 'Would you like the blue one or the green one?'
• 'Shall we deliver it this week or next?'
• 'Would you like the small, medium or large size?'
With the alternative close your prospect has to make a real effort to say no.

Only when the prospect says yes can the deal be described as having been closed.

TOP CLOSING TIPS

• **Maintain eye contact**
• **Never break the silence**
• **Always Be Closing**
• **Smile as if you expect the order**

Experienced salespeople can instinctively tell when the buyer is ready to say yes. You can learn to spot the signals that almost all people give out when ready to buy.

BUYING SIGNALS

Your efforts to close the deal will be all the more successful if you seek commitment when your prospect is already beginning to think that a purchase might be a good idea. Recognizing the **buying signals** will help you pick the right moment to ask a closing question.

Few buyers actually ask you to stop the flow of the meeting so that they can give you the order. However, if you know what to look for, the signs of growing agreement can be almost as obvious.

Verbal buying signals
The experienced salesperson almost instinctively knows when the prospect is coming over to their side to become a buyer. Positive verbal signs include:

- When the prospect starts to ask you questions
- When the focus moves towards the positive
- When the prospect agrees with what you say or even suggests reasons for buying
- When the prospect asks if a colleague can be invited to join the meeting

Non-verbal buying signals
Changing body language will often show you how your prospect's mood is changing. Physical buying signals include:

- Nodding in agreement
- Leaning forward ('I'm really interested')
- Leaning back ('I've decided!')
- Becoming more animated

When your prospect starts emitting buying signals, you need to change the pace of the interview. Slow down and seek commitment. If you have two people in your meeting and one is clearly more interested than the other, encourage them to discuss their concerns between themselves. This can prove much more successful than attempting to manage two prospects with differing degrees of enthusiasm for your offer. They will be far more direct with each other than you can be with either of them.

Non-buying signals

There will be times when it becomes perfectly clear that you're not going to get anywhere with a particular prospect. Reasons for this could include:

- They're not in the market and you didn't spot this earlier
- They've made up their mind not to buy for a perfectly good reason
- There's something more pressing on their mind

When your prospect seems distracted, loses interest or keeps looking at their watch, you can reasonably assume that you are not going to make much headway. There are many good reasons why this should be, and not all of them may be linked to any dissatisfaction with your product or service. If you pick up the feeling that you're between your prospect and something they consider more pressing, stop and ask what the trouble is. Using an open question will help you to identify the issue, and many people will apologize but tell you that, for example, they have an unforeseen problem to sort out. When this happens, use closing questions to get commitment to a new meeting. It is vital that you do not interpret non-buying signals as rejection of you or your offer.

Finally, if the buyer has decided that it really is not for him or her, why not ask them to refer you to someone they feel would be interested. Remember, most people do genuinely want to be as helpful as they can and to see you succeed.

BUYING SIGNALS

✓ DO

- **Stop and seek commitment**
- **Acknowledge by moving to the close**
- **Mirror positive body language**

✗ DON'T

- **Complete your presentation regardless**
- **Acknowledge directly**
- **Oppose positive body language**

Selling is like climbing a ladder. You need to take one step at a time and stop now and again to check where you are. Simply quizzing your prospect and then asking for an order will not work.

TRIAL CLOSING

TOP TIPS

Trial closing is asking for the order before you expect it. You should:

ALWAYS
- **Maintain eye contact**
- **Ask firmly**
- **Let them answer**
- **Accept and understand their objection**
- **Probe their concerns**

NEVER
- **Say they're wrong**
- **Laugh**
- **Ignore an objection**
- **Push**
- **Be surprised if they simply say yes and place the order!**

Closing techniques were introduced on page 62. In the sales interview you need to use these techniques to identify the barriers you must overcome to get the order. Closing is not just about getting the sale.

Of course, much will depend on your prospect and the level of rapport you have established. However, even the friendliest prospect will not welcome being asked for the order before they've even begun to understand the benefits of your offer.

When to trial close
You've reached the stage in the meeting where you've identified the prospect's need and discussed how your product or service can meet those needs. Now, you need to let your prospect suggest the direction of the conversation. Only they know what they are thinking, and you do not want to introduce obstacles they might not even have thought of.

You should therefore trial close when you:

- Want to check if your prospect is ready to buy (they might be!)
- Need to identify your prospect's remaining areas of concern
- Have lost you way and want to pick up the thread of the interview again

How to trial close
Using both open and closed questions, ask if your prospect is ready to order. If they are not, you can go on to ask what is preventing them from saying yes.

The difference is that you are not asking for the order - that would be too big a step to take. Instead, you are asking your prospect to help you by detailing the information they need to make their decision. Consider the following dialogues.

Salesperson: *'OK, so we've talked a lot about your restaurant and the profile of your customers. You've also tasted a few of our frozen desserts and reckon they would suit your menu. Are you ready to give me an order?'*
Prospect: *'No.'*
Salesperson: *'So what is holding you back?'*
Prospect: *'Well, I'm not convinced that they are really going to work out cheaper than making my own'.*

So now the salesperson knows where to focus. Convince the restaurateur that it's cheaper to buy than to prepare the dishes in the restaurant kitchen and the order should be in the bag.

In reality, you may go through several trial closes, eliminating a succession of objections, before the deal can be concluded.

TRIAL CLOSING

- **Identifies barriers**
- **Focuses you**
- **Empowers prospects**

'Can you see how much our product will save you?'

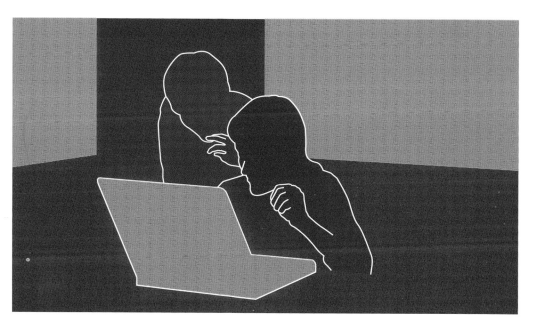

People do not always mean what they say, neither do they always say what they mean. You need to tease out the real issues from those put up as a smokescreen.

TYPES OF OBJECTION

When you try to close a deal your prospect will inevitably raise objections. You should welcome them because they show what lies between you and success.

You will not have reached this stage of the sales meeting if your prospect cannot see some merit in what you are selling. When objections are raised, however, you need to be alert to the fact that your prospect may be concealing their real motive from you. You need to watch their body language – in particular see if they avoid eye contact when they voice their objection.

As we saw on page 52, there are two kinds of objections, sincere and insincere ones. No one likes being less than truthful, but sometimes a hidden issue or agenda will inhibit the prospect from giving you the order no matter what you say. If they are feeling bad about it, they may give you a token small order to 'make you happy'. You will probably then join a large band of suppliers who all work hard to win small orders every time but who never profit from the relationship.

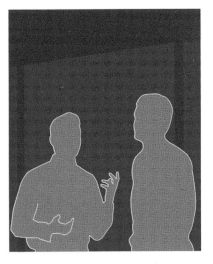

Sincere objections

These are the genuine concerns that you need to overcome before obtaining a prospect's commitment to buy. They arise from reasoned consideration of your offer. Sincere objections are often linked to the performance of your product compared with the alternatives. Examples of typical sincere objections are:

- 'But surely, it will cost more to operate than my current model.'
- 'The cost savings are not great enough to warrant the up-front investment.'
- 'Frankly, I don't like the colour and don't think it will match my décor.'

Insincere objections

Objections of this type are usually offered to mask a motive for not buying that your prospect is choosing, for some reason, to keep hidden, and they are often delivered with more emotion than logic. When you overcome one, it will be followed by another, perhaps quite unrelated objection. Examples of typical insincere objections are:

- 'It's simply too expensive.'
- 'My customers won't like it.'
- 'I'm sorry, but it's really just too grand to fit into my house.'
- 'My wife wouldn't like it.' (Here the blame is projected on to someone not present)

The genuine barriers to a sale that can be found hidden behind insincere objections are often facts the prospect is too embarrassed to share. They include:

- 'I cannot afford it.'
- 'I am not the decision-maker.'
- 'My wife wears the trousers and we both need to be here.'
- 'I gave your rival the order yesterday so am no longer in the market.'

Remember, too, that consumers and business buyers will often have different priorities and concerns.

SPOT THE DIFFERENCE

SINCERE OBJECTIONS

Logical

Often quantified

Reveal genuine concerns

Overcome by explanation

INSINCERE OBJECTIONS

Emotional

Rarely quantified

Conceal a genuine objection

Explanation leads to new objection

	CONSUMER	BUSINESS BUYER
Price	Buys with taxed income	Buys with 'company' money
Payback	Will it last until I'm bored?	Will it make me a profit?
Value	Do I like it?	Do I need it?

Handling objections forms perhaps the most challenging area of the sales interview.

DEALING WITH OBJECTIONS

10 TOP TIPS FOR HANDLING OBJECTIONS

1 Know your product
2 Respect the prospect's view
3 Check that you understand
4 Think before you answer
5 Use visuals
6 Use testimonial
7 Don't waffle
8 It's OK to check facts
9 Have the prospect help you
10 Accept that you won't win them all!

Reflecting objections

Sometimes, particularly if the reasoning behind the objection is difficult to understand, it is useful to seek the prospect's help in overcoming it. The chances are that they know the answer but are simply stalling to give themselves time to think. If you want to reflect an objection, pose the question to your prospect that encourages them to suggest how the point raised might best be dealt with. Here is an example:

Prospect: 'My drivers won't like your vans.'
Salesperson: 'Tell me, why do you feel your drivers won't like these new vans?'
Prospect: 'Well, they're used to driving Mercedes vans and your marque is not so prestigious.'
Salesperson: 'What would help them to make the transition?'
Prospect: 'Well, they've always said we should have our vans sign-written all over rather than simply putting our name across the back doors.'
Salesperson: 'And why haven't you had your current fleet sign-written?'
Prospect: 'Because it was too expensive. £500 a vehicle.'
Salesperson: 'But my vans are £1,000 cheaper, so you could sign-write them and still bank the difference. What's more, it would raise your profile and generate leads.'
Prospect: 'Now I hadn't thought of that ...'

And our salesperson is one large step closer to a sale.

Helpful phrases

It's always useful to have a few helpful phrases committed to memory that you can draw on when challenged by an objection. It's perfectly all right to use the same words many times, because even though they may come to sound rather trite to you, they will not be so when heard for the first time by each prospect. Next time you are confronted by an objection, try one of the following phrases:

- 'I'm really interested you feel that way, could you tell me why?'
- 'Very few people pick up on that issue. Why is it clearly so important to you?'

WHAT		WHY
Trial close	>	Prompts the prospect to raise an objection: 'I'm not convinced that it will clean my ovens.'
Paraphrase what they've said	>	This checks that you've got the exact message: 'So you're concerned that it won't be effective?' Prospect agrees.
Explore the issue	>	'What is your biggest problem with oven cleaning? 'Prospect tells you more: 'We do a lot of high-temperature work and the grease gets baked on hard. We've never really sorted it.'
Clarify the issue	>	'So you want to know how our product works in those really tough situations where other cleaners have let you down?' Prospect agrees. You now have to convince them.
Provide evidence	>	You could: demonstrate the product; refer to existing satisfied users (testimonial); describe why your product is superior.
Check satisfaction	>	Use a closed question to see if the prospect is happy: 'Can you see now how it actually works in tough situations?' If prospect disagrees, you need to probe some more. If prospect agrees, move on.
Identify next objection	>	'Are there any other points we need to cover before you can place the order?'

You can be more convincing if you can show what your product looks like. It also helps to be able to explain complex operations and benefits using pictures, charts and graphs.

VISUAL AIDS

The art of using visual aids is to tailor their use to support, not lead, your sales interview.

You've probably heard the saying that a picture is worth a thousand words. It could have been written with selling in mind, for pictures, graphs and diagrams are an invaluable part of every salesperson's armoury, and it's now easier than ever to produce and display visual aids that will help your prospect see the point you are making about your product. Always avoid showing every prospect everything you have brought with you. There is little point in helping someone understand features or issues that are of no interest to them.

There is an almost endless list of ways you can illustrate your presentation, but some of the more frequently used are described below.

Flip-over presentation folders

These are often prepared by helpful marketing colleagues. Used wisely, they can enable large sales teams to make the same presentation to every prospect. This is useful in terms of consistency, but unless it is adapted to suit your own style, it will simply erode your effectiveness. Always try to sit beside your prospect and point out the relevant parts or pages that you want them to focus on.

Presentation on laptop

Many salespeople choose to demonstrate their software skills with complex presentations incorporating sound, video and hyperlinks to additional information. Remember: when you're selling, it is always good to keep your presentation simple. Too much technical wizardry can detract from the strength of the message.

Brochures and leaflets

Company literature (or a competitor's literature for that matter) can be useful if you need to illustrate a particular point that you know is covered. You should use a rival company's literature only in response to a particular objection, when you might find it easier to show your prospect how it differs from your product.

Video

Videos are too often used as 'surrogate salespeople' and are shown to prospects in the hope that they will do the selling job. A good way to use video is to send the cassette or DVD to the prospect before the meeting so that you can discuss how helpful they found it when you meet.

Photographs

Satisfied customers will often let you photograph their investment in your product or service. This is particularly true in sectors such as leisure, where fitness equipment, caravans and the like look all the more appealing *in situ* and in use. Photographic testimonial can be the most powerful of all. However, in many manufacturing environments, photography is forbidden because it may breach commercial confidentiality. Always ask before taking photographs.

Samples

The benefits of almost every physical product can be illustrated by samples. These enable your prospect to taste, smell, touch and perhaps hear your product. A little ingenuity can allow samples to play a part in a sales presentation of products that are seemingly impossible to show in this way. For example, if you are selling industrial machines that are too large to move, you might carry samples that show key details, such as tooling, welded joints and other differentiating features.

In the furniture industry it is not uncommon to organize tours for which a truck is packed with samples and parked in front of the prospect's outlet to provide a travelling exhibition to support the sales drive.

GOOD VISUALS

- **Create an impressive presentation that can introduce your offer**
- **Illustrate benefits**
- **Make complex processes simple to understand**
- **Demonstrate how the seemingly difficult is actually quite easy**

VISUAL AIDS CHECKLIST

- **Bold and graphic**
- **Simple**
- **Colourful**
- **Specific**
- **Relevant**

Selling is rarely black and white. To achieve the sale, there needs to be a degree of compromise on both sides. The skill of achieiving this balance is called negotiation.

NEGOTIATING

KEY DIFFERENCES

SELLING

Wins orders

Short-term gain

Makes money for you

A focused, directed communication skill

NEGOTIATING

Builds relationships

Long-term gain

Makes money for you and the customer

A focused, directed selling skill

Few salespeople are able to meet all of a prospect's demands, and in reality the deal struck is usually a compromise between two sets of ideals. Negotiating to reach this agreement uses all the sales techniques described in this book, but a negotiator also seeks to add value and reduce the costs associated with the order. This is particularly important where you are selling an ongoing arrangement rather than a one-off product or service. Examples could be storage and distribution, contract cleaning or the supply of raw materials or energy.

Negotiation starts when you and your prospect have agreed that you want to do business together. Your product or service meets their needs in terms of specification and performance. What happens next is called **trading concessions**.

Trading concessions

It works like this. You offer your prospect something that is worth more to them than it is to you. In return, they make a concession that makes life easier for you. For example, you might deliver to your customer as you produce, saving you storage space. In return, you might allow your customer extended credit, sharing some of your saving on storage costs. The result is that you both win.

Even in one-off consumer sales there is usually room to enhance the deal for both parties through negotiation. For example, you might choose as a consumer to take the washing machine that is on display in the showroom (and has probably been discounted to the retailer by their supplier). In return for your accepting shop-soiled goods, the retailer will share some of his discount with you. The shop gains display space for a newer model and you, in turn, get a bargain. Both parties are content.

Negotiation is, of course, a far more complex process than can be described here, but this is a book about selling. You need to appreciate that the best business deals result from the trading of concessions that add profit to your bottom line and to your customer's bottom line. Within the context of sales, an understanding of the principle of negotiation is important. You can see some examples of commonly traded concessions in the tinted panel at the bottom of the page.

Negotiation, therefore, is a method of **fine tuning the deal** in a way that maximizes profitability for both supplier and customer. It makes for better, sustainable, and more valuable working relationships. When you are working together in this way you are usually regularly reviewing the performance of the contract and communicating this. This keeps you in touch with new opportunities. It also means that you are closer to the customer should things go wrong and you need to sort out problems.

Negotiating is the process by which you trade concessions to reach the conclusion that best suits you both.

CONCESSION	POSSIBLE VALUE (customer)	POSSIBLE COST (supplier)
Early payment	Increases borrowing	Reduces borrowing
Just-in-time delivery	Reduces stockholding Improves cash flow	Reduces production efficiency Damages cash flow
Weekly delivery	Increases stock holding Levels cash flow	Increases production efficiency Levels cash flow
Agree fixed price/volume	Pegs input costs for the agreed volume of product	Provides guaranteed income Can support investment in new plant

Getting the order is of course your goal. However, too often salespeople stop at that point and overlook the opportunity to sell more to your customer while they are receptive.

CROSS-SELLING

CROSS-SELLING

- **Increases order value by adding additional products and services**

- **Reduces transport costs as you are delivering more with each order**

- **Makes customer servicing cheaper as the cost is spread over more turnover**

- **Excludes competitors who might otherwise sell the additional lines**

It is all too easy to forget the opportunity to add to the order when your customer eventually says yes. It is, after all, an exciting moment. However, you can often boost your profit and commission and greatly enhance your relationship with the customer if you help them to buy more from you.

It may well be that your basic offer has been pared back in terms of specification to make the price appealing – car manufacturers do this all the time – but now that your customer is hooked, it is time to re-introduce all the other things they might want to buy. Remember, too, the difference between cost and value. Looking at car manufacturers again, some paint finishes cost more than others but actually cost no more to apply. The manufacturer has succeeded in creating the illusion that some finishes are more valuable and therefore more desirable.

PRODUCT		POSSIBLE EXTRAS
Car	>	Sell up to next model; add to specification
Suit	>	Shirts, ties, shoes, etc. to match
TV	>	Extended warranty; VCR, DVD
Holiday	>	Optional excursions; flight upgrade
Fuel oil	>	Storage tanks; pumps; fleet management software
Steel	>	Extended credit at a cost; delivery/storage options

Increasing the order

You will have noted the prospect's areas of interest as part of your sales conversation. Once you have obtained the order, you need to revisit some of the options already discounted – see the panel at the bottom of page 76 for examples.

Can you see how you can up the order in your market sector? Often, the profitability of the add-ons is a great deal higher than the initial order. This is, of course, helped by the fact that both the cost of customer recruitment and product delivery have already been covered.

Selling more later

It is good practice to make a note to call your new customer shortly after delivery to make sure they are happy. Most customers welcome this and will be enjoying a 'honeymoon period' when their focus will be on what is different in their lives at home or at work. When you open the conversation it is always good to use a leading open question such as:

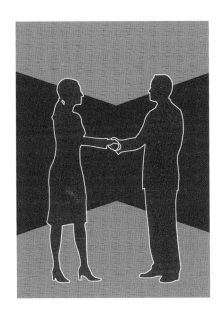

- 'Now that you're using product X, what have you found to be the greatest benefit?'
- 'You've had your new car a week now. What do like best about it?'

Inevitably, your new customer will also have some negative views as well as positive feelings, but you need to encourage them to share the good things. If the bad aspects are of sufficient importance, you will hear about them anyway.

If you see from the notes you took at the time of the sale that additional items were discussed but not ordered, now is a good time to mention them again, especially if they enhance the performance of the product your customer is telling you about. You can be quite directive in this situation – see the panel on the right for an example.

And there you have your sales opportunity – and all because you took the trouble to check that your customer was satisfied.

Salesperson: *'I'm really pleased you're getting on well with product X. Can you remember how we talked about our tailor-made applicators? They can make the product go further, saving you money?'*
Customer: *'Yes, I do remember, but we decided to stick with our old applicators.'*
Salesperson: *'And how are you finding the old applicators with the new product. Are they easy to calibrate accurately?'*
Customer: *'They're ok I suppose, but we have found that your product runs through them faster than we expected.'*

However appealing it is to meet your sales target and agree to a one-off deal, word will soon spread among existing and prospective customers. Sometimes it's best simply to walk away.

WHEN TO SAY NO

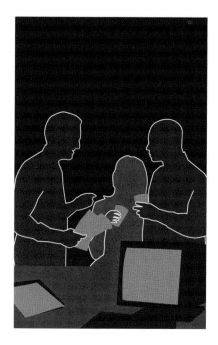

Although it goes against the instinct of any salesperson to walk away from an order, there are times where you simply have to say no and walk away.

Most marketplaces are populated by connected people – that is, consumers of your product or service who network and talk among themselves. These networks can be:

- Members of the same family, because some sectors, notably agriculture, are full of people who are related to each other
- Trade bodies, which share good practice and lobby against unwelcome legislation
- Chambers of trade and other organizations, which represent businesses from all sectors but are based in one locality
- Neighbourhoods, where people chat over garden walls and gossip

You can see, then, that you can never keep secret the details of any exceptional deal you strike to get a sale. If you give too much away to one customer, those with whom you have been less generous will soon find out and become dissatisfied.

The best reason for turning down an order, of course, is that it is simply not profitable to come down to the level of price your prospect is demanding. In sales interviews you sometimes seem to get stuck in an endless loop of trivial objections, and price is always the way your prospect suggests you go if you want to get the order. It can be tempting to say yes and give in, but this can only lead to problems later on. Those buyers who drive ridiculous bargains during the purchase are often those who will give you after-sales problems.

How to sell by saying no

You can sometimes change the course of what seems a failing sales meeting by preparing to leave. If you are convinced that your prospect really wants or needs what you are selling, but is simply trying to batter you into a deal you'd rather not do, tell them. It often works.

Saying no

If you feel that the prospect is asking for too much, be firm but polite and say something like:

- 'I'm sorry, but you're asking too much.
  I cannot agree to that.'
- 'There's no way I can let you have that.
  I'm sorry, I might as well go.'
- 'If you really cannot afford it, then I'm sorry,
  I shouldn't have tried to sell it to you.'

Note that by apologizing you are not blaming the prospect. Instead, it will make them feel that they've let you down and keep the door open for another time.

> Saying no to the customer tells them they've got all the concessions you can give. They have to choose between placing the order or letting you go.

10 REASONS FOR SAYING NO

1 You will lose money by the deal

2 You cannot agree a high enough price

3 The customer needs it before you can realistically deliver

4 You do not believe the product will satisfy the prospect's need

5 You have overstated and misrepresented the benefits

6 The customer still owes for the last delivery

7 The customer wants to break the law using your product

8 You are offered a bribe or other inducement

9 You are physically threatened by the prospect

10 The interview becomes an argument and should be continued another day

Telesales are the quickest and easiest form of selling. However, they demand complete focus as you can easily lose your customer if you do not establish a good rapport straight away.

TELESALES

PRODUCTS OR SERVICES THAT LEND THEMSELVES TO TELESALES

ADVERTISING

- You can post copies of the paper and e-mail rates

FUNDRAISING

- You are targeting interested groups and have advertised

CONSUMABLES

- You ring every day, week or month to build the next delivery

EXHIBITION SPACE

- You need to talk to lots of people many times before they order

Some products and services can be sold over the phone and you may never meet your customer face to face. In this sometimes fast and furious environment you need to work even harder to maintain good relationships.

Common characteristics of products or services that can be sold by phone are:

- You need to make contact several times before the order is placed
- Orders are frequent and your call is to check the details and add new lines
- Several potential buyers need to be 'juggled' over time until one buys
- Your prospects tend to enquire and ask you to prepare a quotation

Telesales is quite different from telemarketing, the process by which sales appointments are made over the phone (see pages 34-5). You are going through the various stages of the sale but in a simplified form. Here are the stages of a sale, this time with how they are different when making telesales calls.

Approach

Try to call at a pre-arranged time

- Book a time/day to call next when you speak
- Ring at the same time of day, when they are often available
- Become predictable and part of the prospect's routine

Note the names and build relationships
- Use software to record alternative contacts and their roles

Establish rapport

Keep good records of what you have said before
- Become someone your contact confides in
- Take a real interest in them
- Check early on that your last delivery arrived safely and in good condition
- If you've not sold to them yet, did they get the information you sent?

Probe

Find out what has changed, is new, is succeeding, is not working
- Understand the role your product or service has for them
- Find out if they've already been talking to competitors
- Get them to list their needs

Proposition

Create urgency
- Are stocks running low and are they in danger of missing out?

Add something new each time
- This creates interest and suggest you are proactive/innovative
- You can create new sales and increase the customer's value
- You will learn more about them

Close

Keep your closing simple
- If a regular order is usual, assume you have one today as well
- Use various different delivery options as alternative closers
- Always book a day/time for your next call

WHY TELESALES WORKS

- **It's fast — it's possible to talk with between 5 and 15 customers in an hour**
- **It's cheap — you don't need to travel**
- **It's convenient — people still prefer to talk to someone**
- **It's predictable — you can measure success and seek improvement**

5 AFTER THE FIRST ORDER

It is not unheard of for someone to have second thoughts after you have left with their order. There is nothing worse than returning to base to find they've rung and cancelled the deal.

Confirming the order

You need to make sure that you have reinforced in the buyer's mind the commitment they have made. This is particularly important with bespoke products and services, which cannot readily be sold elsewhere if the buyer changes their mind. The ways in which you can confirm an order are summarized below.

Order numbers

Many larger organizations operate a purchase order system, and most buyers have sequences of order numbers that they issue against their budget. This allows the company's finance team to validate invoices that come in and be confident that the goods or services have been ordered. The buyer normally also confirms that the bill can be paid.

Getting an order number from your buyer, particularly in bureaucratic organizations, confirms that the order exists. If they decide they want to change their mind, the buyer has to inconvenience colleagues 'in accounts', which many people will not wish to do.

Deposits

Consumers do not issue purchase orders; neither do they always behave as you would wish. It is vital when you are selling to householders to get real commitment from them. The best form of commitment is a cheque, which represents an up-front payment for what they have just ordered. If they are going to change their mind, they'll do it while they are writing the deposit cheque when you are there to reassure them. Issue a receipt for the cheque. If you take deposits from businesses, they will also need a pro-forma invoice for their books.

It is advisable to avoid taking large cash deposits. Many firms can also take deposits by credit card, even over the phone.

Order forms

Writing out the details of the order is always a good idea, as is leaving a copy of the order with your customer. Always ask them to read, then sign the order to confirm that they agree with what you have recorded. Signed orders can be useful evidence if you have a problem later. Most order forms also allow you to note any deposit you have taken.

Terms and conditions

It is always wise to have some legally drafted terms and conditions of sale. These are usually printed on the reverse of the sales documents you give or send to your customer. Bear in mind, however, that few people will read the small print, and no one will like to have these clauses drawn to their attention because you have chosen to interpret them literally.

A sale is not a sale until the money's in the bank.

CUSTOMERS LIKE YOU TO CONFIRM THE ORDER BECAUSE

- They can relax – the decision is made
- It is now your responsibility – not theirs
- There is no need to search further for a supplier
- You have demonstrated that you know what you are going to do

We all love surprises and your customers will glow with contentment if you give them just a little bit more than they expect. Happy customers keep coming back for more.

DELIVER AND DELIGHT

Winning the sale makes your day. How can you make the customer's day?

In most sales roles you are also responsible for making sure that the customer stays happy, even after the goods have been delivered and paid for. 'Delighting the customer' has almost become a cliché, but the reality is that, with a little effort, you can convert almost any customer into a mine of valuable repeat business and referrals.

During the process of winning a sale you will have persuaded your customer that your business is at once professional, competent, efficient and innovative. To possess these attributes is ultimately the wish of every organization. Making these a reality, certainly for your customer, is very much part of the sales function.

Looking good

Just as you take a pride in your own appearance and take trouble to make a smart, professional impression, so must your product or service show the same care when it is delivered. Even if your product is simply a software download from a website, the ease with which this can be achieved reflects your concern to provide a positive customer experience. If your company's staff visit your customer's premises – whether to deliver, install, service or maintain – their performance is even more important.

Pleasant surprises

You may be surprised to learn that even what seems to be a very small additional investment in your customer at the time of delivery can repay a huge

PURCHASE		POSSIBLE SURPRISE
Gym membership	>	T-shirt
Replacement windows	>	Cleaning kit
Phone system	>	Handset upgrade
Van fleet	>	Cost-monitoring software

dividend. The reason is that even if the purchase has been made for business reasons, a 'pleasant surprise' will provoke an often subconscious positive emotional response. Perversely, it is often the lowest-cost surprises that will create the greatest impact. Some examples are listed in the box above.

Clearly, the surprise note only has to be appropriate to the value of the order that has been placed, but it should also be linked to it in some way. In a business-to-business environment, of course, you must avoid the unexpected extra being misinterpreted as a cheap bribe. Ideally, as with the phone system example in the box above, the **perceived value should be higher than the actual cost**.

Reciprocal trading

Although some people prefer not to confuse their buying with their selling, in smaller communities and in particular within the small business sector, reciprocal trading should always be encouraged. Imagine you run a phone company. How would you feel if the tyre dealer who maintained your fleet purchased a whole new phone system without even asking you to give a quote for the work?

Reciprocal trading builds relationships between businesses and develops the strength of both companies involved.

10 WAYS TO LOOK GOOD

1 Use overprinted envelopes and packaging that conveys your company values

2 Make sure that delivery vehicles are clean, damage-free and sign-written

3 Provide uniforms and ID cards for all staff who work at customers' sites

4 Encourage staff to stay smart and not smoke in any workplace

5 Provide customer-care training to all front-line staff

6 Give incentives to encourage delivery staff to create sales leads

7 Reserve your best parking places for your visitors, not your directors

8 Make your 'front of house' area clean, warm and inviting

9 Make sure a real person, not a machine, answers your phone

10 Keep websites simple, fast downloading and easy to navigate

Planning to win follow-up business from the new customer is as important as gaining the first sale. After ordering, the buyer's focus moves from you to the product. You need to be remembered.

KEEPING IN TOUCH

HOW TO KEEP IN TOUCH

There are many effective customer relation management (CRM) software packages on the market. Choose one that:

- **Suits your needs now and in the future**
- **Is linked to a diary system and can prompt you to call**
- **Is easy to use**

All too often, after the excitement of winning and supplying the first order has subsided, the new customer gets forgotten. This is not desirable, because existing customers usually hold more potential than new ones.

After you have checked that your new customer is satisfied with their first delivery, the time has come to develop the relationship. You can then make sure you contact them when it is most likely to give you a positive result. Keeping in touch with business customers is different from keeping in touch with consumers. The differences are summarized below.

Business customers

No matter how hard you worked on building rapport before the sale, as a recently established supplier your relationship with the customer will be more open and relaxed. The challenge facing you is to become integrated within their business network and thus difficult to dislodge.

BUSINESS CUSTOMERS	INDIVIDUALS AS CUSTOMERS
More potential for extra sales	> More potential for referrals
Order value/profit usually large	> Order value/profit often small
Usually expect you to stay in touch	> Often suspect you if you stay in touch!
Wide circle of colleagues	> Wide circle of family and friends

WHAT		WHY
Business customers		
Direct dial phone numbers	>	You can avoid switchboards and ring out of hours
Organization chart	>	You can see who else you need to influence
Birthdays	>	You can send a card (too few suppliers do this)
Company anniversaries	>	Significant dates can create sales opportunities
Significant shareholders	>	Use them to 'leap' into their other businesses
Family details	>	People love to talk about their children
Partner's name/job	>	Ask for a referral to the partner's employer
Individual customers		
Club memberships	>	You can see who else you may be able to influence
Birthdays	>	You can send a card (too few suppliers do this)
Significant anniversaries	>	Significant dates can create sales opportunities
Neighbours and friends	>	Sources of referrals
Family details	>	People love to talk about their children
Partner's name/job	>	Ask for a referral to the partner's employer

Individuals

When you've sold to someone in their home your focus is usually on generating referrals, although repeat purchases may also, of course, be possible. It all depends on the product or service you are offering. When you're selling to householders you may choose to collect a different type of information.

The best way to collect information about individuals you have converted into customers is to send them a questionnaire. Link the information you are seeking to an assessment of their satisfaction or use an incentive. Both will build your knowledge bank.

If you've impressed the prospect, even if you don't win the order you might find them willing to refer you to someone they think might like what you're offering.

WINNING REFERRALS

REFERRED AND COLD PROSPECTS

REFERRED PROSPECT

Hears of you from an existing contact

Someone they know has bought from you

Can get an opinion from a trusted source

Has faith in your customer's judgement

Is likely to see you when asked

COLD PROSPECT

Hasn't heard of you before

No one they know has bought from you

Has no one to ask an opinion

Bases decision on what you say

Needs persuading to see you

Every business needs a steady flow of new customers both to replace those that are lost and to deliver sales and profit growth. As they develop, businesses also outgrow their customers. The best way to prospect for new customers is to seek referrals or introductions from your existing customers.

Those closest to your existing customers will already know of you and what you do. They may well have experienced your product or service and have discussed its value to them. They may even be ready to buy but currently not known to you. Winning referrals is all about persuading your customer to introduce you to these hitherto untapped sources of orders.

In a social context we build our network or community of contacts through referrals. Think about the last party you attended. The host probably grabbed your arm and steered you towards a stranger. 'This is John. He's as mad about squash as you are. I'm sure you'll have a lot in common.' Then he moved on, introduction made. You talked to John, and before you parted had arranged a game of squash.

The business context is no different — except you need to ask for the introduction because business referrals rarely come spontaneously. Most people make new contacts in this way, both at home and at work, so you should never be embarrassed to ask for a referral. If your customer is happy with you, they will be happy to refer you to others. If they are not, you might have unearthed a hidden problem with your product or service, and solving this problem might actually save a damaged relationship.

Asking for a referral

As with anything you routinely do in your sales role, it is good to have some well-rehearsed lines that come to your lips naturally. The more confident you become, the more you will start to develop your own technique. See the panel below for some examples you might use.

You will notice that in each instance the emphasis of the question is on the benefit to your customer's contact. This is because the customer will be more inclined to want to help them than you. After all, you have just won an order!

Making referrals easier to give

If you're alert and observant you will see clues around your customer's home or office that you can use to help them identify people to refer. Clearly you cannot be too nosy, but things such as golf clubs let you know how your customer relaxes. It's much easier than to ask a leading question. In a business-to-business situation you should ask about suppliers and customers – others who will benefit if they also use what you are selling. The very fact that your customer has purchased from you, can, in some situations, convert their customers into prospects too.

SITUATION		PHRASE
You've just landscaped a garden	>	'Tell me, who do you know that might also be fed up with their garden and need a hand to turn it round?'
You've just built a website	>	'Tell me, which of your customers and suppliers were most impressed with the new site? Would you introduce me to them?'
You're now supplying a haulier with fuel	>	'Tell me, who do you know that might also value the just-in-time delivery deal we've agreed with you?'

You should always be seeking opportunities to collect names of people known to your customers. This need not be as intrusive as you might think. Handled well, customers are happy to share.

MORE ABOUT REFERRALS

Many successful businesses do not market themselves at all. They get all the new business they want by harvesting referrals from existing customers.

Not all referrals are the same, of course, and to make the most of the opportunity, some may be quite tenuous. Clearly, you cannot imply that you have been referred when you have not, but you do need to explore the boundaries.

Referrals can be generated by a variety of methods, one of which, simply asking the question, is explained on pages 88–9. Some other methods you might consider are described below, but remember that none of them is as effective as simply popping the question when you are face to face with the customer.

Collecting names

Any prospect name you can get hold of, along with some link that can be used to hook their interest when you contact them, is good. You can encourage existing customers to share contacts to whom you can mention their name by:

Dear Mr Green
Your friend Mr Brown has suggested
I write to tell you how valuable he finds
our dog-walking service. He said that
as you also dislike cold, dark mornings
and have a dog that needs a lot of
exercise, you might wish to give our
service a try.

Dear Mrs White
Sally Hart at Evergreen Insulations
has suggested that I write to share
with you some of the reasons she
decided to switch to our wall injection
system. She said that as your firm
also supplies cavity wall insulation,
you might benefit from the cost
efficiencies we can deliver.

- Including the request for contacts on a satisfaction survey form
- Offering an incentive should an introduction lead to an order
- Asking who they collaborate with — for example, trade organizations

Once you have some people to contact, you should prepare a pre-approach letter along the lines described on page 30. Nevertheless, your letter needs to open with the introduction. See bottom of page 90 for examples.

You will notice that both examples focus on the benefit to be gained by the recipient of the letter. You can sometimes get testimonial letters from your customer, and enclosing a copy of such a letter adds real impact.

Bouncing from the customer

A less effective method, but worthwhile nevertheless, is to provide marketing materials that your customer can use on your behalf. These are often most suitable for people whose work is visible to passers-by, who then become interested and may enquire for themselves. They include:

- On-site advertising signs, of the type often used by home-improvement companies
- Postage paid 'postcards' celebrating the arrival of a new 'widget'
- Promotional stickers bearing your details that they can use
- Leaflet drops in the neighbourhood of your new customer

Endorsement

In many business sectors important organizations are courted and supplied with goods and services at preferential rates on the understanding that they can be mentioned as customers in sales campaigns. Everyone who aspires to be as successful as your celebrity customer then has the opportunity to be a little like them by buying from you.

LAUNCH EVENTS

For business-to-business selling, launch events are an excellent way to gather referrals. This is what you should do:

- **Suggest that your customer's investment merits celebration**
- **Offer to provide practical and financial support: your marketing people can prepare invitations; you may be able to find someone notable to speak; contributing to the cost earns you the right to be a speaker and so on**
- **Make sure that the customer invites their network of contacts to the event**
- **Organize a speaker who will describe the merits of your product or service**
- **Ask your customer to endorse your organization's support in public**

Afterwards, you should remember to write to everyone who attended and follow up the contact.

Launch events can also win you 'free' publicity in local, regional and trade publications.

There is a growing trend towards building customer, or user communities. Many customers welcome opportunities to share tips and experiences. Enabling and encouraging this helps you too.

SELF-MANAGING CUSTOMERS

You are responsible for winning sales, and the more you can do to make it easy for yourself, the better. Growing success inevitably means an increasing need to service existing customers rather than find new ones, however. Both aspects of your job are important, but it is possible to encourage your customers to manage themselves, allowing you more time to look for new prospects.

In most cases your customers will have a shared interest, possibly even a passion, for the products or services you provide. This is particularly true of technology products, software and travel. You can use a number of techniques to develop your customer base into self-managing communities or **special interest groups**. This can provide you with highly relevant market information and generate sales and referrals. Handled correctly, your customers can, literally, sell your products and services to each other.

HOW TO MAKE GROUPS EVEN EASIER

- Encourage reliable customers to lead the groups

- Make the activity self-funding by user subscription

- Have the customers manage it themselves

- Have them focus your innovation

- Create a system whereby they tell you who wants to buy and when

Consumer groups

Imagine that you operate a fleet of coaches and provide an annual selection of holidays. Your holiday customers are predominantly elderly and all live within a 30-minute drive or your base. Establishing a holiday club, where your customers are encouraged to come together to meet, reminisce and learn about new destinations, could provide you with opportunities to:

- Sell more holidays, with featured packages sold on the night
- Build your database, with members encouraged to bring a friend

- Gather market intelligence, by asking your audience about rival operators
- Innovate, by asking your audience to suggest new destinations

You will be able to influence collectively customers you might otherwise never meet face to face because holidays are usually sold either from brochures or over the phone.

Other opportunities for consumer groups include:

- Furniture – you could perhaps create a 'pine collectors guild'
- Garden centre – a gardeners' club

What's more, you can offer exclusive deals to your members to boost their loyalty and keep them coming back to you.

User groups

In many industries – printing, for example – users of complex technology often subscribe to unofficial, Internet-based user groups, which they use to share practical tips and experiences. Sometimes they are global networks, and these can actually develop more knowledge and expertise than the original supplier, simply by being communicating and being in touch with those working at the 'coalface'.

Establishing a host for user groups – perhaps by allocating a 'members only' area of your website – would enable you to:

- Establish your own user group
- Benefit from users' practical experience
- Innovate by responding to market feedback
- Know when to contact each customer to sell more

An effective, commercially managed user group can not only keep you in touch with your customers but can more importantly provide you with more time and opprtunities to sell to new people.

NEWSLETTERS

Although they are more of a marketing tool than a sales technique, it is nevertheless important to consider newsletters, which are a traditional method to achieve the same goal. The difference is, however, that newsletters are costly and time-consuming to produce. They are not self-managing because you need to gather the information, then publish the contents.

When some people are dissatisfied with your organization, they will simply drift away and withdraw their support. More helpful are those who ring to tell you what they feel you're doing wrong.

HANDLING COMPLAINTS

TOP 10 TIPS FOR HANDLING COMPLAINTS

1 Take the call
2 Show sympathy
3 Get the facts
4 Gather evidence
5 Investigate the cause
6 Take time to think
7 Call back when you promised
8 Offer a solution
9 Think about benefits
10 Remember this is a sales opportunity

Not all complaints result from shoddy goods or poor service. Sometimes the problem lies with the customer themselves who has mistakenly blamed you for some misfortune. When they are handled sensitively and firmly, complaints can often be resolved and the customer relationship strengthened.

Hearing the news

Your customer is incandescent with rage and ranting about your company. This is the fear we all have when we hear that an angry caller wants to complain. Usually, the customer is quite rational and, although upset and a little angry, really only wants the problem sorted out. When you get a complaint by phone – less confident people sometimes write to complain – you need to:

• Say that you are going to write down the details so that you are sure you get them right
• Sound sympathetic but do not accept liability at this stage
• Listen carefully to what is said and interrupt to repeat back the key points
• Read out what you are writing and ask the customer to confirm it is correct
• Summarize frequently and paraphrase to remove the emotion – for example, say, 'So what you are telling me is that a, b and c happened'
• If appropriate, ask for evidence of the problem
• Agree to investigate and agree a time to call back with information

Investigating the cause

You need to be objective and, to an extent, impartial. Gather the facts and perhaps take photographs if appropriate. Recognize that a small problem will often be magnified to encourage you to make a large settlement. Check with your suppliers to see if anyone else has reported experiencing the same problem – for example, if there has been a component failure. Talk to other customers to see if they have used the same product with no problem, because this can strengthen your case.

Plan to act

Complaints fester if they are left too long, and you must call your customer back with a solution at the time you promised. When you are planning your remedial action, be sure that you:

- Carefully consider the cost/impact of what you plan to do
- Are certain you can deliver what you plan to offer
- Be confident that it is your responsibility in the first place

Involve your colleagues as much as you need to. If you've been let down it remains your complaint, but other people need to help resolve it.

Settlements

You need to agree the settlement verbally, then confirm it in writing – perhaps by e-mail or fax so it arrives within minutes, not days. Remember that:

- Money should be paid only in extreme cases
- Faulty goods are always best replaced, not discounted
- Offer extra product or service rather than future discounts
- Brief staff going on site to 'tread carefully' and be constructive
- Link any concession you are making to a future commitment

You cannot please all your customers all the time, and at some point you will have to deal with customer complaints.

REMINDER

Professional indemnity and product liability insurance can protect you should you inadvertently be personally responsible for a major loss.

The more you show willingness to understand and nurture your customer's business, the more they will respect and support you.

BECOMING THE FAVOURITE

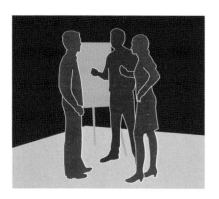

If you are seeking to build a long-term working relationship with your customer, you need to do more than provide superb products and exemplary service. You need to become the buyer's favourite salesperson.

People buy from other people, and you will sell the most to the people with whom you enjoy the best relationship. You don't have to like each other or become close friends. You do, though, need to have a high level of mutual trust and respect. There are a number of ways you can develop the business relationship in this way.

WHAT		WHY
Reinforce	>	Constantly share information that reinforces the perception that you are the best supplier – e.g., competitor analyses
Research	>	Provide regular interpreted knowledge updates because you are (you hope) abreast of what is emerging in your sector
Relate	>	Take a genuine interest in your customer's business and ask to be kept in touch with new developments
Relish	>	Encourage your customer to ask you (or your technical colleagues) for guidance – relish, don't resent, the role
Relay	>	Provided that you are not selling to your customer's competitor, relay any market intelligence you gather

Become an adviser

You might have had to be quite direct and assertive to gain the first order, and this is normal, because many people need help to make the decision to purchase. However, you now need to become your customer's ally. Becoming a trusted adviser is a good way to achieve this. Some of the techniques you might choose are summarized in the panel on page 96.

The advisory role works especially well when you are selling to a distributor who, in turn, sells on your product to their customers. Inevitably, your customer's rivals will be buying from your rivals, so by helping your customer, you are also helping yourself.

Provide a helpline

Helplines are not only of benefit to the customer. If your company provides technical helpline support, you will benefit because:

- Someone else is helping to service your customer, freeing your time to sell
- You have a constant flow of market feedback, which will enhance innovation

Provide training

If you sell training to your customer as part of your package, include the option to buy additional training for new staff members. If you deliver the training yourself, your customer will:

- Regard you as a technical expert, not simply a salesperson
- Be effectively paying for you to visit and reinforce product benefits

Be a local hero

Even if you are selling one-off services to householders, you can do much to become a favourite supplier. Your goal in these circumstances, however, is to generate endless referrals rather than to find repeat business from a single customer. Some ideas to get you thinking are listed in the panel above right.

BEST ON THE BLOCK

BUSINESS SECTOR

Contract gardening

Cleaning company

Home improvements

OPPORTUNITY

Give your customer a framed photograph of your handiwork in their garden, which they will show to their friends, your prospects

Provide a doormat with your logo to catch visitors' eyes

Mail 'knowledge' bulletins to avoid being forgotten

FIVE THINGS YOU SHOULD NEVER DO

1 Offer or accept bribes
2 Sleep with your customer
3 Divulge confidential information about other customers
4 Exploit naïveté
5 Criticize the buyer to their staff

6 WIDENING YOUR HORIZONS

Successful salespeople are alert to opportunities wherever they go, and they never miss a chance to put themselves in a position where serendipitous selling can take place.

Serendipitous selling

You will, of course, be a regular visitor to the conferences, exhibitions and events that your prospective customers attend. This keeps you in touch with the mood of your chosen sector and can also provide valuable networking opportunities. To stimulate your imagination, however, here are a few sales situations you might not have thought of before.

On the train

Imagine that you're sitting on a train going to visit a distant client or are travelling on other business. The chances are that you'll be sharing a table with up to three other people, and if they use their mobile phones, you'll have no choice but to overhear their conversation. You might also notice the logos and company name on the paperwork they're studying. The following are some proven icebreakers:

A good salesperson makes their own luck.

Successful salespeople are always selling.

Good salespeople are powerful communicators.

- 'Excuse me, I'm going to get some coffee. Can I get you anything?'
- 'I couldn't help but overhear your phone call. I've been interested in the x industry for a while. Tell me, what do you do?'

And if you sell to the general public, where everyone is a prospect, you simply need to strike up a conversation and then steer it towards your product. Classic openers are:

- 'My, look at that rain. Do you have far to travel?'
- 'I've finished my newspaper, would you like it?'

At social events

It is unprofessional to make a sales pitch at a social event, but you're almost certain to find out about people's likes, dislikes and their work. The trick is to assume that they will be interested in talking to you at a more convenient time. Here are some lines that might help:

- 'I really think I can help you with that, but now's not the time or the place. I'll call you tomorrow to set up a meeting.' (assumptive close)
- 'From what you've told me, I think I know a way that you can save money and be more comfortable at home. I need to talk to you about this, but now's not the time or place. Should I phone you tomorrow morning?' (alternative close)

Once you have commitment, you need to move on and talk to someone else.

At the gym

You'd be surprised how many business deals are done at the gym. After all, you want to do business with people who share your commitment to fitness, don't you? Have some T-shirts printed with your company name and a benefit statement that links your product to where the message will be read. If you are in the car business, your T-shirt could say 'Every car I sell runs better than I can!' Never miss an opportunity to sell – it gives you more time for other things in your life.

NETWORKING TIPS

- **Always carry business cards**
- **Introduce yourself clearly**
- **Remember names**
- **Focus on one person at a time**
- **Keep moving, no matter how interesting people appear to be**

BEING PERSONABLE

To leave someone without causing offence when you want to move on, touch their arm gently as you say, 'I'm sorry, but I've just spotted someone I really must talk to ...'

Many people find selling to formal committees as daunting as giving evidence in court. You must retain a degree of control and not let your audience intimidate or daunt you.

SELLING TO GROUPS

You need to do more than simply answer questions.

Particularly if you work in the public sector, you will often find yourself presenting to groups because bureaucratic organizations like to include many people in the decision-making process.

By the time you get to this stage, you will already have completed the sales process with a representative of the organization. You will have gone through the various stages of the selling process and have convinced at least one person that you can deliver what they want. But you may not be the only contender, and you might have been invited to present your case to a committee that will make the final decision. It is, however, virtually impossible to interact with everybody in a group and it is unwise to focus on just one or two people – those you exclude may become aggrieved. Here are some of the things you need to do.

Introductions

You will, of course, have arrived in good time and checked that you are presentable. You will then have been invited into the committee room, and these can be daunting arenas. You find yourself exposed and alone in front of rows of sometimes dour-looking people in tiered seating behind tables.

Make sure you introduce yourself clearly and say exactly what you do. You need to know who you are talking to, so if it has not been done, ask if those present could also all introduce themselves to you. This will give you an immediate feel for who is in the room and the nature of their role.

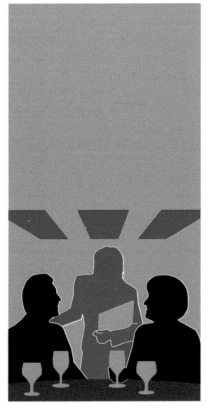

Establish rapport

The next stage is to get everyone on the same wavelength and also to prevent the meeting from becoming too rigid and formal. Equally, you must not appear frivolous and insincere. You need to find out how they want you to play the meeting, so ask them.

Present your argument

You have taken control of the meeting and now need to present the key benefits that your proposal offers their organization. You need to be sure to get eye contact with everyone there so that they know you are talking to them. Excluded people can become negative.

Identify the key people

From the moment you arrive and throughout your presentation, you will pick up on the key players in the meeting. Key people tend to:

- Show more interest
- Make more notes
- Glance at colleagues more often
- Ask questions

Invite questions

You need to encourage everyone with a concern to have their question answered.

When you are answering questions, speak to the whole group and watch for signs of agreement or dissent. If you feel a question is not fair, ask if other people feel the same way before answering it. Difficult questions can sometimes be taken out of the meeting by other members of the group. Use a phrase such as: 'I'm not sure if that point is really relevant, What does everyone else think?'

Seek feedback

At the end of the meeting summarize your key points and those that were raised by the group. Ask if there is anything else they want to know. It's also worth asking them if they can give you an indication of how they will respond to your proposal.

OPENING LINES

- 'I'd like to talk you through our proposal, then take questions at the end. Is that all right with you?'
- 'I'm sure you've been through my proposal, but I'd like to summarize the key points for you before taking questions.'

Selling to a group of people is quite different from selling to an individual or couple.

You should welcome invitations to formally present your proposal. It means you will have time to make your points clearly. What's more, you can use question time to close the deal.

PRESENTING TO GROUPS

TIP

The technique of crossing out objections as you counter them also works well in a one-to-one sales meeting. Simply list the various points on a piece of paper and eliminate them one by one.

The fact that you have been invited to make a presentation to a group means you have been shortlisted. Your audience will already have seen – they may even have read! – an outline of your proposal, so you need to summarize the key points, rather than repeat your whole sales pitch for the group. If you are selling to a committee or group, it makes sense to use visual aids to emphasize the points you want to make.

Powerpoint™

This piece of software has become globally adopted as the standard presentation package. Here are ten ways to make it work to its best advantage when presenting to a group:

- Be bold – a few striking visuals are better than a complex slideshow
- Be graphic – use pictures and graphs, not words, to illustrate your point
- Be consistent – create a distinctive and appropriate master slide
- Use few colours – avoid strident combinations and make it easy to see
- Use few words – avoid bullet points that are really just your notes
- Use large text – you may be presenting in a large room
- Avoid all capitals – upper and lower case text is easier to read
- Use a remote mouse – walk about and engage your audience

- Import images – the Internet offers lots of royalty-free images, which are more impressive than clip art
- Do not give out copies of your slides before you present them

Handouts

It is useful to provide handouts that summarize what you have just said. Do not, however, simply make a copy of your slides.

Flip charts

If the room you are using has a flip chart or whiteboard and your audience is challenging, use it to list, then dismiss their concerns one by one. This is what you do:

- Make your presentation
- Ask for questions and find out if there are many concerns
- List any problem areas on the board
- Ask if there are any other concerns
- Explore each point that is raised in turn, presenting information and using closing techniques to confirm that each issue has been dealt with
- As the issues are resolved, cross them out on the board
- When none are left ... go for commitment

The beauty parade

Another name for presentations to groups is the 'beauty parade'. This is because sometimes all the potential suppliers are lined up and asked to perform one after the other. If you have a choice, it is always best to go last because:

- By the end of the list, the first will have almost been forgotten
- The panel can objectively compare you with the rest
- You can, sometimes, lead question time into a negotiation and obtain the deal on the day

TENDERS

When you are asked to tender in writing, remember that you must always:

- **Answer all the specific points raised**
- **Provide additional suggestions that will encourage a meeting with you**
- **Keep it short, compliant and interesting to read**
- **Have someone proof-read the document before you send it**

Imagine compressing a month's sales activity into one day. If you think this is impossible, try exhibiting at a trade or consumer show. You might make dozens of presentations in one day.

SELLING AT EXHIBITIONS: PREPARING

TENDERS

At all but the smallest events it is worth having literature specially printed. Your literature should:

- **Be factual, simple and professionally produced**

- **Contain testimonial and product benefits**

- **Encourage the reader to contact you for case studies, prices, free estimates and a free audit**

For many people, even those on business, a day out at an exhibition, show or event is a great day's entertainment. For you as an exhibitor, however, it is a major investment of time, money and effort, and you must make the most of every opportunity.

When there is a lot going on around you it's very easy to miss the opportunities that arise as prospects visit your stand and you fail to generate the sales or leads you expect and deserve. At a consumer event, on the other hand, you may speak to many people before finding a prospect.

Boost your success when you plan an exhibition

Planning a successful exhibition will be easier if you remember to do the following:

Make your message explicit
Someone walking past your stand should be able to tell at a glance what it is you are selling and why they should stop.

Movement matters
If you can introduce motion to your stand it will attract the attention of everyone who passes by. Ideally, the moving object needs to be linked to your product or service, but lights that move or change colour can be just as effective. Water features can also pull a crowd.

Dress for success
Wear clothing that promotes your product. It makes you easier to spot on your stand when it is full of visitors. It also acts as an advertisement for your stand when you are walking around and away from your stand.

Invite your prospects
Write to everyone who has shown interest in your product but has not bought and invite them along. They will all feel flattered, some will visit, and enough will buy to make the exercise worthwhile.

Stage a competition
At consumer events a simple quiz with the answers to the questions 'hidden' among your display boards will get people reading your message. Helping them complete their form can be a good entrée to a sales conversation.

Arrange to cross-sell
Agree to pass people from your stand to other stands that are selling products that complement your own. They will do the same for you.

Collect names and addresses
Inevitably, you will not be able to talk to everyone who visits your stand, but you will want to write to everyone afterwards, so make sure that you record names and addresses. At business-to-business events, collect cards.

Stay alert
If the show runs for several days, avoid the late-night sessions in the bar that are loved by so many salespeople when they gather together. Eat light meals and get plenty of sleep. You can party when you get home.

Never assume
You may be talking to a rival posing as a prospect, an unshaven millionaire in scruffy jeans … or a genuine prospect.

Major exhibitions will present you with literally thousands of prospects a day. Selecting then influencing those with the greatest potential will stretch your selling skills and your stamina.

SELLING AT EXHIBITIONS: WINNING ORDERS

You are there to meet, greet and influence. Be welcoming and people will want to talk with you.

Orders
Once you have set out your stall, the success of your investment in attending an exhibition will depend on your ability to juggle visitors and gain commitment. It is hard work, and you have to be constantly alert to what is happening around you.

Boost your success when you sell at an exhibition
Make sure that you are rested and relaxed and that you have refreshed your memory by reading your own and your competitors' literature. The doors open and the visitors flood in. At major consumer events, you can see tens of thousands of people a day and talk to hundreds. It is easy in these circumstances to forget that each one is an individual, with different interests and needs. Try to avoid being blasé and second-guessing those who approach you.

Adopt positive body language
Crossed arms and frowns will discourage visitors. Look relaxed and use your arms to gesture people towards your stand.

Don't invite rejection
Never say 'can I help you?' It is a classic mistake and gives your prospect the chance to say 'no thanks' and escape from your stand. Instead, ask an open question. Ask them to comment on what they are looking at. This will give you a clue about where their interest (and potential) lies.

Keep conversations focused
Unless there are only a few visitors, you need to find out quickly who you're talking to and what they're interested in and then gain their commitment to follow up after the event.

Get help
If your stand proves to be busier than you expected, consider having colleagues or even temporary staff on hand to take down people's details after you have spoken to them. This will mean that you can gather people from the front of the stand, qualify them and pass them back.

Spot golden geese
When the 'chance in a million' prospect comes along, be prepared to be flexible and change your plan to give them some time.

Involve the partner
At consumer events one of a couple will usually do the talking. You need to involve both of them in the sales conversation if you are to be successful. Ask the silent partner if they agree or if they have a view on what is being discussed. The quiet one is often the real decision-maker.

Make appointments
At business-to-business events it is common to make appointments for sales meetings and negotiations. You will find that even in a private room sales interviews take less time and are more focused in the usually frenetic atmosphere. Speed the pace and aim for 30 minutes, rather than the more usual hour, for each meeting.

Confirm what you've agreed
It can be useful to have self-carboning enquiry pads so that you can write down what has been agreed and give your prospect a copy. Remember that they may visit your rival's stand before they go home, and you want them to feel committed.

DON'T STALK OR POUNCE

When someone pauses and takes an interest, approach from within their line of vision. They will see you coming and expect you to open a conversation.

People go to conferences in the expectation that they will discover something new and beneficial. You must not disappoint them.

SELLING AT CONFERENCES

No matter what type of business you are in, there will be conferences that will be attended by those you want to influence and perhaps sell to.

Get noticed
Wear distinctive clothing and be sure to ask plenty of good questions. Always preface your question with an introduction: 'I'm Ashwin Kumar from Ace Garments, we make corporate uniforms. My question is ...'

Be identifiable
Make sure your name badge has your first and family name, company name. If you are wearing a pin-on badge, highlight your name. People will notice.

Get involved
Volunteer to chair a break-out session or propose a toast at the conference dinner. Anything you can do to get noticed will make you easier to identify.

Research the list
A quiet hour spent researching the delegate list will help you to select your top 10 prospects. Be realistic and only select a few people. You want to be sure to meet them.

Stalk your prospects
Check which syndicate sessions the best prospects are in and book the same ones. Alternatively, seek them out during the coffee break and ask them about the session they've just attended. Show interest and listen.

CONFERENCE

CONFERENCE	OPPORTUNITIES
Academic	> Discover new technologies and opportunities Find academics that can endorse your products or processes Sell to other delegates Demonstrate your thirst for knowledge
National trade body	> Understand the key debates in your sector Meet those able to influence your success Sell to other delegates Demonstrate commitment to your industry sector
Professional institute	> Understand the key debates in your profession Discover how to develop your skills Sell to other delegates Demonstrate a desire for intellectual growth
Regional business	> Understand the key debates in your region Meet people who are able to influence your success Sell to other delegates Demonstrate a commitment to your community
Philosophical	> Develop yourself and your confidence Meet and learn from others treading similar paths Sell to other delegates Demonstrate a commitment to yourself

Organize a fringe event
If the topic you feel is most relevant is not covered, hire a room yourself and organize a fringe debate.

Enjoy breakfast
Early morning is a good time for networking. The gym, pool, promenade and breakfast restaurant are all good places to be seen and to be alert. If you're cheerful in the morning, people will notice.

Stay sober
Conferences have a reputation for alcohol excess. Deals struck in the bar rarely make sense the next day.

TIP

Most people get home from a conference, put the pack to one side and go back to work. Everyone you meet that showed promise should be contacted within a week of the conference.

Global business travel is far less glamorous than it might appear. You have to sell to people you've probably never met, in unfamiliar surroundings, against a backdrop of cultural differences.

SELLING OVERSEAS

OVERSEAS VISITORS

If an overseas prospect or customer visits you, you need to be aware of their country's customs and make provision for them. However, do make sure you give them a good insight into the way your own culture works.

TIP

Alcohol can sometimes represent an even greater risk. In some countries business entertaining can involve being plied with copious amounts of strong liquor. Your hosts may be hardened drinkers, and it is far better to refuse politely than to lose all self-control.

Travelling abroad on a sales mission sounds exciting. Indeed, it can be rewarding, both in terms of winning business and experiencing a foreign culture. It can also be embarrassing if you fail to recognize the different ways that business is transacted around the globe.

Do your homework before you set out. Even if you are selling to a country that speaks the same language as you do, you might inadvertently miss an opportunity for a sale or make a *faux pas* because you have misread non-verbal signs. If you can, talk to other people who have experience of selling in the country you will be visiting. Listening to their horror stories may stop you perpetrating any of your own.

Language

The greatest barrier that you will have to overcome is language. English is widely spoken as a second language, so communication is usually possible and you will have an advantage if English is your first language, but you need to recognize that:

- Discussions about your offer may take place in a language you don't understand
- Subtle nuances may be lost, so you need to keep your message clear, explicit and simple
- Learning a few words of your prospect's language will earn you respect

You should also have translations made of all key documents, just in case.

If you are planning to conduct a lot of business in a

particular country, consider learning the language. Chambers of commerce and other similar organizations can introduce you to language courses that include business vocabulary.

Culture

You need to recognize and allow for the fact that the culture of the country you are visiting may be different from your own. The differences are simply something you have to accept if you are to sell there. It is worth researching the customs and cultural differences before you visit, but never be critical and try not to be frustrated. Always be tolerant of what may seem annoying. Examples of customs you might encounter are:

- In Japan 'Yes, I understand' can sometimes really mean 'No, I do not'
- In China you should present and accept business cards with two hands
- In the Republic of Ireland you should accept that punctuality is not valued as much as it may be in other countries

If all else fails, be sure to buy some good guide books to the country you are visiting and make sure you prepare thoroughly beforehand.

Security

Although you will read horror stories about kidnappings, murders and worse, if you are visiting major business centres and are sensible you should be perfectly safe. Heed the advice of your host and do not take unnecessary risks. Some countries, particularly in Africa and South America, do experience more violent crime than you are probably used to. Again, research and common sense are recommended.

Food and drink

It is clearly going to be difficult to conduct a sales meeting if you are confined to your hotel bathroom by a tummy bug. Take care about what you eat and drink and follow all the usual precautions.

TOP TRAVEL TIPS

- **Acclimatize – jet lag can numb your ability to negotiate**
- **Research – speak to people with experience of the place you're going to**
- **Be cautious – it's better to be too formal than too informal**
- **Be aware – in some places business gifts are routinely exchanged**
- **Practise – you need to be able to pronounce your host's name if nothing else**

An effectively managed distributor relationship means that their people are selling on your behalf. You need to make sure that they are fully equipped and able to do this for you.

SELLING THROUGH DISTRIBUTORS

Because distributors sit between you and the end-user, they have power over your destiny.

It might be that your customer is a distributor who buys from you and then sells on your products to their own customers. Your distributor thus has the relationship with the user of your product or service. They also probably sell for some of your competitors, too, preferring to give their customers as wide a choice as possible. Yet despite this seeming lack of loyalty and focus, distributors are essential in many business sectors.

It is fair to say that distributor salespeople are often generalists, whereas those representing their supplier, because they deal with fewer products, are more specialist. The strength of a distributor salesperson lies in their relationship with the customer. Because a high level of trust is placed in distributor salespeople by their customers, they often do not need to follow a structured approach to their selling. The exception, however, is when they are recruiting new customers.

CHARACTERISTIC		PRODUCT/SERVICE
Only sold at certain times of the year	>	Tinsel
Many small orders placed by many customers	>	Building materials
Goods sold through retail outlets	>	Greetings cards
Low margin, low price, infrequent purchase	>	Insurance

Selling skills

Selling through distributors demands different skills from selling in other areas. Here are five ways you can help your distributor sell more of your product:

Use incentives

Distributor salespeople often respond to sales incentives that reward performance. If the incentive is good enough, they will switch users of rival products to your product. This can also work the other way.

Dual call

Accompanying a distributor salesperson for the day can help to build your own relationship with them and develop their understanding of your product. It can also enable you to help them win difficult orders and demonstrate your willingness to support your customer.

Stage events

Encourage your distributor to arrange an open day or evening presentation that will allow you (or your technical colleagues) to share new ideas and generally raise the customers' awareness of the benefits your product can deliver.

Provide sales support

The type of activity can include sales training (plus perhaps copies of this book), marketing support to generate enquiries and point-of-sale display material for their showroom.

Factory visits

Organize tours of your production or research facilities for them and perhaps their key customers. This both informs and bonds.

Sales campaigns

It is not realistic to expect your distributor to focus on your product every week of the year, but running sales campaigns is a good way to encourage people to concentrate for a short time on specific opportunities.

WHEN DUAL CALLING

ALWAYS

- **Let the distributor lead the meeting**
- **Be honest and supportive**
- **Prepare so that you know your subject**
- **Say you'll find out if you don't know**
- **Discuss each call in the car afterwards**

NEVER

- **Take over**
- **Contradict**
- **Guess or waffle**
- **Forget to get back to them**
- **Criticize or dismiss**

Sometimes, distributors are not the answer. Sales agents, with their portfolio of products and usually well established relationships with a buyer, can provide a valuable route to market.

SALES AGENTS

Sales agents provide a flexibility that employed salespeople and distributors cannot match. If you want to set up a network of sales agents, follow the steps described below.

Research

The best agent in the world will not succeed with a 'mission impossible' product in either a saturated or an uninterested market. Before you even start to think about hiring an agent, you need to do some preparatory groundwork.

- Find out what market exists for your product
- Identify and understand your competition
- Explore how your rivals sell
- Sell it yourself to at least four different individuals or organizations
- Seek the advice of those in the know in your sector

CHARACTERISTICS OF PRODUCT OR SERVICE	EXAMPLE
Products with a high demand/interest for a short time	> System upgrades
Where there is insufficient market to justify a salesperson	> Wholesale furniture
Where enquiries are sporadic and demand varies	> Conservatories
Where you are testing a new market	> Almost anything

Develop a package

How will your agent make a living and how will you make a profit? To find your product or service attractive, your agent will need to see:

* A realistic commission per sales level
* The potential to earn enough to make learning about the product worthwhile
* Marketing support to create sales leads
* Compatibility with other lines they already sell

Recruiting agents

Sales agents come in all shapes and sizes. They may be semi-retired industry 'figures' with a strong network, salespeople who have chosen the freedom of self-employment or users of the product who also sell to non-competing users. Good ways to recruit sales agents are to:

* Advertise in relevant trade journals
* Ask your customers if they know any agents
* Search the Internet and consult the various registers and agency brokers the search brings up
* Ask producers of complementary products if you can approach their agents

When you meet prospective agents, you need to be sure that they have the time to devote to your product, the intellect to convey your product message, an existing network of contacts and the motivation to succeed.

Managing agents

Even though their income is directly linked to their activity, agents need careful management and motivation. Remember that they have no peer pressure and operate in isolation. When you are managing agents:

* Agree targets that make you both a fair return
* Provide plenty of information
* Give them commission on everything in their territory, not just on the orders they personally deliver so that they will them manage all accounts
* Make them feel a valuable part of your team
* Have a formal contract that defines the relationship

Finding others to share your enthusiasm and sell as members of your team is an exciting step. However, you need to remember that they will not always see things as you do.

HIRING SALESPEOPLE

Most people in sales roles at some point need to recruit help. This could be because the business has grown to the point where it needs more sales activity or simply because you have taken on a new role.

Of all employees, salespeople have jobs where their performance can be easily measured in terms of return on investment. Even in complex organizations where sales result from the combined efforts of sales, technical and design people, it is still the salesperson who inevitably is the most visible. Surprisingly, then, many salespeople are not thick-skinned extroverts but the complete opposite. The best, most perceptive and sensitive salespeople are often quite shy. Rather like an actor, they create a professional persona that enables them to push themselves into the selling role. The first point about recruiting salespeople is to be open minded. Who would your customer warm to the most?

GOOD SALESPEOPLE ARE:

- Self-motivated – able to work alone and away from the office
- Determined – unlikely to give up easily
- Resilient – able to accept rejection as part of the job
- Personable – easy to get along with and generally good company
- Materialistic – able to translate goals into things they want to own
- Flexible – willing to work odd hours and to travel if required

Sales myths

You need to be a technical expert to sell a technical product

The reality is that too often technically proficient salespeople focus too hard on the features of their product and overlook the benefits. A salesperson without technical expertise will explore, interpret and translate everything into customer benefits.

You need to know the industry before you can sell in it

Why do people simply recruit from within their industry? Selling is a process that can be applied in any situation. People new to your industry will:

- Have fresh ideas from their previous world
- Be less influenced by 'baggage'
- Not be seen as a recycled competitor

Salespeople are finished at 40 and you should hire young people

Although employment law may prevent you from discriminating on the basis of age, there is a tendency to favour younger applicants. Ideally, you need to recruit salespeople who will relate best to your customer group. Some markets – retirement homes, for example – are better served by older salespeople.

YOUTH VS. AGE

YOUNGER	OLDER
More energy	More experience
Creativity	Gravitas
Enthusiasm	Credibility

10 RECRUITMENT TIPS

1. Create an attractive, achievable benefits package
2. Advertise the target earnings and list the benefits
3. Encourage people to send a photograph with their CV
4. Interview those who show initiative
5. Allow two hours between interviews
6. Conduct interviews where you won't be disturbed
7. If interviewing 'out of hours', use a hotel, not a deserted office block
8. Encourage candidates to sell themselves to you
9. Use your instinct as well as your brain
10. Provide objective feedback to all candidates

We are a social species and are more relaxed away from the office environment. It necessarily follows that taking your prospect away from their day-to-day situation can pay handsome dividends.

ENTERTAINING CUSTOMERS

Selling is in many ways a sociable activity, but salespeople have the overriding objective of winning orders.

In some sectors nearly all the business is done over the lunch table. In others, every gift or benefit given has to be declared and may be taxed as a 'benefit in kind'. Whatever the custom in your sector, you need to consider how you can develop relationships by entertaining your customers.

Socializing with your customer or prospect should be regarded as an investment, just like advertising and producing marketing material.

Profiting from business entertainment

Remember that the money you spend on entertaining at work should be linked to the likely return. In other words, you probably won't negotiate a multi-million contract in a fast-food outlet or over a take-away meal, nor will you sell an encyclopaedia over a gourmet dinner. Pitching the activity at the right level will avoid embarrassment all round. It is also important to be realistic and not find yourself out with customers every evening to the detriment of your family relationships.

Let your guest choose

Allow your prospect to select the venue for lunch. They will usually choose somewhere where they feel comfortable and you won't get fleeced.

Arrange breakfast meetings

Agreeing to a breakfast meeting in a local coffee shop can be both cost-effective and extend your selling day. Many people are happy to meet at eight o'clock in the morning, or even earlier.

Avoid lunchtime alcohol
Even if you are a hardened drinker, alcohol will affect your selling skills and make you less effective.

Go somewhere different
Alternatives to meeting over lunch are to share a workout at the gym, tour an art exhibition or simply walk along the beach. You can learn a lot about someone by engaging in activities that are totally unrelated to work.

Organize a charity event
Your customers and prospects will pay to attend the event, admire your philanthropic streak and applaud when you present the cheque to a worthy cause. Once you have deducted your costs, you will have effectively entertained your entire network for free.

Let the customer pay
If your customer feels that your product or service has saved or even made them money, they may be quite prepared to take you out for lunch to say thank you. When this happens, offer to pay for the drinks.

Small can be beautiful
Western custom dictates that you are inevitably always offered coffee or tea when you arrive for a meeting. Why not stop and buy some cakes on the way and share them with your customer? But make sure they are attractively packaged.

Remember the receptionist
Don't forget that the odd box of chocolates for the people who traditionally stand between you and the customer can make sure you enjoy unrivalled future access to the buyer.

Don't just do it at Christmas
Remember that your client might not be Christian and will celebrate festivals at other times of year, In any case, everyone else entertains at Christmas, so why not take your customer out in January instead?

TIP
If you're staying in a hotel, why not invite a customer and a prospect to join you for dinner? Both may be flattered and the customer will do the selling. Your alternative is an evening on your own watching TV.

BUSINESS ENTERTAINING SHOULD BE

- **Viewed as an investment**
- **Appropriate to the business potential**
- **Interesting and different**
- **Shared**
- **Enjoyable and not an excuse for pressure selling**

There is an awful temptation to indulge in one-upmanship when it comes to giving gifts to customers. However, as in the social context, it's the thought and not the cost that counts.

SALES GIFTS

SALES GIFTS

- **Keep your brand in front of the customer**
- **Are important to users as well as buyers**
- **Should be less expensive than they look**
- **Must not constitute a bribe**

As with entertaining, corporate gifts can maintain awareness of your product or service. They can, however, also be interpreted as bribes and so you should always make sure that they are as appropriate as possible to both the value and type of business you are engaged in. Wherever possible, corporate gifts should be:

- Linked to your product or service
- Appealing enough for the recipient to use at work but not at home
- Less expensive than it looks
- Personalized to the recipient

As with any gift, it's the thought, not the price, that counts. Some corporate gifts end up as highly prized collectibles – Pirelli calendars, for example. Always screen-print the items you give with your product message.

Finding corporate gifts

Numerous companies produce glossy catalogues that are full of interesting and unusual items that they can print and deliver to you. Although these are useful if you are in a hurry or short of ideas, there is always the danger that other sellers in your market will buy the same items for the same customers. It is always better to try to source your own items and ask a local screen-printer to add your logo and product slogan. A search on the Internet or a chat with your local chamber of commerce will identify many small local businesses and suppliers, all of whom may be eager to meet your needs.

GIVING CORPORATE GIFTS

✓ DO

- Buy things that will be used
- Buy practical things
- Have your logo/message printed on the item
- Link the gift to the benefit you're selling
- Consider it an investment
- Use the item to merchandise
- Keep it work-related

✗ DON'T

- Buy things that try to do everything
- Buy gadgets
- Save on printing
- Simply buy from a catalogue
- Consider it a cost
- Use the item to reward
- Make it too personal

Keeping up with the competition

As with entertaining, Christmas sees countless salespeople doing the rounds with bottles of drink and other seasonal gifts for their customers. Although less common than a few years ago, it is still tempting to join in with all the rest and feel that if you don't do it you will somehow lose out. In reality, few people are sufficiently influenced by seasonal gifts to place an order, and some people even find them irritating.

The public sector

Remember that some organizations do not allow their staff to receive gifts, no matter how relevant they may be to their role. Often, the organization has to be seen to be impartial and will demonstrate this with draconian rules that reduce the risk of being accused of showing favour or bias. Equally, public sector organizations are often underfunded, and appropriate, branded merchandise can be welcome. If in doubt, ask your customer or prospect for advice.

Why not place your sales message where your prospect will always see it?

Unless you've been a salesperson, you will not fully appreciate the anxieties and pressures that can cloud what might at first appear to be an idyllic career. Always keep work in perspective.

CELEBRATING SUCCESS

Selling can be stressful. The pressure to perform is always there.

Most salespeople live for the successes and accept the failures as an unavoidable part of the job. The old saying that 'every no takes you closer to a yes' is true, but the highs and lows remain an everyday fact of life when you are selling.

When targets are met, it is important to celebrate your success. If you are paid commission or if you own the business, there will be a financial reward associated with the achievement. If you employ salespeople, consider funding a celebration. Having fun when you've won makes the journey worthwhile.

Individual success

If you work on your own and face a challenging set of targets, translate the financial rewards of success into something tangible. Perhaps you would like a better car or a bigger house, or you want to take your partner on an exotic holiday. Explore the options, test drive the car, visit the house and buy a guide book for your dream destination. Place reminders of your personal goals around your workplace. A small photograph beside the phone or on the dashboard of your car will be a constant reminder of how your hard work will be rewarded, in a personal way. If others have contributed to your success, thank them as well.

Team success

Rewarding teams is more difficult. You want to encourage every member to play their part, but equally important is the need to recognize collective success. Often the best solution is to structure your targets in the following ways:

- The team goal has to be achieved for everyone to benefit
- Outstanding personal contributions are recognized and rewarded

This avoids the unfortunate situation where although some members have over-achieved, the team has fallen short of its overall target.

Team celebrations should contain a training and development element that builds the capacity and motivation of the team to work together and perform. Organized outdoor activities – involving ropes, trees and water, for example – can be structured to combine team building with fun.

Become even better at selling

Selling is like life itself – you can only take out what you put in. The best salespeople invest in their cusomers, their products, their knowledge, their skills, but most importantly, they invest in themselves.

This book has introduced you to some sales techniques, tips and ideas that will enable you to become more effective and therefore more successful. For anyone wanting to achieve real success, however, the self-development process needs to become a routine part of everyday life. Not everyone wants to drive around everyday listening to sales gurus drawling words of encouragement over the car's sound system, although they do work for some. There are plenty of ways you can develop your skills.

Stay fit

Regular physical exercise increases your energy levels, stamina and resilience and raises your self-esteem. The endorphins released make you feel positive and confident both about yourself and in turn about what you are doing.

Eat well

A diet of hastily snatched fast food from roadside outlets is not ideal. Seek out a balanced diet and always eat breakfast: it fuels the day.

TIP

Successful salespeople

- **work hard**
- **take holidays**
- **satisfy customers**
- **make time for their kids**
- **look after themselves**

Why not celebrate your success with the customers who made it possible?

KEEP THINGS IN PERSPECTIVE

Selling is about work and work is what we do to stimulate our intellect and pay the bills. Always put yourself and your family first.

Drink water
Dehydration is a real threat if you only drink coffee and branded soft drinks. Try to drink a litre of water a day as well.

Watch TV
Stay abreast of current affairs and be able to hold an intelligent conversation on the topic of the day.

Read books
Sales technique books, self-improvement books and industry reviews are important, but also read novels. They broaden your mind and your vocabulary.

Talk to strangers
Striking up a conversation with those you meet at work, in hotels, queues, bars and conferences will widen your network and introduce you to new ideas and concepts. You will also find new customers.

Play hard
Selling is stressful and your working life needs to be balanced with a range of interests away from work.

Volunteer
Spending time helping others will help you put your life and its challenges in perspective. You will also network with other volunteers.

Learn
Exploring a new interest or simply becoming more knowledgeable about emerging technologies in your world enables you to apply your sales skills in a different environment. Ask questions, learn more, then share it.

Share
If you've read this book from the start, you will have absorbed many new ideas. Now it's time to share the with those around you. Lend them the book and arrange to meet and talk with them when they return it to you.

INDEX

ACKNOWLEDGEMENTS

Executive Editor: **Trevor Davies**
Editor: **Kate Tuckett**
Executive Art Editor: **Karen Sawyer**
Design: **'ome design**
Illustration: **David Beswick at 'ome design**
Production Controller: **Aileen O'Reilly**

About the author

Robert Ashton is an entrepreneur, writer and speaker. This is his third business book. You can learn more about Robert by visiting www.robertashton.co.uk

Tourism and Gastronomy

In recent years, a growing emphasis has been placed on tourism experiences and attractions related to food. In many cases eating out while on holiday includes the 'consumption' of a local heritage, comparable to what is experienced when visiting historical sites and museums.

Despite this increasing attention, however, systematic research on the subject has been nearly absent. *Tourism and Gastronomy* addresses this by drawing together a group of international experts in order to develop a better understanding of the role, development and future of gastronomy and culinary heritage in tourism.

Particular attention is paid to the relationship between the forces of globalisation, localisation and the use of gastronomy and to food as a source of regional and national identity, and a source of economic development.

The first part of the book discusses important issues in the relationship between tourism and gastronomy, introducing the themes important to the understanding of case studies. The second part presents a wide range of case studies of gastronomy tourism development, featuring development programmes, marketing activities and networking between tourism and agriculture. The case studies, drawn from a range of countries, including Australia, New Zealand, Singapore, Spain, Portugal, Greece, Italy, Scotland and Wales, are used to explore further themes, including intellectual property and sustainability

Students and researchers in the areas of tourism, heritage, hospitality, hotel management and catering will find this book an extremely valuable source of information.

Anne-Mette Hjalager is an independent consultant and contract researcher based in the Science Park in Aarhus, Denmark. Over the past ten years she has worked intensively with and for the tourism industry and she has keenly pursued labour market and innovation issues. She also advises the Danish government and the EU in policy planning for tourism.

Greg Richards lectures in leisure studies at Tilburg University in the Netherlands. He is co-ordinator of the Association for Tourism and Leisure Education (ATLAS) and has led a number of EU projects in the fields of tourism education, cultural tourism, sustainable tourism, tourism employment, conference tourism and ICT in tourism. His main research interest is cultural tourism.

Routledge Advances in Tourism

Series Editors: Brian Goodall and Gregory Ashworth

Tourism and Gastronomy

**Edited by Anne-Mette Hjalager
and Greg Richards**

London and New York

First published 2002
by Routledge
2 Park Square, Milton Park, Abingdon, Oxon, OX14 4RN

Simultaneously published in the USA and Canada
by Routledge
711 Third Avenue, New York, NY 10017

Routledge is an imprint of the Taylor & Francis Group

First issued in paperback 2011

Typeset in Baskerville by RefineCatch Limited, Bungay, Suffolk

British Library Cataloguing in Publication Data
A catalogue record for this book is available from the British Library

Library of Congress Cataloging in Publication Data
A catalog record for this book has been requested

ISBN13: 978-0-415-27381-7 (hbk)
ISBN13: 978-0-415-51099-8 (pbk)

Contents

Illustrations

Contributors

Magda Antonioli Corigliano has a B.Sc. in Economics from Bocconi University (Milan) and an M.Sc. in Financial Economics from the UNCNW (UK). She is Professor of Economic Theory and Policy and Professor of Economics of Tourism and the Behaviour of Firms at Bocconi University, where she is also responsible for the tourism activities of the Research Centre for Tourism and Regional and Transport Economics (CERTET). She is Visiting Professor of Environmental Economics at Kyoto University (Japan), of Tourism Economics and Policy at the ESADE (Barcelona, Spain), of Economics of the European Union and Tourism Economics within the European Studies Programme of the University of Chulalongkorn (Bangkok, Thailand). She is also the author of various studies on industrial economics and the economics of tourism and of the environment.

Sean Beer has a B.Sc. in agriculture from Reading, a Dip. Ag. Sci. from Massey University, in New Zealand, and a Cert. Ed. from Wolverhampton, as well as considerable practical experience in agriculture and marketing. He is currently Senior Lecturer in agriculture at the Centre for Land-Based Studies at Bournemouth University. His current research interests include retailing and the food supply chain, marketing and co-operation in agriculture, small family farms, the producer/consumer relationship, hill and upland farming, education and curriculum development.

Steven Boyne is a researcher within the Leisure and Tourism Management Department of SAC (the Scottish Agricultural College). His work centres on issues relating to the development of tourism in rural areas, particularly in the Scottish context. Currently he is involved in research relating to tourism community relationships; tourism, food and gastronomy and skills and training issues for small tourism businesses. He maintains an ongoing interest in research theory and in VFR (visiting friends and relatives) tourism.

Jonathan Edwards is Head of the Centre for Land-Based Studies at the University of Bournemouth and he has been involved in a number of co-operative training and research initiatives concerned with the agri-food industries in western and eastern Europe. His research interests relate to the development and diversification of rural economies particularly in regard to the development of the service sector. He has worked extensively in Portugal and has witnessed and written upon the changes that affected Portugal's rural areas following their accession to the European Community.

Carlos Fernandes is an assistant professor in the Tourism Course at the Polytechnic Institute of Viana do Castelo (Portugal). He completed his BA at Syracuse University (USA), his MA at Rutgers University (USA) and is currently enrolled in the Ph.D. programme at Bournemouth University (UK). Research interests include tourism as a strategy for local development and cultural tourism. He has participated in numerous EU projects related to tourism, presented papers at major international tourism conferences and published widely in the English and Portuguese languages.

Kevin Fields has lectured for the past eleven years in hospitality and tourism-related subjects at Birmingham College of Food and Tourism. He is also programme manager for BA (Hons) Hospitality and Food Management.

Derek Hall is Professor of Regional Development and Head of the Leisure and Tourism Management Department of SAC (the Scottish Agricultural College). He has undertaken a wide variety of research relating to tourism and rural and regional development including work in socialist and post-socialist countries. Additionally, Derek has research interests relating to the role of animals in tourism; tourism and transport; gender and welfare dimensions in tourism. His Ph.D. was focused on perception and evaluation of local community.

Michael Hall is Professor and Head of the Department of Tourism at the University of Otago in New Zealand. He is also co-editor of *Current Issues in Tourism* and Chairperson of the International Geographical Union Study Group on Tourism, Leisure and Social Change. He has published widely on areas relating to tourism, heritage and environmental history. Current research interests include tourism as a component of economic restructuring, particularly in rural areas; contemporary mobility, second homes, wine and food tourism, gastronomy and lifestyle.

Anne-Mette Hjalager is an independent consultant and contract researcher based in the Science Park in Aarhus, Denmark. Over the past ten years she has worked intensively with and for the tourism industry, and she has keenly pursued labour market and innovation issues. Anne-Mette Hjalager advises the Danish government and the EU in policy planning for tourism.

Ian Jenkins is a Senior Lecturer at the School of Leisure and Tourism, Swansea Institute and is currently Co-Director of the CELTaS tourism and leisure research unit. This unit has produced a number of articles and research reports on subject areas such as food tourism, heritage, museums and urban areas. He is also Director of the SAIL Research Unit, which has produced leading edge research on Tourism and Leisure Safety Management. Ian is currently co-ordinator of the School's Socrates and Erasmus programmes. He has carried out numerous research and consultancy projects relating to tourism and leisure and his specialisms include: Geography of Tourism, Tourism and Leisure Philosophy, and Risk and Safety Management.

Andrew Jones is a Senior Lecturer and Co-Director of the CELTaS tourism and leisure research unit at Swansea Institute. He has professional experience in planning at regional and local levels and has been involved in the professional body – the RTPI. Andrew is currently Course Director for the M.Sc. in Tourism Resource Management. Andrew has also completed a fourteen month sabbatical as a research fellow at the University of Brunei. Here his research centred upon conservation, heritage and eco tourism development. Subject specialisms include Tourism Planning; Urban Regeneration; Conservation; Cultural Tourism Development and Environmental Policy.

Richard Mitchell is a Senior Lecturer in Tourism Marketing at La Trobe University, Melbourne, Australia. He has undertaken extensive research on wine tourism in New Zealand and has recently commenced researching wine and food tourism in Australia, with a special focus on the Yarra Valley and Coldstream Hills.

Neil Ravenscroft is Principal Research Fellow at the Chelsea School, University of Brighton, England, where he is currently working on a number of projects related to people's everyday experience of leisure. Neil has written extensively on leisure, culture and environment, and is currently a member of the editorial boards of *Leisure Studies* and the *Journal of Leisure Property*.

Greg Richards lectures in leisure studies at Tilburg University in the Netherlands. He is Co-ordinator of the Association for Tourism and Leisure Education (ATLAS) and he has led a number of EU projects in the fields of tourism education, cultural tourism, sustainable tourism, tourism employment, conference tourism and ICT in tourism. His main research interest is cultural tourism. He has edited books on *Cultural Tourism in Europe* (1996), *Crafts Tourism Development and Marketing* (1999), *Tourism and Sustainable Community Development* (2000) and *European Tourism and Cultural Attractions* (2001).

Francisco Sampaio is the co-ordinator of the Tourism Course at the Polytechnic Institute of Viana do Castelo and President of the Regional Tourism Board of the Alto Minho. He completed his *Licenciatura* at the University of Porto (Portugal), a post-graduate degree at the University de Navarra (Spain) and is currently enrolled in the Ph.D. programme at the University of Aveiro (Portugal). He has published extensively on the subject of gastronomy and has co-ordinated numerous regional gastronomy events and congresses in the last few years and is chairman of the Fraternity of Gastronomers of the Minho region.

Rosario Scarpato is a food and wine writer and gastronomy researcher. He has lived and worked in Melbourne (Australia) since 1989 and regularly contributes to media in Italy (*Gambero Rosso, Corriere della Sera*), Australia (*Divine, The Age*) and Argentina (*Cuisine & Vins*). Rosario is the author of path-breaking essays on gastronomy as an independent academic discipline and sustainable gastronomy. He holds a Master of Arts and is Ph.D. candidate at Melbourne La Trobe University, School of Tourism and Hospitality.

Jetske van Westering is Lecturer in Hospitality Management. Her research interests include Gastronomy, Food and Wine Tourism, Food and Wine Marketing and Hospitality Operations Management.

Fiona Williams is a researcher within the Rural Policy Group at the Scottish Agricultural College (SAC). Her research remit is rural development with a responsibility for tourism. Currently, Fiona is working on an EU FP5 project (co-ordinated by SAC), 'Aspatial Peripherality, Innovation and the Rural Economy'. Fiona was previously a lecturer on advanced level Tourism/Leisure Management courses at Herefordshire College. During her early career she was employed by the University of Wales Institute, Cardiff and completed her M.Phil. at this time.

Preface

The aim of this book is to provide a theoretical analysis of the growing relationship between tourism and gastronomy, supported by practical examples of gastronomy tourism development and marketing from different countries and regions.

The book is a result of a transnational collaboration between members of the Association for Tourism and Leisure Education (ATLAS). A group of researchers from different disciplinary backgrounds was brought together in Portugal for the First International Gastronomy Congress staged by the Regional Tourist Board of the Alto Minho. The papers presented at the congress were prepared in advance, allowing the group the luxury of substantial discussion and debate regarding the content of individual contributions and the text as a whole.

The process of meeting in Portugal was also extremely useful in informing the development of the text, since the staging of the congress itself was stimulated by Portuguese efforts to protect their gastronomy from the effect of EU regulations and to develop gastronomy tourism as a means of preserving gastronomic heritage. By bringing together a transnational team of scholars in Portugal we could contrast the Portuguese approach to gastronomy tourism with those adopted in other parts of the world. Discussions among the research team and with congress delegates helped to inform the issues dealt with in this book.

In our discussions in Portugal the team also tried to clarify what the function of the text should be. It was agreed that it was beyond the scope of a single book to present a geographically comprehensive review of the relationships between tourism and gastronomy worldwide. Instead, we have tried to emphasize some of the major issues in the relationship between tourism and gastronomy and to illustrate these with a limited range of case studies. In bringing together authors from different regions and disciplinary backgrounds we also sought to highlight common themes as well as the value of a comparative approach. Because of the previous lack of academic work in this field, we felt it was important that the book should be given a theoretical emphasis, but we have also tried to illustrate the practical implications for the development and marketing of gastronomic tourism where possible. We have also been conscious of the significant gaps in our knowledge, and directions for future research have therefore also been emphasized.

Anne-Mette Hjalager and Greg Richards
September 2001

Acknowledgements

It goes without saying that thanks are due to all the contributors to this volume for their sterling efforts in producing the text, but in this case their contributions to the debates and discussions held by the authors in Portugal were also crucial to the whole production process.

For the opportunity to meet in Portugal we are extremely grateful to the Regional Tourist Board of the Alto Minho and in particular Franciso Sampaio for the hospitality we received in the region. Carlos Fernandes also played a key role in initiating and organizing the whole event, in his usual inimitable style.

Of course the whole exercise would not have been possible without the support provided by ATLAS, and in particular the ATLAS Project Manager Leontine Onderwater.

We are grateful to the Wales Tourist Board, the Welsh Development Agency and Sainsbury's Supermarkets for permission to reproduce the figures in Chapter 7.

Part I
The relationship between tourism and gastronomy

1 Gastronomy: an essential ingredient in tourism production and consumption?

Greg Richards

Introduction

As competition between tourism destinations increases, local culture is becoming an increasingly valuable source of new products and activities to attract and amuse tourists. Gastronomy has a particularly important role to play in this, not only because food is central to the tourist experience, but also because gastronomy has become a significant source of identity formation in postmodern societies. More and more, 'we are what we eat', not just in the physical sense, but also because we identify with certain types of cuisine that we encounter on holiday.

As tourists become more mobile, so does the food they eat. The comfortable association of certain foods with particular regions is being challenged by the growing mobility of food, culinary styles and the increasing de-differentiation of dishes and cuisines. Far from producing an homogenized gastronomic landscape, the tension between globalization and localization is producing ever more variations. Not only are global drinks and foods emerging, such as Coca-Cola and McDonald's, but local and regional food is thriving, and new 'fusion foods' are also being created to feed the 'global soul' (Iyer 2000). Tourists themselves are contributing to gastronomic mobility, by creating a demand in their own countries for foods they have encountered abroad.

Gastronomy has developed considerably through the ages, and there are numerous studies that chart the development of gastronomic styles and tastes over time. For example, Mennell (1985) traces the development of eating in England and France since the Middle Ages, and Parsa (1998) has summarized the development of Western cuisine in America. In Chapter 4 of this volume Rosario Scarpato examines the development of the concept of gastronomy in some detail. Gastronomy is not only extremely difficult to define, but the term, just like 'culture', has become more heavily laden over time.

As Scarpato shows, the original definition of gastronomy has broadened in recent years. The *Encyclopædia Britannica* (2000) defines gastronomy as: 'the art of selecting, preparing, serving, and enjoying fine food'. Originally gastronomy was for the nobility, but over time the concept has also come to include the 'peasant food' typical of regional and local cuisine. As well as including a wider range of foods, the growth of cultural practices related to food has meant that the concept of gastronomy has begun to encompass cultural practices also, so that Scaparto argues that we can now talk about 'gastronomic culture'. More recently, the serving and consumption of food has become a global industry, of which tourism is an important part. In common with other services and 'experiences' offered to (post)modern consumers, a distinct system of production, distribution and presentation has emerged that can be characterized as one of the 'cultural industries'. In the cultural industry of gastronomy the value chain is being extended to include a wide range of economic activities, many of which are related to tourism (Hjalager, Chapter 2 this volume).

In this volume the development of gastronomy as a socio-cultural practice and important cultural industry is examined from the perspective of tourism. The various ways in which gastronomic experiences are created, developed and marketed to tourists and the importance of gastronomic experiences for tourists are analysed in a variety of different settings. In this introductory chapter we introduce some of the main points of discussion surrounding the relationship between gastronomy and tourism which are tackled in more depth in subsequent chapters.

A question of identity: we are what we eat?

As Giddens (1990) and Bauman (1997) argue, the modern condition is characterized by an increasing level of social and personal insecurity. With the disintegration of established structures of meaning, people are searching for new sources of identity that provide some security in an increasingly turbulent world. As Hewison (1987) and other commentators have observed, heritage and nostalgia have provided a rich source of signs of identity, particularly in tourism. Food has also become an important factor in the search for identity. Food is one of our basic needs, so it is not surprising that it is also one of the most widespread markers of identity. We are what we eat, not just in a physiological sense, but also in a psychological and a sociological sense as well. The 'comfort foods' of childhood become the refuge of the adult cocooner. Any attempt to change our eating habits is seen as an attack on our national, regional or personal identity.

There is of course a close link between food and the body. As Bell and Valentine (1997) show, eating is not only a means of sustaining the body, but becomes an essential part of the politics of the body. As people in developed countries increasingly gain weight, the 'ideal' body shape is getting thinner, exerting pressure on people to lose weight. This pressure is particularly strong for women, exposed to the gaze of their partners and friends, and continually measured against the 'ideal woman' as portrayed in the media. The surveillant gaze may become even more crucial on holiday, as bare flesh is exposed to the view of strangers on the beach. As Valentine (1999) argues, we are caught between such discourses of self-control in relation to food, and the pleasurable, hedonistic and social aspects of eating, which are also related to identity, bodily pleasures and sexual desire.

Food is also one of the important aspects of the 'environmental bubble' that surrounds most tourists on their travels. Many tourists eat the same food on holiday as they would do at home. Mass tourist resorts can often be divided spatially on the basis of cuisine – English tourists in English pubs, German tourists in the *Bierkeller*. Some tourists still engage in the habit of taking their own food with them on holiday. Dutch tourists are still renowned for this, even to the extent of taking their own potatoes with them when they go camping in Southern Europe.

Food has been used as a means of forging and supporting identities, principally because what we eat and the way we eat are such basic aspects of our culture. As Leigh points out, eating habits are parochial behaviours that are learned and culturally bound:

> Some Catholics still avoid meat on Friday, as an act of contrition, and so often eat fish on this day. Japanese love raw fish. Chinese eat dogs and monkeys. Moslems and Jews do not eat pork. Hindus do not eat beef. French eat frogs, snails, horses and raw meat. Arabs eat camel meat and drink camel milk. Aborigines eat earth grubs. Greeks drink sheep's milk. Some African tribes drink blood. Yanamamo Indians of South America eat fresh uncooked lice and fried insects.
>
> (Leigh 2000: 10)

Such differences are the source of much of the diversity upon which tourism thrives.

The growth of the nation-state has also been paralleled by the development of different national cuisines. Their influence has to some extent reflected the power of national cultures, as exemplified in the extension of French haute cuisine through the elite of Europe, or the relative obscurity of Portuguese gastronomy. Food is a support for images that bind nations, and they may also be the source of negative 'they-images' and stereotypes, such as 'Frogs', 'Limeys' or 'Krauts' (ERICarts 2000).

Given the strong relationship between food and identity, it is not surprising that food becomes an important place marker in tourism promotion. One of the basic reasons for this is the strong relationship between certain localities and certain types of food. As Hughes (1995: 114) points out there is a 'notion of a natural relationship between a region's land, its climatic conditions and the character of food it produces. It is this geographical diversity which provides for the regional distinctiveness in culinary traditions and the evolution of a characteristic heritage.' This link between location and gastronomy has been used in a number of ways in tourism, including promotional efforts based on distinctive or 'typical' regional or national foods (see the case studies in Part II of this volume). Food can also be used as a means for guiding tourists around regions or countries.

In his classification of cultural attractions, Munsters (1994) identifies regional gastronomic routes as a specific cultural tourism product. The routes he identifies in the Benelux include an asparagus route, a mussel route, a hops route and a gin route. Many of these routes are seasonal, reflecting the link between agricultural cycles and local food production. The season for most of these products also coincides with the main tourist season. The idea behind such routes is that specific products can be linked to particular locations and/or seasons – the 'natural' order of things referred to by Hughes.

Globalization and localization: we are where we eat

The close association of gastronomy and local, regional and national identities is apparently threatened by the process of globalization. As foods such as 'French fries' become available everywhere and previously seasonal foods are sold all year round there is an apparent dissociation of food and place.

In a rapidly changing gastronomic landscape, the forces of globalization and localization are both exerting pressures on our eating habits. The rise of fast food has come to characterize the globalization of culture and economy encapsulated in the term 'McDonaldization' (Ritzer 1993). McDonald's franchises more than 25,000 outlets in 120 countries worldwide. The Big Mac has become such a standard culinary product that it is used to measure the purchasing power parity of national currencies (Ong 1997). While some tourists have welcomed the homogenization of the gastronomic landscape as a means of eating cheaply, predictably and safely across the world, others have attacked the standardization and homogenization of fast food as unhealthy and unnatural and for depriving locals and tourists of a sense of place.

Of course, the extension of global foods has its advantages, not least for tourism:

> Homesick American tourists in far-off countries can take comfort in the knowledge that they will likely run into those familiar golden arches and the restaurant they have become so familiar with.
>
> (Ritzer 1993: 81)

Not only do tourists seek the 'comforts' of home in their travels, but the tourism industry has been only too glad to provide McDonaldized products of its own to meet those needs. For Ritzer, the package holiday itself is a classic example of McDonaldization. Even if some authors have heralded the unpackaging of the package holiday, travel is still highly McDonaldized. Ritzer and Liska (1997) argue that package holidays can become more flexible precisely because the rest of the world has become more McDonaldized. If there is a McDonald's in every tourism destination, tourists no longer have to worry about their food, and won't need it included in the package.

This development challenges the common hypothesis that tourism behaviour is a 'compensation' for activities or experiences that are missing in our everyday lives. In fact, Ritzer and Liska argue, much tourism is an extension of our everyday lives. A similar conclusion has recently been reached in an analysis of cultural tourism behaviour (Thrane 2000). Those people with a high degree of cultural capital will also be likely to undertake cultural activities in their leisure time and in their holiday time, rather than looking for different tourism experiences. Not only is tourism is increasingly like the rest of our lives, but our everyday lives are increasingly like tourism. The cultural capital that we develop on holiday regarding foreign food is utilized in our leisure time to distinguish ourselves from others and to develop our identity.

The fact that many people seek the comfort of the familiar on holiday is one factor that helps to support the spread of global foods. Tourism is one of the forces of globalization in what Castells (1996) terms the 'space of flows' or the global network economy. Increasing integration of the global economy favours increasing economies of scale and scope in food production and distribution just as in tourism. The result is a growing standardization of food in the 'homogeneous spaces' of tourism worldwide (Edensor 1998).

At the same time, however, there is a countervailing force towards more localization in what Castells call the 'space of places' – the local environments in which the bulk of the world's population live their everyday lives. It is being realized that there are real limits to the homogenization of globalization, precisely because global flows of capital, people and culture interact with the specific features of the locality to produce new, locally-specific mixtures of the local and the global. A resurgence of the local is also being stimulated by growing resistance to what many perceive to be the homogenizing forces of globalization, Disneyfication and McDonaldization.

We are already seeing specific reactions to McDonaldization in the growth of the Slow Food Movement, which is particularly strong in Italy (see Scarpato, Chapter 8 this volume). The Slow Food Movement sees food not just as a question of nutrition, but as part of a broader lifestyle statement. To this end, the 'slow cities manifesto' has been created. Slow cities are dedicated to slowing down life in general to improve the quality of life for their citizens. Slow food and slow cities also offer tourists the chance to sample 'real' local food instead of globalized versions of it.

The relationship between globalization and localization is not a diametric opposition, but a dialectic one (Green 2001). Exchanges and cross-fertilization between the global and the local to produce new foods and eating practices have been going on for centuries. The introduction of the potato to Ireland from the New World in the seventeenth century produced a new national food, over-dependence on which among the peasantry laid the foundation for widespread famine in the nineteenth century. The Dutch *rijsttafel*, is 'an elaborate meal of Indonesian dishes developed during the Dutch colonial era'. But 'because of its political overtones, the *rijsttafel* is seldom served today in Indonesia, but it is popular in The Netherlands and at both Dutch and Indonesian restaurants abroad' (*Encyclopædia Britannica* 2000). This type of 'creolization' has become common in the cuisines of former colonizing countries, as the prevalence of Indian food in the UK and couscous in France attest. Globalization has also ensured that many creolized foods have become international, and are being developed as new products on a global scale. Ruis (1996) for example has charted the development of the Irish pub in The Netherlands and other countries. Seen as a typical marker of Ireland, the Irish pub has now been globalized as a standard product by Guinness, who see the pubs as a vehicle for selling their products worldwide. Pub owners receive advice on how to make their pubs 'typically Irish', including the intimate layout of the bar, hiring Irish staff, choosing appropriate music and serving 'traditional' Irish food.

As well as the global becoming localized, the local is also becoming globalized. Many commentators decry the apparent standardization of culture, cuisine and eating that the globalization of the Irish pub represents. However, there are abundant signs that such cultural pessimism is overly dramatic. Although cultural signs can easily be reproduced, standardized and globalized, the way in which people use those signs is often specific to their own culture. Irish pubs may exist in many different countries, but an Irish pub in Dublin is culturally a very different experience from an Irish pub in Valladolid (Spain) where the standard 'Europop' music played during the evening is replaced late at night by Spanish dance music and local youth culture takes over (Richards 1999a). The product may be global, the staff may be able to speak English, the beer may be served in pints, but the experience is local.

Global cultural reproduction is not just affecting the way in which we consume food; it is also having a profound effect on our experience of tourism. Holidays used to be a break from everyday life. The beach, for example, created a liminal space in which the rules of everyday life disappeared, or at least could be bent (Shields 1991). As tourism experiences have become democratized and more widespread, Urry (1990) has pointed to the emergence of a 'tourist culture'. One of the important features of the tourist culture is the creation of specialized settings in which tourist consumption occurs – the homogenized spaces of the tourist industry (Edensor 1998). These spaces used to be restricted to tourist destinations, but the de-differentiation of work, leisure and holidays is ensuring that these 'holiday' environments are becoming a part of our everyday lives. We can visit a Spanish restaurant to re-live the culinary experiences of a holiday in Spain. We can visit a 'beach bar' to re-live the joys of a Mediterranean holiday in the depths of winter. Après-ski bars allow us to sample the delights of *Gluwein* and fondue all year round. This hedonistic proliferation of 'tourist' spaces might be termed 'Californication', in homage to the de-differentiated tourism-work-leisure lifestyle typified by *Baywatch* and other American soap operas.

These trends even leave their mark on the urban fabric. As cities transform themselves into leisure stages through 'festivalization', the architecture of holiday destinations is recreated too. At a basic level there is an extension of cafe terraces and al fresco dining, even in winter. Food, which has so long been confined indoors in Northern Europe, reclaims the streets. These processes are so tied up with the consumption of food that Zukin (1995) referred to the gentrification process in New York as 'pacification by cappuccino'.

A matter of taste

The importance of food and eating in all cultures is emphasized by the import-ance of 'taste'. Having good taste is a matter of being educated or cultivating the 'right' habits in eating, drinking, table manners and other areas of life.

Food has a central role in discussions of taste because of its communal character. Mealtimes are often the central focus of social occasions and family gatherings. Our choice of food, the way we present it, the way we serve it and the way we eat it speak volumes about who we are and our position within the group.

The study of difference is essential to our understanding of society. In the past, class was seen by many as the essential division. As the traditional signifiers of class have begun to blur, attention has turned to the way in which differences are signified through consumption. In particular the work of Bourdieu (1984) on the sociology of taste has been crucial in shaping this area of research.

In his classic work *Distinction*, Bourdieu examines the role of taste in forming and maintaining and legitimating class differences. Not surprisingly one of the main arenas in which these distinctions are developed and underlined is in eating. Bourdieu shows us that the physical necessity of eating is also a cultural practice:

> ... cultural practices also appear in eating habits. The antithesis between quantity and quality, substance and form, corresponds to the opposition – linked to different distances from necessity – between the taste of necessity, which favours the most filling and most economical foods, and the taste of liberty – or luxury – which shifts the emphasis to the manner (of presenting, serving, eating etc.) and to stylized forms to deny function.
>
> (Bourdieu 1984: 6)

The culinary triumph of form over function is more than gastronomic. Food and eating form part of a symbolic universe in which the working class 'ethic of convivial indulgence' is counterposed with the bourgeois 'ethic of reticence and restraint' aimed at producing a socially acceptable body form as well as acceptable table manners.

> ... the taste of the professionals or senior executives defines the popular taste, by negation, as a taste for the heavy, the fat and the coarse, by tending towards the light, the refined and the delicate.
>
> (Bourdieu 1984: 185)

These divisions are also engrained in the way in which we consume food and drink. Bourdieu contrasts local cafes frequented by workers with the restaurants catering to the bourgeoisie. Of course, these differences in eating habits are merely expressions of complete lifestyles. In the past, the preference of the middle classes for foods requiring elaborate preparation was supported by the division of labour, with the 'time reservoir' provided by the wife in bourgeois households allowing complex dishes to be prepared.

The division between elite and mass consumption is continued in modern tourism through the distinction between mass tourism (a democratized, popular form of travel) and independent travel (a personalized, reflective mode of travel) (Munt 1994).

Of course, the basis of distinction can shift over time. In the past, the restaurant as described by Bourdieu was a middle-class preserve, in which class distinctions were maintained through table manners or the requirement to dress appropriately. As 'eating out' has become popularized, so distinctions between class factions have had to be underlined in ways other than simply visiting restaurants. Today it is essential to visit the 'right' restaurant – the hip, happening place. To be caught in a restaurant that has fallen out of favour with one's peers can be social death. Even if one manages to choose the right venue, it is important to have sufficient cultural capital to order the 'right' dishes, and in the case of foreign food to be able to pronounce their names properly.

In the struggle to maintain distinctions, foods, just like restaurants, may go through cycles of elevation and popularization as the masses attempt to emulate the consumption patterns of higher classes, who in turn seek to maintain their distinctiveness by finding new areas of culinary exclusivity. This cycle has been illustrated in the case of cider by Augustyn (2000). She shows that cider was in the seventeenth century considered to be on a par with modern champagne. Payment of farm labourers in kind with cider led to the image of the drink being downgraded in the eighteenth century, and cider was further eclipsed by the rise of beer in the nineteenth century. In recent years cider has been positioned as a traditional niche product in an attempt to distinguish it from beer and add value to the product. In so doing, the drink is again becoming popular with the middle classes. The tendency for 'forgotten' traditional foods to be rediscovered and turned into gastronomic products has accelerated in recent years, as the rise of *polenta* and *pa amb tomàquet* illustrate.

Our desire for distinction becomes conflated with the modern appetite for novelty in a ceaseless wave of 'food fads':

> We don't eat from dishes any more, but from fashion plates, subject to the whims and fancies of designer chefs forever looking for new ways to catch media attention with their artistic urges. Heaven forbid you may want to eat the same thing twice.
>
> (Durack 2000: 45)

The development of food as fashion has been supported in recent years by the rise of the culinary media. In the search for new recipes and stories, food critics and media chefs have increasingly begun to scour the world for 'new' styles of cooking, new ingredients and new backdrops. Food and travel have become inseparable in the travels of TV personalities such as Keith Floyd, Ken Hom and Antonio Carluccio. The relationship between their cooking and the destination is synergetic – the destination provides the recipes, the cultural context and the scenic backdrop, the television chef promotes the destination that is encapsulated by its cuisine. These effects are discussed in more detail by Hall and Mitchell in Chapter 5 and Scarpato in Chapter 8.

Food becomes the ideal sign of tourism consumption. Eating is an obligatory part of the holiday experience, and therefore lends itself as a tool of distinction for everybody. We can show off our cultural capital relating to the destination by eating 'authentic' food in the destination. The traveller can escape from the mass tourist hordes by finding that 'hidden' local restaurant where only 'locals' go.

Creating experiences

Food structures the tourist day. A large proportion of most tourist experiences are spent either consuming food and drink, or deciding what and where to consume. However, many of these experiences are taken for granted, because we often regard eating as a necessity rather than a leisure activity. One of the essential tasks in developing and marketing gastronomic tourism, therefore, is to find ways to add value to the eating experience in order to make it memorable.

Tourism is one of the quintessential experience industries that Pine and Gilmore (1999) argue will come to dominate the economy in future. As the basis of the economy shifts from delivering services to staging experiences, the quality of the basic elements of the product will increasingly be taken for granted by consumers, who will demand engaging absorbing experiences as part of the tourism and gastronomy product.

The development of gastronomic experiences is evident in the appearance of restaurants that offer a total package of food, entertainment and atmosphere. The Rainforest Cafe, for example, claims

> Rainforest Cafe® is A Wild Place to Shop and Eat®! Our unique restaurant and retail concept is an adventure through the most realistic indoor rain forest ever created! Discover amazingly lush surroundings, cascading waterfalls, live birds, and beautiful giant aquariums. Savor our fresh, original menu selections, influenced by the cuisines of Mexico, Asia and the Caribbean. Your Adventure is About to Begin!
>
> (Rainforest Cafe 2000)

The adventure is spiced up by a thunderstorm every 15 minutes, rainforest educational tours and of course countless merchandising opportunities for those essential souvenirs of your visit. Even in less aggressively themed surroundings, the preparation and serving of food is being turned into an experience. Kitchens are being opened up to the gaze of the visitor, and waiting staff may be expected to sing or offer other forms of entertainment when serving.

As Kevin Fields shows in Chapter 3, creating saleable experiences also becomes part of the art of developing tourist destinations. As global competition between tourist destinations increases, so the search for distinctive products becomes more intense. Gastronomy is seen as an important source of marketable images and experiences for the tourists; and as Antonioli Corigliano argues in Chapter 10, experiences can be developed through linking resources in a single region or in different regions through gastronomic routes or paths. The tourist can experience a range of gastronomic products linked to the cultural and agricultural resources of a specific region, or compare the way in which culture interfaces with similar gastronomic products in different regions. Creating such experiences necessitates not only linking different locations but also linking different producers in the value chain.

Gastronomic experiences for tourists are usually developed from the perspective of 'unique' aspects of the gastronomy that can only be found in that particular location. As more destinations develop gastronomic experiences for visitors, however, so the issue of intellectual property becomes more acute. Ravenscroft and van Westering (Chapter 9) point out that countries or regions will need to protect the intellectual property bound up in their gastronomic culture in order to maintain the distinctiveness of their products. They show how Spain has reinvented itself as a destination partly through employing gastronomic products such as *paella* and *Rioja*. However as the gastronomic products of Spain and other countries become more widespread, there will be a growing need to identify the essence of these products and protect them from reproduction elsewhere.

Selling the destination

If gastronomy can be linked to specific countries or regions, it becomes a powerful tourism marketing tool. Authenticity has always been viewed as an important aspect of tourism consumption, and seeking out 'authentic' local and regional foods can become a motive for visiting a particular destination. Many countries and regions around the world have begun to realize this, and are using gastronomy to market themselves, as many of the chapters in this volume show.

For example Boyne *et al.* (Chapter 6) and Jones and Jenkins (Chapter 7) show how food has been used as a vehicle to reposition Scotland and Wales respectively. Both have developed similar marketing programmes: 'A Taste of Scotland' and 'A Taste of Wales'. The Taste of Scotland initiative created a marketing scheme in which participating establishments would agree to provide dishes which were either 'traditional or using recognizably Scottish produce, to provide the visitor with a meal of Scottish food' (Hughes 1995: 114). Hughes argues that the Taste of Scotland scheme constructed a food heritage for Scotland which could then be used as a marketing tool. Similar schemes are evident in other areas as well. In the Alto Minho region of Portugal, for example, a recipe book was produced by the regional tourist board to give visitors the opportunity to 'carry away with [them] an enduring memory of the tasting, the pleasures of the dining, in these lands of the Minho' (Sampaio 1985: cover text).

Much of the marketing effort directed at developing rural gastronomy is aimed at establishing and increasing the 'authenticity' of the local cuisine. An important aspect of developing authentic local products is an appeal to nostalgia and the virtues of a traditional, simpler and more wholesome rural past. As Sampaio argues in the case of the Alto Minho:

> Because of the constraints of modern life and technological progress our grandparents' recipes are often put away in the drawer, forgotten, to be replaced by other more practical (?) and more modern (?) menus . . . in this

way damaging and even sacrificing, an expression of our ancestral heritage, truly representative of our heritage.

(Sampaio 1985: 4)

Edwards *et al.* (2000: 294) have also argued that gastronomy is an important element of the brand image of the Alto Minho, which 'contains an agriculturally based society set in a particular landscape, with particular ways of social behaviour and with a distinctive gastronomy'. These relationships are explored further in Chapter 12 of this volume.

With such resources, Portugal is in a position to use its extensive role in European gastronomic tradition to develop attractive gastronomic products for tourists. Not only can these products be positioned as uniquely 'Portuguese', but the role of Portugal as a trading nation means that the Portuguese have had a role in developing the gastronomy of the countries from which many of their tourists come.

In contrast to the appeal to tradition and pre-modern forms of gastronomy found in rural areas, the urban marketing of gastronomy is often based on positioning cuisine at the cutting edge of fashion and (post)modern life. Gastronomy has for example been one of the reasons for the rise of Cataluñia as a fashionable region in Europe (Richards 2000). The cuisine of Cataluñia not only matches the current taste of many consumers for simple, wholesome food, but is also associated with a dynamic region full of modernist architecture, modern art and contemporary fashion.

Marketing destinations through gastronomy also brings a range of benefits through complementary activities and linkages, such as stimulating local agriculture, food processing and retailing, raising food quality and strengthening local image and identity.

Tourism and food production

Tourism is intimately linked to local food production. Tourists, just like local people, need to eat. If their demands can be met from local resources this can provide an important boost to the local economy. If not, tourism can add to the demand for imported foods, harming local agriculture, increasing imports and reducing the economic benefit of tourism. Strong linkages between tourism and local food production can, as Hjalager shows (Chapter 2), create considerable added value; but poor linkages can be fatal.

Because local food production depends on agriculture, hunting and fishing, the appropriate development of linkages with tourism can aid the stimulation of indigenous entrepreneurial activity and stimulate the 'bottom-up' development of community-based tourism initiatives. As Telfer (2000) has shown in the case of Indonesia, tourism not only provides a market for the final products of agriculture, but also offers the potential of further income generation through developing experiences for tourists in the form of 'agritourism'.

In some cases, however, the preference of tourists for familiar foods can be a major drain on the economy. This is a particular problem for areas with a limited capacity for agricultural production, such as many small island destinations. Where local agricultural production is better developed, tourism can be an important market. As Michael Hall and Richard Mitchell demonstrate in Chapter 11, innovation has been vital in developing the gastronomic products of Australia and New Zealand, and has had considerable spin-off effects for agricultural production and food exports. Maximizing these benefits has been dependent on the creation of effective networks incorporating both vertical and horizontal integration.

Another important aspect of food production in the modern 'risk society' (Beck 1992) is the extent to which our food is safe to eat. In the 1970s food safety fears in the developed world often related to unprocessed foods, such as unpasteurized milk, which almost disappeared as a result. The development of modern factory farming methods and food processing has now created a situation in which the risks associated with mass-produced processed food have actually increased, and the demand for 'safer' foods, such as biological or unprocessed foods have grown as a result. This is in turn likely to increase the demand for gastronomic tourism in regions which can show that their food products are 'safe' and/or rely on traditional production methods. This may become increasingly important in peripheral areas where farmers apparently at a disadvantage through lack of mechanization and modernization may actually be able to turn their 'old-fashioned' production methods into an advantage. The increasing awareness of food risks will also strengthen calls for labelling and quality schemes that guarantee the origin and production methods of foods, which is already an important element of marketing strategies in many of the regions analysed in this volume.

Take-away food

Not only is consumption of food and drink important at the destination, but much food and drink can also be taken home as a souvenir. Drink is particularly important in this respect, although the recent abolition of duty free sales in the European Union may have curtailed this habit for some.

There is considerable potential for tourism regions to develop this gastronomic souvenir market, particularly where distinctive food and drink products are available. For example, research conducted by the EUROTEX crafts tourism project in Greece, Finland and Portugal (Richards 1999b) indicated that 84 per cent of tourists in rural regions purchasing souvenirs had bought food or drink to take home. Food products are particularly important as souvenirs because they are relatively cheap and easy to carry. Not surprisingly, food and drink souvenirs tended to have a very high use value, with 45 per cent of purchasers indicating that their souvenir was 'useful'.

Food and drink were particularly likely to be bought by those aged over 30 and under 60, and those with higher educational attainment and higher status occupations or craft workers. There was also a strong relationship between having a cultural occupation and food purchases. In terms of income, however, it tended to be those on median incomes who were most likely to buy.

As far as motivations were concerned, those interested in cultural traditions and hospitality were particularly likely to buy food. Authenticity was also confirmed as being fairly important in the decision to buy gastronomic products. Over 75 per cent of respondents buying food and drink said that the authenticity of the products was 'important' or 'very important' in their decision to buy. As suggested by May (1996), however, the importance of authenticity is not confined to independent, 'postmodern' tourists: 95 per cent of those on package holidays bought food and drink, and 68 per cent of these indicated that the authenticity of these products was important to them.

The relationship between specific regions and the souvenirs purchased was also important. In Crete, for example, many of the food purchases related to Cretan olive oil. This strong relationship between tourism and olive oil production has since been exploited through the establishment of a specific olive oil marketing project, aimed both at tourists visiting the region and those purchasing olive oil once they returned home. It is hoped that the experience of tasting Cretan olive oil on holiday would help to strengthen the image of the Cretan product relative to its competitors from other parts of Greece and other Mediterranean countries.

Gastronomic products are therefore confirmed as important souvenirs that appeal to a wide range of tourists. Part of the appeal of buying food and drink on holiday is arguably the ability to share these with friends and relatives on your return. Almost half of the food souvenir purchasers in the EUROTEX study indicated that having a memento for friends and relatives was important in their decision to buy. Food products can also be used to display the cultural capital gained on holiday, by cooking for and entertaining friends on our return from holiday. Local dishes can be prepared using authentic ingredients, accompanied by local wines and perhaps even served on local ceramics purchased on the holiday.

In the Portuguese case, however, other research evidence indicates that gastronomy is not currently developed as a strong element of the tourism product. In her study of rural tourism in Northern and Central Portugal, Kastenholz (2000) found that gastronomy was ranked as the fifth most important motivational factor for tourists visiting the region, and in terms of satisfaction it was rated only eighth. The relatively poor satisfaction level is of concern because word of mouth is one of the most important ways in which tourists gain information about potential destinations.

As part of the experiential baggage that tourists take home, gastronomy can also play a role in making their consumption skills and cultural capital visible to others. As Schor (1998) points out, the status role of leisure consumption is often undermined by our inability to show others what we have consumed. Because tourism experiences are unique and intangible, we have to find ways of capturing, preserving and displaying them to our peers if we are to capitalize on their value as status symbols. Suntans, photographs, holiday slides and videos all serve to display our consumption. If we want to emphasize the cultural capital we have gained, however, our knowledge of foreign foods and eating habits is a useful means of distinction. Unless our friends have also been to the same destination they will probably not recognize the food products we have brought back, they may have trouble using the chopsticks that we have mastered during our Far Eastern tour, they may be unwary of the fiery *wasabi* lurking in the dainty Japanese dish on the table, and they may not know that Japanese custom dictates that you do not fill your own *saki* cup.

Signs of consuming food become just as important status symbols as the food itself. The Hardrock Cafe, for example, makes a great deal of its turnover from the sale of T-shirts and other souvenir items. The sales outlets are placed outside the restaurant so that you don't even need to eat there to collect these signs. Because the Hardrock is a globalized product, collecting T-shirts with different Hardrock locations becomes a way of emphasizing the breadth of your travel experience rather than the narrow focus of your culinary taste.

Conclusion

Gastronomy has considerable potential as a means of developing and marketing tourism regions worldwide. While the tourist may be an eager consumer of gastronomic products, however, the analyses presented here also indicate the many tensions surrounding the production, reproduction and consumption of gastronomic culture. As with many aspects of the tangible heritage, some people feel they must 'save' the gastronomic heritage before it is washed away by the tide of globalization or McDonaldization. The Slow Food Movement is a prime example of how gastronomic culture is becoming emblematic of a whole way of life that many consider to be worth saving. The homogenization produced by McDonald's is also an easy target, as the popularity of the Slow Food Movement shows. But McDonald's is also about rationalization, and as Ritzer (1993) has pointed out, rationalization has many benefits that people want, as well as the irrationalities they don't want. Modern omnivorous tourists may well want to sample local gastronomy, but they are not averse to eating at McDonald's as well.

Gastronomic heritage is also not the same as the tangible heritage of sites and monuments. Gastronomy evolves and develops precisely because the living culture around it changes. It is therefore important to realize that sustainable development of gastronomic tourism is not just about preserving the past, but also about creating the future. To fossilize culinary products is to make them as distant and inaccessible to the modern consumer as blackbird pie or roast swan. The strength of gastronomy as a cultural resource is precisely its propensity to change, whether through creolization, globalization or localization.

Gastronomy is also a fertile breeding ground for 'creative tourism' (Richards and Raymond 2000). Tourists are increasingly willing to learn and eager to increase their cultural capital by creating rather than just consuming. Gastronomic holidays are therefore an important aspect of the emerging creative tourism sector, as tourists can learn to cook, can learn about the ingredients used, the way in which they are grown and appreciate how culinary traditions have come into existence.

In developing gastronomic experiences for tourists in an increasingly competitive tourism market, it is important not just to base the product on the culture and traditions of the destination, but to provide a link to the culture of the tourist. This means not just their own local or national culture, but also the culture of tourism that is generated by Castell's space of flows. The developers of gastronomic tourism in the future will have to spend more time building bridges between spaces of flows which provides the global market for gastronomy and spaces of places where that gastronomy is produced and maintained.

A guide to reading this volume

Given the range and diversity of material and approaches presented here, we felt it may be useful to outline the structure of the text, as well as the guiding principles we used in writing it. Although one of the strengths of this book arguably lies in the fact that it presents a range of different views on the relationship between tourism and gastronomy, we have made some attempt to develop areas of common ground.

One of the discussions among the authors concerned the terminology of the text. There is a bewildering array of food-related terms to be found in the book, including gastronomy, eno-gastronomy, sustainable gastronomy, cuisine, meals, agro-alimentary products, foodways, food paths, taste trails and wine routes. This diverse terminology reflects the wide range of disciplinary and geographical backgrounds of the authors, and rather than attempting to standardize the definitions, each author has defined these terms in their own chapters. The only exception to this is the term 'gastronomy', which is so central to the text that we decided to adopt a common definition for the purposes of this book. We have therefore defined gastronomy as 'the reflexive cooking, preparation, presentation and eating of food'. This definition is dealt with in more detail by Rosario Scarpato in Chapter 4.

In putting together the chapters in this volume we have tried to be analytical and illustrative rather than comprehensive. The case studies presented here are not designed to cover all types of gastronomy or tourism, but rather to focus on specific issues and case studies that reflect what we consider to be important issues in the relationship between the two fields. The chapters in Part 1 of this volume consider some of the theoretical perspectives on the relationship between tourism and gastronomy in more detail. In Chapter 2, Hjalager applies value chain theory to the analysis of culinary tourism development. She shows how regions and nations have increasingly had to shift towards higher order levels of value added as food supplies and culinary tourism have become globalized. In Chapter 3 Kevin Fields examines the relationship between tourist motivations and the gastronomy tourism product. He points to the need to tailor gastronomy products to individual tourist needs and to weave them into total gastronomic experiences. Rosario Scarpato then deals with tourism from a gastronomy studies perspective in Chapter 4. He argues the need for tourism researchers to adopt a trans-disciplinary gastronomic approach in order to analyse the relationship between tourism and gastronomy effectively. Michael Hall and Richard Mitchell place the development of gastronomy and tourism in the context of globalization and localization in Chapter 5.

The case studies in the second part of this volume analyse some of the issues that have arisen in developing and marketing gastronomic products in a wide range of tourist markets. Chapter 6 (Boyne, Williams and Hall) and Chapter 7 (Jones and Jenkins) provide comparative cases studies of two marketing and branding schemes in Scotland and Wales respectively. These chapters demonstrate how important the local context not just of gastronomy, but also of tourism is in determining the success of these developments. In Chapter 8 Rosario Scarpato deals with the issue of making gastronomy sustainable, analysing three case studies of 'gastronomic tourist products' in Australia, Singapore and Italy. He illustrates that in the context of sustainable gastronomy, the drive towards small-scale and 'authentic' products often argued for in the field of sustainable tourism may have negative consequences. Magda Antonioli Corigliano analyses the development of Italian food and wine routes in Chapter 10, focusing on the need to develop effective networks to sustain producers and to market the product effectively to tourists. In Chapter 11, Hall and Mitchell demonstrate how Australia and New Zealand have developed new food products and styles of cuisine, and used these to develop food tourism. Tourism has in turn provided an important link between networks of local producers and global markets. Beer, Edwards, Fernandes and Sampaio compare two case studies from rural regions of the UK and Portugal in Chapter 12, focusing in particular on the relationship between regional agriculture, regional food cultures and marketing and branding food for tourists.

In the concluding chapter, Hjalager and Richards draw together a number of strands from the preceding chapters, and fit these into an epistemological framework that indicates how new knowledge about the relationship between tourism and gastronomy may be created, and indicates a research agenda for the future.

In discussing the themes of this volume, we were struck by the similarities between tourism and gastronomy. We have attempted to pull a number of these parallels together in Figure 1.1, which places tourism and gastronomy in the context of the development of the 'experience economy' as defined by Pine and Gilmore (1999). As Kevin Fields points out in Chapter 3, both fields are characterized by a production–consumption chain that results in the creation of experiences. Gastronomy tourism can be related in its many forms to different parts of the production–consumption continuum, from sampling the 'raw' product at the farm or vineyard (food and wine tourism) to the gastronomic experiences provided by restaurants. In the former case the 'quality of opportunity', or the basic product is most important, whereas in the restaurant much more hinges on the whole 'quality of experience' (Crompton and Love 1995). Arguably, adding more elements to the basic product will enhance the experience for the consumer, and add more value to the product. We therefore see the convergence of gastronomy

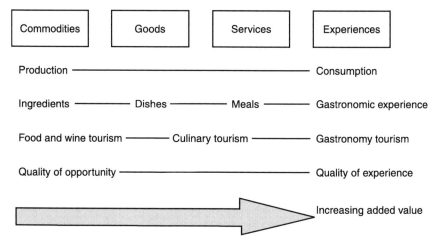

Figure 1.1 Relating consumption and production in gastronomy tourism experiences

and tourism as being closely linked to the rise of the experience economy and the constant need to innovate and distinguish products and services in order to add value for the consumer.

References

Augustyn, M. (2000) 'From decline to growth: innovative strategies for manufacturing small cultural tourism enterprises – Westons cider case study', *Tourism, Culture and Communication*, 2: 153–164.

Bauman, Z. (1997) *Postmodernity and its Discontents*, Cambridge: Polity Press.

Beck, U. (1992) *Risk Society: towards a new modernity*, London: Sage.

Bell, D. and Valentine, G. (1997) *Consuming Geographies: we are where we eat*, London: Routledge.

Bourdieu, P. (1984) *Distinction: a social critique of the judgment of taste*. Routledge: London.

Castells, M. (1996) *The Information Age: Economy, society and culture. Volume I: The rise of the network society*, Oxford: Blackwell.

Crompton, J.L. and Love, L.L. (1995) 'The predictive validity of alternative approaches to evaluating quality of a festival', *Journal of Travel Research*, 34(1): 11–18.

Durack, T. (2000) 'What's cooking?', *Independent Magazine*, 20 October, 45–47.

Edensor, T. (1998) *Tourists at the Taj: Performance and Meaning at a Symbolic Site*, London: Routledge.

Edwards, J., Fernandes, C., Fox, J. and Vaughan, R. (2000) 'Tourism brand attributes of the Alto Minho, Portugal', in G. Richards and D. Hall (eds) *Tourism and Sustainable Community Development*, London: Routledge, pp. 285–296.

Encyclopædia Britannica (2000) www.eb.com, accessed December 2000.

ERICarts (2000) *The European Food Project*, www.ericarts.org, accessed December 2000.

Giddens, A. (1990) *The Consequences of Modernity*, Cambridge: Polity Press.

Green, M. (2001) 'Urban heritage tourism: Globalisation and localisation', in G. Richards (ed.) *Cultural Attractions and European Tourism*. Wallingford: CAB International, pp. 173–197.

Hewison, R. (1987) *The Heritage Industry: Britain in a climate of decline*, London: Methuen.

Hughes, G. (1995) 'Food, tourism and Scottish heritage', in D. Leslie (ed.) *Tourism and Leisure – Culture, Heritage and Participation*, Brighton: LSA, pp. 109–128.

Iyer, P. (2000) *The Global Soul*, London: Bloomsbury.

Kastenholz, E. (2000) 'The market for rural tourism in north and central Portugal: a benefit-segmentation approach', in G. Richards and D. Hall (eds) *Tourism and Sustainable Community Development*, London: Routledge, pp. 268–284.

Leigh, J. (2000) 'Implications of universal and parochial behavior for intercultural communication', *Intercultural Communication*, 4: 1–17.

May, J. (1996) 'In search of authenticity off and on the beaten track', *Environment and Planning D: Society and Space*, 14(6): 709–736.

Mennell, S. (1985) *All Manners of Food: eating and taste in England and France from the Middle Ages to the present*, Oxford: Blackwell.

Munsters, W. (1994) *Cultuurteorisme*, Leuven: Garant.

Munt, I. (1994) 'The "other" postmodern tourism: culture, travel and the new middle classes', *Theory, Culture and Society*, 11: 101–123.

Ong, L.L. (1997) 'Burgernomics: the economics of the Big Mac standard', *Journal of International Money and Finance*, 16: 865–878.

Parsa, H.G. (1998) 'Cultural heritage of American food habits and implications for the Hospitality industry', *Marriage and Family Review*, 28: 23–48.

Pine, B.J. and Gilmore, J. (1999) *The Experience Economy*, Harvard: Harvard Business School Press.

Rainforest Cafe (2000) http://www.rainforestcafe.com/RFC/, accessed December 2000.

Richards, G. (1999a) 'Polícas y actuaciones en el campo del turismo cultural europeo', paper delivered at the conference Turismo Cultural, Valladolid, November 1999.

—— (1999b) *Developing and Marketing Crafts Tourism*, Tilburg: ATLAS.

—— (2000) 'Demand evolution in cultural tourism', *ATLAS News*, 24: 21–29.

Richards, G. and Raymond, C. (2000) 'Creative tourism', *ATLAS News*, 23: 16–20.

Ritzer, G. (1993) *The McDonaldization of Society*, Thousand Oaks: Pine Forge Press.

Ritzer, G. and Liska, A. (1997) ' "McDisneyization" and "post-tourism": complementary perspectives on contemporary tourism', in C. Rojek and J. Urry (eds) *Touring Cultures: Transformations of travel and theory*, London: Routledge, pp. 96–109.

Ruis, A. (1996) 'Creolisering in Nederland: de Ierse pub: een explorerende analyse binnen het marktraamwerk', unpublished MA Thesis, Tilburg University.

Sampaio, F. (1985) *The Good Food of the Upper Minho*, Viana do Castelo: Regional Tourist Board of the Upper Minho.

Schor, J.B. (1998) *The Overspent American: Upscaling, downshifting, and the new consumer*, New York: Basic Books.

Shields, R. (1991) *Places on the Margin: Alternative geographies of modernity*, London: Routledge.

Telfer, D. (2000) 'Agritourism – a path to community development?: the case of Bangun-kerto, Indonesia', in G. Richards and D. Hall (eds) *Tourism and Sustainable Community Development*, London: Routledge, pp. 242–257.

Thrane, C. (2000) 'Everyday life and cultural tourism in Scandinavia: examining the spillover hypothesis', *Society and Leisure*, 23: 217–234.

Urry, J. (1990) *The Tourist Gaze*, London: Sage.

Valentine, G. (1999) 'Consuming pleasures: food, leisure and the negotiation of sexual relations', in D. Crouch (ed.) *Leisure/Tourism Geographies: practices and geographical knowledge*, London: Routledge, pp. 164–180.

Zukin, S. (1995) *The Cultures of Cities*, Oxford: Blackwell.

2 A typology of gastronomy tourism

Anne-Mette Hjalager

Some basic assumptions

This chapter attempts to provide a cross-analysis of gastronomy tourism from an economic point of view, linking to the theories, evidence and examples in the other chapters. The aim is to develop a general typology of the extent and nature of value added in a value chain which can then be applied to the description and analysis of tourism and gastronomy worldwide.

The value chain, a common approach in tourism studies (Desinano and Vigo 1994), is used to analyse the accumulated needs of a tourist during the holiday (accommodation, catering, transport, information and entertainment) for the purpose of assessing, for example, the regional implications of tourism. Here, however, the value chain is used in a slightly different way than in most tourism studies.

The chapter starts with basic food production, taking the entire production process into account, from the initial supply of raw materials, e.g. cattle in the fields, to the presentation of the food on the table, even including souvenirs, such as the shells of seafood taken back home. Even more careful attention is paid to the immaterial facets of the production and consumption of food, and to the value added in the different phases of the process. This is where gastronomy and tourism, in particular, come into the picture. In principle, service elements, information, etc., can be added at any phase during the production of the food, from the basic ingredients to the point of eating. Sometimes, as we shall see, these service elements are only very remotely connected to the food as a physical substance.

For decades now, research has acknowledged that tourism is full of symbolic consumption that goes far beyond the satisfaction of bodily needs (Brown 1992; Urry 1990). Food consumption is no exception. Pillsbury (1990) divides food catering into two categories: body food and soul food. Body food comes from fast food restaurants, which fulfil the need to feed the stomach rapidly in standardized environments that do not challenge the intellectual capacities in any way. Soul food has another appeal. The food is prepared more slowly, possibly accordingly to special wishes, sometimes exotic and different – at the very least with some distinct qualities. The pleasures of the environment and the company of other people is an essential part of the eating experience. For Pillsbury, it is decisive that the patterns of food consumption are determined by the situation rather than by demographic or economic factors. Sometimes, at work, sports, etc., body food is chosen; on other occasions, for example in connection with celebrations, soul food is preferred.

Beneath the surface of Pillsbury's dichotomy of restaurant types, there is a continuous development and restructuring of the value chain. In the fast food sector, the value chain is split up, extended to include still more producers, and globalized. For example, McDonald's ships ingredients across many borders, since suppliers for even small items must be selected carefully (Business Trends Analysts 1991). Soul food restaurants are also developing their concepts, not only in terms of new ingredients and recipes, or any other specifications of the food itself, but their efforts are also increasingly concentrated on the environments and atmospheres of the restaurant itself.

From an economic point of view, the integration and sophistication of such production systems could be regarded as vital for continued value adding. The tendency seems to be that the more complex and tightly knitted structures of interdependencies, the more advanced the economies. In relation to food and food provision, the more complex systems represent a refined division of labour between various segments of the economy. The process leads to the creation of new clusters of collaborating enterprises. The intensification of the service aspect over the material part of the product is a more general and widely recognized symptom of modernity, and it is of crucial importance for the analysis of food for tourists. These modernization processes do not take place uniformly as a dehumanized 'McDonaldization' (Ritzer 1993); many other outcomes are possible (Smart 1999).

Tourists are not always provided with high-quality food and eating-related entertainment. The previously abysmal quality of food provision in the former Soviet bloc countries still springs to mind; but quality is also lacking in many other places in otherwise highly developed countries. Why, for example, is fresh fish not served in restaurants in Icelandic fishing villages? Catering enterprises and food producers do not always harvest the highest possible value added along the totality of the value chain. Such paradoxes have generated academic speculation; witness Johns and Tyas (1996), who focus on managerial issues, Hjalager and Antonioli Corigliano's (2000) analysis of political explanations, and Telfer (2000), who has looked at local collaborative structures.

This chapter attempts to systematize some of the important driving forces and barriers to the creation of 'gastronomy tourism'. The development of gastronomy tourism is discussed in a hierarchical model, which systematically defines the 'four orders' of gastronomy tourism, reflecting the increasing sophistication and complexity in the food value chains:

- **First order: Indigenous development.** The building up of gastronomy tourism within the existing economic structures, collaborative networks and knowledge base.

- **Second order: Horizontal development.** Adding steps in the production process and integrating suppliers backwards and forwards, but only in the material part of the production chain.
- **Third order: Vertical development.** Developing and adding analogous services elements to the material provision of food. Creating new types of linkages and collaborations, integrating food in other economic activities.
- **Fourth order: Diagonal development.** Enhancing the knowledge base of the gastronomy experience and creating 'intelligent' gastronomy clusters in the economy.

The reader may object that this hierarchy masks some of the traditional dependency logic: the higher the order, the higher economic performance. The more globalized, the more advanced, etc. (Beck 2000). While it is true that, in general, economic driving forces tend to work more or less in this way, convergence does not mean that, eventually, all food regions will become equally sophisticated and diagonally integrated gastronomy regions. Nor does it mean that a place cannot survive perfectly well without heavy linkages to the surrounding economy, whether local or global. It is precisely this variation and non-uniformity in development patterns that is likely to encourage people to experience foreign food cultures in the future.

First-order gastronomy tourism development: the indigenous

This order of value added represents a basic development of gastronomy and tourism in a region. The economic activities are based on resources, material or immaterial, already established, and very little else.

Increased value added is created in the primary sector in regional food processing industries, and in restaurants by increasing availability and awareness *vis-à-vis* tourists. Their markets are expanded with increasing numbers of tourists, but nothing else is changed. In 'first-order gastronomy tourism development' it is assumed that the resource more or less already exists, but that tourists must be helped to understand the gastronomic particularities. The relevant parameters here are scale and visibility.

Lack of communication between customers and food providers is regarded as the main problem. The availability of sufficient amounts of food and infrastructures such as restaurants are secondary concerns. Expansion takes place along exactly the same trajectory, without changing the basic concepts and without affecting the nature and extent of the business linkages. The Portuguese protective strategy, as described by Beer *et al.* in Chapter 12 of this volume, operates much along these lines.

The following types of activities are regarded as supporting the aim of developing higher value added in the indigenous institutional frameworks.

Including gastronomic aspects in promotional materials of the region/country

Promotional efforts take many forms. Pictures of colourful and lively markets illustrate special atmospheres, and convince tourists that food is available and fresh. Some dishes make good photographs; for example lobsters and other types of seafood, and they often go hand-in-hand with the promotion of coastal destinations. Typically, travel brochures illustrate eating situations. If the food is very exotic, it might be convincing if someone who looks like a tourist seems to enjoy eating it.

Gastronomic nomads are the target group of more classy and specialised PR and marketing. Positive relations to magazines and television programmes are essential to attract this type of tourist. However, food quality will probably have to be considerably higher than average if a region wants to appeal to food connoisseurs.

Campaigns for particular products, connected to a region or season

For example, some British localities have had success in attracting tourists during the apple season, possibly as part of a combined effort to prolong the standard tourist season well into the autumn. The apples and ciders are for sale in shops, and are also included in restaurant menus – exactly as they would have been without the media and tourist attention. Nothing specific is done to develop new recipes that will increase demand for particular local products.

Introducing food trade marks with regional features/names, etc.

A more comprehensive effort consists of combining several products and labelling them with the name of the region. No matter whether the label is a quality label or not, the batching increases product visibility and may enhance the qualities of the region for food lovers.

The most effective trade marks have been developed over decades and based on solid production traditions, as in the case of Italian specialities from the Parma region. It is doubtful how much the recognized qualities of parmesan cheese and parma ham attract tourists to this particular region, but, as noted by Antonioli Corigliano in Chapter 10 of this volume, tourism in Italy is definitely dependent on cuisine and food ingredients in more general terms.

Creating tourism appeal for existing food fairs and events

Every year, large international food fairs take place in, for example, Germany and France, and these annual events attract a heavy inflow of (business) tourists to the regions. In all likelihood, these mega food fairs mainly support the continued specialization in food production and globalization of the markets. In contrast, cattle shows in rural settings are usually opportunities for local and small-scale producers to display their products. Contrary to what might be thought, these events are not entirely eclipsed by large international fairs, since their existence is based on another economic logic. Originally, cattle shows and other events were started to serve the food and agriculture sector, but they have increasingly become open to others outside the sector. The interest of a larger audience of tourists may ensure the survival of these events, but might also lead to changes in the products presented and entertainments provided.

Public/private planning for the restaurant sector in new urban/resort developments

Making gastronomy tourism feasible may require an expansion of restaurants, food stores and other facilities where tourists can buy and experience the produce. In new developments, not least in shopping malls, coastal resorts and urban regeneration projects, the integration of the food element is absolutely essential and the location of major importance (Melaniphy 1992). But also in rural settings, planning for physical facilities, from signs, to parking lots, walking trails and picnicking areas, can be considered part of an indigenous and incremental development of food provision for tourists.

Second-order gastronomy tourism development: the horizontal

The second-order development of gastronomy tourism expands the vision of the first order to include an improvement of product quality. Improvements are introduced not only because tourists are critical, but also because higher quality is assumed to create higher revenues.

Changes in quality, particularly upgradings, are potentially painful and costly for suppliers. Pursuing quality objectives can change the division of labour among producers throughout the entire value chain. A second-order development will thus disrupt existing relations and create new ones. New institutions in charge of tasks not previously defined in the production system will be established, mainly in the area of marketing, quality control and other business services.

In spite of the growth in volumes and expansion of institutional frameworks, the value added is still largely based on the distinct gastronomic traditions and resources of the region concerned. Some examples of the development logic in the second order of gastronomy tourism are mentioned below.

Implementing and marketing quality standards

Sometimes, regions have an interesting cuisine, but the produce has become impoverished for many reasons, e.g. being part of the local population's basic diet, menus might have become trivialized. If such products are to regain their reputation as noble expressions of a regional food culture, more attention will have to be paid to ensuring consistent and controlled quality. Particularly in wine districts, the vineyards and their associations have been trying to improve quality for decades in order to obtain higher prices. The connections between wine quality and a region's tourism image may be more blurred, however.

Certification is generally of great value to producers, but only if it is recognized by the market. The establishment of workable certification systems puts substantial pressure on the producers, and discipline is not always easy to maintain in a community of many small and individual producers. In Chapter 6 of this volume, Boyne *et al.* address a more gentle methodology to improve local qualities, combining measures such as training and joint promotional efforts. The authors also reflect on the need to generate more innovative linkages between restaurants and their suppliers, though they acknowledge the difficulties of such efforts.

Certification and branding of food providers and restaurants, based on various criteria and values

Michelin stars are too rare to play any important role for the majority of tourists, and the Michelin seal of approval may have only a minor impact on the regions in which the restaurants are situated. Michelin's rather elitist accreditation is thus increasingly being supplemented by numerous other certification systems. And quality is not the only criterion used. The rating and branding can be based on any point along the entire value chain, from the raw materials used, the cooking methods, the seasoning, to the interior decoration of the restaurants and the availability of a playground for the children. Historical food, or food based on regional cuisine, may be among the criteria (Engelseth 1998).

The important elements in a workable certification are:

- Precise criteria, easy to follow for any food provider who wants to obtain or increase a rating.
- Efficient control and advisory organizations, able to motivate and guide the food providers to take steps that improve quality. The combined efforts of control organizations and proprietors should lead to a rise in standards for the region as a whole.
- Marketing of the system to the tourists, using it to increase interest, create competitive advantages for accredited suppliers, and enhance value added among food producers throughout the value chain.

A certification system can also include suppliers of raw materials and other input, thus possibly generating new alliances in the horizontal production system.

Reinventing, modernizing and commodifying historical food traditions

The industrialization and globalization of food production has led to the obliteration of many food traditions and recipes. However, what was once thought to be lost or to have disappeared from daily life can later be revived in tourism activities. Food is a clear and simple starting point for interpreting stories, myths and traditions of the past. Food becomes a historic time machine and a refuge from McDonaldization. Food not only appeals to the nostalgic or intellectual mind, but also provides a challenge to the senses, such as smell and taste.

Heritage relies on faith rather than rational proof. We select and exalt our legacy not by weighing its claims to truth, but by a feeling that it must be right (Lowenthal 1996). Historic food is full of fakes and manipulations, and even political intentions affect the reconstruction of regional cuisines, as shown by Csergo (1996) in the case of France. In preparing herrings in vinegar, a traditional Nordic dish, the curing process is speeded up by use of chemicals. Tastes and aromas can be added to the food without the need for time-consuming processes such as smoking. In the consumption of these products, the environment and the glimpse of history they afford might be of greater importance than their actual authenticity.

The need for a variety of tourist products has intensified the search for any usable historical traces of regional cuisines. The same need has challenged the creativity of cooks and food producers not only to reinvent and modernize the old traditions, but also to invent brand new regional cuisines. This creative practice is still a largely urban phenomenon, used, for example, by trendy London cooks looking for a place in the international travel literature. London is placing itself on the map, in spite of its questionable gastronomic traditions, but only as a consequence of the city's connection to globalization processes in other respects (Friedman 1990).

Third-order gastronomy tourism development: the vertical

The third order of value added in gastronomy tourism goes a step further by integrating other peripheral activities that enhance the experiental values of food. Food is one part of a larger and more complex tourism experience, possibly the most important part, but in many cases only a contributory element. Food is moving out of restaurants, markets and food stores to become a component in other activities that occupy the tourists' time and attention. This component is not trivial, and its potential is being rapidly developed.

Value added can be increased throughout the tourism sector by emphasizing the food element. It is possible, for example, to combine the sale of food with any tourism activity. Eating and drinking in public transport has exploded, and drive-in facilities turn cars into dining rooms. No museum is without a café, a place that is usually more crowded than the exhibition rooms. Even on difficult trails in the Himalayas, food is available at regular intervals.

The erosion of the food monopoly of restaurants and restructuring in new vertically integrated systems create losers as well as winners. In particular dedicated catering enterprises that are not able to satisfy the need for entertainment and experiences are in danger of being pushed out of the market. Inns and restaurants that are stagnating (but not old enough to be of historical interest) will disappear, change ownership or concepts. Not surprisingly, the restaurant sector is one of the most turbulent sectors in the economy (Hjalager 2000). On the other hand, entrepreneurs base new businesses on integrated concepts, which replace old types of food outlets.

Third-order restructuring of the gastronomic food experience

This includes opening up food producing plants and sites for tourism. Although they are not often regarded as important actors in the tourism industry, farms, food manufacturers, fields, etc., are perfect tourism attractions. However, as mentioned by Hjalager (1996), modern farms with industrialized production methods are hardly (ethically) fit to cater to a nostalgia-driven audience. Thus, tourism is mostly restricted either to enterprises with outdated production methods, which may be more or less forced to look for income sources through tourism, or to new types of politically correct food producers. Niche producers, politically correct or not, may utilize tourism as a window for public relations and marketing. Both types could be attractive for tourists and perfectly viable in economic terms.

Some producers generate considerable income by selling samples of the produce after visitors have spent time watching the production processes, participating in the work, and tasting the results. Farm shops are becoming more and more sophisticated, with an assortment far beyond the production capacities of any single farm (Bushby and Rendle 2000).

Tourists are often reluctant to buy because the product is difficult to handle when travelling, needs cooling, etc. New packaging is now emerging to solve such problems, e.g. tube containers with water for live fish, and delivery systems at airports.

Establishing and marketing routes

These will link several facilities of the same category in order to create a synergy effect. Wine routes in Canada and Australia are described by Telfer (2000) and Hall and Mitchell (in Chapter 11, this volume), who both stress the ideas of co-operation. Producers are reorganizing themselves into networks, and they either have to hire external marketers or co-operate with regional tourism offices as supporting resources. There are now beer, whisky, cider and other types of drink routes; but more solid types of food are also offered in 'Taste Paths', as described by Antonioli Corigliano in Chapter 10. To avoid the risks of drinking and driving, a French trail provider is organizing bicycle wine trail tours.

Particularly successful wine routes seem to have been established in many places, and vertical conceptualization is prevalent. A North Carolina trail offers dining, bed and breakfast, scenic walks, pottery, and Friday-night jamborees. Napa Valley in California has developed as a wine trail over many years, and diversification has gone as far as including the development of skin care products from grape pips; these products seem to sell to the same category of customers as the wine.[1]

Establishing visitor centres, museums, etc.

These could tell the story of the produce and production processes, including sometimes with hands-on experience. Food has moved into museums and heritage sites. The preparation of daily meals has been a main task throughout most times of history, and the story of the use of tools, the types of produce, the cooking methods and menus are ideal for exhibitions. Opportunities not only to observe, but also to participate, for example in baking, are increasing tourists' attention and satisfaction (Prentice 1993).

A number of attractions have food or food ingredients as the main subject of the concept, e.g. exhibitions on the importance of salt at the Salt Centre in Mariager, Denmark. The connections to the local food traditions are very obvious. The lack of food is exhibited in the Museum of the Famine in Roscommon, Ireland.

At other tourist sites, food provision is adapted to the attraction, e.g. restaurants in aquaria serving fish dishes. Beef goes naturally with Wild West attractions, and safari lodges in Kenya serve game. On the other hand, food concepts in some national parks with wildlife protection boast of keeping as far away from the main theme as possible.

Creating events based on food and tourism

Festivals, themed events, parties, fairs, competitions, etc., can be conceptually linked to food. In this volume, Scarpato (Chapter 8) analyses the developments and characteristics of food festivals and food awards, focusing on the festival as an opportunity to promote the sustainability issue more widely and increase awareness of local foods.

Events and festivals could, for example, be related to national or regional feasts, such as harvest celebrations. Church festivals and religious ceremonies are often connected to social events and the consumption of traditional food and specialities (Getz 1991), as are ethnic events. Many festivals and fairs are invented, and have only a tenuous connection to local agriculture and food processing. Ideas tend to be mobile; Halloween pumpkin pies and other commercialized symbols are rapidly spreading all over world. Festival set-ups can move from one place to the next.

Fairs and festivals allow the integration of numerous commercial and non-commercial side activities that challenge, and possibly activate, visitors. In addition to the presentation of food and drink, possibly of local origin, such events also enable cooking utensils and food-processing equipment to be displayed and sold. Festivals also feature cookbook signings, appearances by celebrity chefs, lectures and demonstrations, cooking competitions, auctions, etc.

Cooking classes and cooking holidays

Cooks and owners of hospitality facilities organize tours and classes for people who want to learn the art of cooking. The Internet helps to launch these typically very small-scale resources to a geographically widely spread special interest audience.[2] To judge from the advertising on the Internet, regional food traditions, local products, the agricultural landscape and hands-on experience of cooking are a familiar mix of most cooking holiday concepts. The majority of cooking schools are in France and Italy, indicating that a reputation for the cuisine is essential.

Some of the schools and courses are linked to the names of popular TV cooks; the role of the media is probably growing. The phenomenon of combining cooking with the holiday is largely unresearched, in spite of the interest in studies of food culture.

Fourth-order gastronomy tourism development: the diagonal

In the third order of gastronomy tourism, the scope of food-related activities was widened to include food as an element in a comprehensive tourism experience. We also indicated that, through this process, new linkages between food producers and other actors were created, and that the old division of labour and specialities were likely to break up and be restructured into new constellations. The diagonal logic includes one more dimension: the development and commodification of the knowledge base connected to food and tourism.

In the fourth order of development, a region goes beyond the simple expansion of scale and scope of gastronomic resources. Additional knowledge resources and innovative capacities must be developed and brought to interact with the totality of the food and tourism sectors.

The diagonal approach aims at ensuring the creation and transfer of knowledge across the food, gastronomy and tourism sectors, compensating for the structural deficiencies in these typically SME-based sectors, and taking into account the reluctance to network among small enterprises, who:

- need to build up trust with their potential partners – this takes time and requires (informal) contacts;
- are reluctant to spend valuable time and effort on a network if the objectives and potential benefits are unclear;
- fear losing strategic assets and information to other network members;
- have varying needs and expectations of networking depending on their own capabilities;
- will be disillusioned if their experiences with networking are negative (Boekholt and Thuriaux 1999: 390).

In this order of gastronomy tourism, the target group of visitors is no longer exclusively holidaymakers, but also professionals in the food and tourism industries. The items marketed and sold are not only food and entertainment/experiences related to food, but also knowledge, visions and concepts that can be modified and implemented in other regions. Accordingly, the relationship between global and local forces is dynamic and interactive.

Knowledge-building capacities are enforced in the following types of institutional arrangements. Knowledge is the most important ingredient, and these activities are crucial for the innovation process and the dissemination of knowledge.

Training for gastronomy, food science and tourism professionals

Vocational training and chef schools can enhance the capacities to produce and develop food-related tourism activities. However, this requires continuous and lifelong learning, particularly in a rapidly changing sector. The Swedish initiative, *Grythyttan*, and the Danish 'House of the Meal' both attempt to establish open learning environments for those professionals responsible for the quality of food in the catering and restaurant sectors. *Grythyttan* is also open to the public (particularly school classes) for cookery tourism experiences, and the Danish House will occasionally hold similar events, assuming that the response from consumers can give important feedback to producers.

Learning environments include updated facilities such as libraries, electronic sources, and access to advanced equipment for production and analysis, and, eventually, connections to relevant strands of food research. Guest teachers and researchers are invited to co-operate and give inspiration.

Research and development (R&D)

Food processing is not a particularly research-intensive sector; nor is tourism. Most of the research in the food sector, for example, is dedicated to biotechnology or to the development of food additives, etc. Important research with relevance to tourism is carried out across a wide range of disciplines. As a result, there is little enhancement of the knowledge base and targeting of research towards needs in the combined tourism and food industries. We have not been able to identify such combined research units, although many universities around the world include hospitality departments that might be moving in this direction.

The opportunities for a commercialization of R&D are quite limited in tourism, since products and processes are usually very simple to imitate. Patenting and intellectual property rights are not easy, as shown by Ravenscroft and Westering in Chapter 9. This means that, in most cases, R&D for food and tourism is applied research.

Media centres

As noted above, the development of gastronomy tourism is heavily dependent on a well-disposed media. A genuine fourth order of gastronomy tourism development will thus have to try to take control of the media in a more comprehensive way. Regional tourism organizations responsible for marketing will probably not be sufficient if regions want to develop food brands as well as gastronomy tourism brands. Regions launching sustainability concepts might need to cultivate closer relations with the media, as suggested by Scarpato in Chapter 8.

Developments in communication and exhibition methodologies, such as interactive media, will be more and more decisive. Food and gastronomic cultures are highly suited to new media approaches, not least electronic ones, but development has hardly got off the ground yet.

Demonstration projects

A number of visitor centres, festivals and other food-based tourist attractions include ethical or political considerations, and sometimes they demonstrate less harmful ways to produce or consume.

Such projects appear to be more *ad hoc*, however, and not connected to other initiatives. Projects in opposition to the mainstream food conglomerates will be in particular need of cross-national alliances and networks. Initial steps have been taken by some governments (local and national) and the European Union (EU) to set up demonstration sites, for example within the framework of Local Agenda 21 programmes. However, gastronomy and food aspects seem to be only marginally integrated in official initiatives.

Demonstration projects may be designed to raise new issues in gastronomy tourism, e.g. food safety and food therapy. Demographic trends will increase the need for restaurants and food providers who specialize in medical values (Cetron *et al.* 1996), and combinations with tourism and leisure seem obvious.

Conclusions and perspectives

Table 2.1 summarizes the main elements of the typology presented in this chapter, and a specific application of the typology in the UK and Portugal is presented by Beer *et al.* in Chapter 12 of this volume.

This chapter has described a development logic of gastronomy tourism from the most simple resource mobilization to the creation and utilization of sophisticated knowledge and innovation capabilities. It is assumed (but hardly proved anywhere in practice) that, if a region can travel along this development path, still higher value added can be earned, for the benefit of the local population – or capital owners, so to speak. The scarcity of examples in the fourth order of diagonal developments also indicates that opportunities are still unexploited. There are many reasons for this. One of the most important is that, on the one hand, gastronomic cultural capital is linked with the circulation of financial

Table 2.1 Typology of value added in gastronomy tourism

	First order	Second order	Third order	Fourth order
Main input resource	Food production resources	Resources in the service sector	Entrepreneurial resources	Knowledge
Expected tourist behaviour	Enjoy the food	Understand the food	Experience the food	Exchange knowledge about the food
Principal strategies	Higher revenues through boosted production and marketing	Maintaining revenues through quality and reinvention of traditions	Offering new products and services to tourists	Selling know-how to professionals
Collaborative structures	Unchanged	Enforced co-operation between existing organizations	Creating new structures and service organizations, still localized	Creating new structures in a global context
Examples of initiatives to enhance value added	Culinary aspects in regional promotion Campaigns for particular products Regional food trademarks Marketing food fairs and food events	Quality standards Certification and branding Reinventing and commodification of historical food traditions	Opening production plants and sites Routes and trails Visitor centres and museums New events based on tourism Cooking classes and holidays	Research and development Media centres Demonstration projects

capital in investment and production. There is a physical and mental distance from rural actors to urbanized capital providers. On the other hand, the utilization of gastronomic traditions and resources is dependent on the demands of new and more affluent customers. Compared with mass tourism, the markets are small and difficult to target. These observations suggest that new organizations for gastronomic resources and consumption will have to be examined in terms of *spatial embeddeness* and *global mediation* simultaneously.

The typology borrows from research in industrial districts and clusters, an issue also raised by Antonioli Corigliano in Chapter 10 of this volume. Well-established clusters possess a tightly knit set of horizontal and vertical business interdependencies. The balancing of localism and globalism is becoming more crucial, demonstrated not least by IT clusters, where the markets for ideas, products and labour cannot be restricted to any one local area. Nevertheless, it is possible to sustain localized learning and development environments.

It has often been asked whether it is possible to nourish such clusters by means of public intervention. A recent OECD report assesses the experiences of the past decades in terms of government intervention in the creation of clusters. It identified several pitfalls:

- The creation of clusters should not be government-driven, but should rather result from market-induced and market-led initiatives.
- Government policy should not be strongly oriented to directly subsidizing industries and firms or to limiting rivalry in the marketplace.
- Government policy should shift away form direct intervention towards indirect inducement. Public interference in the marketplace can only be justified in the presence of a clear market or systemic failure. Even if clear market and systemic imperfections exist, it cannot necessarily be concluded that government intervention will improve the situation.
- Cluster policy should not ignore small and emerging clusters; nor should it focus only on 'classic', or existing clusters.
- Clusters should not be created 'from scratch'. The cluster notion has sometimes been appropriated by (industrial) policy-makers and used as an excuse to continue more or less traditional ways of defensive industrial policy-making (Roelandt and Hertog 1999).

An evaluation of the cluster perspectives will have to be based on careful studies in single regions. The contributions in this volume seem to indicate that more comprehensive gastronomy tourism regions are likely to emerge. However, the creation of such regions is difficult as a political project.

Notes

1 http://www.travelfood.com/
2 http://dmoz.org/Recreation/Travel/Specialty_Travel/Culinary/ and http://cookfor fun.shawguides.com/

References

Beck, Ulrick (2000) *What is Globalization?* Oxford: Polity Press.

Boekholt, Patries and Thuriaux, Ben (1999) 'Public policies to facilitate clusters: background, rationale and policy practices in international perspective', in OECD (ed.) *Boosting Innovation: The cluster approach*, Paris: OECD, pp. 381–412.

Brown, Graham (1992) 'Tourism and symbolic consumption', in Peter Johnson and Barry Thomas (eds) *Choice and Demand in Tourism*, London: Mansell, pp. 57–72.

Bushby, Graham and Rendle, Samantha (2000) 'The transition from tourism on farms to farm tourism', *Tourism Management*, 21(6): 635–642.

Business Trend Analysts, Inc (1991) *The Fast Food and Multi-Unit Restaurant Business. Past Performance, Current Trends, and Strategies for the Future*, London: Business Trend Analysts.

Cetron, Marvin J., DeMicco, Fred J. and William, John A. (1996) 'Restaurant renaissance', *The Futurist*, Jan–Feb: 8–12.

Csergo, Julia (1996) 'The emergence of regional cuisines', in Jean-Louis Flandrin and Montanari Massimo (eds) *Food. A culinary history*, New York: Columbia University Press, 500–515.

Desinano, P. and Vigo, C. (1994) 'Developing information technology options in the hotel industry: the value chain approach', in A.V. Seaton *et al.* (eds) *Tourism. The State of the Art*, Chichester: John Wiley & Sons, 275–282.

Engelseth, Per (1998) *Food from Finnmark. Building brands based on regional ethnic symbols*, Højskolen i Finnmark, report 1998: 8.

Friedman, Jonathan (1990) 'Being in the world: Globalization and localization', in Mike Featherstone (ed.) *Global Culture. Nationalism, Globalization and Modernity*, London: Sage, 311–328.

Getz, Donald (1991) *Festivals, Special Events, and Tourism*, New York: Van Nostrand Reinhold.

Hjalager, Anne-Mette (1996) 'Diversification in agricultural tourism. Evidence from a European Community programme', *Tourism Management*, 15: 103–111.

—— (2000) 'Organizational ecology in the Danish restaurant sector', *Tourism Management*, 21(3): 271–280.

Hjalager, Anne-Mette and Antonioli Corigliano, Magda (2000) 'Food for tourists – determinants of an image', *International Journal of Tourism Research*, 2: 1–13.

Johns, Nick and Tyas, Phil (1996) 'Use of service quality gap theory to differentiate between foodservice outlets', *The Service Industries Journal*, 16(3): 321–346.

Lowenthal, David (1996) *The Heritage Crusade and the Spoils of History*, New York: Free Press.

Melaniphy, John C. (1992) *Restaurant and Fast Food Site Selection*, New York: John Wiley & Sons.

Pillsbury, Richard (1990) *From Boarding House to Bistro*, Cambridge MA: Unwin Hyman.

Prentice, Richard (1993) *Tourism and Heritage Attractions*, London: Routledge.

Ritzer, George (1993) *The McDonaldization of Society*, Thousand Oaks: Pine Forge Press.

Roelandt, Theo and den Hertog, Pim (1999) 'Cluster analysis and cluster-based policy making: the state of the art', in OECD (ed.) *Boosting Innovation: The cluster approach*. OECD Proceedings, Paris: OECD: 413–427.

Smart, Barry (ed) (1999) *Resisting McDonaldization*, London: Sage.

Telfer, Davis J. (2000) 'Tastes of Niagara: Building strategic alliances between tourism and agriculture', *International Journal of Hospitality & Tourism Administration*, 1(1): 71–88.

Urry, John (1990) *The Tourist Gaze: Leisure and travel in contemporary societies*, London: Sage.

3 Demand for the gastronomy tourism product: motivational factors

Kevin Fields

Introduction

As many of the case studies presented in this volume show, a large number of destinations use gastronomy as a tourism marketing tool, and many also use tourism to promote gastronomy. There are signs, however, that such marketing efforts are far less effective than they could be. Because of the separation of the fields of tourism and gastronomy, tourism marketers often do not understand the gastronomic product, and many gastronomers do not understand tourism. What is needed, we argue here, is more knowledge of the gastronomy tourism market. What determines the demand for gastronomy tourism? Are the motivations of individual tourists most important, or is it the total gastronomic experience provided by the destination?

This chapter is concerned with the nature of tourism demand for the gastronomy product. It sets out to establish a framework for analysis of the drivers of gastronomy tourism demand. While foodways, eating habits and geographies of taste are themes of extensive research (for example Scarpato, Chapter 8 and Richards, Chapter 1 in this volume), empirical studies that allow more specific conclusions about the nature of gastronomy tourism demand are missing in the literature. What we might call 'the sociology of tourism and gastronomy' is a relatively undeveloped field. There is insufficient room in this brief review to deal with all the sociological aspects of gastronomy tourism motivations, but an attempt is made to link different motives with social aspects of tourism such as class, gender and lifestyle.

The starting point for our inquiry into the nature of demand for the tourism gastronomy product is the motivations that tourists have to visit different destinations and experience their gastronomy. Gilbert (1993: 81) argues that because motivation links the needs and wants of the tourist to destination choice 'understanding . . . motivation is therefore of fundamental importance since it forms a major influence on tourism demand patterns'. As Hudson (1999: 9) points out, there are two basic aspects to tourist motivation: 'push factors are those that make you want to travel and the pull factors are those that affect where you travel'. Gastronomy can arguably fulfil both functions – pushing people away from their familiar foods and eating patterns, or, alternatively, pulling them towards new and exciting foods.

Although tourism motivation in general has been extensively studied in recent years (e.g. Dann 1977; Crompton 1979; Cohen 1984; Witt and Wright 1992; Baloglu and Uysal 1996) gastronomy has been a relatively neglected aspect of motivation. As the other chapters in this volume indicate, however, the demand for gastronomic experiences among tourists is rising. This chapter seeks to analyse the different motivational factors underlying the growth in gastronomy tourism, which we define for the purposes of this review as being the reflexive consumption of gastronomic experiences by tourists.

The role of food in tourist motivation

What food-related motivations make people want to travel? Inspiration for answers to this question can be gained from the extensive research on tourism motivators.

People travel for many different reasons. Types of tourism motivators are as numerous as tourists themselves. Although the range of wants expressed by consumers is vast, many studies have tried to simplify this picture by looking at the needs that are expressed through individual wants. The relationship of motivations to needs has meant that many studies have used Maslow's hierarchy of needs as a basis. Ryan (1997) for example uses a scheme based on the motivational needs categories identified by Beard and Ragheb (1983) as being fundamental to leisure motivations: an intellectual component; a social component; a competence-mastery component and a stimulus-avoidance component. A similar typology is found in the four categories of motivation suggested by McIntosh, *et al* (1995):

1   Physical motivators.
2   Cultural motivators.
3   Interpersonal motivators.
4   Status and prestige motivators.

The following sections will examine how gastronomy can be placed as a motivator within each of these categories.

Physical motivators

Tourists may be motivated by the physical experiences they will undergo during their holiday. The act of eating is physical in nature, although there are other aspects. Food is experienced through sight, taste and smell. Our mouth may water from the smell or merely the thought of food. Our sensory perceptions play a major part in our appreciation of food – as they do in other physical experiences we may undergo.

Normally, the physical motivators will be connected to some kind of need that cannot be fulfilled in daily life, such as total relaxation, a change of climate, or the opportunity to sample new foods. It is unlikely that modern, well-fed tourists will be motivated by the opportunity for a surplus intake of calories; rather the opposite. The physical need behind trips to health farms, for example, is rather a reduction of calories or stimulants, and change of diet. Many tourist places offer food products or gastronomies claimed to have positive impacts on health and physical condition. The 'Mediterranean Diet' in countries such as Greece and Italy, or the 'Atlantic Diet' in Portugal emphasize the health benefits of their food, and are designed to appeal to Western tourists burdened by weight, cholesterol and other health problems. The appeal of such health benefits as a promotional tool should not be underestimated given the increasing concern with health and the safety of food products in the developed world.

Health concerns are also a reflection of the growing importance of the body in social discourse. Images in the media ensure that we are informed about the ideal body shape, and diet becomes a means of controlling body shape, particularly when we are preparing to visit the beach or when we are trying to work off the excess kilos acquired as a gastronomic tourist. Richards in Chapter 1 of this volume indicates the gendered nature of such control, which is felt much more keenly by women. As Valentine (1999) points out, however, much of the literature on the body in relation to tourism and leisure has tended to ignore the bodily pleasure to be had from eating, which is ultimately one of the most important motives for gastronomy tourism.

A change in diet, eating patterns or the setting of a meal can also be an important motivational stimulus. Gyimóthy's (1999: 64–65) research in Denmark revealed the importance of novel settings for visitors: 'We found this amazing restaurant where only local people go, quite by chance. We couldn't believe that you could just walk in without booking!' For many visitors it was the element of surprise that elicited positive arousal and ultimately satisfaction. There is no need for haute cuisine to achieve this, however: 'The food was different from German [food], with so many sandwiches, coffee and a lot of tea . . . I love it, its different from where I come from!'

Cultural motivators

Food has always been one of the key elements of the culture of any society, but there is no doubting the increased interest in food in contemporary society. Mennell *et al.* (1992) refer to a rise in interest in 'the sociology of culture' as an explanation for increasing levels of interest in food and eating. Eating out has become an important part of people's lifestyles in recent decades and the search for novelty is an important part of culinary-based lifestyles (Riley 1994).

Cultural motivators are therefore strong push factors for the development of gastronomy and tourism. When experiencing new local cuisines, we are also experiencing a new culture. Cultural motivators lead the tourist into learning about, and experiencing, the culture of societies other than their own. What better way than through food?

The search for authenticity has been identified by many researchers as being central to tourism motivation, and gastronomy provides the opportunity for many 'authentic' encounters with different cultures. Many tourism suppliers have tried to meet tourist demand for 'authentic' or 'traditional' food, although in major tourist resorts the food products on offer may be the result of the 'emergent authenticity' accruing to dishes altered to meet the expectations of tourists, as in the case of much of the 'paella' served on the Spanish costas (see Ravenscroft and van Westering, Chapter 9 this volume).

Interpersonal motivators

Although there are many individual travellers, most tourism occurs in social groups. Having someone to share an experience with adds to the pleasure taken from that experience. This is also very true of meals. Warde and Martens (2000) in their survey of eating out in the UK found that people valued the sociability function of meals (95 per cent) higher than the quality of the food (94 per cent) in contributing to their experience. Meals clearly have an important social function:

> Sociologists have therefore argued that the meal in domestic life can articulate not only the identity of the 'family' and 'the home' but also gender roles, identities and power relations between different members of the household.
>
> Bell and Valentine (1997: 75)

Meals taken on holiday can be a means of reproducing such social relations, as Deem (1996) points out in her research on gender roles on holiday. For women holidays are often an extension of their working roles as cooks and carers, rather than leisure experiences. On the other hand, many of Deem's respondents indicated that they gained relaxation and pleasure from the change in environment or daily routine on holiday.

By changing the context of consumption, holiday meals also have the potential to build new social relations and strengthen social bonds. For example, opportunities to eat together may be greater on holiday, where eating may take on an even stronger social function. This is particularly true as the pace of modern living has fundamentally changed the way in which we eat in everyday life. Communal dining is on the wane – few families eat together every day in the way that was once the norm. The more leisurely way in which we are likely to eat while on holiday facilitates the interpersonal aspect of dining, which, for some, has become all too rare.

Food and drinks are means to increase and ease social interactions, also among people who did not know each other before. 'Sundowning' arrangements are ingredients in many charter holiday tours. Galas are prevalent when cruising and conferencing. Many other events based on food and eating give the excuse to come together and socialize and to create a feeling of 'community', and companies such as Club Med take advantage of this by mixing groups during meals.

From a sociological point of view this motivator is of considerable interest. It raises questions about the nature of family life in different cultures, about the extent of loneliness, etc.

Status and prestige motivators

Status and prestige have long been important aspects of the gastronomic field. Many chefs and restaurateurs pursue Michelin stars with the same dedication that tourists collect starred attractions from the Michelin guide.

Eating in the 'right' restaurant and being seen to eat there has always been an important means of drawing status distinctions, as Richards points out in Chapter 1. However, the increasingly indistinct nature of class boundaries has arguably placed more emphasis on lifestyle choices as an expression of status and individual identity. Gastronomic tourism has therefore become an important part of the lifestyles of the 'new middle classes', with holiday destinations being chosen by some because their distinctive gastronomy says something about the 'taste' of the tourist, and therefore their status. This has become particularly important in the development of independent travel, as shown by Munt (1994), and some destinations, such as Tuscany and Provence arguably owe their success to their distinctive and distinguishing cuisine (although as Scarpato argues in Chapter 4, these areas have used culinary myths to underpin their image).

However, the growth of 'postmodern' forms of tourism means that distinction can also be gained from everyday gastronomic experiences. We may build our knowledge of the cuisine of others by eating as the locals do. This may be a simple meal, according to Bode (1994: 198):

> A piece of bread, an apple and a piece of cheese.
> As long as our attitude insists that:
> The bread is good and fresh, the apple is ripe and the cheese mature, and we have the sense or wisdom to know that they are so.
> If we can add to this simple meal, a glass of wine and find a friend to share it with us, all the important factors of gastronomy have been satisfied.

The most basic of meals can therefore deliver a novel gastronomic experience. Such basic gastronomy can also satisfy status-related motivations as tourists explore new cuisines and foods that they or their friends are not likely to encounter at home. While the less experienced or less adventurous traveller may seek comfort in familiar foods in mass tourism resorts, the modern status-conscious traveller is likely to seek out the local cuisine, very often the 'traditional' or 'peasant' food not supplied by the mainstream tourism industry. Although these simple foods are often widely available, most tourists are not aware of the economic necessity that created them, as Scarpato emphasizes in the case of newly fashionable polenta (Chapter 8). Only the wealthy tourist can afford to travel long distances to taste the fruits of poverty.

Finding that 'hidden' little restaurant patronized only by 'locals' is also a goal for many tourists. This type of behaviour can create a paradox however: status can only be gained from the experience if others know about your consumption, but then you run the risk of others finding the location of your 'hidden' gastronomic treasure and therefore destroying its distinctiveness. A similar paradox also applies to gastronomic awards for small independent producers, as Scarpato points out in Chapter 8. An analysis of the ways that people communicate their status through eating is therefore crucial to our understanding of gastronomy tourism (Warde and Martens 2000).

Once the holiday is over, as with the meal, fond memories should be the residue. These memories will also be revisited at will. Again, some of the less enjoyable experiences at the time may be looked back at with amusement, and some experiences will be regarded as status enhancing, others not. Consider the embarrassment of dishes ordered in error due to unfamiliarity with the local language. Avoiding embarrassment may well explain the propensity of many tourists to stick to safe and familiar foods on holiday.

From motivations to experiences

This brief review of the relationship between tourism motivations and gastronomy has indicated the many areas in which tourism and gastronomic motivators intersect. As recent studies of tourism motivation have shown, however, the relationship between individual motivations and the decision to visit a particular destination and undertake specific activities is extremely complex. A number of authors have therefore pointed out the need to understand motivation in a more holistic sense and to look at the entire 'experience' sought by tourists (e.g. Gyimóthy 1999). As Richards points out in Chapter 1 of this volume, many destinations are orientating their marketing towards the experiences that tourists desire rather than motivational drivers. This is arguably one manifestation of wider trends towards an 'experience economy' (Pine and Gilmore 1999) or an 'experience society' (Schulze 1992).

In an age of experiences, tourism and gastronomy will tend to converge as complementary elements in a wide range of consumer experiences. Gastronomic elements have become vital to a whole range of tourism products, from theme parks to independent rural holidays. Meals consumed outside the home are by definition experiences that contain many elements besides the food on the plate. The entire experience of dining out, particularly in a good restaurant, involves some or all of the following: service; cleanliness and hygiene; décor; lighting; air conditioning; furnishing; acoustics; size and shape of room; other clientele; and price. If you disappoint a client in any of these areas then you have spoiled their 'experience'.

In order to determine more precisely the role that food in a wider sense may play in tourism experiences, it is necessary to consider its role as a tourism resource. The resources a destination requires to meet the varied needs of tourists have been categorized by Godfrey and Clarke (2000) as:

Principal Resources – those with the strongest pulling power, representing the key motivating factor in the tourist's travel decision process.

Supporting Resources – those which supplement a destination's visitor appeal, but do not on their own represent a prime motive for travel.

In some European countries, notably France and Italy, gastronomy may be considered as a principal resource. In a study of visitor and non-visitor images of Mediterranean destinations, for example, Italy was found to score significantly higher on 'appealing local food (cuisine)' than Turkey, Egypt or Greece (Baloglu and McCleary 1999).

In most destinations, however, gastronomy is more likely to be considered a supporting resource. Even here, gastronomy can still play an important role, particularly in destinations with undifferentiated primary resources.

The mass-tourist Mediterranean destinations have built their appeal upon similar key determinants: sun, sea and sand. When marketing any product with a high level of competition from identical or similar products, manufacturers strive to differentiate their product in some way in order to gain competitive advantage: '... individual countries and regions are desperately seeking "unique" and "authentic" elements of culture which can distinguish them from their neighbours' (Richards 1996a: 313).

The need for destinations to distinguish themselves is matched by some tourists' needs to seek out unique or different destinations. 'It must also be recognized that many tourists are constantly seeking novelty and different experiences' (Holloway 1998). This is becoming more critical as the homogenization of many cities across Europe is introducing uniform blandness – the same fast-food outlets and retail chains providing a similar vista in all but the most remote of destinations.

For example, standing on Placa Catalunya, in Barcelona, Marks & Spencer, C & A Modes, Burger King and McDonald's are all within sight – without bending your neck. Exactly the same retail and food outlets can be seen when standing on Church Street in Liverpool. This may be an extreme example as Liverpool and Barcelona are still dissimilar in many ways, although both are seaports and do have some common characteristics, but as recently as five years ago the view from Placa Catalunya wasn't quite so globalized.

Montanari (1994) refers to the 'global delocalization of food', in that food production systems often exist to serve the needs of consumers geographically remote from the area of production. He also laments the weakening of economic and cultural links between food and territory, caused by delocalization:

Many products have effectively lost their cultural significance, the door has been opened to every sort of gastronomic combination and experiment, and all foods have been brought into a single unlimited dossier.

(Montanari 1994: 158)

This globalization of gastronomy may provide a visual comfort-blanket for the more xenophobic of tourists but, ultimately, the old adage will become true:

familiarity breeds contempt. If a destination wishes to build a strong identity in the mind of the tourists, it must market its differences along with its main motivational attractors. In an increasingly look-alike world, food with a strong national or regional identity can become one of the vehicles for achieving this. In fact, tourism and gastronomy have much to learn from each other in terms of experience production. For example, there are remarkable similarities, if not direct parallels, between the meal experience and what may be termed the 'tourist experience':

> Consumers in tourism (tourists) typically purchase and consume a whole range of services, which together make up the 'holiday or vacation experience'. Thus, tourists tend to base their judgements on the quality of and satisfaction with a vacation experience on all components of a complex tourism system.
>
> (Weiermair 2000: 398)

The information search process for selecting a holiday may commence many months, or even a year, in advance. Many alternatives may be considered before a choice is actually made. 'Ongoing search for information is conducted both to acquire information for later use and because the process itself can be so pleasurable' (Crotts 2000). Once the decision is made and the deposit paid, the months of pleasurable anticipation, of looking forward to the holiday, are enhanced by talking about the holiday with the people, or person, you will be going with, as well as family and friends. The selecting of new clothes will again be part of the experience.

Just as tourists invest a lot of time in planning their holidays, Warde and Martens (2000) have emphasized that meals eaten outside the home are also seen as important events which are eagerly anticipated and often carefully planned. The 'meal experience' is a concept which has been explored by many that have written texts about food and beverage management (Davis *et al.* 1998; Cousins *et al.* 1995; Jones 1996; Lillicrap *et al.* 1998; Kinton *et al.* 1999).

If gastronomy and tourism are considered as leisure experiences, the pre- and post-elements of the experience gain further significance. As Gyimóthy (1999: 69) indicates, tourists appear to evaluate holiday experiences against vague holiday ideals influenced by general motivations in the 'pre-holiday phase' and re-assessed in the 'post-holiday phase'. Tourist satisfaction is therefore dependent on the image of the destination they have before visiting related to the actual experience they have in the destination. This is important in promoting gastronomy tourism, as research on the destination image of Menorca (Phelps 1986) indicates. Gastronomic elements of the destination product such as gin and cheese were much more likely to be mentioned by repeat visitors than by first-time visitors. As the tourist's level of knowledge of the local gastronomy prior to consumption is likely to be far less than their post-visit knowledge – it is the lack of pre-consumption knowledge that must be addressed in marketing gastronomy tourism.

Focusing on the holiday experience and the meal experience may well be a useful way of tracing the relationship between tourism and gastronomy. Both of these forms of consumption are increasingly important in a symbolic economy dominated by the circulation of images. The following section considers the role of the media in creating images of gastronomic destinations and in shaping our desire for the gastronomy tourism experience.

Destination image – the importance of the media

Destination image is one of the most important 'pull' factors attracting tourists to a particular location. The image of many destinations is also heavily reliant on food. Andersen *et al.* (1997) for example, found that of the top seven freely elicited images of Denmark among British respondents, four related to food.

A great deal of the literature on destination image deals with the relationship between image and motivation (Joppe *et al.* 2001). Because tourism is an intangible product that doesn't exist until the consumer actually experiences it, destination marketers must therefore attempt to build an image in the mind of the prospective tourist. 'Images are built around the unique attributes which the destination can claim. The more these help to distinguish it from other similar destinations, the greater its attraction will be for the tourist' (Holloway 1998: 60). Food, or rather, gastronomy, can aid this process. One of the main ways in which images of a destination and its gastronomy can be fixed in the minds of prospective tourists is through the media.

The modern convergence of destinations and food images is mainly the result of media attention and not the result of individual travellers' experiences. Bell and Valentine (1997: 6) underline the influence of the media:

> Food writers, critics and broadcasters . . . show us not only how to cook, but tell us what, when, where, how – and even why – to eat and drink. We might even go so far as to argue that the food media make stars of the foodstuffs themselves.

Affecting the media is therefore a most powerful tool to attract the attention of future customers, even for those who do not see gastronomy as a dominating motivator for their choice of holiday destination. Seductive images of fresh food, natural ingredients and the landscapes from which they come are all part of the 'gastro-porn' presented by food magazines (Smart 1994, quoted in Bell and Valentine 1997: 6). As befits such an industry, it is replete with exploitative images – the fresh ingredients harvested by a local peasant for the metropolitan celebrity chef to create another masterpiece.

The media has not only made stars of foodstuffs, but also of chefs. For example, in the UK each decade since the 1950s has seen a series of food-related television programmes fronted by a chef/cook who has become nationally, sometimes internationally, recognized. Phillip Harbin and Fanny Craddock in the 1950s and 1960s; Graham Kerr ('The Galloping Gourmet') in the 1970s and 1980s; Keith Floyd, Delia Smith, Gary Rhodes, and Anthony Worral-Thompson and others from the 1990s to the present day. Similarly, Hall and Mitchell (Chapter 5, this volume) and Scarpato (Chapter 8) describe the role of culinary media stars in developing gastronomy in other parts of the world. As many of the recent star chefs claim their expertise on the basis of a particular regional cuisine, it is not surprising that these regions (and the others they visit) also become framed as potential tourist destinations.

Additionally, a brief scan through current television listings will uncover a plethora of food-related programmes. Indeed, there are complete channels dedicated to food, such as Carlton Food Network in the UK. Travel programmes frequently cover dining out when reviewing destinations. Both food and travel programmes usually come under 'lifestyle' or 'leisure' headings when being categorized, helping to connect the two activities in the mind of the prospective consumer.

Gastronomic leisure lifestyles can be important in destination image-building. A benefit of using gastronomy as a promotional vehicle may be that the type of tourist likely to be attracted will be more culturally aware, and less problematic than many types of 'mass' tourist. Alcock (1995) cites the case of tourism in Mallorca and efforts, commencing in the early 1990s, to make the island less reliant on the cheaper end of the tourism market. She comments that: 'One result of attracting a more up-market clientele and promoting a more stylish image is the revival of traditional foods.'

As well as giving the destination a more up-market image, gastronomy may underline cultural distinctiveness and identity. Hegarty and O'Mahony (1999) comment that: '. . . we fail to realise that food is more than just vital for human survival; it is an activity by which culture can be distinguished'. Additionally, 'Food helps us to arrive at an understanding of national identity' (Goldstein 2001). Consequently, when promoting the gastronomy of a region or destination, we are also promoting its culture. Indeed, by promoting tourism via gastronomy, we may also be helping sustain, or re-establish, the gastronomy of a region.

By creating images of culturally distinct and gastronomically attractive destinations, the media also helps to create a sense of anticipation among tourists, which as Goossens (2000: 307) notes, with reference to Bandura, (1986) should in turn stimulate demand:

> Through the exercise of forethought, people motivate themselves and guide their actions anticipatorily. Images of desirable future events tend to foster the behaviour most likely to bring about their realization. By representing foreseeable outcomes symbolically, people can convert future consequences into current motivators and regulators of foresightful behaviour.

So, by facilitating the building of mental images, we encourage the prospective tourist to mentally experiment with different experiences that may satisfy their wants and/or needs. The hedonistic experience that food can deliver would seem to be the ideal focus for image building.

The relationship between the media and the individual needs and wants of the consumer is arguably being transformed by the rise of new media and communication technologies. In particular the Internet is beginning to affect the way in which tourists gather information and images relating to the destination, and the way in which destinations promote themselves.

At the same time consumer behaviour is also changing. In 1984 Krippendorf could still characterize tourists as 'unsure consumers' with no clear idea of their own needs and wants and easily influenced by the media or the travel industry. Recent years have arguably seen an increase in the number of 'skilled consumers' who often have more knowledge of specialist tourism products than the intermediaries who sell them (Richards 1996b).

The rise of the skilled consumer is one factor helping to change the balance of tourism marketing away from traditional mass media such as television and newspapers, towards new media focused on individual consumer needs, particularly the Internet. The Internet has a great potential to link specialist suppliers of gastronomy and tourism products to a dispersed but vast global market of skilled consumers.

Many destinations have been taking advantage of electronic media for some considerable time, developing extensive websites that sometimes include virtual tours. But few of these sites are designed to link with the motivations of individual consumers or the experiences they seek. Although 'kitchen table tourism' (Bell and Valentine 1997: 6) is well developed through Internet sites offering recipes from around the world to prepare at home, the tourism industry has not exploited the potential of the Internet to link gastronomy and tourist motivations.

In particular, those attempting to create gastronomy tourism experiences need to be aware of the importance of communicating the experience offered to individual tourists. Many destinations and their tourism marketers remain lodged in an era when the quantity of experiences offered (the number of museums and monuments, the kilometres of footpaths) was more important than the qualities of those experiences. And even recent attempts to develop 'quality tourism' often miss the point that 'it is not the qualities of the destination which provide the impetus for travel to that destination, it is the image of how those qualities can fulfil the needs and expectations of the potential tourist' (Lubbe 1998: 40). In marketing gastronomic experiences to tourists, therefore, you must consider their individual motivations for travel, and demonstrate how the destination will satisfy their needs and wants. Goossens (2000) has also emphasized that experiences can best be transmitted through the use of emotional cues. It is not enough to offer 'an experience', you need to let the tourist know what they will 'feel' as a result.

For example, the Slow Food Movement (Scarpato, Chapter 8) is closely linked to the Slow Cities Movement. Slow Cities agree to slow down a wide range of different aspects of life, including gastronomic experiences, as part of their resistance to the increasing pace of modern life. The Slow Cities therefore offer not just a gastronomic experience based on authentic, traditional local food, but also a taste of a slower pace of life and arguably a higher quality of life as well. For tourists from time-pressured metropolitan regions such an experience could be highly desirable, and can satisfy a wide range of needs, such as the experience of physical difference in the pace of life, closer contact with local culture and adequate time to socialize. The experience also has a strong nostalgic appeal, suggesting that it is possible to holiday in a time gone by when life was more communal, slower and less penetrated by commercial values.

Such approaches to experience creation have been used in gastronomy for years, arguably with a great deal of success. In fact, many of the examples in Pine and Gilmore's (1999) description of the 'experience economy' are drawn from restaurants.

Making the tourists feel good about being in the destination is one thing, but it is even better to make the tourists feel good about themselves. This is one of the emotional appeals of 'sustainable' tourism, which offers to turn 'bad' mass tourists into 'good' responsible individual tourists. To do this, however, requires an effort on the part of the destination in telling them how to behave and how to interact with the local culture and gastronomy:

> There is a need to educate tourists about what ingredients are available, what they are called in the local language and how they can be turned into tasty local dishes.
>
> (Swarbrooke 1999)

Developing experiences that dovetail with the motivations of individual tourists should ensure that gastronomic tourism will become even more popular in the future. The four-category motivator model presented earlier (p. 37) seems to represent a coherent framework for identifying the motivational factors affecting the demand for gastronomy and tourism. Many questions remain unanswered, however.

Towards a research agenda

Empirical evidence relating to the socio-economic background of tourists, their behaviour, attitudes and social relations is essential for the development of an understanding of motivational factors driving the growth of gastronomy tourism. The range of questions to be answered is very broad, but some basic areas of enquiry are provided below:

- To what extent do selected populations suffer from lifestyle-related health problems? What is the socio-economic distribution of these problems (age, incomes, educational status, etc.)? Are food consumption habits connected to these health problems, and in that case, how widely is that recognized? How are health and tourism behaviour connected? Are people with food-related health problems being catered for by the tourism industry?
- Is food playing a minor or a major part in tourism motivation? To what extent do holidaymakers bring food from home, what do they bring, and for what reasons? For whom (socio-economic categories or lifestyle segments) does food play a major part of the tourist experience? How important are

novelty and authenticity in the food and the total meal experience? At what rate are food products, recipes and ingredients taken back home?

- What is the typical composition of travel groups, and how is this related to social status, education, age, geography, and average expenditure on food and restaurants? How do the travellers spend their days, and what is the importance of meal breaks? How do they prefer to spend their meals, and how are they most often spent? What are the attitudes of tourists towards food-related socializing arrangements?
- What is the relationship between income, status and gastronomic consumption on holiday? Is the gastronomic consumption of those on high incomes dominated by 'prestige' forms of consumption, or a search for simpler, traditional cuisine? How is the prestige and status of such consumption normally communicated?

This chapter has attempted to show that gastronomy can be related to a wide range of motivations stimulating tourists to visit different destinations and is also a vital component of the total experience that tourists enjoy there. In order for gastronomic motivations to work effectively for a destination, however, it is important to link gastronomy to the image of the destination and the experiences it offers.

The growth of the media and the Internet in recent years has greatly expanded the information available about potential destinations to increasingly discerning tourists. The Internet in particular may prove to be an effective tool for marketing gastronomy tourism to the skilled consumer in search of challenging and novel gastronomic experiences. The careful parallel development of gastronomic and tourism experiences may also help regions or nations to differentiate themselves in the globalizing tourism market as well as supporting local gastronomic culture.

Achieving these twin aims will not be easy, however. The media conglomerates and the sponsoring by and collaborations with travel agencies, food producers and other major stakeholders in the globalized economy have consequences for the individual choice and behaviour. We are not aware how these alliances work, nor of their consequences for destinations, segments of tourists and providers of gastronomy services.

We are also relatively unaware of the needs of individual consumers. Relatively few restaurants and destinations ask for opinions from their visitors and of those who do, a minority use the information actively for quality improvements. Systematically gathering information on customer needs, wants and satisfaction could make an important contribution to the development of a quality gastronomy tourism product.

References

Alcock, J.P. (1995) 'The revival of traditional food in Mallorca', *Nutrition and Food Science*, 3 (May/June): 35–38.

Andersen, V., Prentice, R. and Guerin, S. (1997) 'Imagery of Denmark among visitors to Danish fine arts exhibitions in Scotland', *Tourism Management*, 18: 453–464.

Baloglu, S. and McCleary, K.W. (1999) 'U.S. international pleasure travelers' images of four Mediterranean destinations: a comparison of visitors and non-visitors', *Journal of Travel Research*, 38: 144–152.

Baloglu, S. and Uysal, M. (1996) 'Market segments of push and pull motivations: a canonical correlation approach', *International Journal of Contemporary Hospitality Management*, 8(3): 32–38.

Bandura, A. (1986) *Social Foundations of Thought and Action: A social cognitive theory*, Englewood Cliffs, NJ: Prentice-Hall.

Beard, J.G and Ragheb, M.G. (1983) 'Measuring leisure motivation', *Journal of Leisure Research*, 15(3): 219–228.

Bell, D. and Valentine, G. (1997) *Consuming Geographies: we are where we eat*, London: Routledge.

Bode, W.K.H. (1994) *European Gastronomy*, London: Hodder & Stoughton.

Cohen, E. (1984) 'The sociology of tourism: approaches, issues, and findings', *Annual Review of Sociology*, 10: 373–392.

Cousins, J., Foskett, D. and Short, D. (1995) *Food and Beverage Management*, Harlow: Addison Wesley Longman.

Crompton, J.L. (1979) 'Why people go on pleasure vacations', *Annals of Tourism Research*, 6: 408–424.

Crotts, J.C (2000) 'Consumer decision making and prepurchase information search', in A. Pizam and Y. Mansfeld (eds) *Consumer Behaviour in Travel and Tourism*, New York: Haworth Press, pp. 149–168.

Dann, G. (1977) 'Anomie, ego-enhancement and tourism', *Annals of Tourism Research*, 4: 184–194.

Davis, B., Lockwood, A. and Stone, S. (1994) *Food and Beverage Management*, (3rd edn), Oxford: Butterworth-Heinemann.

Deem, R. (1996) 'No time for a rest? An exploration of women's work, engendered leisure and holidays', *Time & Society*, 5, 5–25.

Gilbert, D.C. (1993) 'An examination of the consumer behaviour process related to tourism', in C. Cooper and A. Lockwood (eds) *Progress in Tourism, Recreation and Hospitality Research*, 3: 78–105.

Godfrey, K. and Clarke, J. (2000) *The Tourism Development Handbook*, London: Cassell.

Goldstein, D. (2001) 'The spoon not the scepter', *Gastronomica*, 1(2): Editorial vi–v.

Goossens, C. (2000) 'Tourism information and pleasure motivation', *Annals of Tourism Research*, 27: 301–321.

Gyimóthy, S. (1999) 'Visitors' perceptions of holiday experiences and service providers: an exploratory study', *Journal of Travel and Tourism Marketing*, 8(2): 57–74.

Hegarty, J.A. and O'Mahony, G.B. (1999) 'Gastronomy: A phenomenon of cultural expressionism and an aesthetic for living', *Journal of Hospitality and Tourism Education*, 11(4): 25–29.

Holloway, J.C. (1998) *The Business of Tourism* (5th edn), Harlow: Addison Wesley Longman.

Hudson, S. (1999) 'Consumer behaviour related to tourism', in A. Pizam and Y. Mansfeld (eds) *Consumer Behaviour in Travel and Tourism*, New York: Haworth Press, pp. 7–32.

Jones, P. (1996) *Introduction to Hospitality Operations*, London: Cassell.

Joppe, M., Martin, D.W. and Waalen, J. (2001) 'Toronto's image as a destination: a comparative importance-satisfaction analysis by origin of visitor', *Journal of Travel Research*, 39: 252–260.

Krippendorf, J. (1984) *The Holiday Makers*, Oxford: Butterworth-Heinemann.

Kinton, R., Ceserani, V. and Foskett, D. (1999) *The Theory of Catering*, Oxford: Hodder & Stoughton.

Lillicrap, D., Cousins, J. and Smith, R. (1998) *Food and Beverage Service* (5th edn), Oxford: Hodder and Stoughton,

Lubbe, B. (1998) 'Primary image as a dimension of destination image: an empirical assessment', *Journal of Travel and Tourism Marketing*, 7(4): 21–43.

McIntosh, R.W., Goeldner, C.R. and Ritchie, J.R. (1995) *Tourism: Principles, Practices, Philosophies* (7th edn), Chichester: John Wiley.

Mennell, S., Murcott, A. and van Otterloo, A.H. (1992) *The Sociology of Food*, London: Sage.

Montanari, M. (1994) *The Culture of Food*, Oxford: Blackwell Publishing.

Munt, I. (1994) 'The "other" postmodern tourism: culture, travel and the new middle classes', *Theory, Culture and Society*, 11: 101–123.

Phelps, A. (1986) 'Holiday destination image – the problem of assessment: an example developed in Menorca', *Tourism Management*, 7: 168–180.

Pine, B.J. and Gilmore, J. (1999) *The Experience Economy*, Harvard: Harvard Business School Press.

Richards, G. (ed.) (1996a) *Cultural tourism in Europe*, Wallingford: CAB International.

Richards, G. (1996b) 'Skilled consumption and UK ski holidays', *Tourism Management*, 17: 25–34.

Riley, M. (1994) 'The influence of social culture and innovation', *British Food Journal*, 96(10): 15–20.

Ryan, C. (1997) *The Tourist Experience*, London: Cassell.

Schulze, G. (1992) *Die Erlebnisgesellschaft: Kultursociologie der Gegenwart*, Frankfurt: Campus.

Swarbrooke, J. (1999) *Sustainable Tourism Management*, Wallingford: CAB International.

Valentine, G. (1999) 'Consuming pleasures: food, leisure and the negotiation of sexual relations', in D. Crouch (ed.) *Leisure/Tourism Geographies: practices and geographical knowledge*, London: Routledge, pp. 164–180.

Warde, A. and Martens, L. (2000) *Eating Out: Social differentiation, consumption and pleasure*, Cambridge: Cambridge University Press.

Weiermair, K. (2000) 'Tourists' perceptions towards and satisfaction with service quality in the cross-cultural service encounter: implications for hospitality and tourism management', *Managing Service Quality*, 10(6): 397–409.

Witt, C.A. and Wright, P.L. (1992) 'Tourist motivation: life after Maslow', in P. Johnson and B. Thomas (1992) *Choice and Demand in Tourism*, London: Mansell, pp. 33–55.

4 Gastronomy as a tourist product: the perspective of gastronomy studies

Rosario Scarpato

Gastronomy also brings our minds to what's really important.

Michael Symons

Introduction

This chapter introduces the conceptual tools of trans-disciplinary gastronomy studies into tourism research and planning. This newly emerging perspective does not replace but complements those provided by the many disciplines studying food and culture, food and society, food and marketing.

Gastronomy studies is an answer to the urgent need for research evaluating performances, identifying inadequacies, efficiencies and potential improvements in the gastronomic life of communities. Research with this innovative conceptual framework and methodology focuses on how these communities can evolve socially and economically, keeping an eco-nutritional commitment to environmental sustainability and the optimal health of the community. In this context, both general and gastronomic tourism, and their impact on the life of communities, represent a challenging issue for gastronomy studies. This is certainly an unconventional approach because until now gastronomy has been seen as a topic of tourism research and not vice versa.

The paper is divided in two parts. In the first part there is an analysis of the concept of gastronomy and an overview of some of the most relevant aspects of the framework and methodology of gastronomy studies. Since this is one of the first occasions on which gastronomy studies is presented, there is an emphasis on this part. The second part is devoted to the analysis of tourism issues with the trans-disciplinary perspective of gastronomy studies. They are issues related to the necessity of gastronomic imagination in tourism planning, to the points of contact between tourism research and gastronomy studies, and to tourism as a topic of research focusing on sustainable gastronomy. The concluding remarks identify some practical steps for the immediate future.

GASTRONOMY AS REFLECTIVE COOKING AND EATING

Two hundred years ago the word gastronomy made its first appearance in modern times, in France, as a title of a poem published by Jacques Berchoux (1804). Despite the immense popularity attained by the word since then, gastronomy, the object of gastronomy studies, is still 'devilishly difficult to define' (Santich 1996a: 1). Whilst the origins of the word are undisputed, in ancient Greek *gastros* was the stomach and *nomos* the law, its meanings remain only loosely related to the literal translation of the etymon. The broad spectrum of definitions can be reduced into two main categories with overlapping and blurred borders. On the one hand, gastronomy is simply related to the enjoyment of the very best in food and drink. On the other, it is a far-reaching discipline that encompasses everything into which food enters, including all things we eat and drink.

Gastronomy studies pertains to the second category of definitions and particularly to a comprehensive gastronomy implying 'reflective eating' (Santich 1996b: 180), which, however, it expands to reflective cooking and food preparation as well, maintaining the association with excellence and/or fancy food and drink. Therefore gastronomy studies is related to

> the production of food, and the means by which foods are produced; the political economy; the treatment of foods, their storage and transport and processing; their preparation and cooking; meals and manner; the chemistry of food, digestion and the physiological effects of food; food choices and customs and traditions.
>
> (Santich 1996b: 2)

There is a lack of historical research on the formation of gastronomy as reflective eating and cooking. Archestratus (1994) from Gela (Sicily), who lived in the fourth century BC, is among the first authors who shaped an idea of such a gastronomy. His *The Art of High Living* has been often translated as *Gastronomia*, yet Archestratus' *Hedypatheia* (the pleasure of taste) was mainly concerned with the 'delights of the belly' (Race 1999: 49).

It was Athenaeus, two centuries later, who perhaps left one of the first articulate gastronomic analyses. In his extensive *The Deipnosophists*, the wise men at dinner, he 'contrived to bring into his book an account of fishes . . . ; also vegetables of all sorts and animals of every description' (Athenée 1956). Athenaeus also wrote about the relations that historians, poets and philosophers had with food and dealt with subjects collateral to food enjoyment, such as the shape of drinking-cups, musical instruments and the size of food ships.

The work of many other authors, both in ancient Greece and during the Roman Empire era, was more related to cookery than gastronomy as a separate framework. In any case, the contribution of Latin part-time food-writers cannot be discounted: from Apicius' *De re coquinaria* to the so-called *rei rustica* authors such as Cato, Varro, Columella, Palladius and Macrobius who wrote about the conduct of farms and agriculture (Facciolli 1992: VIII).

Research and a quest for knowledge about reflective good eating and drinking were systematically carried out in Italy in the Middle Ages. An embryonic form of gastronomy was contained in medicine books, herbaria, treatises on agriculture, 'sometimes in the form of dietetic recommendations other times with notes about the quality of ingredients' (Facciolli 1992: IX). The *Regimen Sanitatis Salernitanum* (Gherli 1989) was one of them. Inspired by the physicians of a medical school in Salernum, a town in Southern Italy, this thirteenth century collection of aphorisms was mainly focused on food and health and appeared also under the title *De conservanda bona valetudine* (How to preserve good health). *Valetudine*, good health, was the main aim of reflective and good eating of those times. *De honesta voluptate et valitudine* (Of honest indulgence and good health) was the title of a book published in 1472 by Platina (Bartolomeo Sacchi, 1421–1481). Presented often as a cookery book, perhaps the first ever printed, it was in reality the first modern piece of gastronomic research. In the book, Platina (1967) combined the reasons of reflective eating and cooking with those of pure food and drink enjoyment. Cookery was indeed an essential part of Platina's work but his research was aimed at a 'plan for living well' (Santich 1996a: 177), which is still today the final aim of gastronomy.

Jean-François Revel points out that gastronomy originated only when cuisine ceased to be collective. This happened in the second half of the eighteenth century, when the modern era heralded the 'reign of opinion' in 'cuisine, as in politics' (Revel 1982: 149). However it was exactly two hundred years ago that the ugly word gastronomy made its official debut. In 1801 the French author Jacques Berchoux titled his poem *La Gastronomie, ou l'homme des champs à table* (Gastronomy, or the peasant at the table). Yet Berchoux's gastronomy simply means the enjoyment of the very best in food and drink. The word became popular and in 1835 was included in the dictionary of the French Academy as 'the art of good eating'.

The gastronome or gastronomer in those times was perceived as an artist of good eating and drinking. But the art was not a novelty at all, since the aristocratic classes had practised it for centuries. It was new, instead, that the art was by now also a domain of the bourgeoisie, the middle class of the cities. The gastronomer was not a scientist: there was no body of knowledge, or institutionalized practices, nor training to become a gastronomer. Neither was s/he a practitioner of the culinary art, even if s/he had to have some knowledge of cooking methods to be able to pass judgement and to be familiar with the history of cooking and food of other countries. It was Alexander Balthasar Laurent (1758–1837), a Parisian barrister and writer, who better personified with his works the bourgeois way to gastronomy. Known as Grimod de La Reynière, he was a living result of French social transformation, being the grandson of a pork butcher and the son of a farmer general who had married an aristocratic woman.

Gastronomy, the new science

The basis for gastronomy encompassing the enjoyment of excellent food and reflective eating and cooking, was laid by Jean-Anthelme Brillat-Savarin. A bourgeois himself, and magistrate in his native town of Belley, France, Brillat-Savarin

(1994) published his work *La physiologie du goût* (The physiology of taste) at his own expense in 1825. The book has enjoyed a great deal of popularity since then, yet it has not been immune from criticisms and misinterpretations. Still today, for example, *La physiologie du goût* is seen as an attempt by the author 'to make the culinary art a true science' (Courtine 1996: 167). In reality, Brillat-Savarin was principally concerned with gastronomy – and not cookery – as a science. As he wrote, his aim was 'to determine the basic principle of gastronomy, so that it may take its place among the sciences which is its undeniable right' (Brillat-Savarin 1994: 295).

Many aspects of Brillat-Savarin's work still have a high degree of currency today, starting from his definition of gastronomy as:

la connaissance raisonnée de tout ce qui a rapport à l'homme en tant qu'il se nourrit.

Literally translated, his definition is 'the reasoned comprehension of everything connected with the nourishment of man'. There has been, however, a lengthy debate on what Brillat-Savarin really meant with his words. More comprehensive interpretations have emerged such as:

Gastronomy is the reasoned understanding of everything that concerns us insofar as we sustain ourselves.

(Santich 1996a: 2)

In fact, the foundations of gastronomy as reflective eating and cooking are in these words. Brillat-Savarin, however, links his *science* to the enjoyment of good food and drink as well, reinforcing the association gastronomy/excellence. He makes clear that:

a)   the aim of gastronomy is 'to obtain the preservation of man by means of the best possible nourishment';
b)   its object is 'giving guidance, according to certain principles, to all who seek, provide, or prepare substances which may be turned into food';
c)   these figures are ultimately economic industries: 'Gastronomy, in fact, is the motive force behind farmers, winegrowers, fishermen, and huntsmen, not to mention the great family of cooks, under whatever title they may disguise their employment as preparers of food'.

(Brillat-Savarin 1994: 52)

It is evident that for Brillat-Savarin the gastronomer is no longer just an amateur mastering his own food and drink enjoyment. He is the forerunner of a specific, autonomous and professional gastronomic practitioner. And, since in the organization of modern societies, academics fulfil the role of guidance, he writes that gastronomy will soon have its own 'academicians, universities, professors and prizes' and will take its place among the other sciences.

Despite the success of his book, Brillat-Savarin's scientific gastronomy never took off. The reasons for its missed inception as an academic discipline can be many and are yet to be fully researched. First, Brillat-Savarin's theories have been unsuccessful because they did not fit dominant narratives: food, in modern societies, has always being seen as insignificant. Roland Barthes (1979: 167) warned that 'to the scholar, the subject of food connotes triviality or guilt'. This is largely due to the influence that Plato's philosophy has had on Western cultures. Cooks were placed at the bottom of his *Republic*: the privileged rulers and guardians of his ideal society were not required to learn how to cook, because this subject would not have improved their soul (Plato 1953; Rigotti 1999: 27; Symons 1998: 37).

Gastronomy failed to become an academic discipline because of its *multidisciplinarity*. In the last two years the modernist approach to academic work has been extremely disciplined. Brillat-Savarin's gastronomy implied instead a level of disciplinary cross-bordering which was unacceptable within the dominant schemes of his times and after: 'Gastronomy pertains: to natural history . . . to physics . . ., to chemistry . . ., to cookery . . ., to commerce . . ., to political economy . . .'; it 'also examines the effect of food on man's character, his imagination, his wit, his judgement, his courage, and his perceptions, whether he be awake or asleep, active or at rest'; it 'classifies all these substances (foodstuffs) according to their various qualities, indicates those which may be eaten together . . . and it is no less closely concerned with the various drinks which fall to our lot' (Brillat-Savarin 1994: 52–54).

Finally, the style used by Brillat-Savarin to write the *Physiologie* is closer to literature than academic science writing. So, the French author has been too often superficially liquidated just as a witty storyteller. This resulted in more copies of his book being sold but at the same time it further spoiled the chances that gastronomy would be taken seriously by academia.

Emerging gastronomy studies

The very causes of the previous academic neglect of gastronomy have led today to a revaluation of Brillat-Savarin's ideas within a postmodern framework. In fact, it is with his work in the background that trans-disciplinary gastronomy studies sharing the orientation of cultural studies is now emerging. Food producers, cooks and other professionals who participate in the conception, preparation, promotion and presentation of meals (including gastronomic agents, from restaurateurs to gastronomic tourist destination managers) as a subject of cultural studies, should not come as a surprise. Many authors have stressed that the project of cultural studies should be 'broader than that taught in the contemporary curricula and . . . encompassing a wide range of figures from various social locations and traditions' (Kellner 1999). Cultural studies focused on how subcultural groups resist dominant forms of culture and identity, creating their own style and identities. 'Individuals who identify with subcultures, like punk culture, or black nationalist subcultures, look and act differently from those in the mainstream, and thus create oppositional identities, defining themselves against standard models' (Kellner 1999).

It has been argued that gastronomy is one of these subcultures (Scarpato 2000: 15) and gastronomy studies is based on premises of giving voice to gastronomic identities and discourses oppressed by dominant narratives. These identities include culinary practitioners, either domestic or professional, and all the figures participating in the conception, preparation, promotion, and presentation of the meal, such as food and wine writers, consultants, researchers, educators, but also those working in/for gastronomic agencies, from restaurants to tourist resorts. For a long time they have been silenced by dominant narratives, which have managed to represent their work as 'too common, pervasive, trivial, unproblematic' (Symons 1998). In the past, Brillat-Savarin's gastronomy failed due to the dominant platonic narrative. Today the same is happening with the struggle of small independent food producers, chefs and restaurateurs battling against the almost irresistible advance of industrial food.

> Exemplary is the case of cooks, who are the most significant figures within gastronomy and 'have always been in the background – both ever present and unnoticed'. (Symons 1998: x) Cooks and cooking activities have always had a low profile in the community and have been in powerless positions in their relations with and within society. This does not come as a surprise, since 'cooks generally have been women' or slaves and 'their achievements overlooked as inglorious and private'.
>
> (Symons 1998: x)

Gastronomy studies argues instead that cooks have been always 'in charge', that 'civilisation itself is a culinary act' (Symons 1998: xii). If 'we are what we eat' cooks have not just made our meals, but also made us. They have shaped our social networks, our technologies, arts and religions.

> Cooking is the point where production is directed, where social relationships are formed and maintained, and where the arts and sciences emanate. It is the starting-place of trades, the target of the marketplace, the object of philosophy.
>
> (Symons 1998: 121)

To extend what Symons (1998: xi) foresaw only for cooks, gastronomy studies is oriented towards the finding of new ways to think about gastronomy and gastronomy identities and to revise our views in their light. This involves a commitment to the *gastronomic imagination*, that means 'to place meals at the heart of human affairs' (Symons 2000). Although a field still without boundaries, research within an emerging gastronomy studies methodology should contain at least two main commitments:

(a) re-positioning gastronomy activities in the community and
(b) giving 'a cultural voice' to identities and discourses (gastronomy and

sustainability, gastronomy and tourism) oppressed by dominant narratives.

(Scarpato 2000: 16)

The second commitment is clearly derived from the experience of feminist research, which constitutes a considerable part of cultural studies. Gastronomy studies indeed has many points in common with feminist studies, their approaches to research and their frameworks. By giving priority to the above commitments in this particular stage of its evolution, gastronomy studies builds up its own *cultural capital* to overcome its limited and precarious position within the community and academia.

Like other social and cultural theories, emerging gastronomy studies embrace, of necessity, what conventionally is called a multi-disciplinary perspective. A number of traditional disciplines, mainly within social sciences, including history, sociology, literature, languages, nutrition, philosophy, hospitality and cooking, contribute to gastronomy. However, contrary to how it may sound, multi-disciplinarity is a *foundationalist* approach that invalidates the assumption of a knowledge founded in boundary-defined disciplines (Usher 1997). Gastronomy studies rejects this assumption and promotes instead a trans-disciplinarity that overturns 'artificial academic divisions of labour' whilst creating 'new forms of discourse, critique and practice' (Best and Kellner 1997: 19).

The recent turn to the postmodern in cultural studies is 'a response to a new era of global capitalism'. 'Post-Fordism' (Harvey 1989), or 'postmodernism' (Jameson 1991) has been characterized by 'a transnational and global capital that valorises difference, multiplicity, eclecticism, populism, and intensified consumerism in a new information/entertainment society' (Kellner 1999). Culinary trends, as well as gastronomic tourism, must be evaluated in such a context, at the same level of 'the proliferating media culture, postmodern architecture, shopping malls, and the culture of the postmodern spectacle' (Kellner 1999).

Gastronomy studies approaches gastronomic tourism and tourism in a 'critical and multiperspectival' way, similar to cultural studies' comprehensive approach to other cultural phenomena 'from pornography to Michael Jackson and Madonna, from the Gulf War to Beavis and Butt-Head, from modernist painting to postmodern architecture' (Kellner 1992). Gastronomy studies is the answer to a need for 'more concrete and empirical analysis of . . . the processes of the production of culture; . . . and the incorporation of new cultural theories and methods into a reconstructed critical theory of culture and society' (Kellner 1999). For its concrete and empirical aims, gastronomy studies, at an educational level for instance, should find more space in hospitality and tourism departments in universities, rather than being confined to cultural studies.

A postmodern approach to gastronomy

The split from modern theory or absolutism is represented by many and contrasting relativist postmodern theories. However, above all, postmodern is 'a sign that something is new and needs to be theorised, that . . . requires further thought and analysis, that new and perplexing phenomena are appearing that we cannot yet adequately categorise or get a grip on' (Best and Kellner 1997: 20).

This is specifically the case of gastronomy and its relations with society, on which postmodern gastronomy studies primarily focuses. Although pervaded by a mood of incredulity towards grand narratives, it dismisses radical scepticism, as well as nihilism and apocalyptic visions of a future dominated by panic, spasm and crashes of cultural theories (Kroker and Weinstein 1994). We 'are incompletely cultural creatures', as Symons (1998: 341) warns, and gastronomy – regardless of how complex can it be – is a metabolic world, in which things must be done and happen every day, because we need to eat and drink every day. Therefore gastronomy studies can only adhere to moderate methodological assumptions of the postmodern, in particular those seeing the contemporary situation as a border-land or parentheses between the modern and the postmodern in an unending state of transition, permanent tension and strife (Best and Kellner 1997).

In any case, gastronomy studies contrasts with the dominant academic idea of research as 'providing a special kind of methodologically validated knowledge about society' (Usher 1997: 27) and scientifically reflecting the real. Research within the postmodern paradigm 'does not simply embrace the alternative hermeneutic/interpretive' tradition, which is considered as still within the 'framework of objective–subjective, as polar opposites'. It seeks instead to subvert this dichotomy and suggests a number of challenging alternatives.

Gastronomy studies – for example – must take into account that cooking itself, in the postmodern turn, has been presented as a form of inquiry. Lisa Heldke's (1992: 251) exploration of cooking, for example, focuses on the construction and use of recipes. Many aspects of recipe–cook–ingredients relationships escape both absolutism and relativism, becoming a clear example of what Heldke calls the *co-responsible option*, an approach to inquiry that encourages differences, but not all and any differences. Following John Dewey's (1958) modern pragmatism, she also overcomes the dichotomy between theory (the 'knowledge gaining' activity) and practice (the 'getting things done activity').

Her remarks on 'when recipes fail (or when we do)' connect the reflexive/reflective dimension of cooking, theory-making and research. Failures in all three cases may be overcome by 'following the recipe more literally . . . introducing variations only when you have achieved the results you desire . . . asking the recipe's creator for a more detailed explanation . . . asking someone else for suggestions . . .'. All these attempts constitute what Heldke defines as the 'thoughtful practice' (Heldke 1992: 263), which is at the same time an unprecedented way to define cooking activities as well as research. Thus, research within gastronomy studies is not a standardized process or a set of general methods but a *thoughtful practice*. This claim is clearly in opposition to the positivist tradition, since it does not assume that observation is value-neutral and *atheoretical* nor that data are independent from their interpretation. On the contrary, the subjects cannot be separated from their subjectivity, history and socio-cultural location (Heldke 1992: 264).

Gastronomy studies eschews being pinned down to positions. This theoretical opportunism is 'not a search for truth but a form of play, indifferent to old-fashioned matters such as logical consistency' (Best and Kellner 1997). The opportunism is consequently reflected into the techniques for the construction of data and the presentation of them. In particular,

(a) it influences the style of reporting gastronomic research (in whatever format, from text to hypertext or to dishes) and
(b) it requires that the researcher is equipped with personal alternative tools, such as the so-called *gourmandise*.

(Best and Kellner 1997)

In regard to reporting gastronomic research, it must be remembered that, within the postmodern approach, knowledge is not seen as separated from power. Therefore gastronomy studies is aimed at producing a 'powerful' text contributing to the construction and systematization of the world under investigation (Usher 1997: 33). Its methodology rejects the resistance to the existing society in a too serious mode in favour of irony, playfulness and eclecticism, which are characteristics of the postmodern. Playfulness leads to opting for a pleasant text in reporting gastronomic research, a text accessible to both its participants and its consumers. It is a voluntary attempt to be outside the positivist boundaries and enlarge the scope of what is considered acceptable research reporting. In this way, however, unspecialized readers are not excluded as if the text was produced in a strictly academic language.

The pleasure of the text is also very much part of the gastronomy tradition. The importance of a pleasant text was fully realized by Brillat-Savarin in his work. As Symons (2000) points out: 'Brillat-Savarin's secret was to have been serious – *La Physiologie du goût* has sections on obesity, death and the end of the world – while retaining an appropriately light touch.'

For this reason Brillat-Savarin remains much in advance of most contemporary food writing. I'm sometimes surprised at the antagonism among some food historians, especially in England. Their interest seems in the end to be trivial, to be escapist. They can't bear to think about food at the same time as Plato, Marx, postmodernism, etc., etc.

(Symons 2000)

In regard to the personal involvement of the gastronomic researcher, it must be noted that in gastronomy studies the dichotomy objective–subjective is subverted. Neither the 'observer (the subject) nor the observed (the object) are autonomous entities; rather, they are culturally constituted, culturally interpreted, and mutually referred'. The postmodern researcher is particularly conscious of the impossibility of passively and simply reflecting the investigated world. In fact, s/he participates in the construction of it.

It follows that together with a gastronomic imagination, s/he should have a clear commitment to *gourmandise*. The word has a French origin and Brillat-Savarin notes that 'it cannot be rendered by the Latin *gula*, nor the English *gluttony*, not the German *Lüsternheit*'. He says that gourmandise is the 'impassioned, reasoned, and habitual preference for everything that gratifies the organ of taste' and by and large this definition is still valid today. Gourmandise is a tool for the task of understanding gastronomic contexts that communicates no less knowledge than the so-called scientific conventional tool of research. Gastronomy studies researchers must be practically capable of appreciating food and beverages, having some knowledge of cookery and experience in food industry. Of course, their personal preferences will clearly influence their approach but it is on this ground that the gastronomy researcher differs from other academic specialists who provide only impersonal and theoretical approaches.

In his *America*, postmodern author Jean Baudrillard argues that 'the point is not to write sociology or psychology of the car, the point is to drive . . . that way you learn more about this society than all academia could tell you' (Baudrillard 1988: 54). For Baudrillard, participating in American driving behaviour is a better way to understand contemporary American society than through research as conventionally understood. Not only gastronomy studies share this orientation, but without gourmandise, gastronomic researchers are like car drivers who don't know how to drive. Gourmandise represents that 'element of the irrational' that is 'a challenge to the very adequacy of and faith in systematic reason and scientific method' (Usher 1997: 39). It also is a way of putting ontology before epistemology (Usher 1997: 30–31), which is a main characteristic of the postmodern approach.

Finally, by requiring a degree of hands-on experience from its researchers, gastronomy studies becomes a comprehensive thoughtful practice (as both reflective cooking and eating are) and can overcome the modernist division between theory and practice. In one sense, it is the realization, in a postmodern paradigm, of Brillat-Savarin's wish. He dreamed of having gastronomy theory and practice somehow under one roof: 'where the most learned theorists will gather together with practising artists to discuss and examine the various aspects of the science of food' (Brillat-Savarin 1994: 56).

GASTRONOMY STUDIES AND GASTRONOMIC TOURISM

The relationship of food with society, culture and economy has been mostly left to the investigation of social scientists, such as sociologists, historians and philosophers (see for example: Beardsworth and Keil 1997; Geremek 1986; Tannahill 1988; Visser 1986 and 1993; Wood 1995). Although extremely valid, their works are tainted by a *missing gastronomic perspective*. They lack the interface that could enable their practical translation into guidances for the imagination, production, processing, distribution, retailing and consumption of food. Gastronomy studies is coming to fill the gap of this missing perspective.

It is an answer to the urgent need for research evaluating performances, identifying inadequacies, efficiencies and potential improvements in the gastronomic life of communities. Research with this innovative conceptual framework and methodology should focus on how these communities can evolve socially and economically, keeping an eco-nutritional commitment to environmental sustainability and the optimal health of the community. In this context, both general and gastronomic tourism, and their impact on the life of communities represent a challenging issue for gastronomy studies. This is certainly an unconventional approach because until now gastronomy has been seen as a topic of tourism research and not vice versa. It's not by chance that almost all the contributors to this book on gastronomic tourism are tourism researchers.

In the light of what we have discussed above, we will now consider three gastronomic tourism issues from the perspective of gastronomy studies. They pertain to tourism in gastronomic terms, to gastronomy as medium of cultural tourism and to sustainable gastronomy and tourism.

Tourism and gastronomic terms

Michael Symons' (1999) recent analysis of Australian neo-global cuisine is an example of gastronomy studies at work in tourism contexts. The critical examination of this review of 'a current gastronomic debate of particular relevance to the tourism industry' (Symons 1999: 333) will ease the understanding of 'gastronomic terms' of a tourism issue. These terms are of a fundamental importance in any further development of research on gastronomic tourism.

In the opening remarks, Symons explains that gastronomy is most simply 'the study of meals' and 'still scarcely exists as an academic discipline' (Symons 1999: 333). He then makes clear that tourism and hospitality research 'intersects with gastronomy to the extent that they are concerned with meals'. Symons doesn't work within a postmodern framework but he shares the cultural orientation of gastronomy studies. From the outset, he diverges from conventional tourism research. His main concern is for the quality of the gastronomic tourist product *per se*. It is a position in line with his overall commitment to 'his kind of gastronomy, . . . aimed at human well-being rather than industries – better meals rather than tourism dollars' (Symons 2000). In particular, Symons' position is at odds with a vast tourism literature focusing exclusively either on the economic profitability or the organizational aspects of gastronomic agencies. The tourism literature has often dealt with gastronomy rather superficially. The definition of catering businesses, in some instances, has indiscriminately encompassed restaurants with three stars in the Michelin guide in the same category as McDonald's outlets (Urry 1990: 73).

Symons moves from the consideration that 'culinary-opinion makers [. . .] say that a modern Australian cuisine is sweeping the world'. Against this, he argues that 'what the culinary nationalists have celebrated is the emerging dining-out sector within the global food industry'. According to him, although 'culinary globalisation might suit the tourist industry to the extent that procedures can be routinised and staff are transferable . . . Australian cuisine actually belongs to a new global cuisine, which leads to increased sameness'. On one hand this sameness is welcomed by tourists attracted by the 'safety of commercialism', in which the 'financial incentives will save them from confronting or challenging experiences' (Symons 1999: 336). On the other hand, Symons notes that 'when menus become the same the world over, gastronomic tourism becomes redundant'. Now, since Australia's New Global cuisine is 'a non-located "model" for the gastronomy of the world in the next decades', we are facing the grim perspective of having the heart taken out of gourmet travel.

Symons' reading of New Global cuisine seems influenced by overhauled theoretical schemes, evoking Revel's division of cuisine into *paysanne*, *bourgeoisie* and *haute* (Revel 1982). New Global Cuisine is instead 'another ethnic way of cooking, being the regional cuisine of the Global Village, as regional French cuisine was for France or Chinese for China' (Scarpato 2000: 116). It is a 'cuisine that is parallel to the traditional ones' to use a definition given by Malaysian-born Australian chef Cheong Liew, one of the most influential representatives of this cuisine (Scarpato 2000: 141).

Symons neglects the fact that today's global village is no longer only a geographic dimension. It is instead the result of a new cartography drawn according to the characteristics of different lifestyles. 'Cultural' factors have paralleled and often ousted the traditional territorial aggregations of people. 'The Village is an immense consumer zone, transversally criss-crossing idioms, local traditions, religious affiliations, political ideologies, folk and traditional sexual roles, for which New Global Cuisine is catering' (Scarpato 2000: 88).

Tourism research also deals with this village. On a different scale, tourism marketeers dealt with Escoffier's (1957) International cuisine – at the beginning of the twentieth century. That cuisine catered for an army of well-off tourists that – dazzled by the travelling wonders of the first automobiles and trains – crowded the European Grand Hotels, welcoming a cuisine that recreated the grandeur of their aristocratic houses (Smith 1990).

Symons' analysis is much more pertinent to the uniform industrial global cuisine of fast-food chains, franchised commercial cooking or international cuisine served in revolving restaurants atop skyscrapers. These forms of cuisine, too, have all been favoured by the non-geographical global village's consumer zone, which also stimulated the globalization of pseudo-national cuisines. Symons rightly mentions the staging, by large hotels, of 'restaurants resembling Chianti cellars, ancient Chinese pagodas, and so on'.

What is relevant in Symons' work are the 'gastronomic terms' that he identifies. The sense of place, for instance, in gastronomic terms, becomes 'respect for local climate'. Accordingly, Symons argues that 'the climatic variation across Australia would not support one national cuisine, but an interesting variety of regional cuisines' (Symons 1999: 333). He also mentions as gastronomy's role the critical reflection on 'the complex processes of globalisation, underpinned by the free market' and points out that the more important gastronomic responsibilities are 'to understand, evaluate and propose'. When considering journalists and marketeers who intend to promote a distinctive, restaurant-led Australian cooking style, he issues a simple but firm gastronomic warning: 'Even when the aim is unique cooking, then the first step is to make it good' (Symons 1999: 336).

Symons also cites the 'distancing effect' of tourism on gastronomy. 'While it shrinks the world it also increases distance . . . between one specialist and another, between ourselves and our history, between our desires and the needs of healthy bodies, and so on'. And, as there is 'more distance between farm and plate', because of transport demanding 'hard tomatoes, sturdy strawberries and fewer fragile fruits like figs', similarly, in gastronomic tourism, air conditioning 'adds distance of another kind, by taking restaurant customers out of the local environment, and sound-conditioning with Vivaldi restores the calm of a far-off age' (Symons 1999: 336).

For Symons, to be in harmony, meals must be 'in all their elements', and this is certainly another important gastronomic principle: 'authentic meals have to be true to place' (Symons 1999: 336). Only climatically sensitive cooking favours the sense of place and the quest for authenticity of gastronomic tourists, 'who have long sought local cooking and so avoid international hotel fare and the increasingly inevitable McDonald's'.

This claim, however, ignores the existence and the relevance of a new breed of travellers and tourists, who side with the traditional gastronomic tourists. Cheong Liew provides a pertinent definition of them:

> People are travelling more to expand their business, that means they will be experiencing more . . . their palates will demand more and more. We actually have a group of people that have been travelling around the world, whether they're musicians, entertainers, lawyers, corporate businessman or educators (and their travelling) develop an influence of their palate instinct.
>
> (Scarpato 2000: 127)

This is not to deny that the 'sense of place' has a fundamental relevance for the gastronomic tourist experience. It is arguable, instead, that gastronomic authenticity in the postmodern world is given only by either geographical or historical sense of place. Symons seems to share the strong fascination that media and tourism marketeers in New World countries have with the food of the past, the local cuisines, their supposed simplicity and authenticity, in opposition to the inauthentic contemporary eclectic cuisine. This fascination has generated one of the strongest romantic culinary myths of our days, which could be called the 'global myth of Provence', but the 'Tuscan myth', or 'Greek Islands myth' would also be appropriate. Like all myths, however, they have a little historical basis. The rise of Italian *polenta* in the media and on tables around the world happened in the name of these myths. However no nostalgic editors of glossy food magazines ever told their readers the other story of polenta, which in the past killed hundreds of peasants forced to eat only that 'authentic, simple' food (Scarpato 1999).

The push for regions to follow their natural and climatic vocations in terms of production of ingredients is an unquestionable gastronomic principle. What multi-perspectivist gastronomy studies must question instead is the cuisine possible today in regional contexts, which will never again be limited to local ingredients, as in the past. The borders between local, national and global cuisine are blurring. Neat distinctions are possible only on paper, because each single regional cuisine is undergoing endless changes and transformation. Furthermore, when it comes to their meals, the gastronomic tourist seems to suffer increasingly from the 'glob-loc syndrome' in contemporary culture and people incessantly swing from global to local dimensions, often without any apparent justification (Wilson and Dissanayake 1996: 25).

The critique of some aspects of Symons' analyses doesn't diminish its relevance as an example of 'gastronomic imagination' in a tourism context. The limited perspective of some of its points is mainly due to the lack of available research and is compensated by the overall gastronomy studies vision of the author.

Gastronomy and cultural tourism

The gastronomy studies approach to tourism and its impact on communities, have many points in common with research on cultural tourism development. The underpinning position is that gastronomy is culture and definitively a medium of cultural tourism. In a tourism context, this statement may sound unconventional because, whilst art, music and history are commonly seen as cultural tourism resources, gastronomy, together with other areas such as religion, industrial heritage, events, festivals and architecture are considered 'grey zones' of cultural tourism (Prentice 1993).

This classification, however, has been overcome by recent studies into the cultural dimension of the meal, which is the constituent unit of gastronomy. The meal is the point of confluence of the production, treatment, storage, transport, processing, cooking and preparation of food. A meal implies food choices, customs, manners and traditions, a political economy context and many psycho-physiological motivations and effects.

Even in its most minimalist form of nibbling or snacking (Fishler 1980: 947), a meal represents a 'complex and homogeneous dominant feature useful for defining a general system of tastes and habit' (Barthes 1979: 169). With a linguistic analogy, both Barthes and Lévi-Strauss make a parallel between language and cooking, both 'a truly universal form of human activity' (Lévi-Strauss 1966). Cooking's efforts are all directed to the meal, but even when it is not made of cooked food, the meal contains always 'prepared food' which signifies 'a system of communication, a body of images, a protocol of usages, situations, and behaviour' (Barthes 1979: 167).

The meal is therefore a cultural artefact, a product that has prosodic value transcending the physical combination of foodstuffs in the dish. So, the prosody of a meal permits a person 'to partake each day of the national past' (Barthes 1979: 170) as well as present (Scarpato and Daniele 2000), it clusters around the concept of health (which is a mythical relay midway between the body and the mind) and represents 'anthropological situations' (Barthes 1979: 170). Michael Symons goes considerably further, arguing that 'the usual tendency is to say the meals express cultural realities, which is back to front. Culture is an expression of meals' (Symons 2000).

If the meal is a cultural artefact, the industry that produces it is a cultural industry in which are involved not only cooks – although cooking is a central activity – but all the gastronomy professionals who participate in the conception, preparation, promotion and presentation of the meal. Professional production of meals as a cultural industry has been the framework of recent studies. For instance, for a long time it was acknowledged that operating a restaurant has 'cultural value' (Miller 1978), but only recently has research pointed out that 'the economic organization of the restaurant industry permits business to be run for their cultural rewards' (Fine 1996: 11). Fine describes the restaurant as 'an organization in which groups labor to produce physical and cultural objects' (Fine 1996: 231). So, the restaurant meal 'like all food, has an aesthetic, sensory dimension and is evaluated as such by both producers and consumers' (Fine 1996: 13). The aesthetic choices behind the production of restaurant meals 'provide a means by which a cultural analysis informs and is informed by an organizational and economic reality' (Fine 1996: 11). The restaurant, as provider of cultural artefacts, shares the position of other cultural industries, such as the publishing industry (Coser *et al.* 1982: 7).

It has also been argued that the cultural dimension of the work of chefs, in particular those practising New Global cuisine (Scarpato 2000: 176), makes them design professionals like those working in the film, television, music, advertising, fashion and consumer industries. They are *cultural specialists* and, as such, reflect values, philosophies and aesthetics of their common culture, as do architects when designing a building or a painter when painting a picture.

In the light of all this, tourism research must fully acknowledge the role of gastronomy as a medium of cultural tourism. Gastronomic tourism is also a form of *new tourism* (Poon 1993) and not rarely gastronomy is the driving force behind the 'cultural revival' of a tourism industry in a growth crisis, struggling at a critical stage of the tourist product lifecycle.

As a contemporary cultural resource, gastronomy satisfies all the conventional requirements of cultural tourism products. First, it is a viable alternative for new destinations that cannot benefit from 'sun, sand and sea' resources. It adds value to the tourist experience and – at many levels – is associated with quality tourism; it also fits into the contemporary pattern of consumption tourism, in search of new products and experiences which yield a high satisfaction (the boom of wine tourism is a clear example) and finally it offers answers to the increasing demand for more short breaks, and added value for the business traveller (the explosion of Bed & Breakfast accommodation and packaged gourmet escapes are good examples).

It has been argued that developing tourist products based on historical and contemporary cultural resources is now a strategic option for many cities and regions in search of new economic activities. This situation certainly provides new opportunities for the tourism industry and regional and national governments, but it also involves a number of managerial challenges.

One of these opportunities is for tourism research and gastronomy studies to work closer together and allow gastronomy studies to be actively involved in the planning process of communities and businesses. We already noted that the final purpose of gastronomy studies is *practical*, that is to provide *guidance* (direction) to all stakeholders involved in gastronomic tourism: service providers, communities, consumers and tourism researchers. It is possible that this will make many theoretical icons of tourism research redundant, including some obsolete market segmentations that by tradition never paid much attention to the gastronomic motivation of tourists (Smith 1978: 3). This is a challenge for academic researchers, tourism marketeers and especially managers in tourism business. One of the many challenges that they have to face is to understand the 'push' and 'pull' factors affecting tourism demand, as Fields demonstrates in Chapter 3 of this volume.

Sustainable gastronomy and tourism sustainability

In the contemporary world the quest for good eating can no longer be dismissed as trivial. Increasingly, in the future 'a greater appreciation of how quality of food contributes to individual, species and societal well-being' will be needed, according to Wahlqvist (1999). Good eating means quality food and variety and there is growing evidence that this is 'conducive to health'.

Gastronomy studies therefore need to research on ways of narrowing the divide gap between the elite of *foodies* and the vast parts of communities, living in a state of 'gastro-anomie' (Fishler 1980), increasingly alienated from their food supply (Coveney and Santich 1997).

As cultural studies have been part of a 'critical media pedagogy', gastronomy studies should be involved in a critical nutritional pedagogy, enabling individuals to resist food manipulations. Access to quality food is posed to become a political issue as much as an environmental issue. The Italian-based international Slow Food movement, for example, is already positioned in the defence of eco-gastronomy:

> We wish to enjoy the pleasure which this world can give us, we have to give of our all to strike the right balance of respect and exchange with nature and the environment. This is why we like to define ourselves as eco-gastronomes. The fact is that our pleasure cannot be disconnected from the pleasure of others, but it is likewise connected to the equilibrium we manage to preserve (and in many cases revive) with the environment we live in.
>
> (Slow Food 2001)

For this reason community policy-makers should resort to the contribution of gastronomy studies in their planning constructions. Gastronomy studies should contribute to the evaluation of the options available to the industries involved and to the broader community in respect to future 'food security', which is a greater issue than is commonly appreciated. Food security 'is not only predicated on pestilence, famine and conflict' (Wahlqvist 1999) but it pertains, among the other things, to trade, food processing, retailing, human behaviours and food choice, which form the field of gastronomy.

This effort should be translated into research related to the survival of local food outlets and fresh markets, the viability of home cooking, the transmission of culinary knowledge and educating children's taste, and – above all – the impact of tourism on gastronomic authenticity and communities' well-being. 'Authentic meals provide communion or closeness to not only culture . . . but also other persons . . . and the various aspects of the natural world' (Symons 1999: 334). Any gastronomic tourism planning should have in mind these words that negate 'any thought of restaurateurs just "giving the customers what they want", an attitude which disdains guests as not deserving extra explanation and persuasion'.

Gastronomy researchers cannot put themselves above the fields of their investigations. They are politically involved in them and this does not reduce the heuristic value of their research, for their political work is to contribute to practical gastronomic guidance that is sustainable.

In this way researchers are committed to a sustainable gastronomy that 'is about producing food in a way that is sensitive to the environment, and preparing and eating it in ways that nourish the body and the mind' (Coveney 1996: 24).

Sustainable development is a political issue and sustainability is increasingly concerning tourism. Sustainability constitutes a common ground for transdisciplinary relations between gastronomy studies and tourism research. This association may help to overcome the low response to idealistic options of sustainable tourism. The practical perspective of gastronomy studies is essential to integrate the work of tourism planners and academics struggling to translate models and concepts of sustainability into practice. This will also increase the profile of sustainability, which has often slipped down the policy-making agenda.

Conclusion

Gastronomy today is like agriculture without agronomists. There are plants involved in agriculture, so there is work for botanists; there is an exchange of products and money, therefore economists are interested as well; there are historians and sociologists studying communities and individuals interacting within them, and so on. They are all doing a necessary job, but still farmers, rural workers and their communities need the support of agronomists, whichever framework they adopt. Similarly, we have a complex gastronomic reality, but there are no professional gastronomers (or whatever we would call them) i.e. gastronomy studies researchers and scholars.

Gastronomy can also be compared to architecture. Sociologists, economists, historians, archaeologists, all contribute enormously to the advancement of architecture by researching the evolution of design, its interaction with societies, the needs of urban environments and so on. Despite this, not one of these experts – with rare exceptions – is able either to design a building or to produce practical guidelines for architects. Neither do they have an architectural imagination.

In such a context, the main aim of this chapter was limited to the introduction of the very new perspective of gastronomy studies in tourism and, particularly, in gastronomic tourism. This justifies the emphasis on some theoretical and methodological issues. In conclusion, however, it must be stressed that gastronomy studies has practical aims. So, the main question to answer now is: where to go from here? There are many directions for future research and action. However, in respect of gastronomic tourism, the first steps are surprisingly simple and escape academic rhetoric. There are three main areas:

1   *Involvement in planning.* Gastronomy studies should be involved at all levels of analysis, planning and execution of plans related to gastronomic tourism or to the gastronomic part of any form of tourism. Professional individuals, working within the gastronomy studies framework, should be involved in community policy making, training of tourism management and business planning.
2   *Trans-disciplinary collaboration.* Tourism researchers should give a fair go to the gastronomy studies approach and work as closely as possible to gastronomy researchers. Gastronomic tourism research should become a ground of active trans-disciplinary approaches involving other disciplines.
3   *Management gastronomy re-qualification.* Gastronomic tourist resort managers, marketeers and community planners should all be trained to approach their work with an active gastronomic imagination.

The quest for a sustainable gastronomic tourism, which is part of the larger project for a sustainable gastronomy preserving the right to good living, relies on the implementation of these recommendations.

References

Archestratus (1994) *The Life of Luxury: Europe's oldest cookery book*, trans. J. Wilkins and S. Hill, Blacktown: Prospect Books.

Athenée de Naucratis (1956) *Les deipnosophistes*, Livres I–II, trans. A.M. Desrosseaux. Paris: Societé Les belles lettres.

Barthes, R. (1979) 'Toward a psychosociology of contemporary food consumption', in R. Forster and O. Ranum (eds) *Food and Drink in History*, Baltimore: Johns Hopkins University Press.

Baudrillard, J. (1988) *America*, London: Verso.

Beardsworth, A. and Keil, T. (1997) *Sociology on the Menu: An invitation to the study of food and society*, London: Routledge.

Berchoux, J. (1804) *La gastronomie, ou l'homme des champs à table: Poème didactique en quatre chants*, Paris: Giguet et Michaud.

Best, S. and Kellner, D. (1997) *The Postmodern Turn*, New York: The Guilford Press.

Brillat-Savarin, J.-A. [1825] (1994) *The Physiology of Taste*, trans. A. Drayton, Harmondsworth: Penguin.

Coser, L., Kadushin, C. and Powell, W. (1982) *Books*, New York: Basic.

Courtine, J.B. (ed.) (1996) *Larousse Gastronomique*, London: Lewis Esson.

Coveney, J. (1996) 'Eating into the environment: nutrition, health and sustaining gastronomy', in B. Santich, J. Hillier and C. Kerry (eds) *Proceedings of the Eighth Symposium of Australian Gastronomy*, Adelaide: self-published.

Coveney, J. and Santich, B. (1997) 'A question of balance: nutrition, health and gastronomy', *Appetite*, 28: 267–277.

Dewey, J. (1958) *Experience and Nature*, New York: Holt, Rinehart and Winston.

Escoffier, A. (1957) *A Guide to Modern Cookery*, London: Heinemann.

Facciolli, F. (ed.) (1992) *L'arte della cucina in Italia: Libri di ricette e trattati sulla civiltà della tavola dal XIV al XIX secolo*, Torino: Einaudi.

Fine, G.A. (1996) *Kitchens: The culture of restaurant work*, Berkeley: University of California.

Fishler, C. (1980) 'Food habits, social change and the nature/culture dilemma', *Social Science Information*, 19(6): 937–953.

Geremek, B. (1986) *La pietà e la forca: Storia della miseria e della carità in Europa*, Bari: Laterza.

Gherli, F. (ed.) (1989) *Regimen sanitatis salernitanum*, Salerno: Assessorato per il turismo della Regione Campania.

Harvey, D. (1989) *The Condition of Postmodernity*, Oxford: Blackwell.

Heldke, L.M. (1992) 'Recipes for theory making', in D.W. Curtin and L.M. Heldke (eds) *Cooking Eating Thinking*, Bloomington: Indiana University Press.

Jameson, F. (1991) *Postmodernism, or, the Cultural Logic of Late Capitalism*, London: Duke University Press.

Kellner, D. (1992) 'Toward a multiperspectival cultural studies', *Centennial Review*, XXVI,1 (Winter): 5–42.

Kellner, D. (1999) 'The Frankfurt school and British cultural studies: the missed articulation', in: http://www.popcultures.com/theorists/kellner.html

Kroker, A. and Weinstein, M. (1994) *Data Crash*, New York: St Martin's.

Lévi-Strauss, C. (1966) 'The culinary triangle', *Partisan Review*, 33: 586–595.

Miller, D. (1978) *Starting a Small Restaurant*, Harvard: Harvard Common Press.

Platina (1967) *De honesta voluptate et valetudine*, trans. E. Andrews, St Louis: Mallinckrodt.

Plato (1953) *Gorgias*, trans. W.D. Woodhead, Edinburgh: Thomas Nelson and Sons.

Poon, A. (1993) *Tourism, Technology and Competitive Strategies*, Wallingford: CAB Publications.

Prentice, R. (1993) *Tourism and Heritage Attractions*, London: Routledge.

Race, G. (1999) *La cucina del mondo classico*, Napoli: Edizioni Scientifiche Italiane.

Revel, J.F. (1982) *Culture and Cuisine: A journey through the history of food*, New York: Da Capo.

Rigotti, F. (1999) *La filosofia in cucina: Piccola critica della ragion culinaria*, Bologna: Il Mulino.

Santich, B. (1996a) 'Introduction to sustaining gastronomy', in B. Santich, J. Hillier and C. Kerry (eds) *Proceedings of the Eighth Symposium of Australian Gastronomy*, Adelaide: self-published.

—— (1996b) *Looking for Flavour*, Kent Town: Wakefield Press.

Scarpato, R. (1999) 'Food globalisation, New Global Cuisine and the quest for a definition', in R. Dare (ed.) *Cuisines: Regional, National or Global?*, Adelaide: Research Centre for the History of Food and Drink.

Scarpato, R. (2000) 'New global cuisine: the perspective of postmodern gastronomy studies', unpublished MA thesis, Melbourne: RMIT University.

Scarpato, R. and Daniele, R. (2000) 'Effects of media reviews on restaurants: the perception of the industry', working paper for *Peak performance in tourism and hospitality research*, CAUTHE Conference, La Trobe University Mt Buller Campus 2–5 February 2000 (unpublished).

Slow Food (2001) Slow Food Movement web site. (http://www.slowfood.com/cgi-bin/SlowFood.dll/SlowFood_Com/scripts/Chisiamo/chisiamo.jsp?SlowFood = S).

Smith, D. (1990) *Modern Cooking: From the first back-street bistros of Lyons to the finest restaurants of today*, London: Sidgwick and Jackson.

Smith, V.L. (ed.) (1978) *Hosts and Guests: The anthropology of tourism*, Oxford: Blackwell.

Symons, M. (1998) *The Pudding that took a Thousand Cooks: The story of cooking in civilisation and daily life*, Melbourne: Viking.

—— (1999) 'Gastronomic authenticity and sense of place', in *Proceedings of the Ninth Australian Tourism and Hospitality Education Conference*, Adelaide: CAUTHE: 333–340.

—— (2000) *On gastronomy*, Unpublished interview with Rosario Scarpato (December).

Tannahill, R. (1988) *Food in History*, Harmondsworth: Penguin.

Urry, J. (1990) *The Tourist Gaze*, London: Sage.

Usher, R. (1997) 'Telling a story about Research and Research as Story-Telling: Post-modern approaches to Social Research,' in G. McKenzie, J. Powell and R. Usher (eds) *Understanding Social Research: perspectives on methodology and practice*, London: The Falmer Press.

Visser, M. (1986) *Much Depends on Dinner*, Harmondsworth: Penguin.

—— (1993) *The Rituals of Dinner: The origin, evolution, eccentricities, and meaning of table manners*, Harmondsworth: Penguin.

Wahlqvist, M. (1999) 'Food security and health depend on food diversity and sustainability', Keynote address to: *Eating into the Future. The First Australian Conference on Food, Health and the Environment*, Adelaide: Eat Well.

Wilson, R. and Dissanayake, W. (1996) *Global/Local: Cultural production and the transnational imaginary*, London: Duke University Press.

Wood, R.C. (1995) *The Sociology of the Meal*, Edinburgh: Edinburgh University Press.

5 Tourism as a force for gastronomic globalization and localization

Michael Hall and Richard Mitchell

Globalization is a complex, chaotic, multiscalar, multitemporal and multicentric set of processes operating in specific structural and spatial contexts (Friedman 1994; Jessop 1999), affecting everything from communication to office relocation and, of course, food. Globalization is not just a fashionable idea, it is 'a concept with consequences' (Hirst 1997: 424). Contemporary globalization 'refers both to the compression of the world and to the intensification of the consciousness of the world as a whole' (Robertson 1992: 8). Globalization has had the effect of changing the 'rules of the game' in the struggle for competitive advantage among firms, destinations and places within, as well as between, countries and regions (Hall 1997; Higgott 1999). However, globalization should be seen as an emergent, evolutionary phenomenon which results from economic, political, socio-cultural and technological processes on many scales rather than a distinctive causal mechanism in its own right. It is both a structural and a structuring phenomenon, the nature of which depends critically on sub-global processes. According to Jessop (1999: 21) 'structurally, globalization would exist in so far as co-variation of relevant activities becomes more global in extent and/or the speed of that co-variation on a global scale increases'. The idea that concepts of the local, national and the global should be treated as separate spheres of social, economic and political organization and action therefore does not hold, and should not be treated as such. Rather, each should be understood in relational terms in which each is a nexus of multiple and asymmetric interdependencies involving both local and wider fields of influence and interest. As Amin (1997) observes:

> It is the resulting interconnectedness, multiplexity and hybridization of social life at every level – spatial and organizational – that [is] perhaps the most distinctive aspect of contemporary globalization. Viewed in this way, to think of the global as flows of dominance and transformation and the local as fixities of tradition and continuity is to miss the point, because it denies the interaction between the two as well as the evolutionary logics of both.
>
> (Amin 1997: 125)

Global interdependence typically results from processes which operate at various spatial scales, in different functional sub-systems, and involve complex and tangled causal hierarchies rather being a simple, unilinear, bottom-up or top-down movement (Jessop 1999). Such an observation clearly suggests that globalization is developing unevenly across space and time. Indeed, 'a key element in contemporary processes of globalization is not the impact of "global" processes upon another clearly defined scale, but instead the relativization of scale' (Kelly and Olds 1999: 2). Such relativities occur in relation to both 'space–time distantiation' and 'space–time compression' (Harvey 1989). The former refers to the stretching of social relations over time and space, e.g. through the utilization of new technology such as the internet, so that they can be coordinated or controlled over longer periods of time, greater distances, larger areas, and on more scales of activity. The latter involves the intensification of 'discrete' events in real time and/ or increased velocity of material and non-material flows over a given distance; again this is related to technological change, including communication technologies and social technologies (Jessop 1999). All of these characteristics of globalization have deeply affected tourism and gastronomy, often in ways we are only now beginning to comprehend. For example, in relation to the hotel industry, Go and Pine (1995: 13) note that 'globalization is popularly understood as a process designed to establish worldwide a hotel company's presence. Globalization is commonly perceived to have a standardizing impact in that products and institutions originally offered domestically appear on a worldwide scale'. Such perceptions of standardization or homogenization have also come to be regarded as a key influence on world hunger and nutrition (Inter Press Service 2000a) as well as threatening traditional cultures and foodways (Charles 1989). Foodways are the beliefs, cultural practices and customs which affect the consumption and production of food.

The purpose of this chapter is to discuss the nature and characteristics of contemporary globalization in relation to food and tourism. It will first discuss how relationships between food and globalization may be analysed. The chapter notes how foodways have always been changing and how tourism has become a part of this phenomenon; it will then go on to analyse how homogenization and diversity act as two countervailing forces in the food and globalization debate and note how it is impossible to have globalization without simultaneously having localization. One cannot exist without the other. This is regarded as an extremely important point as it indicates how places can in fact use globalization positively to improve their economic condition and sustain their ways of life, food production and eating. And it is here that travel and tourism is regarded as playing a major role in reinforcing local identity and production. Nevertheless, the relationship between food, tourism and globalization is not just academic. The shops of the authors' main street in Dunedin are as much a source of local cheeses, artisan-made pasta from northern Italy, cold pressed extra virgin olive oil from the South of France, Belgian fruit beer, Vietnamese sauces, Baltic pickled herring, and anchovies from Portugal as they are a McDonald's burger or a Starbuck's coffee. All of these items are present in a small city in southern New Zealand because of the process of globalization. Such a situation therefore commends us not only to analyse the relationship between food and globalization at a distance but perhaps also to examine our own food and travel preferences and purchases. As Giddens (1996) has commented:

> Globalization is not just an 'out there' phenomenon. It refers not only to the emergence of large-scale world systems, but to transformations in the very texture of everyday life. It is an 'in here' phenomenon, affecting even intimacies of personal identity . . . Globalization invades local contexts of action but does not destroy them; on the contrary, new forms of local cultural identity and self-expression are causally bound up with globalizing processes.
> (Giddens 1996: 367–368)

Analysing food and globalization

Originally distributed in accordance with environmental factors the availability and distribution of particular foodways has now also become a cultural and economic phenomenon with the pattern of eating and production determined by the interaction between these factors (Figure 5.1). Food therefore provides an excellent means of illustrating the manner in which patterns of production and consumption have moved well beyond the local and into the complex global environment. As Probyn (1998: 161) recognized, 'Whether overly politicized or not, eating scrambles neat demarcations and points to the messy interconnections of the local and the global, the inside and the outside. Food systems (from production to consumption) highlight the singular and current ways in which the private is becoming public, and the public is being privatized.' Arguably, cuisine in much

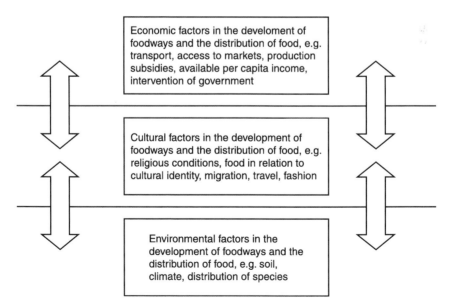

Figure 5.1 The interrelationship of factors in the development of foodways

of the urban, industrialized world is characterized by a wild dialectic of globalism within the local and localism within the global, as seen through the development of 'fusion' or 'multicultural' cuisine (Gordon 1997; Judelson 1997). 'In this the formation of social identities is free to regain localistic, familial and other specific attachments and is increasingly influenced by globalization trends' (Bonanno *et al.* 1994: 5). Nevertheless, it should be emphasized that, while contemporary globalization vividly illustrates economic and cultural time–space compression, the processes of globalization are not new. Indeed, as is well recognized, foodways have been constantly changing through their position within the developing networks of regional and global economic and cultural relations (Sokolov 1991; Bonanno *et al.* 1994).

Hall and Mitchell (1998) argued that since the Middle Ages at least three major periods of rapid change to regional cuisine in the industrialized world can be identified (Figure 5.2). These waves of change occurred as a result of significant factors that affect globalizing processes. The first wave was the period of European mercantilism from the late 1400s to the 1800s. Fruits, vegetables and animals were highly tradable curios and commodities and new foodstuffs were seen as a means to cheaply feed the developing labour forces as well as open up land for exploitation through the availability of new foodstuffs (Innli 2000). This was the period of ecological imperialism (Crosby 1986) in which the produce of Asia and the new worlds of the Americas were brought to Europe and vice versa (Sokolov

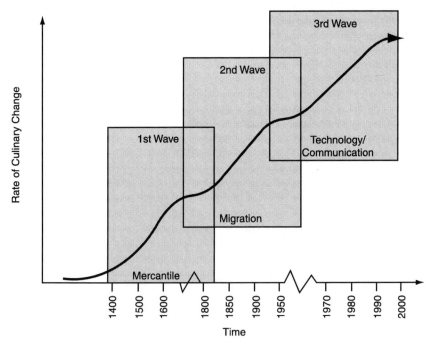

Figure 5.2 Three waves of food change in industrial society

Source: Hall and Mitchell (1998)

1991; Seligman 1994). The medieval menu bore only little resemblance to the national cuisines that evolved in the various nation-states of the continent of the eighteenth century with the codification of cuisine in cookbooks and the development of the restaurant. For example, 'the French, Italian and Spanish food traditions that we now think of as primeval all would be unrecognizable without the American foods sent across the water' (Ripe 1996: 4). Tomatoes, turkeys, corn, potatoes and peppers came to Europe and were later disseminated throughout the European empires and beyond to Africa, Australasia and Asia. Peppers from the Americas became part of Chinese and other Asian cuisines through trading routes (Sokolov 1991).

The second wave of food globalization was the influence of large-scale migrations from the seventeenth century through to the twentieth century. As masses of people settle into new territory they take their food customs and their animals and seeds with them. This occurred not only with the European settlement of the Americas, Australasia and South Africa but also in more modern terms particularly following periods of social and political upheaval in Europe. Perhaps ironically, in the case of the Irish and Scottish migrations to North America and Australasia it was the result of food shortages and new ways of farming owing to the 'potato famine' and the 'clearances' respectively that led to such massive movements of people. More recently, the massive post-first and Second World War migrations, particularly from Southern Europe, to North America and Australia have led to enormous changes in eating habits in the new lands they arrived in. Indeed, the migration of Italians and Greeks to Australia in the 1950s has been seen as critical for the development of a more cosmopolitan Australian attitude towards food and drinking (Newton 1996). Although this position has been challenged by Symons (1993: 12) who provocatively states, 'it is not even an exaggeration to say that multiculturalism also follows the new cuisine, and not the other way around'. Nevertheless, despite Symons' argument, it is widely perceived that migration has led to the widespread transfer of foodways from the old to the new country, albeit often with changes due to seasonal variation in produce and the availability of produce itself.

The third wave of the globalization of cuisine is the current period of contemporary globalization in which advances in communication and transport technology have radically altered the rate at which food and information regarding food is relayed around the world. Clearly, technology has always been a significant factor with respect to food production and consumption. Indeed, Symons (1982), along with others fearful of homogenization (Ritzer 1993), refers to the concept of 'industrial cuisine' with respect to the impact that advances in transport (shipping, railways and automobiles), food production, preservation and retailing have had on what we eat:

> Within the past few decades, production has become global in several senses. Food corporations are truly worldwide. We consume the same hamburgers, pizzas and cola drinks in what has become very much a 'world cuisine'. But most importantly, the food industry is now global in another sense, in that it

typically prepares the total meal. Food technology commands the entire technical battery of growing, preserving, processing, distribution and cooking.

(Symons 1993: 11)

Symons indicates the face of the globalization of food that many commentators rail against and is often related to the McDonaldization of society (e.g. Fishwick 1995). According to Ritzer (1993: 1), McDonaldization 'is the process by which the principles of the fast-food restaurant are coming to dominate more and more sectors of American society as well as the rest of the world' and is marked by five dominant themes: efficiency, calculability, predictability, increased control, and the replacement of human by non-human technology. However, while the changed mode of industrial production is significant, it is clearly not the only influence on cuisine change in the period of contemporary globalization. New cuisines, which may be defined as culturally differentiated culinary features or general products of the kitchen (Goody 1982), are constantly emerging and evolving, particularly with respect to the 'fusion' cooking which is developing as ingredients and cooking styles from all over the world become available to restaurants and cooks. Such fusion cooking – also referred to as Pacific Rim cuisine (Cutforth 2000) in Australasia and North America – is an inevitable outcome of globalization and mobility (Gabaccia 1998; Baker 1999; Hallpike 2000). Seydoux (1986: 6) provides an accurate contemporary description of cuisine as 'non seulement un art de vivre, mais aussi une partie du visage humaine d'un pays ou d'un region'. The hybridization of food styles raises horror in some and admiration in others. Indeed, Australia is promoted as a model of 'postnational' eating (Probyn 1998). Nevertheless, it must be recognized that all regional cuisines have elements of being invented traditions. While availability and environmental factors clearly affect what can be produced in an area, and cultural factors affect how it is prepared, cooked and served, cuisines are not unchanging. As noted earlier, what we now regard as traditional ingredients in European cuisine – peppers, potatoes, tomatoes – are post-Columbus imports. Furthermore, over time such creolization may become identified as a distinctive cuisine style, such as in the Creole cooking of New Orleans and Louisiana. Although, admittedly, notions of creolization 'are often invoked as synonyms for hybridity and celebrated as non-hegemonic, open, creative processes' (Stoddard and Cornwell 1999: 332), they may also prove to have negative associations in certain colonial and post-colonial situations (Young 1995). Such shifts reflect the observations of Tomlinson:

How we live is never a 'static' set of circumstances, but always something in flux, in process. The political discourse of national culture and national identity requires that we imagine this process as 'frozen' and this is done via concepts like the 'national heritage' or our 'cultural traditions'. This 'freezing' conceals a complex historical process in which sorting out the definitive features of 'our culture' becomes highly problematic.

What we take to be 'our culture' at any time will be a kind of 'totalization' of cultural memory up to that point. This totalization will be a particular and selective one in which political and cultural institutions (the state, the media) have a privileged role . . . as a consequence, 'our culture' in the modern world is never purely 'local produce', but always contains the traces of previous cultural borrowings or influence, which have been part of this 'totalizing' and have become, as it were, 'naturalized'.

(Tomlinson 1991: 90–91)

Figure 5.3 indicates a range of factors, elements and indicators of cuisine change, which might be used to identify and/or explain trends in cuisine and which are particular evident in the third stage of cuisine change in industrial society indicated by Hall and Mitchell (1998). By examining the indicators of cuisine change highlighted in Figure 5.3 (i.e. cookbooks, television and radio shows, print media and restaurant styles) it is possible to identify the key factors influencing cuisine and foodways. Most significantly, the figure emphasizes the overarching dominance of mobility as a factor in cuisine change. Increased mobility – of people (labour, tourists and migrants), ideas, images, products, technology and services – is regarded as the key contribution of contemporary globalization processes to cuisine change.

Hall and Mitchell (1998) argue that food, long globalized through international trade and transport, has now become globalized through its symbolic value communicated through a range of productive and consumptive factors and particularly through the related impact of technological developments and modern communication media. Such images are highly mobile over time and space with immediate impact, while changes in transport and technology mean access in the industrial world to more different types of foods and produce than ever. Of immediate significance in assessing change, then, is the role of cookbooks, television and radio shows, print media, food critics and restaurants, to which we can also add the increased role of the critic (e.g. Robert Parker, James Halliday, Jancis Robinson) and chef as superstar (e.g. Graeme Kerr, Julia Child, Robert Carrier, Delia Smith; Jamie Oliver; Gordon Ramsay), and the crossovers that occur between these various influences on cuisine. Indeed, as Randall (2000: 87) notes, 'The food media operate in relationships that are deliberately incestuously intertextual, so that the influence of any individual food text is amplified and legitimized through the production of complementary and supplementary texts in other formats.' Surprisingly, with some notable exceptions (e.g. Strange 1998; Randall 1999), the impact of the media on food consumption and production has been little studied. As Strange (1998: 301) argues: 'This neglect suggests the assumption that cookery programmes . . . are transparent; that they are merely about food and the instruction of cookery methods and as such, do not merit closer examination.' Similarly, there is no analysis of the role of tourism advertising in impacting consumption and production although the role that it plays in influencing tourist expectations would seemingly suggest that it must have an impact.

Media coverage can be vital not only for restaurant success but also for

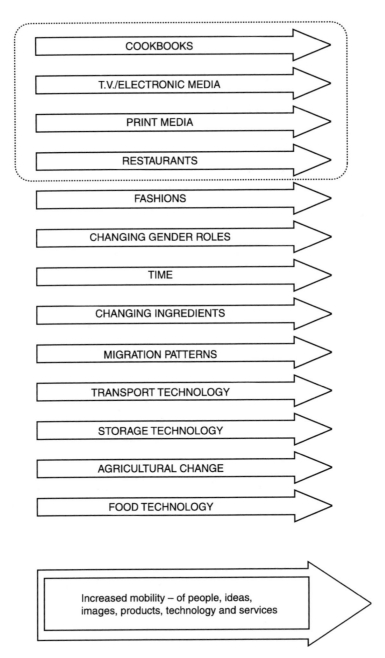

Figure 5.3 Factors affecting culinary change
Source: After Hall and Mitchell (1998)

influencing the popularity of certain foods and cooking styles – and the places where the food is linked too. The likes and dislikes of a relatively small number of key food writers may therefore influence foodways in a manner hitherto unknown since the first mass cookbooks were written. While Mrs Beeton or Escoffier codified a nation's cuisine for the new middle classes, the contemporary food writer also tells us where and what to purchase and what and where is fashionable (Dornenburg and Page 1998). Indeed, it has been suggested that British television chefs' use of seafood led to an increase in fish sales in the United Kingdom for the first time for a number of years (Rowe *et al.* 1999). Table 5.1 illustrates the *New York Times* restaurant reviewers' mentions of foods and cooking techniques in the early 1990s. Though not systematically collected to indicate cuisine change and fashion such data does help reveal the influences, often unnoticed, on dining habits and the sourcing of food. Wood (2000: 150) argues that 'the cuisine of most of the country's top chefs is little more than the McDonald's of the chattering classes – safe, samey and predictable. Such food is the fish and chips of the bourgeoisie . . . a tasteless and vulgar simulacrum of culture and refinement that owes more to the traditions of crassness associated with media cults than it does to culinary intellectualism and skill.' Wood may be correct. However, if the celebrity chef has anywhere near the impact of McDonald's then foodways will clearly shift in response to the new focus on food in the media. As Randall (2000: 87) notes, 'Secondary media texts construct the viewers/"readers" reading formation. It is inevitable that both producers and consumers of new food and beverage texts will adopt a position that has been predetermined, to some extent, by familiarity with the discourse and meanings circulating in other media products.'

Increasingly, restaurants and chefs produce recipe/lifestyle books that may also serve as the basis for radio and television programmes or are simultaneously released as part of total media package. For example, Gary Rhodes produced a series of books on British food along with a television programme that not only shows the food but also introduces place elements, such as countryside scenes and meeting (and eating) with the producers of the foodstuff which he uses. Similarly, Keith Floyd completed a whole series of cooking programmes on world food all cooked *in situ*, while Rick Stein has done similar though focused specifically on seafood (Stein 1995). Place connections and constructions are highlighted in much of the food media and are used to highlight the 'authenticity' of the food that is being presented. Indeed, cooking shows which just focus on what the cook does and the preparation of food rather than an association with place are increasingly in the minority. As Randall (2000: 89) recognized, 'one common and significant feature of food texts is the limited amount of time actually devoted to the cookery/food elements'.

The placefulness of food offers rich potential for tourism through the opportunity for place promotion through various media as well as explicitly connecting place with certain forms of production and consumption (Hall and Mitchell 1998). National and regional tourist organizations are often major sponsors and supporters of food programmes (e.g. Madhur Jaffrey's series on Asian cuisine; and Keith Floyd's travel to Australia) while advertising is also used to connect travel to

Table 5.1 What *New York Times* restaurant critics are eating

Twenty most frequently mentioned foods			
Chicken	236	Bread	171
Greens	228	Salmon	156
Mushrooms	204	Lemon	149
Cream	194	Steak	147
Fish	191	Lamb	138
Garlic	190	Potato	127
Cheese	189	Beef	124
Chocolate	188	Pasta	122
Onion	177	Pork	122
Tomato	177	Tuna	120
Most frequently mentioned cooking techniques			
Grilled	256	Steamed	98
Roasted	223	Baked	63
Fried	213	Braised	57
Sautéd	100		

Source: Derived from Dornenburg and Page (1998), no time period was provided for length of analysis.

the place whether it be on the media or in the supermarket through food promotions. Although such measures are perhaps as much an indicator of the lifestyle characteristics of the consumer as they are of conscious place promotion, they do draw attention to the way in which food has become a component of the tourism product at the level of both the destination and the consumption of the individual tourist. The interrelationship between food and tourism is therefore intimately tied up with the production and consumption of the cultural meaning of place and space.

According to Cook and Crang (1996: 133), such actions are used to 're-enchant' (food) commodities in order to 'differentiate them from the devalued functionality and homogeneity of standardised products, tastes and places'. Geographical product descriptors are therefore being used to brand, differentiate and value food commodities and are highly protected and often related to appellations. Indeed, restaurants and the supermarket shelf (along with media products) are now places to experience globalization. As Arce and Marsden (1993: 304) commented, 'Distant places of production are ... brought together into a network where diverse environments interact ... through the actions of a corporate food industry ... [But the] objective is far from that of producing the homogenized "world scene". Rather, it is necessary to provide a whole range of differentiated food commodities as if instantly harvested from the local field for the suburban and urban platter.' The global-postmodern (Hall 1991: 32) is therefore not marked 'by the homogenizing impacts of a material culture promoted by a monolithic transnational capitalism but by the staging and (re)construction of difference in a "globalization of diversity"' (Pieterse 1995: 49 in Cook and Crang 1996: 133).

Globalization and localization: homogenization and diversity?

The growth of international corporations, such as McDonald's, has been a major feature of contemporary globalization. However, commentators such as Cherry Ripe (1996: 4) see this as potentially leading to 'homogenization of the world diet'. Concerns over homogenization, whether culture or food (in both its nutritional and cultural forms), are a feature of modernity. Although there is evidence that an unprecedented cultural convergence seems to be occurring at certain levels, this cannot be read in the self-evidently negative terms that the critics of 'cultural homogenization' or consumerism assume. The notion of cultural homogenization is far from simple. For those in a position to view the world as a cultural totality, it cannot be denied that certain processes of cultural convergence are under way, and that these are new processes. As Tomlinson recognized 'the problem of homogenization is likely to present itself to the Western intellectual who has a sense of the diversity and "richness" of global culture as a particular threat. For the people involved in each discrete instance . . . the experience of Western capitalist culture will probably have quite different significance' (Tomlinson 1991: 109). Indeed, while there is globalization of the food market, both as a result of international trade and also the result of the same product being simultaneously launched in all countries of the world, major local and regional patterns in our eating remain and, in some circumstances, are even growing.

Homogenization of consumption or production is not a certainty. Indeed, an awareness of cultural differences may become decisive in oligopolistic markets of the kind which transnational consumer goods manufacturers have already created in many countries of the world. For example, in India McDonald's added the 'McKebab Burger' and the vegetarian 'McAloo Tikki Burger' to their menus, while they also developed 'teriyaki' burgers and kosher meat burgers for Japanese and Israeli tastes. In the case of India, Kentucky Fried Chicken, which shrugged off violent attacks on its outlets by anti-globalization protestors, finally folded when Indian consumers rejected its bland offerings. Pizza Hut and Dominos have moved into the niche and have been extremely successful because they have customized their pizza to the Indian palate. For example, Pizza Hut 'runs exclusively vegetarian outlets for strict Hindus. It even offers a "Jain Pizza" for orthodox members of the Jain religious sect who cannot eat roots and bulbs growing below the ground, like onions, potatoes and garlic' (Inter Press Service 2000b).

As Sinclair (1987: 166) points out, 'When global competition is driven by scale economies, at a certain point everyone gets equalized . . . the competitive advantage will go to the companies that are sensitive to individual market developments.' Accordingly, we can find very few products that are true world brands, 'manufactured, packaged and positioned in roughly the same manner worldwide, regardless of individual economies, cultures and life styles'. The logic of capitalist competition may therefore point to cultural outcomes other than homogenization in its crudest form. Nevertheless, as Tomlinson (1991: 135) recognizes, the critique of homogenization itself 'may turn out to be a peculiarly Western-centred concern if what is argued is that cultures must retain their separate identities simply to make the world a more diverse and interesting place' (1991: 135). Even in terms of current debates over the McDonaldization of food (e.g. Fishwick 1995; Probyn 1998), the 'sameness' of the food is quite debatable. For the local inhabitants whether the restaurant or the foodstuffs looks like everywhere else may not be a problem if they are enjoying it. Instead, it may only be a problem with respect to those who are fortunate enough to travel and compare international brands (Hall 1996). Yet even this may be problematic as the cultural significance of a McDonald's for local people in the United States may be quite different from one in Moscow, Beijing, New Delhi or even Dunedin.

National and regional traditions, religious practices, tastes and food cultures are clearly strong limiting factors to the globalization of food. Furthermore, cuisines and foodways have developed, and continue to develop, as a result of the availability of food resources, because of a range of environmental, seasonal, economic or cultural factors. As globalization is impossible without localization, so it must be recognized that food and consumption take place in specific geographical locations and, as a result, some component of localism is always involved. Indeed, one of the great apparent paradoxes of contemporary globalization is the extent to which the local or localization has become significant (e.g. Kearns and Philo 1993). As Porter (1990: 19) noted, 'Competitive advantage is created and sustained through a highly localized process. Differences in national economic structures, values, cultures, and institutions, and histories contribute profoundly to competitive success.' In tourism terms this has meant the promotion and categorization of regional cuisines in an attempt to attract tourists and differentiate the destination in the marketplace.

The production and consumption of difference is as important to food as it is to tourism. In focusing on tourism we can note how food becomes a significant point of difference for tourism promotion. As Jacques (1989: 237) observed, 'There is a new search for identity and difference in the face of impersonal global forces, which is leading to the emergence of new national and ethnic demands.' Tourism is a part of the search for identity and a desire for economic positioning in contemporary globalization. Tourism and food provides identity in terms of provision of the 'other' and in terms of self-reference (Tuchman and Levine 1993). Tourism also assists in the promotion and production of places. The instrumental reasoning of contemporary capitalism, its 'social imaginary', not only provides the initial impetus for much food and tourism promotion and development but also sets the trajectory. However, this is not a one-way relationship; tourism can also have a substantial impact on food production and consumption. Menus may change in order to meet perceived tourist demands (Reynolds 1993; Telfer and Wall 1996). As Hall and Mitchell (1998) noted, guinea pig is less available for eating in Peru because of the influence of Western tourists, similarly dog became less available in Korean restaurants during the time of the Seoul 1988 Summer Olympics because of concerns over foreigner perceptions of Korea. Nevertheless, while such actions may be regarded as a loss of food identity, it should also be noted that such places now have a greater selection of foodstuffs available to them than ever before. As noted above, concern over homogenization presents itself only to the person who has a sense of the diversity and 'richness' of global culture as a particular threat. For the vast majority of the world's population it does not.

The global economic and cultural network in which tourism, food and cuisine are positioned is not unproblematic though. The industrialization of food and cuisine can lead to the loss of biodiversity as some varieties of plant and animal become favoured for properties such as keeping or their ability to produce a consistent product. For example, an American variety of potato – the Russet Burbank – is used almost universally in making French fries (Love 1986; Probyn 1998), to the exclusion of the growing of other types of potatoes. While such massification obviously has implications for the maintenance of gene pools, the obverse also exists in that specialized, rare or highly localized food products can also be attractive because they are highly differentiated and offer substantial symbolic value to the consumer (of course they may also taste good!). Such specialized products also offer the opportunity for the development of visitor product through rural tours, direct purchasing from the farm, specialized restaurant menus, and home stays on such properties (Bessière 1998). Indeed, in these circumstances, outsider interest in local produce may serve to stimulate local awareness and interest, and may not only assist in diversification, and maintenance of plant and animal variety, but also encourage community pride and reinforcement of local identity and culture. Therefore, it is apparent that from the seeds of globalization strong local food identities and sustainable food systems have the potential to grow with tourism playing an important role.

The relationship between food and tourism in productive terms therefore needs to be integrated into a strategy for local economic development that seeks to maximize economic and social leverage between producers and the tourism industry (Centre for Environment and Society 1999). There are several components to such a strategy:

- reduce economic leakage by using local renewable resources rather than external sources, e.g. use local materials for packaging, 'buy local' campaigns;
- recycle financial resources within the system by buying local goods and services, e.g. hoteliers need to purchase and promote local foods and wine, use local banks and credit unions;
- add value to local produce before it is exported, e.g. bottle and package food locally, use local food as an attraction to tourists thereby reinforcing the local economy;
- connect up local stakeholders (people and institutions) to create trust, new linkages and more efficient exchanges, e.g. local farmers and producers' cooperatives, a 'buy local' campaign;

- attract external resources, especially finance, skills and technology where appropriate, e.g. use the internet to connect to customers outside of the region;
- emphasize local identity and authenticity in branding and promotional strategies, e.g. list the place of origin on the label;
- sell direct to consumers via farm shops, direct mailing, farmers' and produce markets and food and wine festivals; and
- create a relationship between the consumer and the producer, e.g. using cellar door or farm door sales.

The drive to create such local economic development strategies has already started in many rural regions. Local food and wine networks, the development of food trails, and the rediscovery of farmers' markets – often frequented by day-trippers and tourists – are testimony to the importance of the local within the global. Moreover, there is now an international movement – the Slow Food Movement – seeking to reinforce diversity, identity and taste (see also Chapter 8). As its founder, Carlo Petrini, states:

> To defend biodiversity we have to defend small producers. The Slow Food Movement is different from ecological movements and from gastronomy movements. Gastronomical movements don't defend the small producers and their products, and ecological movements fight the battles, but can't cook. You have to have both at the same time . . . we need an international move-ment for the defence of microbes – they make prosciutto, salami and cheese.
> (Petrini in Brennan 2001)

Changing places/changing cuisines

Globalization has come to mean many things to many people. It has also come to be blamed for many of the ills that beset national and local economies, as well as national, local and personal identities, and the changing pattern of food con-sumption and production. The reality, as Amin (1997: 124) has cogently argued, is the 'blurring of traditional and social boundaries through the interpenetration of local and distant influences, therefore requiring hybrid and multi-polar solutions'.

Local place-bound and world scale territorial logics are not mutually incompat-ible. Instead, globalization can be conceived 'as a process of linkage and inter-dependence between territories and of "in here–out there" connectivities' (Amin 1997: 124), to utilize the insights of Giddens (1996). Therefore, as Held (1995) has noted, globalization is characterized by first, a growing number of chains and webs of economic, social, cultural and political activity that are global in scope; and, second, the intensification of the levels of interaction and interconnectedness between states and societies in an increasingly dense series of networks of regional and global economic and cultural relations. In building upon Giddens' con-ceptualization of globalization in terms of time–space shrinkage, Held (1995: 20) argues that 'globalisation can be taken to denote the stretching and deepening of social relations and institutions across space and time such that, on the one hand, day-to-day activities are increasingly influenced by events happening on the other side of the globe and, on the other hand, the practices and decisions of local groups can have significant global reverberations'.

Tourism and food production and consumption therefore have the potential to benefit as much from globalization processes as they do to suffer. The importance of tourism as a communicator and modifier of cuisine and foodways is only now being recognized. As an instrument of globalization, tourism has increased the tension between the local and the global, helping to produce global food products and, in some cases, strengthening or rekindling local food traditions, with creolization/fusion cooking arguably representing the development of new localized forms of production and consumption. Tourism and hospitality, like other forms of production, totalizes/represents food in a particular state in order to commodify a product which can, in turn, be recognized and consumed. In examining the relationship between food, tourism, and globalization, the issue of what is significant is not the authenticity of cuisine but rather the spatial settings, social itineraries, networks and patterns of consumption and production that are established through usage. In an earlier attempt at examining the relationship between globalization, food, and tourism the authors (Hall and Mitchell 1998) argued that 'we are what we eat'. This is not meant to be a passive statement regarding the potential to be overcome by globalization. Rather, it is a clear suggestion that it is also possible, through active attempts to purchase local and artisan food, to retain diversity, promote local economic and community development and eat better tasting food.

References

Amin, A. (1997) 'Placing globalization', *Theory, Culture and Society* 14(2): 123–137.

Arce, A. and Marsden, T. (1993) 'The social construction of international food: a new research agenda', *Economic Geography*, 69: 293–311.

Baker, T. (1999) 'Australia's foodways: an overview', *Australian Folklore*, 14: 212–221.

Bessière, J. (1998) 'Local development and heritage: traditional food and cuisine as tourist attractions in rural areas', *Sociologia Ruralis*, 38: 21–34.

Bonanno, A., Lawrence, B., Friedland, W., Gouveia, L. and Mingione, E. (eds) (1994) *From Columbus to Conagra: The Globalization of Agriculture and Food*, Lawrence: University of Kansas Press.

Brennan, G. (2001) *Slow Food Movement*, http://www.sallys-place.com/food/single-articles/slow_food.htm

Centre for Environment and Society (1999) *Local Food Systems: Lessons for Local Economies Conference Proceedings*, Colchester: University of Essex.

Charles, C. (1989) *American Foodways: What, When, Why and How We Eat in America*, Little Rock: August House.

Cook, I. and Crang, P. (1996) 'The world on a plate: culinary cultures, displacement and geographical knowledges', *Journal of Material Culture*, 1(2): 131–153.

Crosby, A.W. (1986) *Ecological Imperialism: The Biological Expansion of Europe, 900–1900*, Cambridge: Cambridge University Press.

Cutforth, F. (2000) 'Pacific Rim cuisine', *Pacific Tourism Review*, 4: 45–52.

Dornenburg, A. and Page, K. (1998) *Dining Out: Secrets from America's Leading Critics, Chefs, and Restaurateurs*, New York: John Wiley & Sons.

Fishwick, M. (1995) 'Ray and Ronald girdle the globe', *Journal of American Culture*, 18: 13–29.

Friedman, J. (1994) *Cultural Identity and Global Process*, London: Sage Publications.

Go, F.M. and Pine, R. (1995) *Globalization Strategy in the Hotel Industry*, London: Routledge.

Gabaccia, D.R. (1998) *We Are What We Eat: Ethnic Food and the Making of Americans*, Cambridge: Harvard University Press.

Giddens, A. (1996) 'Affluence, poverty and the idea of a post-scarcity society', *Development and Change*, 27: 365–377.

Goody, J. (1982) *Cooking, Cuisine and Class*, Cambridge: Cambridge University Press.

Gordon, P. (1997) *The Sugar Club Cookbook*, London, Hodder and Stoughton.

Hall, C.M. (1996) 'Globalisation and tourism: connecting and contextualising culture, environment, economy and place', in *Globalisation and Tourism, 46th AIEST Congress Proceedings*, Vol. 38, St-Gall: AIEST, pp. 487–500.

—— (1997) 'Geography, marketing and the selling of places', *Journal of Travel and Tourism Marketing*, 6(3/4): 61–84.

Hall, C.M. and Mitchell, R. (1998) '"We are what we eat": food, tourism and globalisation', paper presented at Innovative Approaches to Culture and Tourism, ATLAS conference, 22–24 October 1998, Rethymnon, Crete.

Hall, S. (1991) 'The local and the global: globalization and ethnicity', in A. King (ed.) *Culture, Globalisation and the World System*, Basingstoke: Macmillan.

Hallpike, P. (2000) 'Australia's foodways – Botany Bay to the packaged present: an overview', *Australian Folklore*, 15: 166–176.

Harvey, D. (1989) *The Condition of Postmodernity: an Enquiry into the Origins of Cultural Change*, Oxford: Basil Blackwell.

Held, D. (1995) *Democracy and the Global Order*, Cambridge: Polity.

Higgott, R. (1999) 'The political economy of globalisation in East Asia: the salience of "region building"', in K. Olds, P. Dicken, P.F. Kelly, L. Kong and H.W. Yeung (eds.) *Globalisation and the Asia-Pacific: Contested Territories*, London: Routledge, pp. 91–106.

Hirst, P. (1997) 'The global economy – myths and realities', *International Affairs*, 73(3): 409–425.

Innli, K.E. (ed.) (2000) *The Norwegian Kitchen*, Kristiansund: Kom Forlag.

Inter Press Service (2000a) *Food: globalisation differs for needy and greedy*, World News Inter Press Service Press Release, 16 October.

Inter Press Service (2000b) *Globalisation gives in to local tastes*, World News Inter Press Service Press Release, 28 October.

Jacques, M. (1989) 'Britain and Europe', in S. Hall and M. Jacques (eds) *New Times: The Changing Face of Politics in the 1990s*, London: Lawrence and Wishart.

Jessop, B. (1999) 'Reflections on globalisation and its (il)logic(s)', in K. Olds, P. Dicken, P.F. Kelly, L. Kong and H.W. Yeung (eds) *Globalisation and the Asia-Pacific: Contested Territories*, London: Routledge, pp.19–38.

Judelson, S. (1997) 'Introduction: What is East–West food?, in S. Judelson. (ed.) *East–West Food: Food from the Pacific Rim and beyond, with 10 of the world's hottest chefs*, London: Hamlyn: pp. 7–11.

Kearns, G. and Philo, C. (1993) 'Preface', in G. Kearns and C. Philo (eds) *Selling Places: The City as Cultural Capital, Past and Present*, Oxford: Pergamon Press, pp. ix–x.

Kelly, P.F. and Olds, K. (1999) 'Questions in a crisis: the contested meanings of globalisation in the Asia-Pacific', in K. Olds, P. Dicken, P.F. Kelly, L. Kong and H.W. Yeung (eds) *Globalisation and the Asia-Pacific: Contested Territories*, London: Routledge, pp.1–15.

Love, J.F. (1986) *McDonald's: Behind the Arches*, Toronto and New York: Bantam.

Newton, J. (1996) *Wogfood: An Oral History with Recipes*, Sydney: Random House Australia.

Pieterse, J.N. (1995) 'Globalization as hybridization', in M. Featherstone, S. Lash and R. Robertson (eds) *Global Modernities*, London: Sage, pp. 45–68.

Porter, M.E. (1990) *Competitive Advantage of Nations*, New York: Free Press.

Probyn, E. (1998) 'McIdentities: food and the familial citizen', *Theory, Culture & Society*, 15(2): 155–173.

Randall, S. (1999) 'Television representations of food: a case study of "Rick Stein's Taste of the Sea"', *International Tourism and Hospitality Research Journal: The Surrey Quarterly Review*, 1(1): 41–54.

Randall, S. (2000) 'How does the media influence public taste for food and beverage?,' in R. Wood (ed.) *Strategic Questions in Food and Beverage Management*, Oxford: Butterworth-Heinemann.

Reynolds, P.C. (1993) 'Food and tourism: towards an understanding of sustainable culture', *Journal of Sustainable Tourism*, 1(1): 48–54.

Ripe, C. (1996) *Goodbye Culinary Cringe*, Sydney: Allen and Unwin.

Ritzer, G. (1993) *The McDonaldization of Society*, Thousand Oaks: Pine Forge Press.

Robertson, R. (1992) *Globalization: Social Theory and Global Culture*, London: Sage.

Rowe, M., Prestage, M. and Cook, E. (1999) 'TV chefs and their seafoodie fans rescue Britain's fishermen', *The Independent on Sunday*, 15 August: 7.

Seligman, I. (1994) 'The history of Japanese cuisine', *Japan Quarterly*, 41(2): 165–180.

Seydoux, J. (1986) 'L'avenir de la gastronomie suisse: La gastronomie régionale, element de promotion touristique', *AIEST Conference Proceedings*, St. Gallen: AIEST.

Sinclair, J. (1987) *Images Incorporated: Advertising as Industry and Ideology*, London: Croom Helm.

Sokolov, R. (1991) *Why We Eat What We Eat: How the Encounter Between the New World and the Old Changed the Way Everyone on the Planet Eats*, New York: Summit Books.

Stein, R. (1995) *Rick Stein's Taste of the Sea*, BBC Books, London.

Stoddard, E. and Cornwell, G.H. (1999) 'Cosmopolitan or mongrel? Créolité, hybridity and "douglarisation" in Trinidad', *European Journal of Cultural Studies*, 2(3): 331–353.

Strange, N. (1998) 'Perform, educate, entertain: Ingredients of the cookery programme genre', in C. Geraghty and D. Lusted (eds) *The Television Studies Book*, London: Edward Arnold.

Symons, M. (1982) *One Continuous Picnic: A History of Eating in Australia*, Adelaide: Duck Press.

—— (1993) *The Shared Table: Ideas for Australian Cuisine*, Canberra: AGPS.

Telfer, D. and Wall, G. (1996) 'Linkages between tourism and food production', *Annals of Tourism Research*, 23(3): 635–653.

Tomlinson, J. (1991) *Cultural Imperialism: A Critical Introduction*, Johns Hopkins University Press, Baltimore.

Tuchman, G. and Levine, H.G. (1993) 'New York Jews and Chinese food: The social construction of an ethnic pattern', *Journal of Contemporary Ethnography*, 22(3): 382–407.

Wood, R. (2000) 'Why are there so many celebrity chefs and cooks (and do we need them)?,' in R. Wood (ed.) *Strategic Questions in Food and Beverage Management*, Oxford: Butterworth-Heinemann.

Young, R. (1995) *Colonial Desire: Hybridity in Theory, Culture and Race*, London: Routledge.

Part II

Issues in gastronomic tourism development

6   On the trail of regional success: tourism, food production and the *Isle of Arran Taste Trail*

Steven Boyne, Fiona Williams and Derek Hall

Introduction, aims and rationale

The interlinkages between tourism and food are many and deep. In satisfying physiological needs, food is a 'non-optional' component of the tourism experience (Reynolds 1994: 191) and for many tourists, food and eating are important social and experiential elements of their holiday. In rural areas tourism and food production often compete for land, labour and capital, while in many cases, management of the natural and built environments for agriculture and food production provides landscapes and settings for tourists to enjoy, or 'consume'. Research has shown that food and drink can account for up to 40 per cent of tourists' holiday spending (Belisle 1983; Hudman 1986; Waterhouse *et al.* 1995), and as much as 50 per cent of the additional expenditure incurred by hosts entertaining VFR (visiting friends and relatives) tourists in rural Scotland (Boyne 2001). The potential therefore exists for rural tourism destination areas to maximize benefits to the local economy by providing locally produced foodstuffs for purchase and consumption by tourists. Encouraging back-linkages in this way can not only enhance the benefits of tourism to rural destination areas, but also help sustain traditional artisan and industrial-scale food production and processing techniques. Viewed from a tourism perspective, the opportunity to sample high-quality locally produced food products can enhance the visitor experience, raise awareness of a destination region or country and encourage first-time and return visits.

Regional development bodies and tourism planners are increasingly recognizing these synergies between tourism and food production and are implementing niche marketing and development initiatives that build upon local, regional and national cuisines to promote their respective areas as high-quality holiday destinations. In Scotland, for example, public-sector bodies, such as the local enterprise companies (LECs) and, previously, the Scottish Tourist Board, have been using local and regional food products to emphasize areas' attractiveness based upon the quality and uniqueness of these. One such initiative, the *Isle of Arran Taste Trail*, supported by the regional development agency Highlands and Islands Enterprise through the local enterprise company, Argyll and the Islands Enterprise, aims to promote Arran as a niche destination based on the quality of its local catering and oduce. The *Taste Trail*, created in 1998, features those who grow, make, sell, and cook with all the best island produce and encourages cooperation between these sectors towards enhancing both the visitor experience and stimulating back-linkages in the local economy from farm gate to point of sale. While similar in many respects to other 'food trails', 'foodways' or 'wine routes', in so far as visitors are provided with a booklet which provides information relating to producers, caterers and retailers (opening hours, location, etc.), the *Isle of Arran Taste Trail* sets out specifically to benefit the local food production sector through its membership criterion stipulating 'the use and promotion of local and/or Scottish produce by caterers and retailers' (Brown 2000: 2).

This chapter reports on the *Taste Trail* as an example of a gastronomic tourism initiative which embodies a strongly bi-directional approach to regional tourism development. Specifically, the term 'bi-directional' is employed here to describe initiatives which aim to produce or encourage complementary benefits for both the tourism and the food production sectors within a local or regional economy. This can be achieved, on the one hand through stimulating or encouraging the use of locally produced products in tourism-related retail and catering businesses, while, on the other hand, developing a marketing and promotion strategy that draws together high-quality tourism and food-related destination imagery. From a review of the tourism research literature relating to tourism and food, this chapter introduces a new taxonomy of tourism food relationships. Using this taxonomy as an organizing framework, the authors relate the bi-directional development process, described above, to its theoretical domains. In this way, the paucity of academic literature that deals with such approaches in a comprehensive manner, is highlighted. It is argued that future research which addresses the issues relating to these bi-directional development approaches can usefully assist planners, developers and practitioners who require a stronger body of related theoretical and applied research to build upon.

The chapter goes on to evaluate the aims and development of the *Taste Trail* and reports on its progress, drawing upon data from: (a) questionnaire responses from users of the *Taste Trail* guidebook; (b) an economic impact assessment carried out on behalf of the local enterprise company; and (c) interviews undertaken with the *Trail's* coordinator and *Trail* members from the hospitality and food production sectors. Finally, we reflect on the likely role of *Taste Trail* type initiatives in the longer term representation and marketing of rural and peripheral tourism destinations.

Tourism and food interrelationships

Using *CAB Leisure, Tourism and Recreation Abstracts* and their own institutional library resources and databases, the authors carried out a literature search for material relating to tourism, food and food production. The search yielded some forty-six journal articles, conference papers and book chapters published in the tourism, land-based and development-related literature between 1973 and 2000 and in which some form of tourism food relationship was deemed to form the main focus. The temporal distribution of these publications is not uniform: the majority (twenty-eight) were published between 1990 and 2001, approximately half this number (sixteen) during the 1980s, and only two during the 1970s. Analysis of the themes of the individual papers generated a fourfold classification of the literature based on the particular type of tourism food relationship being described. The fundamental division in the framework (shown in Figure 6.1) is between food production-related and food consumption-related interrelationships; within these, theoretical 'direct' and 'indirect' sub-themes have further been identified. The specific nature of each of these domains is described in Figure 6.1.

The remainder of this section explores the four domains in Figure 6.1 in the following order: the *indirect production-related* interrelationships are described followed by the two *consumption-related* domains. Finally, the *direct production-related* domain is described. As it is the literature in this domain which deals most comprehensively with the more tangible tourism and food production relationships, the *Taste Trail* initiative is introduced at this point, along with other examples of this type of initiative being undertaken elsewhere in Scotland. The authors use this juxtaposition of conceptual domain and practical initiative to highlight the

Tourism and food interactions	
Production-related	Consumption-related
Direct	**Direct**
• production of the food that tourists eat including aspects such as: > agri- and horticultural food production; > agricultural management systems; > food processing; > supply chain management; and > impact of tourism on destination areas' food production.	• tourists' consumption of food including aspects such as: > tourists' food choices; > service sector (HORECA[†]) management studies; > food safety issues; and > impacts of tourism on destination areas' food consumption.
Indirect	**Indirect**
• land, labour and capital: competition and complementarity between the tourism and food production sectors; • creation and maintenance of landscapes and settings; • creation of facilities, e.g. farm parks and farmhouse bed and breakfast; • mutually beneficial transport improvements (e.g. tourism-related transport improvements can enhance distribution opportunities for agriculture).	• tourists' consumption of agricultural landscapes and settings; • food as a destination image component or marketing/promotion tool; • consumption of agri-tourism products and services such as farm parks and visitor attractions.

[†]HORECA = HOtels, REstaurants and CAfes

Figure 6.1 Fourfold classification of tourism and food interrelationships with sub-themes

need for a more holistic academic treatment of the tourism food nexuses. In this way, it is suggested that research, policy and guidelines can be more closely related to the ongoing practical developments which are drawing together tourism and food production as synergistic rural development tools.

Indirect production-related interrelationships

Of the texts identified and placed in this domain, the greatest number had foci which can be described as *indirect production-related interrelationships*. Of the four theoretical sub-themes identified (see Figure 6.1) within this domain, the majority of the papers found belonged within *competition and complementarity between the tourism and food production sectors for land, labour and capital*. This strand of the literature is characterized by approaches which view tourism and agriculture either in competition for land, labour and capital, or as co-existing, often with tourism providing complementary opportunities for agricultural and food-related businesses. Belisle (1983), for example, concerned about foreign-exchange leakages in the Caribbean resulting from food imports for tourism consumption, highlighted tourism's competition for agricultural labour and land as a key element of the interface between tourism and local food production. In the United Kingdom (UK), Davies (1983) reported on tourism's role in supplementing farm incomes in less favoured areas (LFAs) in England and Wales; Zizic (1984) described the similar way in which tourism revenues can complement income from food production in rural areas of Yugoslavia; Persuad (1988), writing about tourism in the Caribbean, drew attention to the need for small states' agricultural sectors to adjust to tourism's effects on demand for food and labour; Bel and Ulbricht (1986) examined the (unusual in tourism-related studies) scenario of a slowdown in tourism activity leading to a greater demand for jobs in the agricultural sector in the French Rhone Alpes region; and Hjalager's (1996) research showed that in Denmark the returns from tourism to diversified agricultural holdings often did not match expectations, as in many cases farmers continued to give priority to agriculture. Hjalager also recognized the difficulties in combining industrial agriculture with the commodification of 'traditional' agriculture for tourists' consumption – a point noted in the *indirect consumption-related* literature domain, described below.

The *creation and maintenance of landscapes and settings* sub-theme refers to the way in which many of the rural landscapes and settings that tourists find aesthetically pleasing – and form an integral part of many areas' tourism product – are created and maintained by agricultural land management practices or infrastructure for food production; examples include pastureland and harbourside areas. Socher and Tschurtschenthaler (1994), for instance, in their examination of the economic relations between tourism and agriculture in the Tyrol region of Austria, conceptualized agriculture as having two 'supply values' for the tourism industry: the *direct supply* of agricultural products for the tourism industry's consumption, and the *indirect supply* – via land management, cultivation and maintenance – of landscape for tourists. Significantly perhaps, the six papers identified which emphasize the *creation and maintenance of landscapes and settings* sub-theme are all concentrated geographically in a relatively small area of Europe. Socher and Tschurtschenthaler (1994), Buchgraber (1996), Klasz (1996) and Poschacher (1996) all focused on Austria while Sandrock's (1999) paper described research carried out in the Hesse (Hessen) region in central western Germany. This can perhaps be attributed to the importance of landscape in Alpine and rural tourism imagery and the explicit linkages between food production practices and tourism. In the Swiss Alpine region, for example, summer tourism is represented for many individuals by images of cattle (complete with cowbells) along with the grassy landscapes which have been developed to sustain their seasonal grazing: Popp's (1996) agriculturally focused paper, specifically recognized agriculture's role in landscape maintenance for tourism and recreation in Switzerland.

Included in the *creation of facilities* sub-theme are: Bull and Wibberley's (1976) investigation into the potential for the development of farm-based recreation facilities in south-east England; Frater's (1983) research into farm tourism in England which drew upon the earlier European experience and Lores' (1994) description of women's rural tourism cooperatives in Greece. Also in this sub-theme is Bouquet's (1987) social relations analysis of food, eating and hospitality in farmhouse bed and breakfast in the English parish of Hartland. This work examined, from a production perspective, the incorporation of tourists into family relations within (a) the historical context of domestic hospitality towards farm workers and servants and (b) household gender-relations and farm-business survival strategies. In part, the paper concluded that although rural self-catering accommodation facilities may become more popular than farm-based bed and breakfast, the latter is unlikely to disappear owing to continuing consumer demand.

Finally in this domain, Bowen *et al.* (1991) described how improvements in transport systems, ostensibly for tourism, can benefit agriculture through increasing ease of access to market, while elsewhere Demura (1994) described a similar symbiosis in reverse. Together, these give rise to the *mutually beneficial transport improvements* sub-theme.

Direct consumption-related interrelationships

The literature in this domain essentially relates to tourists' consumption of food and the impact of tourism on residents' consumption of food. Belisle (1984), in his economic impact analysis of tourism in the Caribbean, considered the role of tourist food demand in generating foreign exchange leakages through the associated importation of non-locally produced food. Polacek (1986) described the relationships between different forms of tourism and recreation and patterns of eating out in Czechoslovakia and highlights the importance of high-quality gastronomy in satisfying tourists' expectations. Reynolds (1993) investigated food and eating as part of the cultural environment offered to tourists in Bali, Indonesia. His pilot study found that visitors were being offered less traditional Indonesian cuisine than they desired and that traditional cuisine was being corrupted by the (not necessarily tourism-related) growth in international and 'Western' foods. Basić (1995) identified the need to standardize food quality as an important element of Croatia's efforts to encourage and develop tourism, and Torriani (1999) examined the difficulties in implementing food-safety legislation in the context of Italian Alpine resorts and agri-tourism enterprises.

Included in the *direct consumption-related* domain, although not within the scope of this paper, is the wide range of literature relating to the catering and hospitality aspects of food consumption. This literature includes topics such as, for example, food safety (Dawood 1989; Savignac *et al.* 1992), menu design and marketing (Cattet and Smith 1994), food provision in airline catering (Frapin Beauge *et al.* 1994) and the relationship between tourism and catering in destination choice and holiday experience (Sheldon and Fox 1988).

Indirect consumption-related interrelationships

This theoretical domain contains literature relating to food as an element of destination imagery (see Marris 1986; Moulin 1997; van Westerling 1999; Day and Williams 2000). Marketing and development strategies, for example, can draw upon the image of the foodstuffs themselves and also methods of food-production to promote, often rural, destination areas. In many ways the literature in this sub-theme complements elements of the *direct production-related* domain although, here, the point of departure is from the tourists' perspective as consumer. Similarly, complementing the *creation of landscapes and settings* sub-theme within the *indirect production-related* domain, is the literature describing tourists' consumption of these agriculturally created aesthetics. Bessière (1998) made reference to this type of consumption in her discussion of demand for rural tourism, and Hughes (1995a and 1995b) drew our attention to the tension between the constructed and romanticized rural idyll and modern intensive animal husbandry and food production techniques – which are often far from romantic and usually hidden from the view of those not directly involved in the agricultural process.

Also included in this theoretical domain is the sub-theme relating to the consumption of agri-tourism products and services such as, for example, farm parks and rural visitor attractions and agricultural museums. Although the literature search revealed several papers concerned with agri-tourism products and services in the *production-related* domain (see above), there appears to be a paucity of published research dealing with tourists' related consumption patterns and behaviour.

Direct production-related tourism and food interrelationships

This section of the chapter – describing the organizing framework and exploring in some detail how the literature fits into this – has been structured in such a way that the authors may present this *direct production-related* (DPR) domain immediately following the *indirect consumption-related* (ICR) described above. The reasons for this are as follows. In contrast to the *indirect production-related* literature (the main emphases of which include *post-hoc* tourism impact studies and tourism and food production dynamics within individual businesses) and the *direct consumption-related* literature (which can be viewed largely as the province of catering and hospitality studies rather than tourism research), the DPR and ICR domains together contain the majority of the tourism research which may be proactively applied within regional tourism food initiatives. By presenting these domains together it is intended that the reader can gain an insight into their complementarity.

The DPR (direct production-related) domain contains literature which deals more specifically with conditions that affect food production and processing in the context of supply for tourism consumption. Examples include: Belisle's (1985) research into barriers preventing greater use of locally produced food in Jamaican hotels; Taylor *et al.*'s (1991) assessment of the potential for the implementation of a dual agriculture-tourism policy in the Bahamas; Tagliari and Franco's (1997) description of the benefits of combining home production with rural tourism in Brazil; Waterhouse *et al.*'s (1995) work on the problems of local livestock producers meeting the seasonal demand of rural tourists, and Canut's (1995) discussion of the opportunities for Spanish artisan cheese producers in the light of the anticipated wave of middle to high-income tourists expected to penetrate the Spanish interior in search of high-quality locally produced food products.

Telfer and Wall (1996) contains a useful and comprehensive conceptual analysis of the linkages between tourism and food production, and reports on the attempts of a hotel on the Indonesian island of Lombok to utilize more locally produced food. In their review of the literature, the authors described several of the direct and indirect production-related interrelationships including the competition and complementarity between tourism and agriculture in rural and agrarian areas, the impact of imported food on local economic benefits from tourism, and the opportunities and structural barriers facing the increased use of locally produced food. More recently Telfer (2000) described the *Tastes of Niagara* programme which proactively encourages the use of locally produced food and beverage products through formal strategic alliances between growers, processors, suppliers and retail and catering outlets. Of the texts identified, this is the only one which has examined both the production-related (creation of strategic alliances) and consumption-related (tourism-related promotion and marketing activities) domains of the tourism food relationships in any depth. While Telfer's emphases are on the management and development of the strategic alliances upon which the initiative is built (for further analysis of business interdependencies in this context see Hjalager, Chapter 2 in this volume), and the evolution and promotion of the initiative, the inclusion of a food production perspective in both the literature review and the research results section provides a useful and welcome balance.

Drawing the domains together: practical developments and the research gap

It is perhaps not surprising that such a balance is to be found in Telfer's (2000) paper, as it describes a bi-directional development initiative which seeks what we might call *food production for tourism* as well as *tourism for food production*. In Scotland, several development programmes are utilizing, or have used, tourism food synergies to attract visitors. Examples of these include: the *Taste of Scotland* complemented by *Natural Cooking of Scotland*; *A Taste of Orkney*; the *Renfrewshire and Inverclyde Taste Trail*; and the *Perthshire Food Trail Guide*. These programmes are largely driven by public-sector bodies, in particular the local enterprise companies (LECs) working under the auspices of the Scottish Enterprise Network (SEN) and Highlands and Islands Enterprise (HIE), and in some regions the Area Tourist Board (ATB) works in partnership with the LEC. These authors suggest that the rising incidence of such tourism food initiatives is, at least in part, related to the availability (in some areas) of European Union (EU) and United Kingdom (UK) government assistance available through various development measures. Complementary tourism projects often fare well in the operational programmes devised for areas eligible for assistance. Significantly, perhaps, for rural tourism development studies, the above leads us to note that while the recent emphasis on niche markets for rural tourism (typified by high-spending short-break visitors seeking very specific high-quality, high-value products and services) has been shown to be demand-led (e.g. Poon 1989), there also exists an important supply-led dimension in this process.

At an EU level, Ilbery and Kneafsey (1999) have evaluated the past experiences of, and the future potential for, lagging regions of the EU to successfully market and promote place-specific quality products and services (QPS). Based on an analysis of various place-specific products, environments, culture and identity in twelve EU case study areas, they found that there existed under-exploited potential for regional development in this sphere. Although the synergistic development of tourism and regionally specific products was one of their recommendations, it was not within the scope of their research to develop this relationship in any great depth. Indeed, it is perhaps a reflection of the breadth of scope required to produce a holistic analysis of food-related tourism developments that there are so few comprehensive related academic accounts. Similarly, in practice, not all food-related tourism development programmes encourage such strong linkages between the food production, distribution and catering sectors as does the *Taste of Niagara* initiative described by Telfer (2000). In Scotland, there are several *Food* or *Taste Trail* type initiatives (see above for examples) and, among these, the *Isle of Arran Taste Trail* demonstrates a strong commitment to the local production sector through its insistence on provision of locally or regionally produced goods as a criterion for *Trail* membership. Additionally, the *Isle of Arran Taste Trail* employs a marketing and promotion strategy that draws together high-quality tourism and food-related destination imagery.

It would appear, then, that the tourism research literature lags some way behind practical developments. From the organizing framework which describes the tourism and food interrelationships, we can see that while the literature offers analyses within all four conceptual domains, it does so in a fragmented way. The reasons for this are likely to stem from the breadth of scope required for the type of comprehensive analyses which we call for, and, in contrast, the limitations imposed by standard publishing formats such as journal articles, conference papers and book chapters. Development initiatives are attempting to strengthen tourism food relationships within the DPR (*direct production-related*) domain while at the same time employing elements of the ICR (*indirect consumption-related*) domain to market and promote destinations to visitors. Within this context, we suggest that a useful point of departure for any future research into tourism food development initiatives would be to focus on the DPR and the ICR domains. While not discounting the validity of undertaking research within all four domains of the organizing framework, it is felt that by focusing in the first instance on the issues within, and relationships between, the DPR and ICR domains, several concerns can be addressed:

1   Given the difficulties presented by the breadth of scope required for comprehensive analyses in this area, to attempt to embrace all four domains in one study may prove overly ambitious.
2   These are the two domains being operationalized to the greatest extent within practical developments – subsequent research would therefore be of immediate relevance to the industry.
3   As indicated earlier in this chapter, the issues in the DCR (*direct consumption-related*) domain generally fall within the remit of catering and hospitality studies rather than tourism/regional development research – while the emphasis of the research literature in the IPR (*indirect production-related*) has been on *post-hoc* tourism impact studies. It should be noted that, within the IPR domain, changes in land-use patterns may have an impact on the *creation and maintenance of landscapes and settings* sub-theme – for example, following the outbreak in the UK of Foot and Mouth Disease (FMD) in 2001, changes in the use of rural spaces have been mooted by various commentators and there is a likelihood that many farm businesses will cease to trade permanently. Indeed, recent research undertaken in the UK indicates that 6 per cent of farmers affected directly by FMD would not restock following the slaughter of their livestock and that 36 per cent would restock at lower levels than previously (Tasker 2001). However, while further research into the landscape/land-use tourism food nexus would therefore be appropriate and welcome, as it is unlikely that land-use policy will be driven solely by the rationale of the countryside as an aesthetic backdrop for touristic consumption, such research would probably have restricted relevance within the context of the tourism/food regional/rural development studies being described in this chapter.

While tourism food nexuses are beginning to be examined more closely in tourism research, various practical developments are already drawing upon the synergies which these sectors enjoy. One example in Scotland of a tourism development initiative which seeks to enhance benefits for both tourism- and food-related sectors is the *Isle of Arran Taste Trail* which embraces such a bi-directional approach.

The Arran context

The Isle of Arran (area 43,201 ha) lies in the Firth of Clyde on Scotland's west coast and can be reached year round from the mainland port of Ardrossan via a ferry crossing of some 21.5 km taking approximately one hour. Seasonal (summer) ferries operate from Rothesay on the neighbouring island of Bute and from Claonaig on the Kintyre peninsula. A round trip of the island covers approximately 92 km and takes the traveller past the mountainous peaks of the north of the island and around the more gentle hills and pastureland of the south. The population of the island at the 1991 census was 4,472, down from 4,842 a century earlier when much of this additional population was likely to have been engaged in servicing the then burgeoning Clyde Coast tourism industry. This early form of mass tourism had evolved rapidly in the closing decades of the nineteenth century based on improved transport infrastructure, in the form of steamships and latterly the developing rail network, and fuelled by demand from the population of Glasgow and the surrounding industrial areas in Ayrshire and the Forth–Clyde valley. In the decades following the Second World War, Clyde Coast tourism fell into a drastic decline as UK holidaymakers increasingly took advantage of affordable charter flights and package holidays to Spain and the Mediterranean (Boyne *et al.* 2000: 101).

Today, however, tourism remains a major industry on the island with some 256,000 visitors arriving in 1999, generating approximately £27 million (€44.3 million) revenue for the island (Ayrshire and Arran Tourist Board undated). The island has a robust tourism infrastructure with activities including hill-walking, mountaineering, bird watching, golf and water sports. The island boasts several ancient monuments including ten henges and stone circles and several burial chambers and cairns; the visitor arriving in Brodick Bay might visit Brodick Castle, a sixteenth-century baronial house, or the walled garden within the grounds of the estate; the island has several other visitor centres including a whisky distillery at Lochranza and the Arran Heritage Museum in Brodick.

The island's agricultural industry centres around beef and lamb production. Many of the island's beef cattle are from native Scottish stock, such as the Aberdeen Angus and Highland breeds, although there are some breed mixes which make use of the larger cattle such as Charolais. Arran lamb comes chiefly from the hill-bred Blackface sheep which enjoy a varied diet and are known for the sweetness of flavour they gain from this. The island's largest game resource is wild venison which, along with pheasant, grouse and hare, attracts sporting parties to the island for hunting expeditions. Cheese, milk and ice cream are all made from milk produced by the island's ten dairy farms. Most of the dairy cattle are Holstein Friesan crosses although there is one herd of the native Ayrshire cattle – these produce less milk per head but with a higher fat content than other, more commercial breeds. Arran's largest arable crop is the potato and the island gives its name to several varieties of this tuber including the Arran Pilot, Arran Banner and the Arran Comet – all bred by Mr Donald 'Tattie' McKelvie, Arran's own prodigious potato breeder of the early twentieth century. In addition to its wild berries Arran produces some soft fruits on a commercial scale, and a small amount of vegetables and herbs are also grown locally. Opened in 1995, the Isle of Arran Distillery at Lochranza makes use of one natural resource the island has in abundance – water. In 1997 the distillery opened a visitor centre which has become a popular tourist attraction. Arran's once thriving fishing industry has all but disappeared and, although there remain some lobster fishermen, much of the seafood available on the island is sourced externally.

The *Isle of Arran Taste Trail*

Origins of the Trail

The *Isle of Arran Taste Trail*'s origins lie in Argyll and the Islands Enterprise's (the local enterprise company) Food Initiative which is involved in promoting quality local produce for which there is perceived to be an increasing demand. Coordinated by the Food Initiative Steering Group, this programme also encourages links between the tourism and food and drink industries. The steering group, recognizing the strength of these linkages, prompted the development of the *Trail* as a method of exploiting these linkages, for the benefit of both the locally based food and tourism industries. The Isle of Arran was selected as the geographical location for the *Trail* based on the diversity of its food producers and catering suppliers and the strong linkages which already existed between these sectors.

Aims of the Trail

The *Trail* initiative aims to promote Arran as a niche destination based on the quality of local catering and produce. The *Trail* features those who grow, make, sell, and cook with all the best island produce and encourages cooperation between these sectors towards both enhancing the visitor experience and stimulating back-linkages in the local economy from farm gate to point of sale. In this way the *Trail* aims to encourage visitors to stay longer on the island, disperse more widely within it and undertake return visits in the future.

Specific objectives are:

- to enhance the linkages between the food and tourism industry sectors;
- to educate visitors about the quality, availability and uses of locally produced food and in this way enhance their visit to the island;
- to encourage caterers and retailers to make more use of locally produced food; and
- to promote Arran as a destination where high-quality food is readily available.

Marketing and promotion of the Trail

The *Trail* is based around a guidebook which features members from three of the island's food production and tourism-related sectors. At the time of writing the members include eight food producers, twelve restaurants and seven retailers. Membership of the *Trail* is exclusionary and is offered to those who meet several criteria including high standards of produce and service and, most importantly, a commitment to providing and promoting locally produced food. The guidebook was written and the members selected by the noted Scottish food writer and co-presenter of the long-running television show, *Scotland's Larder*, produced by Grampian Television Ltd. (Aberdeen). The first edition appeared in 1998 and a revised version was produced by the same author for 1999. The guidebook is offered for sale at a cost of £1 (€1.64) to visitors arriving on the island and, during the first two years of its publication, has sold around 5,000 copies. The main point of distribution for the guidebook is through the Ayrshire and Arran Tourist Board (AATB), principally in their network of local Tourism Information Centres (TIC), while many of the *Trail* members retail the guidebook on their premises. Additionally, a small number of guidebooks were displayed in a London TIC – the impact, if any, of this is, however, unknown.

A logo which depicts some of the island's generic food products was developed and is used extensively in the guidebook and by *Trail* members who display this at their establishments. Posters are displayed on the island's connecting ferries and high-quality point-of-sale promotional material is distributed by guidebook retailers. Press articles have appeared in *The Herald*, a Scotland-wide daily newspaper and the British Airways in-flight magazine *High Life*. The *Trail* website *www.tastetrail.co.uk* was launched in January 2000 and details the content of the guidebook with additional features such as recipe information, links to other food-related sites and travel information for visitors to the island.

Management and coordination of the Trail

The *Trail* is supported by the economic development agency Highlands and Islands Enterprise through the local enterprise company, Argyll and the Islands Enterprise (AIE), who have funded the initiative thus far with additional monies coming from the LEADER II Community Initiative. The majority of the development work was undertaken by AIE's local officer who was successful in encouraging participation from twenty-seven local businesses, exceeding the targeted number of twenty-one to twenty-five. The majority of the costs of managing and operating the *Trail* are incurred by the assessment process which requires the use of an independent assessor. At present, AIE believe that to continue to be successful, the *Trail* requires to maintain standards of quality, i.e. to maintain an exclusive membership policy. Therefore, if members are to be selected objectively, an independent assessor is necessary; it is possible, however, that this approach may be revised in the future as the *Trail* evolves and, in the longer term, hopefully becomes self-sustaining. Other costs include the production of the guidebook, promotional activities, general administration and maintenance of the website. As mentioned above, public sector fiscal support for the *Trail* will not continue indefinitely; solutions must therefore be sought regarding its longer-term financial sustainability. Potential methods for achieving this are discussed below under 'Issues for the future'.

Monitoring and evaluation of the **Trail**

Two separate evaluative exercises were undertaken by AIE. First, a questionnaire response card for respondent completion is inserted in the guidebooks. This invites visitors to respond and to enter themselves into a prize draw – a follow-up postal survey was then sent to these respondents. Second, a firm of external consultants were commissioned in March 2000 to carry out an economic impact evaluation of the initiative. This consultancy exercise included a Members' survey which was undertaken not only to elicit their views but also to help engender a sense of ownership in the members through their active involvement. Finally, for this research, the authors carried out interviews with two *Trail* members (one hotelier/restaurateur and one food producer) and the *Trail*'s coordinator, Maureen McKenna. The following results are based on information gained during these interviews and data from the surveys referred to above which were kindly provided to the authors by Ms McKenna.

Results and discussion

Visitors' perceptions

Included in every *Trail* guidebook was a short questionnaire survey in the form of a large FREEPOST card. The questionnaire offered respondents entry to a prize draw with the opportunity to win a bottle of whisky. The questionnaire engendered 225 responses. In general the responses were positive and many constructive comments were forthcoming. In 1998, 70 per cent of respondents said that the information contained in the booklet had encouraged them to eat out more often and in 1999 this figure had risen to 74 per cent. Additionally, a large majority of respondents (90 per cent in 1998 and 89 per cent in 1999) said that having read the guidebook, they were prepared to spend more money on meals consisting of locally produced food. Respondents were also asked about their purchases of groceries and provisions; of those respondents who did not already do so, only 2 per cent said that having read the guidebook, they *would not be* more inclined to purchase groceries directly from producers or small shops selling local produce. When considering a return visit to the island, 70 per cent of respondents in 1998 and 88 per cent in 1999 said that the quality of Arran's food would be a positive factor in their decision to return.

Economic impact of the Trail

During March 2000, a firm of independent consultants were commissioned by AIE to undertake an economic impact assessment of the *Trail* and to identify key areas for consideration with regard to ways forward for the initiative (Jackson 2000). Key findings of this investigation include:

- at least two FTE (full time equivalent) jobs have been created during the first two years of the initiative;
- a growth in turnover of some 25 to 40 per cent has been reported by some businesses and in most cases the *Trail* is having some positive effect on members;
- several examples of spontaneous networking between member businesses point to the capacity of the initiative to stimulate cooperative working practices;
- some members expressed a willingness to become involved in the future planning and management of the *Trail* and would consider making financial contributions to the initiative. Although, as a caveat, thought must be given to quality control issues if the *Trail* becomes a member-operated or sponsored initiative; and
- based upon similar initiatives elsewhere, the *Trail* as at present will require continued support for several years into the future.

Recommendations contained in the consultancy report (Jackson 2000) include:

- for future monitoring and evaluation there is a requirement to establish clearly defined performance criteria;
- the cooperative working practices which have evolved may be built upon and in the longer term the *Trail* may seek to foster and facilitate networking of this type;
- to assist communication between members, and between members and the public, a private forum area may be provided on the website and a newsletter (perhaps quarterly) may be produced either in print or on-line;
- a promotional strategy may be developed in partnership with the Area Tourist Board (ATB); and
- a discrete effort should be placed upon training issues such as management and marketing, skills for chefs and *Trail*-related training for front-of-house staff.

Members' views

As the development process of the *Taste Trail* was undertaken in a substantially top-down manner (Argyll and the Islands Enterprise chose the format and the location while the guidebook's author selected the list of businesses eligible for membership), it was felt that a Members' survey would address two needs: (a) to canvass the members for their views on the *Trail*, and (b) to foster a sense of ownership in these key stakeholders through allowing them a forum for comment and subsequent discussion. Accordingly, an element of the economic impact consultancy was devoted to this. The Members' responses were overall positive. The guidebook was well received and members felt that it afforded the visitor a good impression of the island. There were some critical comments relating to the emphasis of the guidebook in so far as some members thought a stronger focus on food producers might enhance the educational element of the *Trail* by providing more information relating to local production methods.

Primary research

During the course of the authors' research for this chapter, interviews were undertaken with two members of the *Trail* (one hotelier/restaurateur and one producer) and the enterprise company's local officer who was responsible for the implementation and subsequent management and administration of the *Trail*. All interviews were undertaken by one of the authors; two in person and the remaining interview (with the hotelier/restaurateur) by telephone. A synopsis of the information gained from the interviews with the two *Trail* members is presented briefly below.

The Auchrannie Country House Hotel and Restaurant occupies a nineteenth-century holiday home built by a wealthy Glasgow merchant. The accommodation stock consists of some twenty-eight internal rooms and twenty-three holiday lodges located in the grounds of the hotel. There are two restaurants; an all-day cafe bar and a more formal hotel dining room. As with all three of the interviews undertaken for this research, the discussion was semi-structured and based on a short *aide-mémoire* which was customized accordingly for the particular context of each interview. The hotel manager was highly supportive of the *Trail*, and was able to confirm that, in his view, the *Trail* was (at least in part) responsible for increases in the business's turnover and profit, an increased volume of food being prepared and sold and a greater spend per head by customers eating in the hotel's restaurants. The hotel restaurants use goods from all of the producers listed in the guidebook although, of necessity, much of the hotel's supplies come from external sources. When asked if this use of locally produced goods was perhaps assisted by the hotel's distance from external markets and its isolation being on an island (albeit, one with relatively good transport links with the mainland), the respondent agreed that many of the hotel's supplies had been sourced locally prior to the *Trail* being implemented. Importantly, however, the *Trail* had encouraged this, and other hotels, to source more supplies locally. One particularly positive impact on the hotel was that the *Trail* had lengthened the tourism season allowing the restaurants to open for weekends during the winter season. While the hotel does promote itself in the marketplace, it was the feeling of this respondent that the demand for locally produced food created by the *Trail* was a positive factor in the island receiving these off-peak visits.

Arran Dairies are the main supplier of milk on the island, producing around 30 per cent of their output from their own herd and buying in the remainder from other dairy farms on the island. Using unhomogenized milk (unlike most modern milk, the fat globules in unhomogenized milk remain whole, imparting a more creamy flavour in the product) the dairy has recently expanded into making traditional, Italian-style, ice cream. The major benefits of the *Trail* as seen from the perspective of Arran Dairies' Director are its encouragement of cooperative working practices between the island's small and medium enterprises (SMEs) and its creation of a positive image (of both the island and individual businesses) which in the longer term will help increase market-share in external (mainland) markets. Logistical difficulties faced by SMEs in peripheral locations hamper expansion into external markets even where limited demand already exists – it is simply not cost effective to make long distribution trips for relatively small orders. By working in cooperation with other suppliers, however, a critical mass of goods for distribution can be achieved which reduce such barriers to market penetration. The *Taste Trail* type of initiative, by acting as a catalyst to bring together actors in rural areas – who are often reluctant to work together (see, for example, Boyne *et al.* 2000: 108; also Black, personal communication 2001) – has been invaluable in kick-starting this type of SME marketing and distribution-related networking. Additionally, the positive branding image afforded by *Trail* membership – which reinforces individual businesses' images with the high-quality brand image of the island – helps engender demand in external market-places not least in visitors who, having returned home, seek to purchase products discovered and enjoyed during their holiday trip. The logical extension of this type of networking might be a joint-marketing initiative based on a portfolio of locally produced and Arran-branded produce backed up by a structured distribution strategy.

Issues for the future

From the above and from the data collected during the interviews conducted for this research several salient issues can be articulated. As the initiative appears largely to have been a success during the first two years of its operation, our attention can perhaps be turned first to sustaining the *Trail* into the future. The key issue relating to the future survival of the *Trail* is that of financial self-sustainability.

The ongoing costs of the initiative in its present form are described in greater detail above and can be summarized thus: the independent assessment and grading process; production of the guidebook; promotional activities; general administration and maintenance of the website. The *Trail* has been funded for the first two years of its existence by Argyll and the Islands Enterprise (AIE) utilizing their own funds along with a contribution from the LEADER II Community Initiative at a cost of some £26,000 (€42,700). Although this figure includes initial start-up costs and exceeds greatly the annual running costs, based on the experiences of similar regional food and drink groups set up in England during the 1990s by the MAFF-supported (Ministry of Agriculture Fisheries and Food) Food from Britain organization, it is likely that in the short term the initiative will continue to require external support. The most likely route to achieving financial self-sustainability is to gradually reduce public-sector support over, for example, a three-year transition period, at the same time introducing membership charges. Although several *Trail* members have indicated a willingness to pay for membership of the scheme, there are concerns that such a move may compromise the quality of the *Trail* as membership would then be based on willingness to pay, rather than, as at present, on an independent assessment of quality and commitment to using and promoting local produce. A membership fee approach is employed with some success, however, by the regional food group *Middle England Fine Foods*, who have a tiered payment structure based on different categories of membership, specifically producers, retailers and wholesalers and affiliates who provide these groups with goods or services.

Alternative strategies include (a) another agency such as Visit Scotland (the renamed Scottish Tourist Board) taking control – although this would still require public money to be utilized in supporting the initiative and (b) transfer to private sector control where, for example, a private company takes on the role of a DMO (destination marketing organization) in return for a membership fee levied on participating businesses. One major advantage of this method is that experience and professionalism can be brought to bear on the process through the DMO, who may also have a greater depth and breadth of experience and resources than a locally based partnership. Alternatively, however, using a DMO will usually mean money leaving the local economy.

Indirect benefits of the *Trail* for producers and suppliers may come from joint marketing and distribution partnerships, and within local rural economies strategic alliances between SMEs can promote efficient use of locally produced goods (see, for example, Telfer 2000). Strategic alliances have been encouraged by the *Trail*'s development team and some members have formed a consortium offering gift packs featuring their various products and carrying the *Trail* logo. A stronger emphasis on partnership working in the future which might include more formal structures or facilities for cooperation, perhaps following the approach of, for example, the *Tastes of Niagara Quality Food Alliance* which has created a clearinghouse where producers drop off products which are then refrigerated for later purchase by caterers and suppliers (Telfer 2000: 81). To reinforce any such efforts, and to address the concerns raised by the economic impact consultants that members did not fully understand the aims of the *Trail*, an educational package or packages could be devised so that members can more clearly recognize the benefits of working together – although, it should be noted here that attitudes to cooperation amongst SMEs on Arran may be more positive than in other, particularly mainland, rural areas. Such a 'positive community spirit' was highlighted by one respondent to this research and may result from Arran's physical remoteness and islanders' perceptions of their own economic and social peripherality. Orkney, for example, another remote island community in Scotland, has been shown to possess strong levels of 'social capacity' in comparison with less peripheral mainland rural areas (Williams *et al.* 2000).

One characteristic of Arran's tourism industry is its retention of customers: many of those who holiday once on Arran, return. While this is undoubtedly a desirable tourism attribute, in the contexts of general tourism development and the *Isle of Arran Taste Trail*, it poses problems on two levels: first, for the island's tourism developers, retaining existing customers does not increase overall annual visitor numbers (although influencing existing visitors to extend their stay or take additional stays can increase tourism revenue); second, for the *Taste Trail*, repeat visitors are unlikely to buy the guidebook year after year, preferring rather to use the same one again, or perhaps dispensing with it once they have established their favoured facilities. The most obvious solution in response to this quandary is to attempt to attract first-time visitors to the island. Can a *Taste Trail* type initiative achieve this, however?

The *Isle of Arran Taste Trail* aims to influence visitors' behaviour subsequent to their arrival on the island and does not, at present, attempt the more complex and difficult task of attracting them there in the first place. Some destinations can attract tourists on the strength of their regional or national gastronomy. Italy and France, for example, have been successful in this regard (Hjalager and Antonioli Corigliano 2000: 290), although these tourist flows probably evolved through a spontaneous process rather than as a result of any premeditated development strategy. It is notable that in both France and Italy, national and/or regional cuisine had achieved premier status, throughout the Western world and beyond, prior to the late twentieth century emergence of the modern tourism phenomenon. Indeed, it is the contention of this chapter that such a pre-existing strength of gastronomic image will, in most cases, be required if a region is to successfully establish food-related tourism flows. Scotland does possess such a strength of gastronomic image; its seafood (Scottish smoked salmon and fresh shellfish), beef cattle (Aberdeen Angus and Highland) and whisky all enjoy international acclaim as high-quality nationally or regionally branded products. Additionally, however, it is also suggested here that for food-related tourism flows to be generated, a destination must already have a reasonably well established tourism infrastructure. It is unlikely that many tourists, except Plog's more allocentric travellers (Plog 1973), will be inclined to visit a country or region unless a reasonably well developed tourism infrastructure is in place.

If a region does possess some levels of both gastronomic recognition and existing tourism infrastructure, then, it is suggested here, over time the marketing and promotion of the area's tourism and gastronomy (perhaps utilizing a *Taste Trail* type initiative) could enhance the gastronomic (and touristic) image of that area. Eventually, in this way, first-time visitors may be attracted by the strength of image and quality of the local cuisine and food products. A theoretical development scenario (based on the *Isle of Arran Taste Trail* initiative) illustrating such a process is described below. Points 1 to 3 describe the likely context for such a process, Point 4 considers elements of the development process while Point 5 describes the likely outcomes in the longer term. In Chapter 2 of this volume, Hjalager introduces a hierarchical model which describes four orders of culinary tourism where each consecutive order is typified by increasing sophisticated and complex linkages between production and consumption. Future conceptual work could usefully explore the related dimensions with respect to Hjalager's model and the development scenario presented below, not least in the area of supply-chain infrastructure which Hjalager approaches from a 'cluster' perspective.

Point 1. The process may take place in an area which is usually rural, or with a rural dimension, as there must be some food production (or perhaps processing) in the region.

Point 2. The local food resource is widely, perhaps internationally, recognized – examples include Parmigiano cheese and Scottish smoked salmon. Additionally, the region's food products may have an official demarcation or quality assurance label, such as the French *Appellation d'Origine Contrôlée* (see for example, Ilbery and Kneafsey 2000a and 2000b). Such a product demarcation may have aided the survival of the product thus far and/or helped enhance the product image and its desirability.

Point 3. The area has some existing touristic activity – this is necessary as the *Taste Trail* type of rural development initiative is built around the symbiosis of tourism and food production. Both of these elements must be in place as the destination marketing and development process is a bi-directional one. That is, benefits for both the tourism and agricultural sectors are sought – food production for tourism *and* tourism for food production.

Point 4. A gastronomic tourism initiative can be developed, which aims:

(1) in the first instance, to influence visitors upon their arrival in the destination area in, for example, the following ways:

    (a) increase their length of stay;
    (b) increase their spending on locally produced goods;
    (c) increase their dispersal throughout the destination area; and
    (d) enhance visitor satisfaction and in this way encourage repeat visits.

(2) in both the short and longer term, improve the economic outlook for, and help ensure the survival of, locally based primary and secondary sector food-related SMEs by:

    (a) stimulating back-linkages in the local economy from farm gate to point of sale;
    (b) increasing consumer awareness of, particularly high-quality, local products and in this way creating and enhancing opportunities for the development of these products in the wider marketplace;
    (c) building upon this increased consumer awareness and utilizing it to feed back into the destination branding process, thus providing promotional material based around strongly imaged local food and beverage products in addition to other destination characteristics such as the natural and built environments and cultural heritage.

Point 5. Over time the interwoven representations of tourism destination, gastronomic destination and gastronomic-tourism destination combine to create a holistic place-specific destination image which is strong enough to induce first-time visits to the area based on (a) a well developed and strongly imaged tourism product, a major element of which is (b) the availability of high-quality, locally-produced foodstuffs (which will itself be based on a strong locally-rooted supply chain infrastructure).

Point 5 in this theoretical process is the most desirable for a tourism destination area as it can then use the strength of its tourism and food destination imagery to promote itself to new, first-time visitors, rather than as at Point 4 where the tourism food initiative is employed to influence visitors once they arrive. The importance of such an outcome for destination areas such as Arran is that they become less reliant on repeat visits from individuals and families, who may go elsewhere in successive years only returning to one particular destination every alternate year or possibly less frequently. Elsewhere in Scotland, the importance of generating visits based on strongly imaged destination characteristics has been highlighted by research carried out in the then Grampian Region in the North East (now covered geographically and administratively by the Moray and Aberdeenshire unitary authorities). Reporting on this research, Day and Williams (2000: 11) describe how respondents recognized that without such a strong image the region was at a disadvantage compared with other Scottish regions in respect of attracting tourists. For peripheral Northern European destination regions in particular, the ability to utilize destination characteristics other than 'sunny beach scenes' in marketing and promotional material can enhance visitor satisfaction by removing to some extent the potential for disappointment (which may occur when visitors discover that many beaches in Europe's northern periphery are not sunny every day).

Summary and conclusions

This chapter has explored the relationships between rural tourism and food production through an examination of the existing literature and by describing the implementation of a locally based gastronomy tourism development initiative. The *Isle of Arran Taste Trail* encourages back-linkages between the local tourism and food production and processing sectors to enhance the benefits of tourism for all these local industry sectors. The *Taste Trail* employs a guidebook which features those who grow, make, sell and cook with all the best island produce and encourages cooperative working practices within and between the local tourism and food industry sectors. In this way the *Trail* addresses both the production- and consumption-related aspects of the tourism food nexuses which are identified in this paper. These tourism food nexuses were generated following a review of the existing tourism research literature relating to food production and gastronomy and form an organizational framework for the chapter. Specifically, we identified four discrete theoretical domains each containing several sub-themes. Both the production- and consumption-related nexuses (illustrated in Figure 6.1) contain direct and indirect theoretical domains. We argue that while practical developments such as the *Isle of Arran Taste Trail* in Scotland and the *Tastes of Niagara* quality food initiative in North America are drawing together specific, discrete theoretical domains (specifically, the DPR or *direct production-related* and the ICR or *indirect consumption-related*), the tourism research literature is some way behind. While the literature deals with all of these theoretical domains, it does so in a fragmented manner. Accordingly, there is a need for further research which will address the requirement for a holistic approach to regional and local gastronomy-related tourism development. In the first instance, such research should focus on the aspects of gastronomy-related tourism development described in the DPR and ICR domains. Such an approach would: (a) reflect practical developments within the tourism industry; (b) generate outcomes of the greatest immediate relevance to policy-makers, planners, practitioners and academics; and (c) go some way to providing foci for approaching such a wide-ranging and diverse research agenda.

Additionally, based on the aims and implementation of the *Isle of Arran Taste Trail*, and a consideration of how this experience relates to existing gastronomy related destination imaging elsewhere in Europe, we suggest a model which describes how a *Taste Trail* type initiative could, in the longer term, go some way to creating a locally or regionally based destination image within which the interwoven representations of both gastronomy and tourism combine to create a destination image which has the capacity to attract first-time visitors in addition to influencing the behaviour of tourists upon their arrival at the destination.

References

Ayrshire and Arran Tourist Board (undated) *Ayrshire and Arran tourism fact sheet*, Ayrshire and Arran Tourist Board, Prestwick.

Basić, F. (1995) 'Some aspects of sustainable agriculture in Croatia', *Poljoprivredna Znanstvena Smotra*, 60(2): 237–347.

Bel, F. and Ulbricht, T.L.V. (1986) 'The Alps, between tourism and grazing: discussion', *Integrated Rural Development*, proceedings of a European Symposium Wageningen, 23–25 September.

Belisle, F.J. (1983) 'Tourism and food production in the Caribbean', *Annals of Tourism Research*, 10(4): 497–513.

—— (1984) 'Tourism and food imports', *Economic Development and Cultural Change*, 32(4): 819–842.

—— (1985) 'Food production and tourism in Jamaica: obstacles to increasing local supplies to hotels', *Journal of Developing Areas*, 19(1): 1–20.

Bessière, J. (1998) 'Local development and heritage: traditional food and cuisine as tourist attractions in rural areas', *Sociologia Ruralis*, 38(1): 21–34.

Black, L. (2001) Personal communication between first author and Linda Black, Food Partnership Project Officer with Scottish Enterprise Tayside, January.

Bouquet, M. (1987) 'Bed, breakfast and an evening meal: commensality in the nineteenth and twentieth century farm', in Bouquet, M. and Winter, M. (eds) *Who from their labours rest? Conflict and practice in rural tourism*, pp. 93–104.

Bowen, R., Cox, L.J. and Fox, M. (1991) 'The interface between tourism and agriculture', *Journal of Tourism Studies*, 2: 43–54.

Boyne, S., Gallagher, C. and Hall, D. (2000) 'The fall and rise of peripherality: tourism and restructuring on Bute', in Brown, F. and Hall, D. (eds) *Tourism in Peripheral Areas: case studies*, Channel View Publications, Clevedon, pp. 101–113.

Boyne, S. (2001) 'VFR (visiting friends and relatives) tourism in rural Scotland: a geographical case study analysis', in Lennon, J. J. (ed.) *International Perspectives on Tourism Statistics*, Continuum International Publishers, London.

Brown, C. (2000) *Isle of Arran Taste Trail*, guidebook published by Argyll and The Islands Enterprise, Lochgilphead.

Buchgraber, K. (1996) 'Grünland – Bewirtschaftung – Grundlage für Milch- und Fleischproduktion und Basis der Produktion für Landschaft und Fremdenverkehr', *Stocarstvo*, 50(6): 439–448.

Bull, C. and Wibberley, G.P. (1976) *Farm Based Recreation in South East England*. Report: Studies in rural land use, Wye College (University of London), No. 12.

Canut, E. (1995) 'La relation des fromages artisanaux espagnols avec leur demande agro-éco-touristique', in Flamant, J.C., Portugal, A.V., Costa, J.P., Nunes, A.F. and Boyazoglu, J. (eds) *Animal Production and Rural Tourism in Mediterranean Regions*, proceedings of the International Symposium on Animal Production and Rural Tourism in Mediterranean Regions, Evora, Portugal, 10–13 October 1993, European Association for Animal Production, pp. 135–137.

Cattet, A. and Smith, C. (1994) 'The menu as marketing tool', in Cooper, C.P. and Lockwood, A. (eds) *Progress in Tourism, Recreation and Hospitality Management*, 6, John Wiley: Chichester, pp. 149–163.

Davies, E.T. (1983) *The Role of Farm Tourism in the Less Favoured Areas of England and Wales 1981. (A physical and financial appraisal)*, Report No. 218: Agricultural Economics Unit, University of Exeter.

Dawood, R. (1989) 'Tourists' health: could the travel industry do more?', *Tourism Management*, 10(4): 285–287.

Day, G. and Williams, F. (2000) *Tourism, Food and Drink: the potential for branding the North-East of Scotland*, Leisure Studies Association Annual Conference, Glasgow (July).

Demura, K. (1994) 'Multiple functions of agriculture and rural communities in environment, landscape, and tourism – a case study of farm road improvement projects', *Journal of the Faculty of Agriculture*, Hokkaido University, 66(1): 127–137.

Frapin Beauge, A.J.M., Bennet, M.M. and Wood, R.C. (1994) 'Some current issues in airline catering', *Tourism Management*, 15(4): 295–298.

Frater, J. M. (1983) 'Farm tourism in England: planning, funding, promotion and some lessons from Europe', *Tourism Management*, 4(3): 167–179.

Hjalager, A.M. (1996) 'Agricultural diversification into tourism: evidence of a European Community development programme', *Tourism Management*, 17(2): 103–111.

Hjalager, A.M. and Antonioli Corigliano, M. (2000) 'Food for tourists – determinants of an image', *International Journal of Tourism Research*, 2: 281–293.

Hudman, L.E. (1986) 'The travellers' perceptions of the role of food in the tourist industry', in *The Impact of Catering and Cuisine upon Tourism*, proceedings of the 36th Congress of the International Association of Scientific Experts of Tourism (AIEST), 31 August to 6 September, Montreux, Switzerland.

Hughes, G. (1995a) 'Authenticity in tourism', *Annals of Tourism Research*, 22(4): 781–803.

—— (1995b) 'Food, tourism and Scottish heritage', in Leslie, D. (ed.) *Tourism and Leisure:*

Towards the Millennium. Volume 1: Tourism and Leisure – Culture, Heritage and Participation, Leisure Studies Association, Eastbourne, pp. 109–120.

Ilbery, B. and Kneafsey, M. (eds) (1999) *Regional Images and the Promotion of Quality Products and Services in the Lagging Regions of the European Union*. Final Report, RIPPLE Project undertaken for the European Union as FAIR3-CT96–1827.

Ilbery, B. and Kneafsey, M. (2000a) 'Producer constructions of quality in regional speciality food production: a case study from south-west England', *Journal of Rural Studies*, 16: 217–230.

—— (2000b) 'Registering regional speciality food and drink products in the United Kingdom: the case of PDOs and PGIs', *Area*, 32(3): 317–325.

Jackson, R. (2000) *Isle of Arran Taste Trail*. Report by Ecosse Associates for Argyll and the Islands Enterprise, July.

Klasz, W. (1996) 'Die Multifunktionalitat der Landwirtschaft als Motor regionaler Entwicklung', *Forderungsdienst*, 44(10): 301–305.

Lores, C. (1994) 'Las cooperativas de mujeres de turismo rural en Grecia', *Geórgica*, 3: 77–82.

Marris, T. (1986) 'Does food matter', *The Tourist Review*, 41(4): 17–20.

Moulin, C. (1997) 'Gastronomy and tourism: must every tourist wish be our command?' *The Tourist Review*, 1: 19–24.

Persuad, B. (1988) 'Agricultural problems of small states, with special reference to Commonwealth Caribbean countries', *Agricultural Administration and Extension*, 29(1): 35–51.

Plog, S.G. (1973) 'Why destination areas rise and fall in popularity', *Cornell Hotel and Restaurant Administration Quarterly*, November, 13–16.

Polacek, M. (1986) 'Eating habits of Czechoslovak population and gastronomy as a tourist motivation', *The Tourist Review*, 41(4): 22–25.

Poon, A. (1989) 'Competitive strategies for a "new tourism"', in Cooper, C.P. and Lockwood, A. (eds) *Progress in Tourism, Recreation and Hospitality Management*, 1, John Wiley: Chichester, pp. 149–163.

Popp, H.W. (1996) 'Die Landwirtschaft zwischen Freihandel und Ökologie – Leitlinien einer agrarpolitischen Lösung', *Agrarwirtschaft und Agrarsoziologie*, 1: 97–117.

Poschacher, G. (1996) 'Perspektiven für den ländlichen Raum im europäischen Integrationsprozess', *Forderungsdienst*, 44(9): 9–12.

Reynolds, P. (1993) 'Food and tourism: towards an understanding of sustainable culture', *Journal of Sustainable Tourism*, 1(1): 48–54.

Reynolds, P. (1994) 'Culinary heritage in the face of tourism', in Cooper, C.P. and Lockwood, A. (eds) *Progress in Tourism, Recreation and Hospitality Management*, 6, John Wiley: Chichester, pp. 189–194.

Sandrock, A.F. (1999) 'Landwirtschaft, ein wichtiger Partner der Regionalentwicklung – Strukturwandel setzt sich unvermindert fort', *Fulda – eine hessische Region mit beispielhafter Entwicklung*, Fruhjahrstagung der Agrarsozialen Gesellschaft eV, Fulda, Germany, 26–29 May, Materialsammlung, 200: 108–113.

Savignac, A.E. *et al.* (eds) (1992) *Food Safety and Tourism: Regional Conference for Africa and the Mediterranean*, Hotel Abou Nawas, Tunis, Tunisia, 25–27 November 1991: proceedings.

Sheldon, P. and Fox, M. (1988) 'The role of foodservice in vacation choice and experience', *Journal of Travel Research*, 27(2): 9–15.

Socher, K. and Tschurtschenthaler, P. (1994) 'Tourism and agriculture in Alpine regions', *The Tourist Review*, 49(3): 35–41.

Tagliari, S. and Franco, H.M. (1997) 'Industrialização caseira com turismo rural: uma fórmula de sucesso', *Agropecuaria Catarinense*, 10(1): 51–54.

Tasker, J. (2001) 'Farmers plan to quit or scale down', *Farmers Weekly*, 26 April, as viewed online at <http://www.fwi.co.uk/live/news/fwi_news.asp?WCI=Display-&WCE=21618,1> on 17 July 2001.

Taylor, B.E., Morison, J.B. and Fleming, E.M. (1991) 'The economic impact of food import substitution in the Bahamas', *Social and Economic Studies*, 40(2): 45–62.

Telfer, D.J. (2000) 'Tastes of Niagara: building strategic alliances between tourism and agriculture', *International Journal of Hospitality and Tourism Administration*, 1(1): 71–88.

Telfer, D.J. and Wall, G. (1996) 'Linkages between tourism and food production', *Annals of Tourism Research*, 23(3): 635–653.

Torriani, M. (1999) 'L'autocontrollo nelle imprese alimentari: alcuni problemi applicativi del Decreto legislativo 155/97', *Obiettivi e Documenti Veterinari*, 20(11): 26–32.

Waterhouse, A., Ashworth, S.W., Gibon, A. and Rubino, R. (1995) 'Adaptation of local animal production systems to seasonal tourist demands', in Flamant, J.C., Portugal, A.V., Costa, J.P., Nunes, A.F. and Boyazoglu, J. (eds) *Animal Production and Rural Tourism in Mediterranean Regions*, proceedings of the International Symposium on Animal Production and Rural Tourism in Mediterranean Regions, Evora, Portugal, 10–13 October 1993, European Association for Animal Production, pp. 65–70.

van Westerling, J. (1999) 'Heritage and gastronomy: the pursuits of the "new tourist"', *International Journal of Heritage Studies*, 5(2): 75–81.

Williams, F., Copus, A. and Petrie, S. (2000) *Entrepreneur Survey: Scotland*, The Role of Regional Milieux in Rural Economic Development – funded under the Northern Periphery Programme (3107982/15).

Zizic, Z. (1984) 'Développement du tourisme rural en Yougoslavie', *Le tourisme en milieu rural*, Congress de Madrid, 19–20 October: 99–103.

7 'A Taste of Wales – Blas Ar Gymru': institutional malaise in promoting Welsh food tourism products

Andrew Jones and Ian Jenkins

Introduction: the concept of 'food tourism'

The relationship between tourism, environment and cultural resources has been a topic of considerable debate at both national and international levels over the last decade.

Food has always been an integral part of the tourist product or 'package' and a significant part of tourism expenditure in both organized and independent travel. Hudman (1986) suggested that food had become an increasingly important element in the tourist industry and that up to 25 per cent of total tourist expenditure was accounted for by food. Defort (1987) also acknowledged food and gastronomy to be an important element of tourism and discussed how tourists were placing an emphasis on good and well prepared food as part of their overall tourism experience. Despite the growing importance of food in the tourism experience, however, Hudman qualified his statements by suggesting that tourism demand still tended to be determined more by a destination's natural attractions, entertainment facilities or cultural and historic sites than by the attractions of food. This is a scenario that very much reflects the current status of tourism development in Wales.

Since these earlier debates, however, the concept of food associated with tourism has evolved from its historic and more general roots in traditional hospitality, cuisine and gastronomy into the new concept of 'food tourism', where food has become increasingly important in promoting tourism destinations. Food is now used as a means of developing new niche markets, supporting regional identities, developing quality tourism and sustainable tourism. Food has therefore developed from being a basic necessity for tourist consumption to being regarded as an essential element of regional culture. Reynolds (1993) argued that if culture and tradition are to prove sustainable in the face of tourism, then traditional and ethnic foods must be preserved along with other art forms.

Food tourism is not generally well documented in research on contemporary forms of tourism. However, over the last decade, the concept has evolved into a more recognized area of tourism research and tourism product development. Previous studies (e.g. Kaspar 1986; Polacek 1986; Convenant 1991) have tended to concentrate on hospitality and catering experiences, but recent research has begun exploring some of these new food tourism concepts.

More recent literature has concentrated on the use of food as a means of developing and promoting both established and new regional tourist destinations, which are often linked to wider tourism products associated with heritage, cultural and rural tourism. These developments are illustrated by Mallon (1995) who documents the growth of 'gastronomic' tourism, particularly in France. Mallon argues that tourists travel to a particular region specifically for its cuisine and that destinations cannot afford to overlook their regional cuisine when developing promotional strategies. Food tourism is thus seen as means of developing 'high quality' tourism products and markets which are often associated with specialized niche markets and sustainable tourism products. This is a sentiment that has been more recently reflected in a Welsh tourism policy context where such new markets have become a key development objective of organizations such as the Wales Tourist Board (WTB), the Welsh Development Agency (WDA), the food producers and retailers and other smaller stakeholders (Pritchard and Morgan 2001).

The evidence currently available suggests that food tourism is becoming an important means of providing new tourism products that 'sell' the 'distinct character' and 'culture' of a destination. Food tourism is also a potential antidote to stagnating mass tourism demand and a means of supporting and promoting sustainable tourism. In Wales, Banks and Bristow (1999) also point to the growing merits of encouraging quality 'agro-food' and the wider spin-offs this can generate. All of these factors have tended to strengthen arguments for the development of food tourism. Carney (1994) even argues that strategic planning for tourism should include giving a culinary expert an important position within tourism policy making.

Despite the potential advantages of developing food tourism, it is not without problems. Tensions can emerge between the capacity of a local area and the local food distribution system to deliver quality gastronomic products in sufficient quantities in the high season. It would appear that many marketing initiatives pay scant attention to the capacities of the local food production and distribution system and thereby become, at best marginalized and at worst dishonest. Danger signals are already starting to emerge over the disparity between promotion and delivery and there are concerns that branding strategies are little more than marketing gimmicks, which can be very counterproductive in terms of tourism promotion and the tourist experience. Riddell (2001) also decries the lack of quality food provision and co-ordination within British tourism markets, particularly in the hospitality sector. These are sentiments also expressed by Banks and Bristow (1999) in their critique of 'agro-food' supply chains in Wales. Their discussion on the increasing complexity and varying quality within supply chain networks helps to highlight the 'policy malaise' in food tourism. Lack of effective policy has resulted in ineffective institutional or stakeholder networks for developing gastronomic tourism in Wales.

It would appear that food and tourism can frequently provide a potent means for promoting tourism destinations, but there are debates emerging over the extent to which food tourism can bring measurable benefits to a tourism destination.

The choice of Wales as a case study is particularly pertinent as the development of food and gastronomy tourism has been a specific strategic goal for the Wales Tourist Board. The 'Taste of Wales' initiative, which has been devised over the last decade, has had the ambitious aims of introducing both a co-ordinated and an institutionalized approach to promote food as a tourism experience. It has also promoted schemes that link and promote local food quality initiatives. Wales, therefore provides an interesting platform from which to evaluate the issues associated with a holistic approach to marketing and branding food products for tourism and the success and failures that have resulted.

Our analysis of food tourism in Wales is based upon qualitative research using depth interviews with key participants in the present 'Taste of Wales' initiative. The sample has been taken from a range of producers, promoters, retailers and users in order to ensure a representative response from the different sectors (stakeholders) of the food and tourism industry within Wales. The interviews were conducted over a two-week period and focused on the perception and evaluation of both the 'Taste of Wales' initiative and broader issues relating to food and tourism. The research approach was effective in collating a range of discursive material from which a range of common issues emerged and provided the basis for discussion in later sections of this chapter. Although the information gathered is largely based on the subjective views of major stakeholders, the interviews did provide new evidence and material to explore emerging issues relating to food and tourism promotion within Wales.

Welsh gastronomy: past traditions, challenges and changing attitudes

Food in Wales, as in all countries, reflects the changing culture of a nation over time. Traditional Welsh fare is largely attributed simply to the historical vestige of everyday eating and reflects the ability of the location to provide food contingent upon climate and the fertility of the land or sea. So Wales' traditional dishes are clearly rooted in the past but have inevitably changed as technology and society have advanced. For example, Pressdee (1995: 9) links the culinary delights of Wales to its historical and geographical past:

> We begin our tour (of Welsh Coastal cookery) in the Wye Valley at Tintern, renowned as far back as 1188 when Geraldus Cambrensis wrote of the great winter salmon of the River Wye. The monks of Tintern Abbey planted vines here, and in recent decades new vineyards have developed . . . . Wordsworth's sylvan Wye has some fine old mature woodlands that abound in wild mushrooms through the warmer winter months.

Traditional Welsh food tends to be geographically localized. Penclawdd on North Gower is famous for its cockles (*Cerastoderma edule*), where they have been harvested for centuries (Farrington 2000: 4). Laverbread is another classic Welsh food made from seaweed (*lawr* in Welsh) found on rocks between the high and low water marks. These classic Welsh foods are geographically located at Swansea, where the local market has stalls dedicated solely to these so-called gastronomic delights. As if to emphasize the importance of this image to Swansea, the City holds a Cockle Festival every October (CCS 2000: 1), sponsored by the 'Taste of Wales' initiative. To some the West of Wales could be considered to be 'the agricultural heartland of Wales, a landscape of lush dairy pasture slashed by lazily meandering rivers flowing down to a coastline that produces some of Britain's best fish and shellfish' (Farrington 2000: 23).

Pressdee also suggests that the physiognomy of Wales has helped to preserve and enhance the diversity of traditional Welsh food. He notes:

> The topography of Wales and its coastline breaks areas into small patches. Most farms are tiny, and numerous small villages straddle the river mouths. Many areas were virtually self-sufficient until the last few centuries and hence provided everything from dairy milk and bread to bacon, lamb and beef, and vegetables from the land
>
> (Pressdee 1995: 9)

The Industrial Revolution also provided a new influence in Welsh cuisine. As Farrington notes:

> Traditional working class Welsh food is simple, filling and hearty, harking back to an age when meat was a rare treat for the common man. Welsh workers looked for their protein elsewhere in laverbread and dairy produce – cheese was a popular meat substitute in many dishes. It is not surprising then that you have such dishes as Glamorgan Sausages which have no meat and may have been one of the first vegetarian sausages.
>
> (Farrington 2000: 4).

The industrialization of the South Wales Valleys offered a plethora of jobs in mining. It attracted immigrants to the Valleys who had a subsequent impact upon traditional Welsh cuisine. Of particular importance were Italian immigrants and even today Italian names are common in South Wales. Indeed such names have become synonymous with traditional Fish and Chips and Ice Cream. Farrington (2000: 9) notes: 'From the end of the 19th Century there was mass immigration of the Italians into South Wales, lured by booming coal and steel industries. Even today, the majority of the Valleys communities have their own Italian café.'

The historical legacy of an evolving Welsh culture has thus resulted in classic dishes and recipes drawn from different locations and traditions throughout Wales. This legacy is now being developed as a basic resource for tourism development and marketing.

The 'Taste of Wales': new strategies and market approaches

The Wales Tourist Board considers the distinctive appeal of the country to be based on a range of resources that include: natural landscape, flora and fauna, built heritage, small-scale settlements, arts and cultural attractions, cultural events, local private businesses and distinctive local cultural traditions, which include food and local cuisine (WTB 2000). The development of tourism in Wales is, therefore, inextricably linked to the general development of these resources, especially as 'cultural resources' form an integral 'back-drop' and 'motor' for the general development of tourism throughout Wales (WTB 2000; ONS 1999; ETB 1999).

Food tourism: the 'Taste of Wales' initiative

One notable concept that has tried to utilize such resources has been the 'Taste of Wales' Initiative which has aimed at promoting food and food products linked to the hospitality industry throughout Wales.

The concept of the 'Taste of Wales' is difficult to track down in terms of its origins. References were made to it as far back as the 1970s and it seems to have long been identified with the Wales Tourist Board (WTB). However, the

Figure 7.1 Taste of Wales logo

Figure 7.2 Initiative re-launched: co-ordination between Welsh Development Agency (WDA) and the Wales Tourist Board (WTB)

significance and relevance to the tourism product appears to be somewhat ambiguous and woolly in terms of aims and objectives. Real impetus was given to the initiative in 1991 when it was relocated to Welsh Food Promotions (WFP) which were closely connected to the Development Board for Rural Wales (DBRW).

During the early 1990s interest in Welsh food was increased due to media coverage, such as BBC food programmes presented by well-known culinary writers, Gilli Davies and Colin Pressdee. Gilli Davies went on to produce a listing of recommended gastronomic outlets. The 'Taste of Wales' continued under the umbrella of 'Welsh Food Promotions – WFP' until July 1998 when this organization folded due to financial problems. Under WFP Welsh food had a brand image but has little validity due to the lack of an accreditation scheme emanating from the hospitality sector. Its main aim was to promote Welsh food and its production.

In 1998 the Welsh Development Agency took centre stage with the 'Taste of Wales' initiative in partnership with the Wales Tourist Board and Wales' regional tourism companies. 'Taste of Wales' was re-launched in May 1999 under the control of the Welsh Development Agency (WDA), contained within the newly formed 'Food Directorate' (WDAFD), an initiative which is also financially assisted by the European Union. The WDA's remit is to encourage and develop employment in Wales in whatever form is beneficial to the Welsh economy.

The new 'Taste of Wales' initiative has a mission to promote 'standards of excellence in the preparation, presentation and sale of Welsh produce' with a supporting aim 'in surroundings which enhance the reputation of Welsh catering' (WDA 2000a: 3). In addition to production and promotion there is also a link towards quality and hospitality. The WDA notes that the 'Taste of Wales' is 'the sign of the highest quality Welsh food and the warmest of Welsh welcomes' (WDA 2000a: 3).

The launch of the new initiative was accompanied with an accreditation element to ensure that standards and aims were being met. The validating authority is TQS (Tourism Quality Services) which is a privatized company of the WTB. This operates the accreditation of accommodation under the Welcome Host Scheme. Products promoted within the initiative are clearly identified within the categories of:

- Alcoholic Beverages – e.g. Buckley's Bitter and Brains SA beer, as well as a new whisky distilled near Merthyr Tydfil.

- Baked products – e.g. speciality breads.
- Welsh Dairy – farmhouse butters, Cheddar cheeses of Caerphilly, organic yoghurts.
- Fish and seafood – mussels from Bangor, Penclawdd cockles, Laverbread in Swansea.
- Fruit and vegetables.
- Meat and meat products – e.g. Welsh Black beef and Welsh Lamb.
- Non-alcoholic beverages – Welsh teas such as Glengettie and Welsh Brew.
- Poultry and game – Brecon farmed venison and food of the bards such as roast goose and pheasant.
- Preserves and sauces – traditional pickles and eclectic chutneys and Welsh honey.

(WDA 2000a: 4–7)

The number of establishments which have been accredited stands at some 370 out of a possible 8,000 and is rising by approximately thirty each month (WDA 2000b: 3) encompassing 'small guest houses, farmhouse accommodation suppliers, restaurants, country houses and hotels' (WDA 2000c: 1). In order to qualify and become an accredited member there are a number of criteria that have to be met:

- Skilful use of the best Welsh produce with acknowledgement of the sources included on the menu.
- Commitment to high standards of welcome, hospitality, ambience, cleanliness and service.
- Demonstration of factors which enhance the reputation of Welsh hospitality.

(WDA 2000c: 1)

The inspections occur annually and visits can be made at any time through the year. The current cost of membership is £58.75 (€92) and the benefits are:

- a FREE independent accreditation inspection visit;
- entry into the annual 'Taste of Wales' Good Food Map;
- inclusion in the 'Taste of Wales' website;
- scheme promotion in the Wales Tourist board and Welsh Development Agency publications;
- scheme public relations support;
- use of the 'Taste of Wales' logo;
- dated 'Taste of Wales' certificate and decal;
- new product briefing and trends information;
- copy of the 'Taste of Wales' Food and Drink Producers' Directory.

(WDA 2000c: 1)

In essence the 'Taste of Wales' 'initiative provides a universal standard for everyone to aspire to . . . the logo should become a kitemark for the hospitality industry in Wales' (Scott 2000: 17). This statement sets a standard and provides both a challenging and interesting benchmark from which to evaluate the merits of such an initiative.

Food tourism: national tourism strategies

Strategic development and planning for tourism in Wales has, over the last decade, been guided by the Wales Tourist Board Strategic Plan (*Tourism 2000: A Strategy for Wales*) which was published in 1994. The mission statement of the plan said that: 'The Wales Tourist Board seeks to develop tourism in ways which will yield the optimum economic and social benefit to the people of Wales' (WTB 1994: 2). In this context the key objectives of the plan were threefold:

- To offer high standards of product quality and service.
- To sustain and promote the culture of Wales and the Welsh language.
- To safeguard and enhance the natural and built environment of Wales.

Within the plan's framework, a series of initiatives were formulated to implement these key objectives. In terms of cultural attractions, key initiatives were aimed at improving environmental sustainability, involving local communities in tourism projects, encouraging coastal and resort regeneration, creating a marketing strategy for the regeneration of historic and market towns, developing a country holiday programme and facilitating innovative niche product development such as the 'Taste of Wales' (WTB 1994).

In autumn 2000 the Wales Tourist Board published its new updated strategy. Titled *Achieving Our Potential, A Tourism Strategy for Wales* the new strategy aims to build on the achievements and lessons from Strategy 2000 but largely repeats the aims of sustaining the economic, social, cultural and environmental well-being of Wales through effective sustainable development linked to co-ordination and collaboration at all levels of the tourism industry. The new strategy contains four key objectives:

Objective 1: To market Wales more effectively as an attractive all year round tourism destination.

Objective 2: To exceed the expectations of visitors to Wales by providing high standards and ensuring investment.

Objective 3: To improve professionalism and innovation by raising the profile of the industry and by enhancing skills, training and motivation within the industry.

Objective 4: To embrace a sustainable approach to tourism development which benefits society, involves local communities and enhances Wales' unique environmental and cultural assets.

(WTB 2000)

These general objectives all provide opportunities to introduce concepts of food tourism. Objective 4 makes efforts to develop food tourism more explicitly. Under the heading 'Enhancing community benefits of tourism' policy statements make reference specifically to encouraging tourism businesses to locally source a greater proportion of goods and services, including local food produce from local suppliers, to encourage local employment and deliver a distinctive Welsh experience for the visitor. Specific references are also made to the 'Taste of Wales' initiative in implementing the strategy, clearly emphasizing the importance of food within strategic policy objectives (WTB 2000).

The establishment of the Welsh Development Agency Food Directorate (WDAFD) has also added a new dimension to the way policy is directed and co-ordinated for food product development. The remit of the new unit is to raise the profile of Welsh food and drink products within the UK and overseas. The establishment of such a unit is a clear departure from traditional roles and responsibilities that have been generally associated with the Wales Tourist Board and 'Taste of Wales'. It is a situation, however, which begins to raise questions on the role of institutional structures and the effectiveness of policy co-ordination.

The unit is still in its infancy and outcomes are yet to be established, but there are clear implications for food tourism development in Wales. Initial soundings suggest that the promotion of food and quality food products are now being recognized at national government levels as an important economic and cultural resource asset for Wales. On this note the WDAFD has already commissioned London based branding and marketing consultants (Spring Point) to undertake a new branding exercise for food products which was due for completion in 2001. Preliminary findings from Spring Point's initial survey work suggest that there is considerable scope to improve the current approach to food tourism development, branding and promotion. In this respect the consultants highlight poor co-ordination, limited strategic vision, complacency and policy malaise (Spring Point 2000).

Despite these new developments, the relationship between the Wales Tourist Board, the Welsh Development Agency, the new food directorate and the 'Taste of Wales' remains unclear, but this may become more obvious once Spring Point have presented the outcomes of their research. Food and food tourism products are therefore on Wales' political agenda notwithstanding the weak channels of communication and poor co-ordination.

Challenges for food tourism in Wales

Measurable benefits

The results of the qualitative interviews suggest that there are clear benefits in promoting new niche markets or brands, such as food tourism. In broader terms, the ability to support and encourage locally produced products is also generally perceived to have positive impacts in supporting a healthy agricultural community. This, in turn, is seen to have significant benefits in supporting traditional farming practices and 'Welsh agricultural landscapes' which also generate images that can market and brand the country as a whole. Such images are important in promoting the overall 'Welsh character' of Wales.

The promotion of locally produced quality food products can also engage the tourist in experiences that rekindle gastronomic pleasures and tastes lost or diluted through intensive production, the demise of seasonal products and the lack of food with perceived 'authentic' or 'old fashioned' tastes. These are seen as 'products' that Wales can certainly 'exploit' within the food market place. Hence the use of food products to promote tourist destinations is largely seen in a positive light although hard evidence of tangible benefits from implementing such policy initiatives is scarce. Without such evidence both the take-up and support for such initiatives remains weak and results in continued inertia among stakeholder groups.

Policy malaise

It is interesting to note that a recent issue of *The Grocer* (a prominent food industry magazine) is entitled 'Wales: A Food Revival' and the foreword, by the former Agricultural Secretary for the Welsh Assembly, Christine Gwyther, opens by stating: 'The food industry is vitally important for Welsh agriculture and the Welsh economy generally' (Scott 2000: 3).

Emphasis is placed upon the idea of revival, implying that food has not been successful for some years. It is also suggested that devolution may be propitious for the industry especially with the allocation of EU Objective 1 funding, providing the possibility of new money for the Welsh economy. Scott states: 'With much of Wales now following Ireland in winning Objective 1 funding from the European Union, the industry is set to take even bigger strides forward' (Scott 2000: 5). It seems that food may well be the new branding for Wales as 'More than rugby or religion, food is coming home to Wales' (Scott 2000: 4). A strategic policy instrument in this process seems to be the Agri-Food Partnership, co-ordinated by the WDA. Food is clearly an important instrument in supporting employment and improving the Welsh economy. However, the policy linkages to tourism still remain implicit rather than explicit and policy directives remain ambiguous, which leaves the stakeholders within each sector of both the agricultural and tourism industries in a state of continued malaise. Again co-ordination problems appear to be a major hindrance to implementation of food tourism initiatives. Poor communication, inadequate distribution of information and carelessly targeted advertising campaigns have also been major criticisms. These failings have resulted in low awareness and take-up of the 'Taste of Wales' campaign often with muddled implementation which inevitably has had an impact on maintaining quality food products and outlets.

Branding and Welsh identity

It is perhaps a little too simplistic to particularly blame the lack of co-ordination for poor and muddled 'take-up' of food tourism products. As with other associated tourism marketing challenges there remains an image problem, in that Wales continues to have an indistinct image in UK markets when compared to its natural tourism competitors in Scotland and Ireland. The images associated with Wales tend to be based on 'escape' and 'rural space' rather than distinct elements of culture. As a result, food does not feature as a key association with Wales among UK tourists (Pritchard and Morgan 2001). In contrast, Scotland has established food associations with whisky, haggis, shortbread and salmon, and Ireland is associated with whiskey, Guinness and dairy products.

In addition to these general identity problems signals from the quality end of the tourism hospitality sectors also suggest that there is a need to take a cautious line when co-ordinating food initiatives such as the 'Taste of Wales' campaign. Many establishments at the quality end of the market tend to deride and even resent such initiatives as being too prescriptive in drawing up guidelines for traditional Welsh cuisine or Welsh recipes. These can stifle local innovation and creativity and detract from promoting traditional Welsh cuisine 'with a modern edge' or 'contemporary flavour'. This was particularly an issue with some local restaurateurs, who ridiculed the imposition of 'off the shelf' menus that are supposed to reflect typical Welsh cuisine.

There have also been concerns with general food marketing campaigns including the 'Taste of Wales'. The broad-based approach to marketing food products arguably results in over-grandiose schemes that cost considerable amounts of money but ultimately have little impact. There has also has been a concern that a too broadly based marketing campaign can dilute branding for quality food. Suppliers fear that if too many outlets are accredited then this would diminish the aura of high quality and detract from the development of specialized niche markets.

Clearly a paradox emerges between the differing needs of stakeholder groups. The high volume approaches of mass-market food distributors such as Tesco and Sainsbury's may well clash in the long term with the interest of smaller suppliers in maintaining exclusivity.

The local supply chain networks

Sourcing locally has become a critical issue in maintaining quality food tourism products. The relationship between food producers and the hospitality industry remains largely informal, often poorly structured and ill defined. As a result the hospitality industry, especially at the top end of the market, tends to establish locally based networks which rely on personal contacts to acquire and sustain the supply of quality food products. However, these arrangements can be time-consuming, are often unreliable and are subject to last-minute changes or cancellation. This can ultimately impact upon the supply of quality food products.

The fragmented nature of the Welsh hospitality industry, which is based upon small private enterprises, also tends to exacerbate this situation, in that the 'buying power' of such enterprises is often limited and cannot sustain the viable production of locally sourced food products. The lack of quality local food wholesale markets in this context adds to this often complex issue. Even so, the popularity of locally sourced and quality food products among an increasingly discerning public has raised the profile and demand for such products. Supermarket chains have cashed in on these trends by sourcing food from local outlets and independent producers to meet increasing customer demands for indigenous food products. As supermarkets tend to buy in bulk, this has often resulted in upsetting the fragile relationship between local producer networks and the hospitality industry, leading to problems of supply and availability of locally grown food products. Obviously this has had important implications for the wider recognition and development of food tourism products. Within this context the development of effective support infrastructures and the establishment of reliable local network supply chains for both food producers and the hospitality industry is clearly an area for future concern.

Inclusivity or exclusivity

The major supermarket chains in Wales have also embarked upon the sale of local produce. Hence it is not surprising that they see an opportunity in branding some of their products both as local and as representing Wales. Tesco now has a diverse range of local products at its 45 Welsh branches. It has also developed a 'Welsh Office' which is similar to the national structure of its Scottish and Irish Offices, which offer a product range based upon local produce. The main rationale seems to have been adding value to local produce thus benefiting the local community through increased food production and job creation. For example, Bran Bread of Newport has increased its supplies to Tesco from zero to one and a half million loaves of bread within 18 months, which has provided employment for 23 people. The aim is to add new ranges of products, not simply to duplicate products already on sale. In order to increase this product range Tesco has developed the brand, with its own logo 'Quality Welsh product' or in Welsh *Cynnyrch Cymreig O Safon*.

Tesco has also recognized an opportunity to increase sales in Wales by expanding novelty tourism products. Over the last year the sales for the Welsh tourism line have risen from £50,000 to £300,000 (€78,000 to €470,000). The types of products found within this range are such items as confectionery, biscuits, love spoons, rock honey and bottled water, which are considered to be 'impulse buy' products rather than everyday necessities.

Further opportunities have also been identified through its cafes becoming members of the 'Taste of Wales' initiative. They are currently applying for accreditation. Tesco sees the 'Taste of Wales' as a great opportunity, which needs to have its importance fully recognized by the Welsh Assembly and hence possibly closer co-ordination and development. Sainsbury's Supermarkets has also recently embarked upon a marketing campaign to promote Welsh food produce which again reflects growing interest in local quality food products.

These trends however, raise questions regarding the exclusivity and focus of the 'Taste of Wales'. Critical to these debates is the question of whether the initiative should be associated with such national retailers or supermarket chains especially where such a broad association may result in dilution, loss of exclusivity or

Figure 7.3 Sainsbury's campaign to promote local Welsh produce

uniqueness. The key question arises of whether the initiative should be offered to multinational companies such as McDonald's and Burger King if their menus reflected, to some extent, a Welsh cultural content.

Food for future thought

There are clearly challenges concerning the development of food tourism in Wales. Problems remain with branding and identity, leadership and co-ordination and it is these issues that need to be considered further if future policy choices for food tourism in Wales are to be effective.

Branding and identity

Producing recognizable food products that are able to be effectively marketed and branded, and which can clearly demonstrate Welsh 'identity' and 'character' presents some formidable challenges. Clearly it is important to broaden the market appeal of Welsh food culture and extend its attractiveness to the Welsh food industry and beyond. However, care must be taken not to alienate the quality end of the hospitality industry or to dilute the impact of local food promotion through initiatives that may target the wider food industry. Tensions have emerged between the quality restaurateurs and supermarket chains because the former aspire to exclusivity and the latter want inclusivity. This indicates the need to target specific stakeholder groups within the food and tourism industry with specific initiatives which meet their individual needs. The ability to co-ordinate such a programme through effective institutional structures is a fundamental challenge and one that remains unresolved.

The interview respondents also suggested that because the present initiative appears to be driven by producers, full consideration has not been given to the wider tourism product. In order to generate improved economic benefits food products need to be more widely recognized and exported. However, little is known about the needs of tourists in terms of food tourism products. In addition Wales' share of the international tourism is only 800,000 visitors (UKTS 1999) which means that the export of Welsh food products to this market would inevitably be limited.

Leadership and co-ordination

Charting the relationships between the key 'stakeholders' is particularly critical, especially those between the food producers, the hospitality industry and the end users or tourists. Creating effective strategic leadership also requires the establishment of clear roles and responsibilities. This would appear to be particularly important in order to develop sustainable new food product strategies. Positive signs include the decision by Tesco to invest in Welsh food products, but the Tesco initiative also operates largely outside the WDA/WTB 'Taste of Wales' framework, underlining the lack of institutional co-ordination or leadership.

Current initiatives also appear to have a bias towards the food producers within tourism food markets. Although the WTB openly supports the 'Taste of Wales' initiative its exact role within the broader strategy of the WTB still remains somewhat unclear. For example, the strategic objectives of the WDA are not fully reflected in WTB initiatives.

Conclusions

The tensions between the needs of tourists, food producers and the tourist industry identified by Richards (Chapter 1) and Hjalager (Chapter 2) are clearly reflected in attempts to develop food tourism in Wales.

From a marketing perspective, there is a requirement to understand the needs of the tourist with regard to food products. Without this information, it will be difficult to identify potential growth areas for Welsh food products among tourists. In this respect the 'Taste of Wales' initiative seems well placed, but in order to realise its full potential, the scheme needs to pay more attention to gastronomic trends and the needs of individual stakeholders in the Welsh food industry.

The evidence from our interviews suggest that despite industry support for promoting food as part of a quality tourism experience, many of the initiatives operate independently from one another in an institutional vacuum. It is a scenario that can only lead to future tensions between the stakeholder groups, given their increasingly different aspirations for quality assurance.

In terms of Hjalager's typology of gastronomic tourism value added, Wales has not advanced much beyond the first and second order phases. The basic reason for this is the lack of organized structures to encourage commodification, quality standards and certification. However, despite this rather disappointing scenario the picture is not altogether negative. There is a growing patchwork of activities and initiatives that would appear to fit more comfortably in Hjalager's third order phase which identifies 'value added' tourism experiences linked to the development of gastronomy, festivals, culinary attractions, food centres and specialist holidays associated with food. It is a position that does, however, require a greater institutional effort and consolidation in order to move toward food as a comprehensive tourism experience, as envisaged in Hjalager's fourth order of value added development, 'the diagonal'.

In order to achieve this, perhaps Wales needs to pay more attention to Carney's (1994) call for a 'culinary expert' to be present at the high table of tourism planning. This will require the establishment of stronger institutional structures to facilitate and promote Welsh gastronomy and tackling some of the broader or more strategic issues discussed in the earlier chapters of this book.

References

Banks, J. and Bristow, G. (1999) 'Developing quality in agro-food supply chains: a Welsh perspective', *International Planning Studies*, 4(3): 317–331.

Carney, D. (1994) 'The food of North East Scotland', in McKean *et al.* (eds) *Cultural*

Sustenance: Making a Meal of our Heritage, The Robert Gordon University: Donhead, pp. 403–413.

CADW (Welsh Historic Monuments) (1996) *Annual Report and Accounts 1995–6*, Cardiff: CADW.

City and County of Swansea (CCS) (2000) *A Taste of Swansea: A selection of recipes from the 10th Swansea market cockle festival*, Swansea: CCS.

Convenant, M. (1991) 'The flavours of success', *Espaces*, 111: 18–20.

Defort, P. (1987) 'Tourism and gastronomy', *Revue de Tourisme*, 3: 7–8.

Development Board for Rural Wales (DBRW) (1994) *Study of Farm Tourism in Wales*, Newtown: DBRW.

English Tourist Board (ETB) (1999) UK Tourism Statistics, HMSO: London.

Farrington, S. (2000) 'Main Course 2000, Your guide to eating out in Wales', *Western Mail*, Cardiff.

Gwyther, C. (2000) 'Wales: A Food Revival – An Advertorial Supplement', *The Grocer*, 26 Feb.

Hudman, L.E. (1986) 'The travellers' perception of the role of food and eating in the tourist industry', in *The Impact of Catering and Cuisine upon Tourism, proceedings of 36th AIEST Congress*, 31 Aug–6 Sept, Montreux: AIEST.

Kaspar, C. (1986) 'The impact of catering and cuisine on tourism', *Publications de l'AIEST*, 27, Montreux: AIEST,13–16.

Mallon, P. (1995) 'Gastronomy and tourism a difficult but necessary union', *Espaces*, 135: 21–23.

Office for National Statistics (ONS) (1996) *International Passenger Survey (IPS) 1996* London: ONS, HMSO.

Polacek, M. (1986) 'Eating habits of the Czechoslovak population and gastronomy as a tourist motivation', *Revue de Tourisme*, 41(4): 22–25.

Pressdee, C. (1995) *Welsh Coastal Cookery*, London: BBC Books.

Pritchard, A. and Morgan, N.J. (2001) 'Culture, identity and tourism representation: marketing Cymru or Wales?', *Tourism Management* 22: 167–179.

Reynolds, P.C. (1993) 'Food and tourism: towards an understanding of sustainable culture', *Journal of Sustainable Tourism*, 1(1): 48–54.

Reynolds, P. *et al.* (1994) 'Culinary heritage in the face of tourism', *Progress in Tourism*, 6, Chichester: Wiley, 189–194.

Riddell, M. (2001) 'Fatal tourist attraction', *The Observer*, 19 August, 22.

Spring Point (2000) 'Stage one feedback for the WDA Food Directorate branding project', 12 June, London: Spring Point Branding Consultants (unpublished).

Tesco (2000) *A Toast to Wales Ichyd Da!* August, Cardiff: South Wales Publications Ltd.

Welsh Development Agency (WDA) (2000a) *Dining out in Wales, a guide to Taste of Wales Members*, Cardiff : WDA.

—— (2000b) *Taste of Wales, activities since launch*, May, Cardiff: WDA.

—— (2000c) *Taste of Wales, Membership form, self assessment questionnaire and Inspector dining voucher*, Cardiff: WDA.

—— (2000d) *Food for Thought, giving the world a Taste of Wales*, Cardiff: WDA.

Wales Rural Forum (1998a) *Rural Tourism in Wales: Towards Sustainability Draft Report*, Carmarthen: WRF.

—— (1998b) *Rural Services and Facilities Draft Report*, Carmarthen: WRF.

Wales Tourist Board (WTB) (1994) *Tourism 2000: A Strategy for Wales*, Cardiff: WTB.

—— (1995) *White Paper for Rural Wales: WTB Submission Document* WTB, Cardiff: WTB.

—— (1997a) *Tourism in Wales 1996*, Cardiff: WTB.

—— (1997b) *Analysis of the Domestic (UK) Visitors to Wales*, Cardiff: WTB.

—— (1998a) *Survey of Tourism Trends in Wales*, Cardiff: WTB.

—— (1998b) *Visits to Tourist Attractions 1997*, Cardiff: WTB.

—— (2000) *Achieving our Potential*, Cardiff: WTB.

Wales Tourist Board/Scottish Tourism Board/English Tourist Board (1996) *UK Tourism Survey*, London: WTB/STB/ETB HMSO.

8 Sustainable gastronomy as a tourist product

Rosario Scarpato

Introduction

This chapter presents the initial results of a collective case study involving gastronomic events planned to exploit gastronomy as a tourist product. Developed with the innovative conceptual framework of trans-disciplinary gastronomy studies, the work is divided in two parts. The first part describes the three cases analysed, which are:

- The *Melbourne Food and Wine Festival* in Australia.
- The *New Asia Cuisine* in Singapore.
- The *Bologna 2000 Slow Food Award* in Italy.

The second part introduces the concept of sustainable development with regard to tourism and gastronomy. A comparative analysis of sustainable gastronomy issues within the three cases follows. The conclusions contain indications of some actions to be taken towards the gastronomic sustainability of food and wine tourism.

THREE GASTRONOMIC TOURIST PRODUCTS

The cases considered are relevant examples of gastronomy exploited for tourist purposes and can be defined as gastronomic tourist products (GTPs). However, they are not traditional 'bricks and mortar' gastronomic poles of attraction, like restaurants, wineries and food outlets in general. They represent instead a new breed of gastro-attractions within established tourist destinations: they enhance the local tourism on offer not only by promoting the local gastronomic culture but also by building on diversity, multi-ethnicity, international connections and global exposure.

The Melbourne Food and Wine Festival

Born as a brainchild of Peter Clemenger, the owner of a successful Australian advertising agency, the Melbourne Food and Wine Festival (MFWF) was initiated in 1993. Two years earlier, Melbourne had lost the bid for the Olympics that went to Atlanta, and Clemenger, a member of the Committee for the Olympic Bid, 'wondered how he could turn the loss into a gain' (MFWF 2001). Inspired by the positive feedback of visiting International Olympic Committee officials on Melbourne's food, wine and restaurants, he envisaged that the city needed a Food and Wine Festival promoting it as a prime gastronomic tourist destination.

The first edition of the MFWF scheduled only fourteen events. It had limited support from Tourism Victoria, the State promotional board. The 2001 edition programme listed 93 events (MFWF 2001a). The MFWF 'has gained the support and respect of the food and hospitality industry, sponsors, the media and the 350,000 people who attend the near month-long event each March/April' (MFWF 2001b). It has been estimated that the MFWF generates between A$8 and A$10 million (€4.55 and €5.7 million) into the Victorian economy, through food and wine sales, travel, accommodation, consumer items and employment (Johnson 2001). The MFWF has been declared a *Tourist Hallmark* event, like the *Formula One Grand Prix* and *The Tennis Australian Open*.[1]

The major aim of the MFWF is 'to promote quality produce, talent and life-style of this city and State and to reinforce Melbourne as the pre-eminent culinary city of Australia'. After initially targeting only Melbournians, the MFWF man-agement now 'intends to grow the event to appeal to a broader audience, to include increased national and international visitors' (MFWF 2001b).

The MFWF stages events in collaboration with city and country restaurants, special food-shops, fresh markets, wineries and often also artistic institutions, such as regional galleries. The programme includes thematic dinners, lunches and breakfast, cooking Master classes conducted by local and overseas guests, semi-nars and workshops. The MFWF operates on a not-for-profit basis, with substan-tial financial funding from public institutions and the support from private sponsors.[2]

Singapore's New Asia Cuisine

The visitor to Singapore looking for directions for his/her dinner may find useful information in the Singapore Tourism Board's Official Guide to the city. The guide lists an array of cuisines from which the visitor can pick his/her favourite. All the traditional cuisines belonging to the various ethnic communities forming the Singaporean society are included; from the Chinese to the Indian, from the peculiar Peranakan[3] to the Arab. Then it mentions a *New Asia-Singapore Cuisine*, with the following definition:

> The latest entrant to our food paradise is New Asia-Singapore cuisine. An attempt to marry the best of both Asian and Western, New Asia-Singapore

cuisine is for more adventurous palates. Let your adventures begin in Doc Cheng's at the Raffles Hotel and Club Chinois at Orchard Parade Hotel.

(Singapore 2001: 82)

New Asia Cuisine (NAC) is an example of how new cuisines develop. Neither peasants nor fishermen generate them any longer, as happened in the past. On the contrary, as in NAC's case, they stem from the marketing needs of both the hospitality industry and the agencies promoting tourist destinations, such as the Singapore Tourism Board (STB).

The first public discussions on the concept of NAC happened at the end of 1995. However, the birth of this cuisine

took place many years ago when chefs (professionals and home cooks alike) ventured into the realm of combining flavours and techniques, coupled with the right ingredients, into a different entity that had one important objective in mind: variety, the so-called spice of life. Human beings cannot happily function without a variety of any number of things, especially when it comes to their dietary intake.

(Knipp 1998)

The new cuisine was described as 'the ability to combine the best of Oriental styles of ingredients, cooking processes, flavours and, yes, a good amount of Western presentation techniques, which is universally the standard of delivering the food to one's place of intake' (Knipp 1998). Of course, fresh regional ingredients available in Singapore too, imparted some degree of distinctive flavour to NAC, which received the main publicity boost from a magazine carrying the same name, the publisher of which is himself a chef.[4]

The name NAC was then made official in 1996 'at a meeting in St. Moritz which was attended by Singapore Tourist Promotion Board chief executive officer Dr Tan Chin Nam' (Mosley 1996). At that time, the STB began to promote Singapore as New Asia, a brand name still used today to market the city-state. Not only does NAC reinforce the image of Singapore as a food and wine destination, but in many ways it reflects the New Asia spirit: 'a truly inspiring city where East meets West, Asian heritage blends with modernity and sophistication happily co-exists with nature'.

The 1997 Singapore Food Festival and the World Gourmet Summit – both organized by the STB – were specifically designed to launch NAC (Mosley 1997). By doing this, the STB set a historical precedent: it is likely in the near future that any real or fictitious cuisine *distinctiveness* will also depend on the amount of money injected into its promotions by Tourism Promotion Bodies. At that stage, however, no one had defined NAC convincingly, and the magazine *New Asia Cuisine* hosted a forum with the intention of 'providing the backbone to a trend which is here to stay and without stifling its creativity or destroying the ambitiousness of chefs' (Mosley 1997).

Since then, NAC has been practised in many restaurants, mainly in five-star hotels and promoted as a tourist attraction of the city.

Bologna 2000 – Slow Food Award

Since its foundation, in 1986, the Italian-based International *Slow Food* Movement took a position in favour of quality food production. The movement has commended the work of farmers, artisans and caterers and encouraged the enterprise of all those who defend wine and food heritage. In order to spotlight and support them the movement instituted an International Award in 1999. Its aim is to reward those anywhere in the world who defend, promote or enhance produce, knowledge or flavour, with public recognition, cash prizes and promotion of their activities.

The ceremony of the first Award was held in October 2000 in Bologna, the capital city of Emila Romagna Region, in Northern Italy. In the same year Bologna was also one of nine European Cities of Culture. An international jury made up of 450 journalists and food experts, described as the *General Assembly of the United Nations of Gastronomy*, were invited to vote for 'the most distinguished culinary professionals of the world'. In reality the Award Committee, dismissing all the culinary nominations received, short-listed thirteen producers of and researchers on ingredients for a sustainable gastronomy (Slow Food Award 2000). The composition of the jury, formed prevalently by media representatives from eighty-two nations, gave global visibility not only to the Award but also to the host city and, of course, to the Slow Food Movement.

Bologna and the Emilia Romagna Region have always been renowned for their gastronomic culture. This fact was particularly stressed during the Award with speakers noting that it was not by chance that 'the theme of the good table has been included in the celebration of Bologna capital of the European Culture' (Salizzoni 2000). By hosting the Slow Food Award with its global profile, Bologna reinforced its image as a prime gastronomic tourist destination. Representatives of the public institutions supporting the award insisted on the city's gastronomic wealth. The Mayor wrote that 'Bologna is able to propose exceptionally tasty and also healthy food products' (Guazzaloca 2000), whilst the Chairman of the Regional government said that:

> Our own products can speak eloquently for themselves, and for a region intimately linked to the culture of food and its underlying territory. It is not merely a question of love of tradition. It is our way of keeping pace with economic processes.
>
> (Errani 2000)

At the same time, many of the Award's finalists and their activities enjoyed a media spotlight that they never could possibly have in their home countries.

What the GTPs have in common

The three GTPs are significant and complex examples of gastronomy as a *cultural source* of tourism. No longer can gastronomy be considered a *grey zone* of cultural tourism as in the past (Scarpato Chapter 4, this volume). The GTPs also represent opportunities for *new tourism*, which has been described as a 'large scale packaging of non-standardized leisure services at competitive prices to suit the demands of tourists as well as the economic and socio-environmental needs of destination' (Poon 1993: 85). They are also driving forces for the tourism industry revival in their areas. Singapore New Asia Cuisine, for instance, has contributed to a rejuvenation of cuisine in a number of five-star restaurants in the city, as the *Doc Cheng* Restaurant in the Raffles Hotel.

Furthermore, these GTPs generate some typical cultural tourism benefits for their destinations. The MFWF, for example, adds value to a quality tourist experience of the city. It also fits into contemporary pattern of consumption tourism, by promoting experiences yielding a high satisfaction like the wine and food excursions to the rural areas of Victoria.

With their characteristics of mixed codes, even incoherence, and syncretism, these GTPs are by-products of globalized capitalism with its intense streams of culture, products, people and identities. They also represent the overlapping configurations of global and local within gastronomy. Thus, the MFWF 2000 heavily promoted local and diverse produce but at the same time accepted support from multinational manufacturers of industrial food such as Kellogg's, Nescafé and Schweppes. New Asia Cuisine prospered on the syncretism of its eclectic chefs, whilst the Slow Food Award presented on the same stage Bologna's sophisticated gastronomic production and the humble cheese made from camel's milk in Mauritania.

These GTPs play a role very similar to that of mass media, of which they attract the relevant attention. This makes their audience many times bigger than the number of people physically consuming the products. The MFWF has among its sponsors twelve newspapers, magazine, radio and TV stations, NAC is supported by a magazine carrying the same name and by Singapore Tourism Board advertising campaigns, and the Slow Food Award is based on a jury of hundreds of international journalists. For this reason, they have significant large-scale educational potential. In fact, they play a leading gastronomic role. By including or excluding events, people and establishments within their agendas/programmes, they become gastronomy gatekeepers and taste-makers. On a different scale, their role is similar to that of food reviewers, in respect to the market of restaurants, and has the same political and commercial consequences (Fine 1996:154; Scarpato and Daniele 2000).

Methods

This is a collective instrumental case study conducted within a subjectivist, non-positivist perspective and it has a qualitative approach. The researcher is aware of his influence on the issues investigated. The sample chosen is illustrative, although not definitive, since there are no rules for sample size in quality inquiry (Patton 1980). To an extent, the sample is also homogeneous as illustrated in the previous section. Traditional ethnographic techniques have been used to collect data and in particular:

(a) Documentary primary resources: research journal, travel notes, correspondence, unpublished records of an interview with Ms Sylvia Johnson, Director of the Melbourne Food and Wine Festival;
(b) Content analysis – in particular of official programmes of the cases analysed, public speeches, official websites and magazine articles;
(c) Observation and participant observation; the researcher has been a member of the Slow Food Award Jury in Bologna; he has visited and eaten in various New Asia Cuisine's Restaurant in Singapore, including: Doc Cheng's (Raffles Hotel), Fig Leaf (Central Mall, Magazine Road), Jiang-Nan Chun (Four Seasons Hotel) and Club Chinois (Orchard Road); he has participated in a number of Melbourne Food and Wine Festival events.

GTPs AND SUSTAINABLE GASTRONOMY

The meanings of sustainability

One of the aims of this paper is to analyse the three GTPs in relation to sustainable gastronomy. In many ways this is a totally new process and consequently it is necessary to include some preliminary considerations on the principle of sustainability. In general terms, the phrase means to maintain, to keep in existence, or conserve and is regarded as a positive concept since it expresses a value embraceable by almost all members of the society. Sustainability was not foreign to traditional societies where, for instance, farming always preserved rather than destroyed the productive capacity of the land.

When applied to development, however, sustainability becomes a concept with both intrinsic ambiguity and controversy. For this reason it has been argued that it 'defies a simple definition' and becomes a *political* concept. Development is considered sustainable when it 'meets our needs without compromising the ability of people in the future to meet their needs' (World Commission on Environment and Development 1987). This assumption began to reshape global development strategies in the 1950s, when it was realized that short-term gains were being made at the expense of future generations. It was, however, not until 1980 that the International Union for the Conservation of Nature and Natural resources drew up the *World Conservation Strategy*. Seven years later, the United Nations released the so-called *Brundtland Report* (World Commission on Environment and Development 1987), which introduced a comprehensive framework of guidelines for sustainability. Thus, any sustainable development must, at least:

- have ecological limits;
- preserve the basic resources;
- allow an equitable access to such resources.

Concepts new at that time were also introduced, such as:

- carrying capacity;
- diversification of species;
- community control;
- broad national/international policies framework and economic viability.

More than a decade after the publication of the Bruntland Report, however, it seems that sustainable development is still a concept lacking a clear definition. Problems arise every time people begin to use the concept in an operational context and, for this reason, many commentators argue that planning has failed to help us to achieve sustainable development.

The debate on sustainable tourism

The debate about the effectiveness of planning and management in achieving tourism sustainability, as that of all economic activities, has been lengthy and very much alive in the last decade. Moving from the mainstream of the Bruntland report guidelines, the debate has highlighted a stimulating variety of theoretical positions and approaches (Bramwell *et al.* 1996; France 1997; Mowforth and Munt 1998; Murphy 1985; Wahab and Pigram 1997; Swarbrooke 1999). Tourism is generally considered sustainable when it includes the following characteristics:

- it recognizes the importance of the host community;
- it adopts good standards for the treatment of staff;
- it maximizes the economic return for the local communities;
- its development happens at a low speed;
- it is environment friendly;
- tourists adopt responsible behaviour (e.g. mental preparation, learning local languages, quiet, repeat visits).

In any case, sustainable tourism is no longer seen as detached from sustainable development and interacts with all the other components of development (Swarbrooke 1999: 353) such as:

- societies and communities;
- environment and natural resources;
- economic systems;
- conservation;
- agriculture.

Gastronomic tourism indeed reflects the sustainability issues of general tourism. At the same time, however, it 'represents a challenging issue for Gastronomy studies' (Scarpato 2000). This new approach implies that gastronomic tourism becomes a research topic of a gastronomy rather than vice versa. In Chapter 4 of this volume it was demonstrated that gastronomy, a word first used in 1801 (Berchoux 1804), is extremely difficult to define. In 1825, the French author Jean-Anthelme Brillat-Savarin (1994) attempted to give a comprehensive definition of gastronomy as 'the reasoned understanding of everything that concerns us insofar as we sustain ourselves', according to translations that preserve the spirit of his vision.

The work of Brillat-Savarin has suffered almost two centuries of positivist oblivion and misinterpretations and only recently has been re-evaluated (Symons 1998; Scarpato 2000 and 2001b). Accordingly, contemporary gastronomy can be defined as 'reflective' eating and cooking as well as food preparation, production and presentation in general, maintaining the association with excellence. Gastronomy studies 'encompasses everything into which food, taken in the widest sense to include everything we eat and drink, enters' (Scarpato 2000: 36). Gastronomy studies is therefore an answer to the urgent need for research evaluating performances, identifying inadequacies, efficiencies and potential improvements in the community's gastronomy cycle. This can be described as the process involving agriculture, food manufacturing, commercialization and consumption, with all the related social, physiological, cultural and political aspects. The outcome of a possible debate on whether eating is fundamentally an argicultural act or that agriculture is only the beginning of any gastronomy (Scarpato 2001a), will not affect the process of the gastronomic cycle, to which food and wine tourism is only a relatively recent addition.

Sustainable gastronomy and tourism

The main aim of trans-disciplinary gastronomy studies (Scarpato 2000: 12) is to work for a sustainable gastronomy incorporating the traditional principles of sustainable development. Sustainable gastronomy implies that communities can evolve socially and economically whilst keeping an eco-nutritional commitment to environmental sustainability and the optimal health of members of the community (Scarpato 2000: 186). In this sense, sustainable gastronomy can be described also as eco-gastronomy and interacts with all the other components of a developing system, as we also have seen above in the case of sustainable tourism. Temporary visitors to a community, like tourists, are to be considered – and should consider themselves – as members of that community.

On a more specific level, sustainable gastronomy is about producing food that is environmentally sensitive, and preparing and eating it so that it nourishes both mind and body.

This assumption has a vast number of implications in both rural and metropolitan contexts. The most relevant are related to:

- the survival of local food production, outlets and fresh markets;
- the viability of home cooking;
- the transmission of culinary knowledge and children's education to taste;
- the right to pleasure and diversity;
- the impact of tourism on gastronomic authenticity and community well-being.

Sustainable gastronomy, however, means to narrow the divide between the elite of foodies and the vast parts of metropolitan communities still living in a state of 'gastro-anomie' (Fishler 1980), increasingly alienated from their food supply (Coveney and Santich 1997). It also means a greater appreciation of how quality of food contributes to individual, species and societal well-being. There is growing evidence that quality of food, which translates into excellence and variety in eating and drinking, is 'conducive to health' (Wahlqvist 1999). Access to quality food is posed to become a political issue as much as an environmental issue.

The impact of tourism on gastronomy sustainability of communities is an issue of 'food security, which today is not only predicated on pestilence, famine and conflict' (Wahlqvist 1999) but pertains, among the other things, to trade, food processing, retailing, human behaviours and food choice, all traditional components of gastronomy. Gastronomy studies therefore comes as a much needed contribution to the evaluation of the options available to the involved industries, such as the tourism one, and to the broader community in respect to future food security.

A critique of tourism views of gastronomic tourism

Gastronomy studies adds a missing perspective to the quest for sustainable tourism. Besides its traditional theoretical weakness (Britton 1991: 451), the tourism studies framework is particularly insufficient when it comes to the analysis of gastronomic tourism, even when it bravely acknowledges it as a part of cultural tourism. Sustainable gastronomic tourism is often liquidated as 'the food and drink which tourists are offered in catering establishments and the extent to which it is local authentically traditional', in contrast to what are 'international and/or trivialized versions of well-known local dishes' (Swarbrooke 1999: 299).

Thus, concepts such as 'authenticity', 'local food' and 'tradition' are uncritically associated with the sustainability of gastronomic tourism. In reality, authenticity cannot be considered as an absolute parameter in gastronomy, and non-local food can be as sustainable as local food, as we will see below in the case of New Global Cuisine. Consequently, it is also questionable to assert that hotels and restaurants offering either 'international menu or parodies of traditional local dishes, rather than authentic local food' (Swarbrooke 1999: 299) are not sustainable. Besides any other consideration, one must ask what kind of methodological tools tourism research has to assess the 'parodies of traditional local food', which, from a gastronomic point of view, could be delightful, creative and quite sustainable dishes.

Similarly, the uncritical equation of sustainable gastronomy with traditional foods and cuisines is also highly questionable. This fascination with the old food, fuelled by Western media, has generated one of the strongest romantic culinary myths of our times (Scarpato 1999). It can be considered as a part of that 'nostalgia rush' in which postmodern tourists enthusiastically take part (Urry 1990: 109), with enormous benefits to the tourism industry. Like all myths, however, this one has little historical basis. To start, the reality is that most old food is not very old. Recently Rachel Laudan (2001), in a plea for culinary modernism, noted that 'for every prized dish that goes back two thousand years, a dozen have been invented in the last two hundred'. She also confirmed what had already been argued, that is, that old food implied often, among the other things, 'lack of choice, affordability of other foods, awareness of health issues' (Scarpato 1999).

An ill-equipped tourism approach to gastronomic tourism emerges also from other superficial positions. It has been claimed, for example, that 'the use of imported ingredients rather than utilizing local food products' (Swarbrooke 1999: 299) is a sign of unsustainability. Such an assumption totally disregards one of the most important tenets of gastronomy: diversity. Imported food has always played a crucial role in culinary arts and it is widely considered part of the history and philosophy of gastronomy, from Brillat-Savarin (1994: 379) to contemporary chefs (Liew 1995). It would be culturally and gastronomically unsustainable to ban imported products from our tables.

It has also been argued that a 'positive development' towards sustainable gastronomic tourism has been that of 'encouraging tourists to visit local food producers, such as farms which make cheese, and wineries, to buy directly from the producers' (Swarbrooke 1999: 299). Many wineries around the world, as in Australia for example, are concerned by the incessant pilgrimages of 'Non Serious Wine Tourists' who may discourage the 'Serious Wine Tourists' and have negative effects on their business in the long term (Jago 2000).

Issues of sustainability in the cases

What is the relationship between the three GTPs and sustainable gastronomy? The following paragraphs attempt to provide some answers with regards to a number of opportunities and risks presented by each GTP. This analysis is particularly interesting because of the potentialities of these GTPs. In fact, each one represents an opportunity in itself for, as we have seen, it contributes to the creation of lifestyles, cuisines and trends. The achievement of sustainable gastronomic tourism at a global level relies greatly also on GTPs like these.

The Melbourne Food and Wine Festival: opportunities

Introducing the Natural and Organic Food section

Based on the conviction that 'sustainability is becoming more and more important' (Johnson 2001), in the year 2000 the MFWF introduced the 'Natural and

Organic Food section', to promote a 'healthy and sustainable lifestyle'. The section included a two-day Food Fair with seventy stalls of organic producers. A seminar on the future of food, open to the public and the industry, was also held, with international keynote speakers. Thanks to this, the MFWF has therefore become the only stage in Melbourne on which the issue of sustainability and natural produce is promoted with a relevant media and public exposure. In a clear attempt to stress the relevance of the commitment to the eco-gastronomy, the MFWF official programme of the last two editions has been opened by the presentation of the Natural and Organic Food section. In the 2000 edition, however, there were some contradictions and incoherence in the message sent to the community. The sponsorship policy allowed the association of Bertolli, a large industrial olive oil producer owned by a multinational (Unilever), to sponsor The Pancake Parlour, a food outlet chain that recently switched to the usage of organic produce.

Expanding to the country

'In the past three years the MFWF has ventured into Regional Victoria. It has helped to open many doors in food and wine tourism, and as example, the World's Longest Lunch next year will be held in 21 towns.' Expanding the MFWF to the country can be considered another progress towards a responsible gastronomy. The MFWF became a way to introduce a largely metropolitan crowd to the 'vital' understanding of 'where our food comes from and the processes it has been through before reaching our tables and bodies' (MFWF 2001b).

The Melbourne Food and Wine Festival: threats

Community and industry participation

Transparency and accountability are prerequisites of any sustainable development (Murphy 1985; World Commission on Environment and Development 1987), including that related to gastronomy. They are also basic requirements to having a community participation in/and sharing the benefits generated by a GTP. In general terms, any GTP that only 'uses' its stakeholders risks becoming gastronomically unsustainable. In fact, the lack of transparency and accountability may contribute to forming food and wine aristocracies, enlarging the gap that separates them from the rest of the community living in a gastro-anomie.

From a number of circumstances observed, it appears that the MFWF has some problems in regards to transparency and accountability, that, if not addressed, may lead to some gastronomic unsustainability of this GTP. The most relevant are:

- The MFWF has been run since its formation by the same management.[5]
- There is an 'ever-changing' committee of six people overseeing the organization, but they are hand picked by the management.

- The current Director was 'chosen' by the founding Chairman because 'he said anyone who can run a restaurant, raise two kids and write a book, can run a Festival' (MFWF 2001).
- Despite a significant influx of public funding, there is a very little or no community direct participation in the decision process of the Festival.
- No ongoing formal community consultation initiatives are undertaken. Neither Tourism Victoria nor Melbourne City Council, which are the main sponsors of the event, undertook any study to analyse the impact of the MFWF on Melbourne Tourism and Hospitality and on the community.
- The hospitality industry participation in the programme is also very limited. The local catering and restaurant association[6] is involved only with the organization of a seminar.[7] Until the 2000 edition, there was an industry day, which was cancelled for lack of participants, and since then it has not been included in the programme.
- Although the MFWF is a non-profit organization, the Management is reluctant to make public any financial data.

In such a situation the close alliance with the most influential city's media sponsoring the Festival makes public scrutiny even more difficult. The Management is particularly proud of its record of integrity; however, this situation could lead to a misuse/abuse of the MFWF's gastronomic gate keeping role.

New Asia Cuisine: opportunities

Cooking in progress

NAC is a relevant example of both culinary styles and of how contemporary new cuisines form and evolve as expressions of culture. In this case the role and the needs of Singapore's tourism promotion have contributed to the creation of an opportunity for sustainable gastronomy. In NAC chefs have confirmed their new role as 'cultural specialists and as such, reflecting values, philosophies and aesthetics of a common culture, as do architects when designing a building or a painter when painting' (Scarpato 2000: 119). This has some relevant consequences in gastronomy terms. Contrary to the past, new cuisines are today 'conceived' and escape the tyranny of local climate, the biological constraints and the social barriers. This translates into a better diet and an improved quality of life. NAC chefs have argued that New Asia Cuisine 'is faster to cook and fresher, with no loss of flavours or vitamins. It is less oily, has less salt and sugar and is healthier' (Mosely 1998). In the Singapore context, which has one of the highest rates of heart disease per capita in Asia, this is a real contribution towards the community's food security and, ultimately, towards sustainable gastronomy.

Euphoric globalization

NAC exhibits all the characteristics of New Global Cuisine, which is 'a new non-geographical and trans-ethnic cuisine generated by the current globalization' (Scarpato 2000: 5). This cuisine is also part of what can be defined as the global culinary equation, whereas behind the different names of various cuisines (e.g. Modern British, New American, Contemporary Australian), there is only one, yet not uniform, emerging style which attains to the chef's vision. 'Purity and authenticity in New Global Cuisine have an extra-geographic dimension' (Scarpato 2000: 134). Accordingly, NAC dishes have a cultural homogeneity, which, however, does not imply sameness as in traditional cuisines. In fact, New Global Cuisine has been built on the diversity of both ingredients and cooking techniques from every corner of the globe. This cuisine 'is the result of a new cartography of the world prevalently drawn according to cultural factors, which have paralleled and often ousted traditional territorial aggregations of people' (Scarpato 2000: 116). The world is divided between global consumer groups, in which television preferences, musical tastes, fashion, magazine readership, shopping mail and internet surfing have the same if not more importance than geographical, religious and sexual distinctions.

Among the potential visitors to Singapore, many belong to the vast consumers zone for New Global Cuisine. They have 'been exposed for more than 40 years to television, are computer and telephone addicted, fly regularly to every destination in the world and live side by side with many ethnic groups' (Scarpato 2000: 116). NAC, therefore serves a global marketplace of mobile professional people.

In this sense New Global Cuisine belongs to a positive view of globalization. This implies the transcendence 'of rigid ideological and political divisions, and the worldwide availability of cultural products and information' (Kellner 1999), which in gastronomy terms has contributed to the fulfilment of the old global dream of cooks and diners in almost every culture. The euphoric version of gastronomic globalization contrasts the melancholic one, represented by 'the repetitive and unhealthy fast and industrial cuisine, insensitive to the warnings of ecological catastrophe, which translates into unsustainable gastronomy' (Scarpato 2000: 169).

New Asia Cuisine: threats

Forsaking local traditions

Many observers have pointed out that NAC is 'a distortion of culture', forsaking 'traditions for the benefit of something so unidentifiable' (Knipp 1998). This risk was considered serious, particularly at the beginning of the STB promotional campaign (1996) in which the new culinary style was included. However, these remarks were addressed by the supporters of NAC, who made clear that 'in preparing a new way (or thought), we have to evaluate and appreciate the past, for without the past, there will be no future' (Knipp 1998). Today, after more than five years from its launch, NAC coexists with the traditional cuisines. In many ways it is now part of the panorama of local culinary traditions and its once 'unidentifiable' identity needs to be protected as well as that of old cuisines.

Local community involvement

NAC is a gastronomic product targeting elite tourists, discerning business travellers and well-off locals. It can be reasonably said that the new culinary style has passed unnoticed by a good part of the Singapore population. At least two factors contributed to keep the local community's involvement very limited. They are:

- the already mentioned diffused perception that it was a 'distortion of culture';
- its relatively high costs. Being served mainly in five star hotel restaurants, New Asia Cuisine could not be afforded by the majority of Singaporeans. Some freelance, inexpensive restaurants, run by former hotel chefs adopted this style, however their number remained limited.[8]

Consequently, it must be concluded that the innovatory benefits brought by chefs – for example those at a dietary level – haven't spread evenly.

Bologna 2000 – Slow Food Award: opportunities

The appeal of eco-gastronomy

Bologna's Slow Food Award has been indeed a unique opportunity, possibly the first of its kind, to promote sustainable gastronomy at a global level and in a comprehensive way. The message that the Award has delivered is synthesized in the words of the Slow Food Movement President: 'You can't be a gastronome without being an ecologist any more. You can't just exalt food and great wine and great beer without being aware of the great environmental disasters around us' (Elies 2000). The Award put culinary activities at the centre of the human life and contributed to the re-positioning of their related figures (cooks, food artisans and produce-growers) within our contemporary society. For too long cooks and cooking activities have had 'a low community profile and have been in powerless positions in their relations with and within society' (Scarpato 2000: 16). 'Cooking is the point where production is directed, where social relationships are formed and maintained, and where the arts and science emanate. It's the starting-place of trades, the target of the marketplace, the object of philosophy' (Symons 1998: 121). The Award represents a new way to think about gastronomy and cooks and revise society's views in this light. Without this revision the achievement of sustainable gastronomy would be highly problematic.

Benefits for the city

By hosting the Award, Bologna and its Region reinforced their image as a prime worldwide gastronomic destination. The programme of the Award cleverly included a number of 'local' promotions. Thus, the International Jury cast its vote in a historic city building, surrounded by a showcase of artisan food productions (*prosciutto* and other traditional foods), local wines and gourmet sweets. In fact, the Award has been a much needed boost to the gastronomic reputation of the city, which has suffered a number of setbacks in the recent years. Bologna for example, has scored unsatisfactorily in Italian independent restaurant guides: not one of the local establishments got the maximum score in prestigious guides (Bonilli *et al.* 2001). The generally positive media coverage that the city enjoyed by hosting the Award (Slow Food 2001) reveals that the future association of other cities to such a global eco-gastronomy event is poised to generate a significant food and wine tourism return to them.

Bologna 2000 – Slow Food Award: threats

Neo-colonialism and negative spotlighting

We will focus only on a major risk that events like the Slow Food Award may face. It is not related to the hosting city, but to the future of the initiatives rewarded. The association of the Award with Bologna might also have unforeseen perverse consequences, because, in order to maximize the media visibility of the hosting city, the rewarded initiatives are also heavily promoted. This is recurrent in the contemporary post-modern situation, where local and global codes and signs combine and clash. On the other hand, without a global exposure, the city of Bologna – and any other city that in future will host the Award – would not have been interested in providing its financial support.[9] Not to mention the fact, that what made news on the Bologna stage, was 'alternative' gastronomy, initiatives either almost forgotten, such those in Third World countries, or overlooked, like those in Western and developing nations.

Far from suggesting that we are in the presence of a form of gastronomic neo-colonialism, that is, an exploitation for marketing purposes of disadvantaged communities, it cannot be denied however that there is a strident disproportion between the agenda of a 'first world' gastronomic city like Bologna and Rancio Grande, a small community of vanilla beans growers in the remote Chinantla (Oaxaca) region of Mexico, a representative of which was an Award recipient. The chances that, after the exposure in Bologna, the Chinantla community would become a tourist destination are high. If so, there may be negative consequences for the sustainable gastronomy project carried out by the community.

At least another three rewarded initiatives spotlighted in Bologna face the same risk, for they can quickly attract the interests of tourism developers. One of them is the project of the Spanish *Transumancia y naturaleza* association that has revived long-distance transhumance in Cantabria. Since 1992, the passing of huge numbers of transhumant sheep in cities and villages of Spain (including Madrid, Seville and Valladolid) has already generated 'welcome parties and ceremonies' (Scaffidi and Kummer 2000: 80). They could easily be transformed into festivals or gastronomic tourist events, which, if not appropriately managed, will have obvious consequences for their gastronomic sustainability. Finally the two Turkish communities of Çamlihemsin and Dalyan, which respectively produce honey and *haviar* in harmony with the local eco-system, could find themselves in the same situation.

It must be questioned, therefore, whether the traditional public award models, with their broad and sudden exposure to media, are beneficial to sustainable gastronomy projects. This means that it must be questioned whether awards, like Slow Food in their current format, are themselves sustainable. In the current mediascape (Appadurai 1990), spotlighting remote areas, even only to praise their positive records in sustainable gastronomy, is equivalent to a vigorous marketing action and may pave the way to upsetting tourist exploitations. At the current stage, with tourism 'de-marketing' (Swarbrooke 1999: 221–226) invoked as an extreme but unavoidable measure to protect also sustainable gastronomy, it is necessary to begin a quest for alternative forms of public recognition. Indeed they should provide economic incentives and support to the rewarded initiatives, but at the same time should avoid exposing them abruptly to a potential unsustainable media assault.

In its commendable fight to establish a sustainable gastronomy, the Slow Food movement is faced with many similar dilemmas. Just after the Bologna awards, the Movement held the Torino's Salone del Gusto (The Hall of Taste), a successful fair celebrating good and natural food (Borri *et al.* 2000). One of the Hall's main attractions was the area dedicated to the Presidia of the Ark project, for which people are invited to adopt foods, cultivations and produce in danger of being lost or extinct. Also in this case, however, by heavily spotlighting the endangered gastronomic items, Slow Food increases the risk of their extinction, since the media make them fashionable (Borri *et al.* 2000: 133).

Conclusions

The GTPs analysed belong to a new breed of cases representing gastronomy exploited for tourism purposes. For their gatekeeping and tastemaking characteristics, they can play a considerable role in establishing and promoting sustainable gastronomic practices, habits and procedures. Their role is relevant not only within their respective local communities but also at a global level. Two key elements contribute to the enhancement of such a role:

- Their high public visibility; they cluster and combine the interests of the hospitality industry, the media and the community, including both direct consumers and non-consumers of the product.
- Their economic viability; although they perform within an economy of market, they enjoy a substantial financial support from public institutions. Their

viability as sustainable gastronomy products is therefore not at risk as that of other strictly commercial gastronomic tourist products, such as restaurants.

The three GTPs, in particular, appear as ideal stages for the introduction of policies and style of management oriented towards a sustainable gastronomy, both within their own and associated organizations. For instance, they can promote new policies for the recruitment and the training of human resources and operations management in the hospitality industry. Traditionally, the workforce of the industry of preparing and serving meals has always suffered from scarce competence and preparation, due to a relatively easy access to some jobs (waiting, for example) and high labour turnover. Contrarily to the industrial food of McDonald's (Swarbrooke 1999: 235), sustainable gastronomy requires qualified 'reflective' staff. The issue of staff qualification needs to be addressed by sustainable food and wine outlets.

The three GTPs can also contribute to the introduction of changes in the operational management of restaurants and food outlets. Through them, sustainable gastronomy practices can be promoted and tested, such as:

- alternative purchasing policies ('buy local');
- waste management and recycling;
- ending old industry practices, for example, replacing 'à la carte' menu, particularly when it does not coincide with the needs and the often limited availability of local produce, with short fixed menus including limited dishes but with a vast range of flavours;
- ethical and responsible marketing;
- educational programmes for tourists.

In any case, sustainable gastronomy is on shaky ground and the risk that GTP practices can become suddenly unsustainable is always high. A restaurant[10] in rural Victoria (Australia), had on the menu a tasty wild perch from the local river, as a commitment to the promotion of regional and fresh food. The restaurant soon became famous, attracting a large number of customers wanting that fish. As a direct consequence, the general consumption of the fish increased, contributing to making the fish an endangered species.

A contribution to the reduction of these risks could come from the creation of comprehensive guidelines functioning as sustainable gastronomy codes of conduct, as we will see below.

Gastronomy studies and GTPs

Gastronomy studies can be of a great assistance to sustainable gastronomy gatekeeping initiatives, like the three GTPs analysed. As cultural studies have been part of a 'critical media pedagogy', gastronomy studies should be involved in a critical pedagogy in respect to their management. This critical pedagogy should be extended to all the stakeholders of gastronomic tourism, from the media to

industry practices and tourists' behaviour. Media scrutiny is particularly important, due to the poor qualifications and lack of gastronomic imagination of specialized and general media, in which the space given to food and wine topics has
grown enormously in the last few years. Media, in which paid advertising plays a
large role, can be highly unsustainable in gastronomy terms, exactly like tourism
can be.

Possible actions

There are many possible actions to improve the standards of sustainable gastronomy in these and other GTPs. At a general level, the introduction of a gastronomy educational philosophy, including the concerns and the aims of a sustainable
gastronomy, should no longer be delayed. Hospitality studies curricula and
research aims should be re-designed in function of this philosophy, which should
also permeate a re-thinking of the GTPs management processes and the subsequent training programmes. The problem is that 'educational philosophy' has
always received scant attention from academics, policy-makers and educators,
who have liquidated it as a 'non pragmatic' approach, like in the case of rural
schools in the United States (Theobald 1992). A discussion on this topic would be
complex and beyond the aims of this paper, so we will focus on the two actions
that can be considered as priorities.

Policy-makers and gastronomy

There is an increasing need for community policy-makers to support only those
gastronomic tourism developments that are committed to sustainable gastronomy.
In particular, they should privilege and support financially initiatives like the three
GTPs we have considered. Gastronomy research can make a significant contribution to the planning and the execution of community policies on sustainable
development. Far from being only theoretical, such a contribution should imply
that professional gastronomers are finally involved at every decision-making level,
including participation in boards and executive management responsibilities.

Codes of conduct

The role of gastronomy studies can be substantial in creating local, national and
international sustainable gastronomy codes of conduct for all the stakeholders
involved in gastronomic tourism: industry, voluntary organizations, media, the
host community and tourists. These codes should contain economically viable
'terms of references' for business and communities in regard to the exploitation
of food, wine and related traditions as tourist 'poles of attraction'.

In particular, the codes should carefully consider concepts such as spotlighting
and heavy marketing of sustainable gastronomy enterprises by festivals, media
and other promoters. Without creating economic hardship for the stakeholders,
the codes should also acknowledge, for instance, that the de-marketing of a

gastronomic tourist area doesn't translate automatically into discontinuing the efforts to market the area's rural production nor to arresting its economic development

Gastronomy tourist products like the GTPs analysed should make legally binding pledges to the codes of sustainability in order to get either ordinary or special public financial support. Finally, the codes should be branded, widely advertised and associated to GTPs as quality marks, to which the tourist industry and the consumers can refer.

Notes

1 Among the other Victorian Hallmark Events there are: the Melbourne International Flower and Garden Show; the Melbourne International Comedy Festival; the Spring Racing Carnival; the Melbourne Festival.
2 According to Mrs Johnson (2001), one-third of the Festival budget comes from the State Government, but a substantial contribution also comes from Melbourne City Council.
3 Peranakan or Nonya cuisine is a fusion of regional Malay and Chinese culinary tradition. It began in the fifteenth century, when Chinese merchants came to Singapore and married local women. The typical nonya (wife, woman) melted in her cooking her preferred flavours and those of her baba (man, husband), who often had another wife in China.
4 A profile of Peter Knipp and his activities can be found in the website: www.asiacuisine.com/
5 Mrs Johnson said in the interview: 'Pamela Bikes and I have given almost our whole lives to the MFWF as it does permeate through every living day.' Mrs Bikes is the Manager of the Festival.
6 Restaurant and Catering Association of Victoria (RCAV).
7 The title of the seminar is: 'So you want to be a restaurant caterer'.
8 The Fig Leaf Restaurant was opened in 1997 with Anderson Ho and Jimmy Cheok, former chefs at the Raffles Grill in the Raffles Hotel.
9 The financial support involved the payment of all costs of travel, transfers, meals and accommodation for all Jury members.
10 The restaurant operates in the north of the State of Victoria.

References

Appadurai, A. (1990) 'Disjunction and difference in the global cultural economy', *Theory, Culture & Society* 7, nos. 2–3.

Berchoux, J. (1804) *La gastronomie, ou l'homme des champs à table: Poème didactique en quatre chants*, Paris: Giguet et Michaud.

Bonilli, S., Perrotta, G. and Barra, C. (2001) (eds) *Ristoranti d'Italia 2001, Roma-Novara*: Gambero Rosso Editore – De Agostini.

Borri, B., Burdese, B., Perona, F. and Petrini, C. (2000) (eds) *Salone del Gusto, Catalogo Ufficiale*, Bra: Slow Food Editore.

Bramwell, B., Henry, I., Jackson, G., Prat, A.G., Richards, G. and van der Straaten, J. (1996) (eds) *Sustainable Tourism Management: Principles and Practice*, Tilburg: Tilburg University Press.

Brillat-Savarin, J.-A. (1994) *The Physiology of Taste*, trans. A. Drayton, Harmondsworth: Penguin.

Britton, S. (1991) 'Tourism, capital and place: towards a critical geography of tourism', *Environment & Planning D: Society & Space*, 9(4): 451–478.

Coveney, J. and Santich, B. (1997) 'A question of balance: nutrition, health and gastronomy', *Appetite*, 28: 267–277.

Elies, L. E. (2000) 'Slow Food fan dipping ladle in New Orleans', in *Times Picayune*, 23 June 2000. Available on line: www.slowfood.com >Press office > International Press Review.

Errani, V. (2000) 'Introduction', in Scaffidi, C. and Kummer, C. *Slow Food Award Bologna 2000 for the Defence of the Biodiversity*, Bra: Slow Food Editore.

Fine, G.A. (1996) *Kitchens: The culture of restaurant work*, Berkeley: University of California Press.

Fishler, C. (1980) 'Food habits, social change and the nature/culture dilemma', *Social Science Information*, 19(6): 937–953.

France, L. (1997) (ed.) *The Earthscan Reader in Sustainable Tourism*, London: Earthscan Publications.

Guazzaloca, G. (2000) 'Introduction', in Scaffidi, C. and Kummer, C. (eds) *Slow Food Award Bologna 2000 for the Defence of the Biodiversity*, Bra: Slow Food Editore.

Jago, L. (2000) 'Wine tourism in Victoria', working paper for peak performance in tourism and hospitality research, CAUTHE Conference, La Trobe University, Mt Buller Campus, 2–5 February 2000 (unpublished).

Johnson, S. (2001) Interview with the author, unpublished.

Kellner, D. (1999) 'The Frankfurt School and British Cultural Studies: the missed articulation', in http://www.popcultures.com/theorists/kellner.html.

Knipp, P. (1998) 'New Asia Cuisine: Revolution or Evolution', *New Asia Cuisine*, March, also available on www.asiacuisine.com/

Laudan, R. (2001) 'A plea for culinary modernism: why we should love new, fast, processed food', *Gastronomica Quarterly*, 2–01: 36–45.

Liew, C. (1995) *My Food*, Sydney: Allen and Unwin.

MFWF (2001), Brief history of the Melbourne Food and Wine Festival, Melbourne: MFWF.

—— (2001a) Melbourne Food and Wine Festival Official Program, Melbourne: MFWF.

—— (2001b) Melbourne Food and Wine Festival Sponsorship proposal, Melbourne: MFWF.

Mosley, J. (1996) 'New Asia Cuisine Singapore', *New Asia Cuisine*, September, also available on www.asiacuisine.com/

—— (1997) 'World Gourmet Summit', *New Asia Cuisine*, September, also available on www.asiacuisine.com/

Mowforth, M. and Munt, I. (1998) *Tourism and Sustainability: New tourism in the Third World*, London: Routledge.

Murphy, P. (1985) *Tourism: A community approach*, London: Methuen.

Patton, M.Q. (1980) *Qualitative Evaluation Methods*, Beverly Hills: Sage.

Poon, A. (1993) *Tourism, Technology and Competitive Strategies*, Oxford: CAB.

Salizzoni, G. (2000) The Deputy Mayor Welcoming Address to the Slow Food Award Jury, Bologna, 24 October 2000, unpublished.

Scaffidi, C. and Kummer, C. (2000) *Slow Food Award Bologna 2000 for the Defence of the Biodiversity*, Bra: Slow Food Editore.

Scarpato, R. (1999), 'Food globalisation, New Global Cuisine and the quest for a definition', in Dare, R. (forthcoming) (ed.) *Cuisines: Regional, national or global?*, Adelaide: Research Centre for the History of Food and Drink.

Scarpato, R. (2000) 'New global cuisine: the perspective of postmodern gastronomy studies', Master's thesis, Melbourne: RMIT University (unpublished).

—— (2001a) 'Gastronomy as a tourist product: the perspective of gastronomy studies', paper for the Atlas Expert Meeting on Tourism and Gastronomy, Esposende 22–25 March 2001, unpublished.

—— (2001b) 'Figli dei fiori? No, di cavoli e fornelli', *Gambero Rosso*, Monthly, April: 41–43.

Scarpato, R. and Daniele, R. (2000) 'Effects of media reviews on restaurants: the perception of the industry', working paper for peak performance in tourism and hospitality research, CAUTHE Conference, La Trobe University, Mt Buller Campus, 2–5 February 2000 (unpublished).

Singapore (2001) *Singapore New Asia: An insider guide*, Singapore: Singapore Tourism Board.

Symons, M. (1998) *The Pudding that Took a Thousand Cooks: The story of cooking in civilisation and daily life*, Melbourne: Viking.

Swarbrooke, J. (1999) *Sustainable Tourism Management*, Wallingford: CAB International.

Theobald, P. (1992) *Rural Philosophy for Education: Wendell Berry's Tradition*, Eric digest ED345930: www.ericir.syr.edu

Urry, J. (1990) *The Tourist Gaze*, London: Sage.

Wahab, S. and Pigram, J.J. (1997) (eds) *Tourism, Development and Growth; the challenge of sustainability*, London: Routledge.

Wahlqvist, M. (1999) 'Food security and health depend on food diversity and sustainability', keynote address to: Eating into the Future. The First Australian Conference on Food, Health and the Environment, Adelaide: Flinders University.

World Commission on Environment and Development (1987) *Our Common Future*, Oxford: Oxford University Press.

Websites

http://www.melbfoodwinefest.com.au/
http://www.slowfood.com/
http://www.slowfood.com/activities/award/index.html/
http://www.slow-food.com/award.html/
http://www.bologna2000.it/
http://www.asiacuisine.com/
http://www.newasia-singapore.com/

9 Gastronomy and intellectual property

Neil Ravenscroft and Jetske van Westering

Introduction

The increase in foreign travel and holidays witnessed throughout the second half of the twentieth century has generated a heightened awareness of alternative cultures. In particular, interest has focused on alternative eating traditions. This has prompted an increase in demand for foreign gastronomic produce. The opportunities for trading imitation produce have grown likewise: Canadian 'cheddar', Danish 'feta', Japanese 'whisky' and Californian 'Chablis' afford examples of products associated with one place being produced and branded by another. Trade negotiations such as the General Agreement on Tariffs and Trade (GATT) aim to globalize the legislation affecting agricultural produce. The growth in use of geographical indications (negotiated in GATT under intellectual property) on gastronomic products such as wine, cheese and butter reinforces that there is, indeed, a need for producers to protect their produce, possibly in the form of intellectual property. In addition to the threat posed by imitation produce, globalization creates internal and regional pressures on countries (as exemplified by Spain in this chapter) leading to the potential homogenization of regional gastronomies.

In this chapter we will explore whether and how intellectual property law can be extended to cover regional gastronomy. Whilst acknowledging that a region's gastronomy is rooted in its produce, gastronomy consists of more than that. Recipes, set combinations of dishes and drinks, questions of how, where and in which order dishes are eaten, as well as eating/drinking traditions make up the gastronomic culture of a region. They are, we suggest, as much part of the intellectual property of a region as is its produce. To recognize gastronomy as intellectual property would serve to make an inventory and raise awareness. It would help to profile and distinguish regional culture and emphasize its unique nature – that combination of atmosphere, cultural mores, climate and local people that cannot be reproduced authentically elsewhere.

It has been argued (van Westering 1999) that gastronomic experiences and memories (produce, recipes, traditions) are the most powerful souvenirs of a holiday. They are recalled long after the holiday is over, reinforcing the critical nature of the food experience. Gastronomic culture can also be used to market and sell a region's cultural product to tourists, as instanced in the case of Spain. This country has successfully re-branded itself as a tourist destination with a worthwhile culture – where sun, sea and sand are equal partners to *paella*, *gazpacho* and *Rioja*. Until recently, the gastronomy of Spain has not been a significant attraction for tourists. This is ironic when the global impact of its gastronomy is surprisingly high. Spanish gastronomy has influenced the gastronomy of other countries, notably Mexico, which has one of the world's major cuisines. Despite this, it has never been judged a major European cuisine equivalent to that of Italy or France. Until tourists adopted the country for their holidays on a regular basis, Spanish cuisine remained relatively unknown. Since then the demand for culinary products such as olives, olive oil or cava has been rising steadily. Spanish agricultural products are also exported to many countries with increasing success. Equally, tapas restaurants can be found in many European cities.

Although this may seem a positive development, it will be argued here that the success of Spain in reinventing itself as a cultural holiday destination has put under threat its very regionalized gastronomies. As international recognition and consumption of Spanish products increases, it will matter less – to the world outside Spain at least – from where in Spain they originate. Unless the individual regions are able to protect their gastronomic intellectual property, external pressures (from tour operators for example) may lead to the creolization of regional foods into an inauthentic reflection that lives up to marketed expectations rather than reflecting the real gastronomic differences between regions.

Tourism and Spain: the early years

The emergence of Spain as a tourist haven since the early 1960s is legendary – the key tourist centres roll off the tongue: the initial popularity of the French/Spanish border towns (Frejus, Rosas), then the love affair with the Costa Brava (Lloret del Mar and Tossa del Mar) – both areas opened up through the development of Gerona Airport. These beginnings appear to have swept like a tourist wave down the coast with the improvement of tourist routes (roads and airports) – this wave taking in Tarragona, Salou and Cambrills and extensive tourist development, whilst the explosion of the southern Costas (Torremolinas, Benalmendena, Fuenerola, Malaga) is a renowned phenomenon.

After this growth in tourism and the associated boom in hotel construction, the Spanish government realized the need to intervene and reconstruct tourism to and in the country. Away from the coastal areas to the south and east and the industrial areas in the north, much of Spain was inhospitable to tourists. In order to open up Spain, and to spread the tourist wealth more equably across the regions, the infrastructure of the country had to be improved. With help from the EU a network of roads and airports was built making inland Spain gradually less remote.

After these crucial improvements a number of other significant initiatives were taken to market Spain, in its entirety, to tourists. These initiatives all emphasized that the brand Spain incorporated more than just sun, sea and sand, i.e. the coastal regions. Four of these initiatives are worth mentioning briefly here:

- The development of major tourist attractions in touristically less popular areas. These include the National Museum of Roman Art in Merida (in the Province of Extremadura) and the more recent Guggenheim Museum in Bilbao, in the north of Spain. The latter attracted 1,300,000 visitors in its first year (of whom 25 per cent were foreigners) and helped to transform the Bilbao economy from one based on heavy industry to one that is more service-based.
- The development of *paradores* (small or medium sized hotels), usually located in historic buildings in scenic or culturally attractive locations. The emphasis in these *paradores* is on traditional Spanish interior decoration and cuisine, albeit with a degree of modernism.
- 'So you think you know Spain': an advertising campaign that highlighted a number of aspects and places in Spain, mainly inland. Each advert represented a lesser known town or region, seeking to convince potential visitors that the authentic Spain could be found in places away from the popular areas.
- *Spain Gourmetour*: a glossy brochure promoting food, wine and travel, published in English, French and German, three times a year, with the fiftieth issue in early 2000. The journal is sponsored by the Spanish Institute of Foreign Trade (ICEX) of the State Secretariat for Trade and Tourism and distributed free for trade professionals. Articles which feature both major and minor tourist products including regional cuisines and foods and wines are particularly detailed often including information on varieties (of e.g. olives, tuna, rice) not easily found elsewhere.

From these initiatives it becomes clear that the Spanish authorities are determined to emphasize aspects of Spain other than sun, sea and sand: its traditional, multifaceted regional side is placed alongside the modern, sometimes separately, sometimes harmoniously, blended. As, for instance, in the case of the Guggenheim Museum, where challenging modern architecture is matched in the restaurant with modern Basque cooking which is, however, still deeply rooted in tradition.

Culinary Spain

Modern Spanish cuisine, unlike modern British cuisine, is firmly rooted in the traditional regional cuisines of Spain. Products, combinations, ways of preparation and service show the influence of the chef's origins, more than an international approach. Although some dishes such as *lomo de cerdo*, *chuletas de cordero* or *tapas* such as *boquerones*, olives and *tortillas* can be found on the menu almost everywhere in Spain, eating in a Spanish restaurant in Spain means eating regional dishes: local produce is used and local ways of production are adhered to.

Such culinary tradition is based on locally produced ingredients. Most regions are well known for their produce: Valencia means oranges, lemons, rice and nuts; the Galician coast is renowned for fish and seafood; Jerte for its picota cherries; Leon for beef, beef products and lentils; and Andalusia for green asparagus: to name just a few. Many regions also have a cheese or one or more wines with which they are identified.

Spain, like France, has made ample use of the legislation on geographical indicators; *Denominacion de Origin* (D.O.) is used for a wide variety of products. Examples include Serrano ham (D.O. Jamon de Teruel), Iberico ham (D.O. Guijuelo, D.O. Dehesa de Extremadura, D.O. Jamon de Huelva), raisins (D.O. uva de mesa embolsada Vinalopo), cherries (D.O. Cereza del Jerte), cheese (D.O. Idiazabal, D.O. Manchego, D.O. Roncal – for example), as well as for some rather unknown products such as *horchata* (D.O. Chufa de Valencia) a drink not unlike a milk shake produced from earth almonds (small tubers). For D.O. products of outstanding quality a further system (the green star), especially meant for export produce, was devised in 1994. Premium produce with unique qualities is often hard to sell at top prices in established markets abroad – customers need convincing that the product not only looks good, but has outstanding flavour as well. The idea behind the green star system was to give produce a sense of place by forging a two-way information and quality control chain that would link producers to their customers abroad. Each box or pack carries a label of guarantee identifying the producer, the date of harvesting and the packer of the produce: thus complaints can be referred directly to the company responsible. Existing quality controls, laid down by the D.O., are strictly adhered to and often surpassed by the producers and exporters of green star products, for instance in the limited use of chemicals. To date only four products (table grapes from Vinalopo in Alicante, asparagus from the lowlands of Andalusia and Extremadura, cherries from Jerte and nisperos or loquats from the south of Valencia) have been accorded this elevated status.

Local produce is the basis for Spanish regional gastronomy – evidence of regional gastronomic identity and pride can be found on the menu of most restaurants. Not only the local specialities are mentioned; the whole of the menu reflects the gastronomic traditions of the area. In addition, the numerous fiestas related to gastronomy warrant mention: festivals such as the annual *romescada* in Cambrills near Tarragona for instance, offer the challenge to produce the best *romesco* sauce; the festival of *calcots* in the same area sees small spring onions grilled over a wood fire and eaten with *romesco* sauce. As much as *romesco* sauce forms part of Cataluna, so too does *vizcaina* (Bisquay) sauce reflect its Basque identity, *arriero* sauce the identity of Castile-Leon and *ajada* that of Galicia. These four sauces, *romesco, vizcaina, arriero* and *ajada* are all red pepper sauces. Yet all are different and all are part of the distinctly different regional profiles.

Nutritional studies also expose differences between regional diets; these in turn reveal the differences between the regional gastronomies. Gracia and Albisu (1999) record interesting variations in consumption between the regions: Madrid and the Basque countries have a similar diet with a high amount of fruits, meat, fish, eggs and dairy products eaten. The regions along the Ebro river (Aragon, Navarre, and La Rioja) have a high consumption of fruits, vegetables and meat, although the diet is low in cereals and potatoes. In the Mediterranean areas (Catalonia, Murcia, Valencia and the Balearic islands) consumption of rice, vegetables, fruits and meat is high, whilst consumption of fish, eggs and dairy products is lower. The north and northwest have a high consumption of potatoes, fish and dairy products, with lower consumption of rice, vegetables and meat.

The emphasis on regionality in Spanish gastronomy can also be gleaned from the Spanish answer to a recent survey by the World Tourism Organization (WTO 2000). Member countries of the WTO were asked to list the dishes that best represent their country. From the list produced by Spain's National Tourist Office it transpires that 17 of the 20 dishes listed are a regional speciality, with 10 of the 20 giving the region in its name or description. The list incorporates both well-known dishes, such as *paella* and *gazpacho*, which have become national icons, as well as dishes such as *quesada pasiega* (Cantabrian cheesecake) or *marmitako* (tuna with potatoes), known only to those who have visited the region. It seems that the list was deliberately construed to represent each region, as other particularly Spanish icons such as *sangria, tapas, jamon serrano, cochon de leche* and *zarzuela* are missing.

Lurking threats

The threat to regional cuisine is exemplified by the case of *paella. Paella* became an iconic dish when it was featured in advertisements for holidays in Spain. The dish is originally from the country around Valencia, hence it is often seen under the name *paella valenciana*. Due to its success, it can now be found in different versions (and with varying quality) everywhere along the coast, as well as inland. Under such circumstances dishes tend to change, usually in order to suit perceived tourist tastes, or due to the interpretation of the chef, particularly where the chef's origins are different from those of the cuisine itself. Reynolds (1994) describes how, under similar pressures, the cuisine of Bali changed into a cuisine rejected by both tourists and the indigenous population. Similarly, under these influences the distinct differences between the regional gastronomies in Spain could be lost.

Regional cuisine is not only under external pressure. There are equally serious threats from inside the country. Gracia and Albisu (1999) describe how the consumption pattern of (especially young) Spanish people is changing. Typical Mediterranean food products are no longer highly rated and the consumption of cereals and pulses is on the decrease. Cookies and hamburgers have been incorporated, and in general a more Northern European diet, with a higher consumption of meat and saturated fats, seems to have become popular. This trend is underlined by the changing consumption of drinks in the country. Traditionally water and (locally produced) wine were consumed with meals other than breakfast. However, according to World Drink Trends (1998), the consumption of beer and soft drinks in Spain is increasing, while there has been a dramatic decline in the consumption of wine. These dietary changes could eventually lead to changes in regional cuisine. As a consequence, one of the distinguishing features of regions – the associated gastronomic culture – could disappear.

Evidence of cultures changing under tourist pressures is also given by Howard (1998). He describes how the *flamenco* was originally danced by locals at evening gatherings in village squares. Demand for the dance from the tourist trade led to courses being run for foreign visitors, as well as to a much more self-conscious dancing in the evening by the villagers. As visitors were invited to join in the evening dance, the level of difficulty was reduced to suit the foreigners. The result is twofold: *flamenco* dancing on evenings in the villages is reduced in quality as well as in its exclusivity. In addition the dance has been lifted to the international stages, danced by professional flamenco dancers. Howard argues that the outcome of this process is that the common inheritance of the village has been lost both upwards to the professional world and downwards to the lowest common denominator of the tourist world (Howard 1998).

Intellectual property

The World Trade Organization cites intellectual property rights as those rights given to persons over the creations of their minds. These creations include symbols, signs, names, images and designs. Such property therefore shares much in common with real and personal property, to the extent at least that it is, in theory, an asset that can be bought or sold (Hefter and Litowitz 2000). Unlike these other forms of property, the intellectual variety is intangible, meaning that it cannot be defined or identified according to its own physical parameters, and thus must be expressed in some alternative and discernible way in order to be protected (Gikkas 1996; Hefter and Litowitz 2000). Hence the intellectual property *right* is a convention or claim made by or on behalf of a person or persons with respect to use of the intellectual property by a third party.

The significance of intellectual property therefore lies less in its own individual parameters than it does in the ways in which rights are attached to it. It is these rights that signify the importance and value of the intellectual property just as surely as they do for other types of property (Seabrooke 1985). Establishing a right to intellectual property gives the owner of the right the ability to establish barriers to prevent others using the property – unless they pay for the privilege. It is thus the right, rather than the property, that gives rise to the potential for commercial exploitation. For Tansey (1999), this utilitarian approach offers the possibility of (temporarily) transforming what is essentially a public good into a private one. This allows the 'creator' of the good to benefit from the creation in ways that would not be available without the ability to exclude others.

Gikkas (1996) suggests that there are two ways in which wealth can be generated from intellectual property: the incorporation of the intangible intellectual property into a tangible product that can be sold; or licensing others to use the property to make a similar, or different, product. In terms of the second option, licence agreements often revolve around the right to use brand names or other types of trademarks, usually in franchise or concession arrangements. These types of arrangements can also involve supplying know-how, and may be linked to product supply deals, marketing and other forms of publicity. Moran (1993) gives the example of *Bleu de Bresse* cheese, where the French owners of the intellectual property right sold a licence agreement to New Zealand producers, involving French know-how and branded packaging (although of course with a different country of origin).

In official terms, intellectual property can be of two principal forms: industrial property; and copyright (World Intellectual Property Organization 2000). Industrial property includes a category termed 'geographical indication of source', which is defined as:

> a sign used on goods that have a specific geographical origin and possess qualities or a reputation that are due to that place of origin.
> (World Intellectual Property Organization 2000)

This is very much a two-part test: one of origin, and the second of quality. While the first of these is essentially a matter of provenance (Moran 1993), the second is a more exacting test, which implies that the quality and characteristics of the product are due predominantly to the geographical environment in which it was produced (Bodenhausen 1968). This is very much the case with wine production, in which the individual terrain is, in Bell and Valentine's (1997) terms, literally bottled. As Moran (1993) argues, it is thus of little surprise that much of the development of geographical indicators has been based on the practice of the French *appellation d'origine*, a system codified over several centuries and enshrined in law for most of the last one.

Geographical indicators

Geographical indicators are therefore a territorial rather than a sensory brand of intellectual property. As such, they are neither portable nor the preserve of an individual, but are open to all those with access to the territory. Indeed, they are hardly intellectual property at all, given that the territory has a physical presence that is wholly separable from the minds of those who occupy it. Yet, of course, it is not so much the physicality of the territory that forms the intellectual property, but the branding of the goods that are produced in (and by) the territory. The territory is thus, in Fitzpatrick's (1992) terms, a 'mute ground', defined by those with access to it according to its use and signification. As a result, it is not enough for a product to have come from a particular place. It must, in addition, represent the character of the place, as it is portrayed by the rights' holders, such that the product is emblematic of the place just as the place is emblematic of the product. Moran (1993) suggests that the Burgundy region of France is a fine example of this symbiosis.

Moran (1993) goes on to suggest that these types of geographical indication assist small family firms in resisting the industrialization of production, by countering the standardization implicit in the globalization of the agro-food industry.

While multinational corporations may be able to buy the brands (as has been the case with some of the major French wine producers), they cannot escape either the terrain or the individualized skills of the wine maker, thus limiting their ability to exact large-scale economies in production. Equally, the growth of wine and other forms of rural tourism has allowed many small-scale producers to sell directly to the final customer, thus cutting down on the need for the distribution infrastructure offered by the large corporations (Mitchell *et al.* 2000). Greater use of internet ordering could take this a stage further.

While, at one level, being no more than a means for 'the social and industrial groups with rights to them (intellectual property) to protect . . . their products' (Moran 1993: 264), the territoriality of geographical indications is highly symbolic of deeper panoptic and disciplinary codes. By linking notions of quality with those of location, Bodenhausen (1968) argues that existing operators are able to safeguard their rights from abuse by outsiders. However, probably more important is their ability to exercise a similar, but more immediate, level of control over other existing rights holders. By insisting on certain levels of quality (denoted in the French wine *appellations* by input and output measures such as the planting regime, choice of grape varieties and maximum size of harvest), the leading producers are able to discipline the intellectual property to suit their own requirements, particularly control over the market.

Although now encoded in statute, Moran (1993) shows that the French wine *appellations* evolved over centuries of custom, with the leading producers able to dictate the terms and conditions for the award of the *appellation*. Allied to this discipline is an overarching ability to police the system, through the distribution of predetermined numbers of bottle seals. This provides, in Foucault's terms, a panoptical ability to 'oversee' what is going on, in the process 'persuading' the smaller producers to accept the prevailing disciplinary codes in order to maintain their own prestige and exclusivity. Just as surely as OPEC, the oil producers' cartel, determines the global level of oil supply, the major players in any individual *appellation* control both the quantity and the quality of the produce, as well as defining the character of the brand.

Wine production, particularly in France, has dominated the development of geographical indications as a branch of intellectual property. While some authors see the potential for extending the system into biotechnology (Fowler 1997; Tansey 1999), Moran (1993) suggests that it has little further application, given that few products exhibit the significance of terrain in the way that wine production does. However, this is probably to interpret too narrowly the definition of geographical indicators, and to misunderstand the disciplinary motives of those seeking to assert their rights claims. Moran (1993) does, to some extent, recognize this failing, in claiming that intellectual property rights will spread to other products, even if there is little evidence to support this form of legal colonization. This is indeed what has happened over the last five years: almost all EU countries have established claims to the production of certain produce.

Gastronomy as intellectual property

As argued above, gastronomy, although rooted in regional and local produce, is more than produce alone. This is reinforced by the World Intellectual Property Organization (2000) in the suggestion that, rather than being limited to agricultural products, geographical indications can also relate to the specific qualities of a product that are due to human factors found in the place of origin. The examples given relate to manufacturing skills and traditions, such as Swiss watch making. This is already recognized, to some extent, by the French *appellation d'origine* system, in which the skills of certain producers, allied to the their specific *terroir*, is given particular prestige or significance.

It is intriguing to consider how far this definition of intellectual property can be taken. Can it take on specific cultural meanings, for example, where the skill might lie in the preparation of authentic foods, or the dancing of a particular dance or the wearing of authentic costume? From a cultural standpoint, van Westering (1999) has argued that the gastronomy of one region is not transferable to another; that *gazpacho* made in Deptford is not *gazpacho* as it is eaten in Spain: the loss of the environment changes the eating experience. This corresponds with similar debates (and subsequent litigation) about Spanish or New Zealand champagne (see Moran 1993). Yet there is an apparent difference: the issue with respect to wine is where and how it is made, not where and how it is consumed, while the issue with *gazpacho* is effectively the reverse. A Burgundy wine remains a Burgundy wine regardless of where it is consumed; the intellectual property lies in the branding of origin and quality, not distribution and consumption. *Gazpacho*, or other gastronomic products, is not tied to the place of origin in the way that wine is. But is this distinction really valid? Is *gazpacho* not as much a part of its terrain as wine is of its? Is the issue not more about cultural understandings about the production, distribution and consumption of different products? Since wine making on any scale is a skilled and technical undertaking, and since wine has always been kept in transportable containers, it has defined sites of production, from which it can be moved to different sites of consumption. Making a branded copy, as in the case of Spanish or New Zealand champagne, is thus exposed as a fraud, regardless of its taste, since it is possible (in theory at least) to obtain bottles of the authentic original.

The case with *gazpacho* is less clear-cut. It is not made at fixed sites and transported elsewhere, but produce is acquired from different sources, prepared in different kitchens and, generally, consumed close to the point of preparation. The intellectual property in this case resides not in individual bowls of food (although maybe it once did), but in a broader cultural understanding of the link between the food and the region in which it has traditionally been prepared. Unlike wines, in which each producer retains a unique quality, even within a single place of origin, regional gastronomy is the creation of many, both privately and commercially. The outward movement of this gastronomy, which has occurred organically over time, is largely the result of people taking recipes with them on their travels, or bringing recipes home from their travels (what Lury (1997) terms the objects of travel). The process here is not the fraudulent attempt to capitalize on a prestigious brand, but to enjoy the heritage of a region without diminishing its culture.

Perhaps more insidious is the potential for one region to annex the culture or gastronomy – the symbols of intellectual property – of another as part of its own branding exercise. This type of appropriation is seen by Moran (1993) as an inherent part of the evolution of geographical indications as intellectual property. He shows how the practice of naming wines after localities still required legal protection after centuries of development, as neighbours indulged in illegal naming, labelling and over-production of their own wines to capitalize on the intellectual property of an established wine area. This has led – and can still lead – to intense regional conflicts, competition and issues of dominance, as the products or outputs of one region are claimed by another.

As such, it is not the gastronomy of a region that can acquire intellectual property rights. Gastronomy is not essentially the creation of mind or terrain in the way that wine purportedly is, and no one will go out of business in Spain as a result of *gazpacho* being prepared in a private house – or even a restaurant – in Deptford. To demarcate ownership of (gastronomic) culture is not possible although it is clear that ownership of (gastronomic) culture lies with its users, and the longer the use the greater the ownership. Rather, the intellectual property right lies in the branding of the region and the extent to which a specific gastronomy can be linked to that region. Following Gikkas' (1996) arguments, the exploitation of the intangibility of the intellectual property of a regional brand can best be achieved by incorporating it into tangible products that can be sold globally. Gastronomy itself is too intangible to be an appropriate vehicle for this process. Rather, tangibility lies in the brand itself, as Moran (1993) demonstrates, with respect to the Burgundy region of France:

> Burgundy gives its name to one of the best known wines in the world but at the same time the region of Burgundy becomes known because of its wine. Moreover, the little bits of it, often only a few hectares, also derive their prestige from the wines that are produced there. In Burgundy, the process has developed to the extent that in order to capitalize on the reputation of their most famous wines many of the communes . . . have taken the name of their most famous vineyard. Corton was added to make Aloxe-Corton, Montrachet to make both Puligny-Montrachet and Chassagne-Montrachet, Romanee to make Vosne-Romanee, St Georges to make Nuits-St Georges and so on.
>
> (Moran 1993: 266)

The Burgundy case demonstrates that branding (and the annexation of the intellectual property rights associated with it) is not an end in itself. Rather, it is a means to an end: the commercial exploitation of the brand. This is the purpose for which intellectual property rights are commonly protected. The suitability of wine as a geographical indicator is therefore less about its 'exclusive or essential' relationship to the terrain (Bodenhausen 1968: 23) than it is about its tangible representation of the terrain. Culture and gastronomy do not share this same tangibility and thus cannot be used in the same way. Yet they are important to a region in establishing its branding, particularly if it is attempting to develop its tourist industry and potential.

However, the significance of intangibles such as gastronomy lies less in the physical reproduction of the food than it does in the symbolic links that the gastronomy has with the region and its branding. Placing *gazpacho* on the menu in Deptford will not undermine its cultural links to its place of origin, nor will it necessarily compromise the ability of its place of origin to benefit commercially from its gastronomic culture and heritage. Indeed, such product placement may enhance the regional brand. Yet, the ability of the region to capitalize on this will depend to a large extent on the degree to which it can distinguish itself from other Spanish regions and, in doing so, can attach *gazpacho* to its regional identity in the way that Burgundy has capitalized on its wines.

Conclusion

It is widely accepted that current systems to protect intellectual property are insufficient, especially in the areas of culture and traditional knowledge (Weatherall 2001). Mould-Iddrisu (2000) states that intellectual property rights can help galvanize the industry of 'developing' nations while protecting local cultures and customs. No discussions have taken place yet whether intellectual property rights should be extended to gastronomic heritage. Culture, and thus gastronomic culture, is one of the main distinguishing factors between regions and as such of prime importance in the tourism product; it can be used to market and sell a region's overall brand to tourists. The branding of a region and the extent to which its gastronomy is interwoven with that region will emphasize that region's intellectual property rights.

However, a lack of regional distinction outside the country could lead to a generalized branding of what are, internally, seen as distinct regional variations as exemplified, above, in the case of Spanish *paella*. Two other products have equally been branded externally as generically 'Spanish' due to the need for national icons; *gazpacho*, originally from Andalusia, and *Rioja*, the wine from the district with the same name, are seen by most tourists as 'Spanish' – they have almost lost their regional roots. Although as icons these products have given Spain large benefits – as part of the brand Spain they initially attracted tourists to the country – the final outcome of this process is the erosion of regional culture. Not only will this process affect regional profile and morale, but also it dilutes the intellectual property of the individual regions and facilitates a greater degree of creolization of individual gastronomies.

Spain's strong regional cultures have given it a strong competitive advantage which it would therefore do well to preserve. To stimulate regions claiming their gastronomic heritage and intellectual property rights, subsidies could be given and prizes awarded for small and medium sized producers of traditional products.

Preservation must be sought in a wide variety of areas; produce, recipes, food combinations, local life and traditions related to eating/drinking such as opening hours of shops and restaurants as well as working days, regional fetes and festivals are together the backbone of regional cultures. All these elements should be considered part of a region's intellectual property – to consider these as a region's intellectual property would serve to make an inventory and it would help to profile, contrast and distinguish the region's culture and emphasize its uniqueness.

References

Bell, D. and Valentine, G. (1997) *Consuming Geographies: We are Where We Eat*, London: Routledge.

Bodenhausen, G.H.C. (1968) *Guide to the Application of the Paris Convention for the Protection of Industrial Property*, Geneva: United International Bureau for the Protection of Intellectual Property.

Fitzpatrick, P. (1992) *The Mythology of Modern Law*, London: Routledge.

Fowler, C. (1997) 'By policy or law? The challenge of determining the status and future of agro-biodiversity', *Journal of Technology Law & Policy*, 3(1). http://journal.law.ufl.edu/~techlaw/3-1/fowler.html

Gikkas, N.S. (1996) 'International licensing of intellectual property: the promise and the peril', *Journal of Technology Law & Policy*, 1(1). http://journal.law.ufl.edu/~techlaw/1/gikkas.html

Gracia, A. and Albisu, L.M. (1999) 'Moving away from a typical Mediterranean diet: the case of Spain', *British Food Journal*, 101(9): 701–714.

Hefter, L.R. and Litowitz, R.D. (2000) 'What is intellectual property?' *Introduction to Intellectual Property Rights*, Washington DC: US Department of State. http://usinfo.state.gov/products/pubs/intelprp/support.htm

Howard, P. (1998) 'Heritage and Art', *International Journal of Heritage Studies*, 4(2): 61–63.

Lury, C. (1997) 'The objects of travel', in C. Rojek and J. Urry (eds) *Touring Cultures*, London: Routledge, pp. 75–95.

Mitchell, R., Hall, C.M. and McIntosh, A. (2000) 'Wine tourism and consumer behaviour', in C.M. Hall, L. Sharples, B. Cambourne and N. Macionis (eds) *Wine Tourism Around the World: development, management and markets*, Oxford: Butterworth-Heinemann, pp. 115–135.

Moran, W. (1993) 'Rural space as intellectual property', *Political Geography*, 12(3): 263–277.

Mould-Iddrisu, B. (2000) 'A developing country's perspective', *Introduction to Intellectual Property Rights*, Washington DC: US Department of State. http://usinfo.state.gov/products/pubs/intelprp/support.htm

Reynolds, P. (1994) 'Culinary heritage in the face of tourism', in C.P. Cooper and A. Lockwood (eds) *Progress in Tourism, Recreation and Hospitality Management*, Vol. 6, 194–198.

Seabrooke, W. (1985) *Land management or great expectations?*, Inaugural lecture, Portsmouth Polytechnic.

Tansey, G. (1999) *Trade, intellectual property, food and biodiversity*, a discussion paper, London: Quaker Peace & Service.

van Westering, J. (1999) 'Heritage and gastronomy: the pursuits of the "new" tourist', *International Journal of Heritage Studies*, 5(2): 75–81.

Weatherall, K. (2001) 'Culture, autonomy and *Djulibinyamurr*: Individual and community in the construction of rights to traditional designs', *The Modern Law Review Limited*, 64(2): 215–242.

World Drink Trends (1998) *World Drink Trends*, Henley-on-Thames: NTC Publications.

World Intellectual Property Organization (2000) *About intellectual property*. www.wipo.org/about-ip/en/overview.html

World Tourism Organization (2000) *Local Food in Tourism Policies, preliminary findings of a WTO Secretariat survey*, Madrid: WTO.

10 The route to quality: Italian gastronomy networks in operation

Magda Antonioli Corigliano

Introduction

Over the past few years, trends in tourist demand and consumer behaviour have shown that tourists not only want to visit cultural and historical sites, but also to explore regions and landscapes as a whole. They increasingly select destinations not only on the basis of climate, art and historical heritage, human landmarks and environment-based activities in general, but also in terms of eno-gastronomic resources.[1] Gastronomic supply is therefore increasingly shaped by tourist demand, highlighting the considerable potential wine and gastronomic products have in national and international tourist markets. Taking the region as the basic context of all tourist products, this chapter analyses wine and gastronomic components of the product in detail, trying to underline the added value of an aggregating or network logic in the development of typical agro-alimentary products[2] and tourism. The examples presented in this chapter are drawn largely from the Italian experience.

In many European countries, the situation of wine and gastronomic tourism appears to be complex and variegated, but also dynamic and rich in social, cultural and economic implications (Antonioli Corigliano 1999: 27). In order to realize its potential, it is essential that all actors involved implement a common entrepreneurial logic integrating wine and gastronomic tourism into the global tourist offer. In theory, this would allow them to take advantage of the strong synergies that can be achieved and to transform local land planning into a crucial instrument for sustainable development policy.

Wine and gastronomic tourism is now emerging as one of the most promising segments of the tourism sector. Nevertheless, organizational and managerial capabilities lag behind in many places. It is highly likely that networks are needed to build an efficient and competitive network, to market high quality products and to safeguard the region's positive image.

It is also an assumption in this chapter, that it is important to identify and encourage agricultural development through specialized and typical regional products, which can be protected and promoted through legislation, such as the Common Agricultural Policy (CAP) of the European Union. This will provide the basis for a solid and durable success both in tourism and agriculture, engendering revenue and employment benefits, especially in less developed areas.

Rural tourism and wine tourism: new trends in the tourist market

Alternative forms of tourism, which place emphasis on greater contact and understanding between tourists and the environment, emerged relatively recently. The various forms of environmental tourism can be grouped under the generic term of 'rural tourism', mainly practised away from traditional tourism destinations such as seaside and mountain resorts and art cities. Rural areas provide the backdrop for various forms of tourist behaviour, including sports, horse-riding, hunting, tasting wine and gastronomic products and learning about cooking, bird watching, photography, etc. (Martinengo and Savoja 1999: 135–142).

Rural tourism has long been considered a second-choice product, reserved for people with limited resources, who chose the countryside because they could not afford more attractive destinations. The re-discovery of tradition essentially based on typical products and rural lifestyles has only recently brought about a new rural tourism which is quite often able to offer high-standard services in terms of prices and quality.

The new specific demand for environmental interaction in authentic settings (Perez de las Heras 1999) is deeply entrenched in the rural environment: tourists are interested in nature and tradition. 'Real' rural tourism only started to develop in the 1980s (Grolleau 1987: 90–100). From this point of view, local culture and the natural features of a rural environment become the real highlights. In the specific case of wine tourism, wine and other typical products of the local cuisine become real tourist attractions and a motivation to visit the countryside. Such motivations can be either exclusive – gastronomic trips or tours of wine cellars – or complementary to other interests (recreation, sport and fitness, culture). This explains the progressive growth of the gastronomic offer, as it targets not only tourists explicitly demanding it, but also tourists visiting the region for other reasons.

Hence, public sector promotion of different forms of tourism in the rural environment has shifted to meet changing consumer demand. In Italy, Law No. 730 of 5 December 1985 relating to farm tourism was initially aimed at encouraging farmers to remain in rural areas, improving their living conditions and fostering the development and balance of the agricultural region through tourism. Furthermore, rural tourists were encouraged to work together with the farmer. Today, the law is used for valorizing typical regional products, safeguarding and promoting traditions and cultural heritage in the rural environment in order to respond better to the changing trends in tourist demand. The guest is no longer an 'extra farmer', but a tourist taking a holiday in the countryside.

Thus, the countryside has definitely become comparable to many other typical tourist destinations; it has become an all-purpose cultural destination. Rural tourists seek a mixture of attractions and activities, in order to qualify their holiday as distinctive, if not unique. They need to have a 'noteworthy experience' they will remember and talk about once they return home (Antonioli Corigliano 1999). This is only possible if tourists can experience the region as a whole, discover its identity and traditional values and come into direct contact with the local community. Such experiences will also encourage tourists to consume the same gastronomic products in their own countries of origin. In fact, eno-gastronomic tourism strongly fosters the export of traditional and unique agro-food products. In Italy, for instance, tourism was the key to successful exports of olive oil, pasta, mozzarella cheese, etc. (AA.VV. 1998: 1–22).

Furthermore, besides being an attractive market niche, wine and gastronomy can be considered as a transversal component of all kinds of tourism and, therefore, an important feature of national identity and differentiation in the marketplace. Italy, for instance, has integrated gastronomic elements into its multifaceted national cultural heritage, which is internationally celebrated. Let us remember that there are over 500 varieties of cheese, 300 kinds of salami and hams and over 2,000 varieties of wine (Antonioli Corigliano 1996b: 198).

Wine and gastronomic tourism can thus be considered as forms of cultural tourism (Antonioli Corigliano 1996a: 2), as they aim at preserving and valorizing agricultural territories – especially those producing wine, oil and other typical products – and suggest a new way of holidaying: gourmet tours around farms and wine cellars to taste typical regional gastronomic products. Gastronomic tourism allows tourists to come into contact with the culture of the region and to establish a tie with its past, its traditions, its historical and cultural heritage. A region's cultural heritage is embodied in its agriculture, its environment, its social patterns and its farming tradition. Gastronomic tourism can make a contribution to relating the distinctive culture of a region to the wider social, economic and environmental context of the location.

The development of gastronomic tourism will probably be favoured by changes currently taking place in the tourism market. In particular the growth of short breaks and additional holidays has led to a predominance of short stays scattered throughout the whole year. In other words, tourist trends reveal an increasing customization of the tourist 'package' leading to a highly fragmented demand that Italy's regional resources, which are very articulated and differentiated, seem to be particularly suitable for (Antonioli Corigliano 1988; Candela 1988: 105–110).

Furthermore, the tourist sector is highly influenced by globalization and progressive liberalization; as a result, many new destinations – several of which are situated in developing countries where investment and management costs are significantly lower – have arisen, slowly eroding the market share of more established destinations such as Italy.

In order to meet competition from these countries, it is necessary to promote the distinctive features of the national heritage. Italy is internationally renowned for its unique blend of natural and cultural resources, which has a significant role in global culture. Thus, a relaunch of the national tourist product based on wine and food elements becomes crucial: supply needs to be reorganized and oriented not only towards traditional segments of demand, but also towards new consumer groups (Candela 1996: 50–79).

Figure 10.1 shows the general framework of the tourist supply system of this

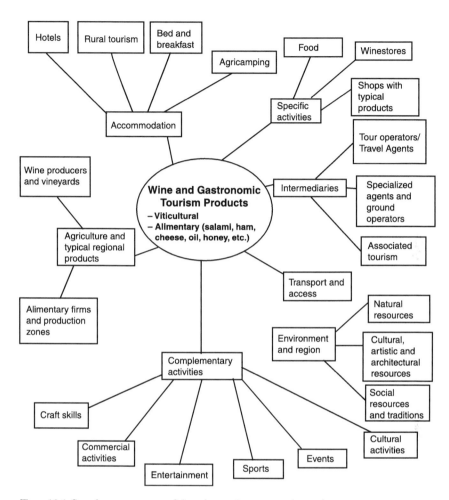

Figure 10.1 Supply components of the wine and gastronomic tourism system

particular 'agricultural product' including all the different components and participants. These include accommodation suppliers, tour operators, primary regional resources (such as agricultural produce, agricultural products and restaurants) and secondary resources (such as sport activities, visits to artistic and cultural sites, folklore parades, events and exhibitions). The presence of a variety of producers does not automatically make networks emerge. Such 'networks of actors' are hardly viable without the coordination of an organizing unit, as we shall try to demonstrate.

Wine and taste routes or paths[3]

The aforementioned evolution of demand has brought about a radical change in supply: the tourist value of various regions has been significantly enhanced and development initiatives – such as the creation of wine routes and taste paths – have been carried out. Such initiatives are aimed at developing a wine and gastronomic tourism production system by offering an accessible and attractive tourist product that is clearly recognizable by tourists/consumers.

A wine route or taste path usually integrates the typical regional raw materials such as wine and oil with all other environmental, cultural and tourist resources to ensure the tourist utilization of the region. The route becomes a common thread linking the tourist/consumer and the tourism supply system.

Tourist motivations are diverse and related to the individual's needs. Gastronomic tourism is definitely not a mass tourism phenomenon since many routes/paths are not physically able to host more than a certain number of tourists at one time. Nevertheless, in order to develop the tourist potential of such routes, it is necessary to identify the underlying needs of individual tourists. Some previous studies on tourist motivations for visiting wine routes/taste paths intended as integrated tourist products have identified different aspects of demand (Antonioli Corigliano 1996b: 52–55; Leed 1992: 48):

- *psychological*: the vacation or trip is perceived as a revealing moment for personal resources and motivations to change;
- *sociological:* cultural and aesthetic values highlight aspects related to the quality of life and of the environment, setting off comparisons between tourist and non-tourist destinations;
- *economic:* personal income and vacation expenditure are also very important factors, but rural tourists pay particular attention to the quality level of the product and to the price/quality ratio.

A route/path is a complex tourist product, involving an interaction between different material and immaterial components: facilities, services, environment, local communities. Despite the high fragmentation of demand, the complexity of a route is determined by the number of decision-makers and actors involved in organizing it. One of the most critical issues arising in the creation of a route/path is managing the relational dynamics among actors, as they go beyond a purely managerial logic or an enterprise-to-consumer or enterprise-to-enterprise relationship. In fact, numerous stakeholders are involved: internal actors such as local authorities, the resident population and local enterprises and external actors such as tourists, tour operators and investors.

Hence, the route is both a path linking the internal actors and the means of managing the tourist product. In the following paragraphs, we shall analyse some of the key aspects of gastronomic routes/paths identified in studies carried out in the last few years:

- Path patterns as a function of relationship between signs and regions.

- The underlying pattern of regional organization (the concept of a specific district).
- The management structure and strategic development potential of the coordinating service unit.

Sign–region relationships

A major feature of a gastronomic route/path is that it links places of interest through their products, history and landscape. Two variables need to be taken into account in managing the route/path: the resources of the region and its specific markers (information about the distinctive resources of a region). The main goal is to identify, interpret and decode components of tourists' behaviour so as to explain the motivations behind their visit. In this way it is possible to establish relationships between different places and elements composing the tourist product, to identify spatial patterns of demand and to promote specific features of the region. Spatial aspects of demand, which will not be dealt with in detail here, include tangible product components – such as the spatial and geographic context of the region, its physical and built attractions – and subjective aspects – such as the response to tourist motivations, the tourist's experiences in the area, etc. The tangible products of the region and the subjective experience of the tourist can be combined into a route/path map which relates the resources of the region to the markers for those resources, mainly in terms of communication. Actually we can have four different situations with regard to the relationship between regions and markers:

1   One highly profiled marker or resource in one region, such as Chianti wine in the Chianti region. The path map will include places where the resource is present (this case is quite simple and it will be touched on only briefly).
2   One region with multiple markers: wines and other products all in the same region (this chapter concentrates on this case).
3   One marker covering multiple areas: such as the *Via Franchigena*, the Silk Route (routes crossing different regions) or wine routes crossing various regions.
4   Multiple markers in multiple territories: this example is not considered here since it is necessary to define first the priorities within a targeted authentic setting.

The different ways in which gastronomic routes/paths can be developed through relating regional supply, gastronomic markers and tourist motivations will be illustrated in the following sections.

The tourist district

In order to establish an effective network among different actors, the route/path should be placed in a specific spatial context, where interactions among different categories of participants take place. This is the so-called 'tourist district', intended as a delimited area characterized by a common local identity based on historical, social and economic elements and containing a range of enterprises producing and distributing the local tourist product.

In order to define the tourist district and its related externalities, it is useful to refer to some of the general features of the industrial district. Research on industrial clustering has shown that added value is achieved primarily by a network of actors as opposed to individual enterprises (Pyke *et al.* 1990: 1–27). This implies that:

- An area (i.e. village, county or region) is considered in terms of its outward network relations and not just the external relations of individual actors.
- The enterprise's internal and external economies become internal for the network (Beccatini 1979: 120).

All the definitions of a 'district' make reference to the following features (Antonioli Corigliano 2000: 107–115):

(a) a *distinct and delimited geographical area*, with specific features in terms of regional morphology, population, regional products, etc.;
(b) a *characteristic historical, social and cultural identity*, as well as an economic structure typical of the local community;
(c) an *active role is played by local institutions*, in terms of distribution of services, infrastructure, education, etc.;
(d) an *interacting population of enterprises*, interested in establishing a formal network of relations with different hierarchies.

(Becattini 1979: 83)

Such elements are crucial in a context where enterprise competitiveness does not wholly depend on the capabilities of the individual enterprise any more, but it also depends on the external conditions characterizing the overall social and economic system (Roelandt and den Hertog 1999: 5).

However, the features of the tourist product present specific challenges for the tourist district. First of all, the production chain mainly spreads out horizontally rather than vertically and this significantly limits work flexibility, specialization and efficiency, as production and consumption are simultaneous. Secondly, a horizontal chain does not exclude the presence of a vertical one. In fact, each component of the tourist product is the result of a vertical process, not necessarily occurring in the tourist area. If a tourist region is to benefit substantially, the distribution stages or downstream relations need to be handled efficiently by dedicated intermediaries.

A third typical feature of the tourist district concerns relational networks with specific characteristics:

- the *increased importance of extra-economic networks* is determined by the weight of resident communities and the power of local authorities;
- the *complexity of decision-maker networks*, as they involve different hierarchic levels and decision-makers belonging to different industries (agriculture, tourism, transport, environment, etc);
- the *extraterritoriality of many actors* in the tourist production process, having interests which may clash with those of local communities (especially in the tour operating field).

Accordingly, the comparison of a tourist region with an industrial district is promising, but it is questionable whether one can – yet – identify very successful examples of this model of economic organization.

Organizational aspects

Connections among actors, which constitute an essential part of the tourist production process, prove to be crucial for the existence of a tourist district. The plurality of actors involved – as well as their level of co-penetration and interrelationship – and the centrality of human resources in every step of the process, require strong coordination, able to create added value and produce economic benefits for the whole region. In creating an effective gastronomic route/path, therefore, it is important to coordinate public sector intervention and to activate synergies among all the many small actors involved (Associazione Nazionale Città del Vino 1997: 10–30).

With effective coordination, the gastronomic route/path can act as a 'service centre' or coordinating unit, providing the expertise and logistic support necessary to allow network participants to benefit from the scale economies engendered by the integration of agricultural, gastronomic, rural and tourism assets and resources. The route/path provides scale economies that are not available to individual enterprises: system economies related to information management – a major asset in tourist competitiveness at local level – and system economies related to specialized communication channels.

At the very practical level, the organization of a gastronomic route/path involves the following major elements:

- organizing committee;
- management committee;
- disciplinary regulations;
- signage system;
- tourist guides and illustrative, advertising and promotional material.

However, the quality of a system does not depend exclusively on the quality of its single components, but also on the quality of its overall organization as well as the quality of the relational networks among actors.

In the specific case of a route/path, two quality levels call for great attention. The first level refers to the individual enterprises associated with the route/path and two crucial aspects of the tourist experience:

1   Quality of the product offered (regional gastronomic products).

The second level refers to the overall quality of the route/path, to its organization and management.

2   Quality of the tourist components of the visit (single components such as accommodation, activities, etc.).

Where quality issues are concerned, it is essential that individual partners as well as associations comply with standard checking and control procedures, as these are crucial for the success of the network. Standard checking and control procedures of *products* can be carried out by for example:

- Associations formed by the businesses involved in order to verify that eno-gastronomic products meet quality standards.
- Chambers of Commerce for those products covered by specific regulations.
- Trade associations for those sectors which are not subject to regulatory controls, such as tourist information, transport services, tourist farms, etc.

The Management Committee of the route/path can either choose to carry out reception standard checks and controls itself or entrust them to appropriate bodies outside the Association.

In such a context we will concentrate our attention on the steps required to develop the organization's structure, without any account being taken of supply or demand. A more detailed analysis would add a number of steps linking the organization to the region, in particular to the various aspects of tourist planning and to the specific bodies involved such as agriculture, industry, transport, environment, etc. as well as to potential tourists. In particular, efficient observation can help in the identification of the resources to be employed and also in the constant monitoring of the results (Antonioli Corigliano 2000: 110).

Such linkage of demand and supply can be achieved through implementing the following steps:

- supply inventory (both gastronomic and tourism elements);
- identification of relevant internal/external actors (e.g. enterprises and public sector/community groups);
- assessment of tourism market needs relevant to the products available in the region;
- identification of appropriate communication channels relevant to identified market segments (Antonioli Corigliano 1999: 249–255).

The organizational steps required to establish a route/path as defined above, can be summed up as follows:

Establishment of the 'Association'

(a) Establishment of the route/path Organizing Committee with the aim of assigning its management to the operators themselves.
(b) Establishment of the route/path Association.

Start-up of route/path activities

(a) Design route/path logo.
(b) Produce informative and advertising material about the route/path.
(c) Develop common signage system, usually guided by regional or national laws.
(d) Draw up an exhaustive annual activity plan and related financial scheme.

In conclusion, the key goals of a wine route/path should be to:

- Satisfy the increasing demand for rural and wine and gastronomic tourism.
- Supply efficient and accessible services, both for network members and tourists.
- Develop local tourist products distinct from 'industrial' or conventional tourist products. Valorize locally produced or locally managed products characterized by the local landscape, region and culture in order maximize benefits at local level.

Partnership: the role of the different actors

As previously argued, the institutional function of a wine/taste route or path is to ensure the best fit between the needs of demand and supply, the former aimed at satisfying tourist motivations, the latter aimed at promoting a region and its distinctive features in the most suitable way.

It is important to remember that routes/paths or local tourist districts are set in a wider regional or national context, where second-level networks are created. Second-level networks can definitely bring about added value, in terms of scale and system economies for some specific functions, and act as privileged interlocutors with higher institutions such as state and international bodies. But the success of such actions depends largely on an efficient role division between the first and second levels.

Figure 10.2 presents a functional scheme where actors and relationships among different action levels are schematized in a general framework, from international institutions to tourists and local residents. The figure sets out the Italian case in order to give a practical illustration of the networks and actors involved. Particularly relevant in the Italian context are the Wine Tourism Movement (*Movimento*

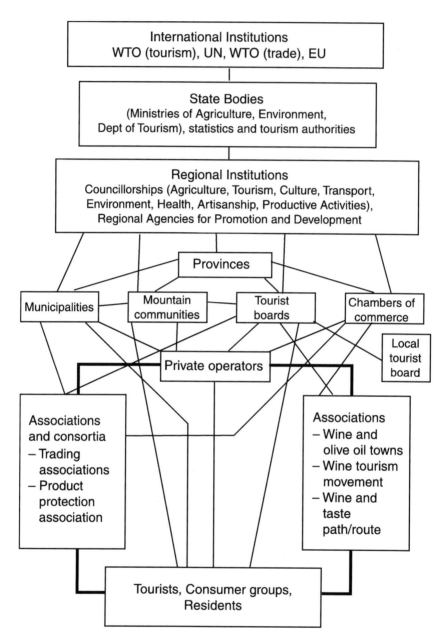

Figure 10.2 Interactions among wine and gastronomic tourism actors in Italy

del Turismo del Vino) and the Wine Towns Association (*Associazione Città del Vino*), two organizations that in Italy have contributed strongly to the creation of a wine and gastronomic culture and have fostered connections among local and national actors.

Institutional actors

Given the environmental, social and cultural impacts of tourism, public sector intervention is needed at all levels: from the European Union to the nation-state and all local institutions as shown in Figure 10.2. Each of these bodies has a specific role, but the involvement of the public sector also confers more importance to the initiative and has a significant effect in terms of land utilization and regional valorization, if we assume that the region is a public good and its promotion is a task for the public sector. Recent studies of industrial districts tend to emphasize the role of the public sector as a facilitator, delivering its services directly as well as indirectly (Roelandt and Hertog 1999).

Co-operation with the public sector is essential to:

- develop tourism and agriculture individually;
- obtain further external financing, for example from the European Commission;
- develop necessary information sources in the standard tourist promotion system (from road signs to joint promotion and advertising campaigns abroad);
- decentralize tourist flows from more crowded areas by various means, for example planning and visitor management;
- to provide learning and innovation resources.

Suppliers

As previously mentioned, one of the main features of a tourist product is its sectoral transversality. In fact, in order to offer a product able to satisfy tourism demand, a number of economic actors from different sectors need to be involved. However, a successful combination between tourism and wine and food production and the production of other services will be possible only if these actors adopt a new entrepreneurial logic, centred on a wider economic vision. The producers have to recognize, accept and utilize their mutual interdependencies. Entrepreneurs who decide to join a route/path need to diversify their activities, will have to re-orient them towards the tourist services market and contribute to the innovation of high quality regional products (Antonioli Corigliano 1996b: 24).

Producing wine, olive oil or other typical regional products does not necessarily establish a basis for wine and gastronomic tourism. Only those destinations able to transform their high-quality products and variegated local cuisine into a territorially, culturally and historically specific product can use wine and gastronomic tourism as an additional means of enhancing the distinctiveness of their region (Viganò 1998: 12–18).

Therefore, high-quality products and regional distinctiveness need to be combined with an efficient accommodation/hospitality system. In addition to an appropriate mix of accommodation facilities, qualified staff are needed to give information about typical local products and all wine/taste route or path-related sites (cellars, historical places, crafts shops, restaurants, etc.) and to hand out informative materials as well (Viganò 1999: 1–10).

The most relevant categories of suppliers are:

- *Cellars and other producers of typical regional products*
  The viticultural farm and its environment – from vineyards to cellars – is the crucial meeting point between wine production activities and their territorial and cultural context. The cellar in particular has a strategic role as it represents the culmination of the production process and it contributes to the marketing process by allowing tourists to gather and learn about wine and viticulture.

  The quality of facilities offered to the consumer/tourist is one of the fundamental criteria to evaluate wine and other tourist-oriented producers. There are three crucial aspects: the *path*, that should start from a welcome point and be sequential, offering all necessary information about the production process; the *tasting* intended as the natural conclusion of the visit, to be held in an appropriate location respecting all hygienic standards; and the *purchase of products*, that should not conflict with other sales channels such as wine suppliers, supermarkets, etc.

- *Rural tourism*
  'Rural tourism' is defined here as accommodation and hospitality offered by agricultural entrepreneurs and their families in their own farms. Rural tourism suits wine and gastronomic tourism perfectly, thanks to its close connection with the region and with the alimentary production processes. It also significantly enhances the route/path offer by satisfying the tourist's need to relax. It can also be complemented by additional activities, such as sports, cuisine classes or other courses related to the local products, gastronomic culture or ecologically sustainable activities.

- *Restaurants*
  Restaurants can offer the real typical flavours of a wine/taste route or path. Wine, for instance, is the beverage which best highlights the solemnity and pleasure of convivial meetings and is therefore closely related to the culinary arts. This connection has to be embodied in local gastronomy, in order to provide tourists with an experience that goes beyond its alimentary and culinary meaning, enabling them to taste the whole gastronomic atmosphere of the route/path. Restaurants should guarantee the quality and typicality of their dishes, using local products and offering traditional recipes. Specific regulations are needed to control them (Bemporad 1990: 14–33; Camporesi 1980: 42–57; Capatti and Colombo 1990: 29–45).

- *Accommodation and other facilities (hotels, B&B, private houses)*
  In order to develop overnight tourism along the route/path and not only

excursion tourism, different accommodation facilities are needed in order to meet the needs of all demand segments and widen the range of lodging choice. Hotels should also offer information about local gastronomic products, cellars and other production sites, paths to follow, etc. Furthermore, accommodation facilities may engender stimulating synergies, for example by allowing other suppliers along the route to present their products directly to tourists.

- *Tour operators and travel agencies*
  Wine and gastronomic tourism is a particular kind of tourism, requiring special attention and care. For this reason, it is often neglected by travel agencies or tour operators, who usually prefer all-inclusive packages to more traditional destinations. Instead, tourism intermediaries should become central to developing an integrated gastronomic tourism product, helping to avoid overcrowding problems at certain times of the year and also to differentiate gastronomic tourism from mass tourism products. The tourist packages created by tour operators to combine wine and gastronomic products may be twofold:

  1 Packages centred exclusively on wine and gastronomic tourism and route/path visits.
  2 Packages where visits to the route/path are part of a multifaceted tourist product (e.g. cultural tourism, thermal tourism, mountain tourism) and represent a complementary highlight.

- *Crafts producers*
  Crafts producers can offer typical products – not exclusively alimentary – able to enhance the authenticity of the tourist experience and to create memories that can be taken home. Relating gastronomic products to other traditional crafts widens the economic impact of the route, as well as ensuring the survival of a wider range of traditional products fundamental to local culture (Ceresini 1992: 86–91).

- *Events, cultural activities, and animation organizers*
  Events, cultural activities and animation play an important role in completing the gastronomic tourism supply system. Event organizers should act according to a common concept of the main product, the sponsorship of events should support local products (rather than those of a bigger foreign company) and the events should support the promotion of other local attractions.

The rest of the chapter illustrates how some of these principles have been applied in the development of wine and food networks in Italy.

The Italian case

The management and valorization of the wine and gastronomic patrimony by public authorities and private operators in Italy is fragmented and differs from area to area. Therefore, wine/taste routes may become the ideal model to promote the region and its resources as a tourist location.

In order to support their development, a national law has been approved to define the concept of routes/paths and illustrate the minimum quality standards required (Law No. 268/1999). This law aims at valorizing wine-producing territories through the creation of 'wine routes/paths' as described in subsection 2 of article 1 'paths advertised and marked by appropriate signs enhancing natural, cultural and environmental values as well as promoting vineyards, single or associated agricultural wine cellars open to the public as the key element to diffuse, commercialize and utilize wine-producing territories as a form of tourist offer'.

One of the most remarkable achievements of Law No. 268/1999 is its enlarged scope, extending from wine tourism to other tourist forms supported by high quality regional products such as olive oil, as provided by article 5, 'the provisions of [. . .] law are also to be intended for the creation of Routes/Paths aiming at valorizing concurrently other quality productions with specific reference to olive oil and other typical products in general'.

Hence, Law No. 268/1999 represents a valuable instrument to enhance entrepreneurial culture and foster collaboration among different actors. Its provisions strongly promote collaborative action at national level able to interrelate tourism and agriculture, two sectors both having a huge potential at local level, a high degree of environmental vulnerability and a relatively weak representation at national level. Thus, Law No. 268/1999 represents the starting point for the creation of a gastronomic path which is both a physical itinerary linking cultural resources and a virtual path linking the various actors involved in it.

The new law has been preceded by several interesting and original initiatives carried out by private enterprises or by regional authorities themselves, as in the case of Tuscany. Tuscany officially created wine and taste routes and approved a related law in 1996 (Regional Law 69/1996). By the end of 2000, Tuscany had fourteen wine routes/taste paths covering a wide part of the region.

The case of Tuscany has been used as a model for similar initiatives in other regions and provided the basis for the national law mentioned above. Numerous regions – such as Piedmont and Emilia Romagna – have followed Tuscany's example and have passed regional laws in order to guide private initiatives for the creation of routes and paths. The experience from these initiatives demonstrates that routes or paths are usually non-profit associations set up by different operators (wine producers, rural tourism farmers, restaurant owners, crafts producers, etc.). Such associations are financially supported through membership fees, often differentiated by membership category. Apart from the management of the route/path itself, communication and event organization are the key activities of the Associations. Their activities are not exclusively intended as general information and promotion initiatives but also as specific promotion aimed at identifying the path or the sign system. However, significant weaknesses are still present in the exploitation of the route/path offer, which is intended as an all-inclusive package formed from different components, which can be tailored according to tourist demand.

The region in the tourist production system: a policy framework

This final section of the chapter intends to focus on some of the main points discussed so far, highlight the role of typical products in potential tourist areas, and give some hints for the strategic development of wine routes/taste paths in order to meet the needs of a new kind of tourism oriented towards healthy lifestyles. This is quite a topical issue since in the last few years the countryside, local traditions and wine and gastronomic tourism have generated more and more interest. These trends are complemented by excellent examples of heritage management and adding value to productive activities, fostered by the increasing recognition gastronomy has achieved in Italy. Thus, itineraries have been created in regions celebrated all around the world such as the Chianti region, but also in less renowned areas such as Piedmont, Marche and Sicily, wrongly considered less 'noble' in the rural tourism panorama.

Nevertheless, successful examples of regional valorization and improved production quality can sometimes be counteracted by hurried development and improvisation that has no other intention than turning a fast profit. Initiatives in the tourism sector also risk the free-riding mechanism where some producers benefit from the investments of others, while not contributing anything themselves. Therefore individual or networked enterprises need to take into consideration the negative reactions generated by such developments by forming dedicated and viable associations. Without institutional frameworks, the development of high quality sustainable gastronomic products becomes almost impossible.

Quality control mechanisms for regional products represent important assets to diffuse through regional networks. It is therefore important to create and foster a real *culture* of alimentary and gastronomic products – whose uniqueness and exclusiveness is enhanced by the knowledge of their region of origin – especially where this still does not exist. The wine route is not asphalted, can host a few people at a time and should never become a highway!

Gastronomic tourism needs specific planning and promotion, and stable partnerships to exploit economic synergies, meet residents' needs and develop professional education and qualifications. It is crucial to remember that the development of rural areas depends not only on agriculture, but also on tourism and other productive activities. Therefore, policies, rules and strategies should be designed for both sectors jointly and should aim at a common target.

Different policies for different territorial areas

There is no universal 'recipe' suitable for every case and every situation. Each locality has its own typology in terms of resources, products, producers, development and tourist growth, and each area calls for different policies. A wine route/

taste path can fulfil an important coordination function by linking regions offering similar or complementary activities, services and products.

With reference to the Italian case, four main types of areas can be identified:

1   Areas particularly renowned for excellent wine or other regional products, but disregarded by tourists. These areas are celebrated for their high-quality wines and gastronomic products, but tourist aspects need to be developed mainly in synergy with nearby locations, and local reception facilities (such as accommodation, information, etc.). Local initiatives could well be included in a wider tourist package and theme itineraries should be created (this is the case in Piedmont or the less developed areas of Tuscany).

2   Areas strongly positioned on the market, both for wine and gastronomic products and tourism, not subject to seasonality and situated close to other tourist attractions, especially cultural ones. The organization of promotional events becomes crucial here and the promotional benefits could for reasons of ecological and economic sustainability be extended to less-known neighbouring areas (a typical example is 'The Gallo Nero' area of the Chianti region).

3   Areas in the vicinity of renowned tourist locations (seaside, mountain and lake resorts) where wine and gastronomy represent additional highlights for other kinds of tourism, but can easily become products in their own right. Therefore, connecting wine and gastronomic resources to tourism, developing tasting activities and rural tourism is important. For out-of-season periods, a wine and gastronomic tourist model might be feasible (this is the pattern in Valtellina (Lombardy), or the Riviera Adriatica in Emilia Romagna).

4   Economically depressed areas or those totally disregarded by tourists, but able to offer high-quality wine and gastronomic resources. A major event or a range of annual events is needed to create a tourist product, to counteract negative images of the region or its culture. In such areas in particular, wine and gastronomy represent a way to develop economy and employment (as in many areas in Southern Italy, such as Calabria or Sicily).

Operators and stakeholders, however, should harness and enhance such opportunities by implementing a planned development process based on environmental protection, synergies between public and private operators and the ability to generate a virtuous circle of development. Furthermore, the contribution of professionals with different skills and capabilities will prove to be crucial within the wider system of local environmental components and their interactions.

In order to fulfil the tourist's expectation to have a *life experience*, wine cellars, restaurants or production places should be ready to give information about local culture, history and traditions. This would enable wine and gastronomic tourism operators to interpret the specific needs of tourists and add value to their products.

Priority issues

Is it possible to create industrial regions, districts or clusters through political willpower? This question has been asked many times by researchers as well as politicians, and it is highly relevant also in the case of tourism and gastronomy. This chapter shows that there are many opportunities for public sector intervention, for example through financial subsidies, regulation or by establishing appropriate institutions. In establishing appropriate structures and networks for the development of gastronomy tourism it is important:

1   To create, diffuse and safeguard a specific culture of quality regional products among consumers and producers.
2   To develop the supply of gastronomic products according to the needs of tourists and of residents as well.
3   To develop a homogeneous and univocal 'welcome culture' among actors, that shares the key objectives as well as quality criteria, programmes and competencies of the different policies implemented.
4   To reach cooperation agreements on marketing and communication projects within the tourist district involving operators, public authorities, agricultural and tourist bodies on the basis of the issues discussed in this chapter.
5   To facilitate the introduction of the concept of area quality to the tourist district as a strategic factor able to integrate the various competitive advantages.
6   To improve human resources in the sector and provide professional training for specific professional roles.

As Hjalager has indicated in Chapter 2, however, there is less optimism concerning the public role on the part of some observers of industrial districts (e.g. Roelandt and Hertog 1999). The top-down approach taken by national and regional governments in Italy (and also described in Chapter 12 in the case of Portugal) has not always been the most effective means of developing innovative gastronomy tourism products. In deciding where and how to intervene in the development of gastronomy tourism, therefore, policy-makers should carefully consider whether intervention is necessary, and if so, what form this should take. Borrowing from the lessons learned in the development of industrial districts, initiatives should be market driven, should avoid direct subsidies and should be geared towards inducement rather than direct intervention. This is the approach described by Hall and Mitchell (Chapter 11) in the case of New Zealand, which has developed healthy gastronomic networks in the face of considerable challenges in global markets. Just as wine-makers in the New World have learned from Italy and France about wine-making, perhaps the Old World also has something to learn from its New World competitors in this respect. Italy, with its enormous gastronomic heritage, tradition of innovation and established networks of small entrepreneurs, is perhaps in a better position than most to benefit from such developments.

Notes

1 Eno-gastronomic is a literal translation of the Italian word 'enogastronomico' which identifies products or production processes that are exclusive to a delimited region and therefore distinguish the same region. The products and production processes are unique and strongly influenced by history and tradition. They are generally thought to be the opposite of mass production.
2 Agro-alimentary products are not the result of mass production but are agricultural processed foods centred in a specific region, with its history and traditions, and are particularly quality oriented.
3 'Route' is used as a synonym of 'path' or connection among different actors. Thus, route is also intended as a path among operators and not only as a geographical link.

References

AA.VV. (1998) *Il turismo enogastronomico in Italia: risorse e potenzialità*, Project Works del XII Corso di Perfezionamento in Economia del Turismo, Milan: Università Bocconi, Mimeo.

Antonioli Corigliano, M. (1996a) 'Risorse economiche dal turismo culturale in Italia: ruolo e prospettive', in *Decongestione e capillarità. Un nuovo equilibrio per il turismo culturale italiano nel XXI secolo*, Naples: FAI.

—— (1996b) *Enoturismo. Caratteristiche della domanda, strategie di offerta e aspetti territoriali e ambientali*, Milan: Franco Angeli.

—— (1988) 'Uno studio microeconomico sulla domanda turistica e delle implicazioni di metodo per la politica del turismo', *Commercio*, 29.

—— (1999) *Strade del vino ed enoturismo. Distretti turistici e vie di comunicazione*, Milan: Franco Angeli .

—— (2000) 'I Distretti Turistici e le aggregazioni fra attori per lo sviluppo del prodotto destinazione', in Colantoni, M. (ed.) *Turismo: una tappa per la ricerca*, Bologna: CNR, Progetto strategico 'Turismo e Sviluppo Economico'.

Associazione Nazionale Città del Vino (1997) *In che strada siamo? Vademecum per la corretta istituzione di una Strada del Vino*, Siena: Associazione Nazionale Città del Vino.

Becattini, G. (1979) 'Dal settore industriale al distretto industriale, alcune considerazioni sull'unità di indagine dell'economia industriale', *L'industria: Rivista di economia e politica industriale*, 1.

Bemporad, C. (1990) *Storia della gastronomia italiana*, Mursia: Milano.

Camporesi, P. (1980) *Alimentazione, folclore, società*, Parma: Pratiche Editrice.

Candela, G. (1988) *Contributi all'analisi economica del turismo*, Bologna: Clueb.

—— (1996) *Manuale di economia del turismo*, Bologna: Clueb.

Capatti, A. and Colombo, C. (1990) *Occhio al cibo. Immagini per un secolo di consumi alimentari in Italia*, Milan: Coop.

Ceresini, A. (1992) *La sfida artigiana: prodotti tipici e mercato unico*, Milan: Franco Angeli.

Grolleau, H. (1987) *Le tourisme rural dans les 12 Etats membres de la Communauté économique européenne*, Bruxelles: TER.

Leed, E.J. (1992) *La mente del viaggiatore: dall'Odissea al turismo globale*, Bologna: Il Mulino.

Martinengo M.C. and Savoja L. (1999) *Il turismo dell'ambiente*, Milan: Guerini Studio.

Perez de las Heras (1999) *La guia del ecoturismo*, Madrid: Mundi-Prensa.

Pyke F., Becattini, G. and Segenberger, W. (1990) *Industrial districts and inter-firm co-operation in Italy*, Geneva: ILO Publications.

Roelandt, Theo and Pim den Hertog (1999) 'Cluster analysis and cluster-based policy making: the state of the art', in OECD (ed.) *Boosting Innovation: The cluster approach*, Paris: OECD: 413–427.

Viganò, G. (1998) *Il turismo enogastronomico. Strumenti operativi e strategie di valorizzazione*, in materiali del Corso di Perfezionamento in Economia del Turismo, Milan: Università Bocconi.

—— (1999) *Strade del vino e territorio. Strategie di valorizzazione e strumenti operativi*, Milan: Università Bocconi, Mimeo.

11 The changing nature of the relationship between cuisine and tourism in Australia and New Zealand: from fusion cuisine to food networks

Michael Hall and Richard Mitchell

> Australia today is an exhilarating place for anybody interested in cooking, a new world with new perceptions and all the appropriate skills to develop and fuse the best aspects of the diverse food cultures that make up the global kitchen.
>
> (Webb and Whittington 1997: 6)

Until recently Australia and New Zealand have not been considered as countries with strong national cuisines nor of explicit links between cuisine and tourism. However, in recent years this situation has changed with New World wine and foods having a strong appearance in the international market and cuisine-related tourism becoming a key component of tourism and primary produce marketing and development strategies. The chapter argues that tourism has been a key component in the changes in Australian and New Zealand cuisine from both a demand and a supply perspective and examines the manner in which cuisine has now become a central component of the Australian and New Zealand tourism experience. The chapter is divided into two main parts. The first examines the history of Australian and New Zealand food systems and the way in which travel by Australians and New Zealanders overseas plus the impact of migrant populations has led to new styles of cuisine. The second part of the chapter discusses how wine and food tourism acts as a link between the tourism sector and the traditional agricultural sector and focuses on the economic, branding and product relationships between wine, food and tourism. The second part of the chapter therefore focuses on strategies by which the relationships between the two sectors can be maximized for greater local return. Case studies are drawn from several areas of Australia and New Zealand, highlighting topics including factors behind innovation and entrepreneurship in food and wine tourism, the role of key individuals as innovators, barriers to network development, techniques of network development and the role of the state as a facilitator of network creation and in promoting gastronomy and rural produce.

The relationship between the changing cuisine of Australia and New Zealand

and the development of strategies to maximize locally sustainable food systems is highlighted in Figure 11.1. The inputs into the food system are regarded as the various institutional, economic, technological, cultural and environmental structures that affect local food systems. These are broadly discussed in the first part of this chapter in relation to how change has occurred. The strategy component of the figure broadly responds to the second half of this chapter. However, it is important that the iterative nature of the local food system is recognized and that consumption and production be seen as two sides of the same coin, in that actions in one sphere lead to changes in the other. Indeed, a key point to emerge from examining local food systems is that the problems of globalization for local food production and gastronomy present an opportunity as much as they do a threat (see Chapter 5 by Hall and Mitchell).

The changing cuisine of Australia and New Zealand

The cuisine of Australia and New Zealand is the product of globalization, dominated by migration from Europe and, more recently, Asia. The two countries' foodways have become substantially affected by the consumption patterns of its migrants and production for both the domestic market and for export (Halliday 1994; Newton 1996). The commonalities between the two countries go beyond their migrant connection though. Both countries were a part of the British Empire and, until Britain joined the European Common Market in the early 1970s, agricultural produce from the two countries had preferential treatment in the United Kingdom. This link to the United Kingdom is extremely significant as not only did it mean that the food heritage of both countries lay with the cuisine of the British Isles but that the set of institutional relationships established between Australia and New Zealand and the United Kingdom also influenced the food that was produced.

Table 11.1 identifies some of the important historical aspects of food in Australia and New Zealand. Until after the Second World War the foodways of the two countries were dominated by the British migrants and their descendants (Baker 1999; Simpson 1999; Hallpike 2000); wines tended to be sweeter, fortified varieties while the most common alcoholic beverage was beer. One notable exception to the argument of British domination of Australian cuisine is Symons (1993) who argued that 'it is more to the point that England led industrialization. This was the epicentre of the Industrial Revolution. It was in the British Isles that the earliest attempts were made to systematically destroy traditional cuisine.' Nevertheless, the dominance of the British, and the English in particular, meant that the food of the indigenous populations tended to be ignored (except perhaps in New Zealand where the hangi was a tourist novelty in Rotorua). Indeed, significant indigenous crops, such as the macadamia nut in Australia, were not utilized until foreign interests had discovered them. Similarly, the foodways of the substantial Chinese populations became increasingly Anglofied although, arguably, they did survive in some of the Chinatown areas thanks in part to the food interests of the intelligentsia, bohemians and, more recently, tourists.

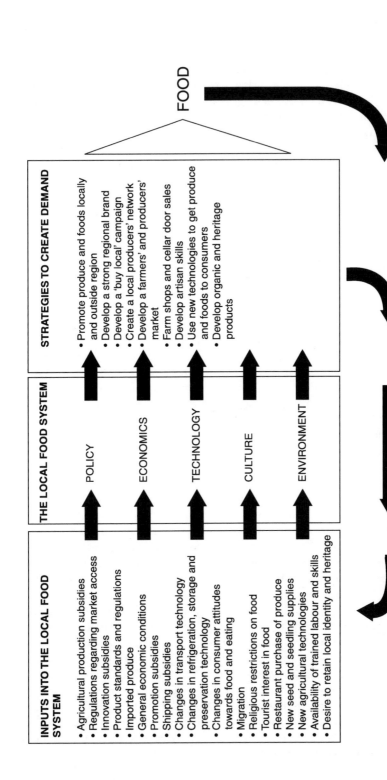

INPUTS INTO THE LOCAL FOOD SYSTEM

- Agricultural production subsidies
- Regulations regarding market access
- Innovation subsidies
- Product standards and regulations
- Imported produce
- General economic conditions
- Promotion subsidies
- Shipping subsidies
- Changes in transport technology
- Changes in refrigeration, storage and preservation technology
- Changes in consumer attitudes towards food and eating
- Migration
- Religious restrictions on food
- Tourist interest in food
- Restaurant purchase of produce
- New seed and seedling supplies
- New agricultural technologies
- Availability of trained labour and skills
- Desire to retain local identity and heritage

THE LOCAL FOOD SYSTEM

POLICY

ECONOMICS

TECHNOLOGY

CULTURE

ENVIRONMENT

STRATEGIES TO CREATE DEMAND

- Promote produce and foods locally and outside region
- Develop a strong regional brand
- Develop a 'buy local' campaign
- Create a local producers' network
- Develop a farmers' and producers' market
- Farm shops and cellar door sales
- Develop artisan skills
- Use new technologies to get produce and foods to consumers
- Develop organic and heritage products

FOOD

Figure 11.1 The local food system

Table 11.1 Overview history of Australian and New Zealand foodways

Year	Australia	New Zealand
1778	Arrival of first fleet in Sydney, first major introduction of European foods and livestock; initial use of indigenous meats, e.g. kangaroo	European whalers introduce pigs, rabbits and goats
1800s	Large areas opened for sheep grazing for wool	
1820s	Cereals grown on widespread basis; first production of grape wine	First production of grape wine
1840s	Gold discovered in the 1850s Large-scale migration and creation of a more substantial domestic market Arrival of Chinese settlers	Increased land opened for agriculture
1860s	Refrigeration revolutionizes meat exports, increased emphasis on sheep meat and cattle production Sugar cane and pineapple production commences in Queensland as does production of butter and cheese	Gold discovered in New Zealand, substantial migration and arrival of Chinese settlers Refrigeration revolutionizes meat exports Sheep meat and cattle production expands for export
1880s	Increased production of foodstuffs for British Empire market Victorian vineyards ravaged by disease	Increased production of foodstuffs for British Empire market Salmon and trout naturalized
1900s	War creates demands for agricultural produce Strong prohibition movement	War creates demands for agricultural produce Strong prohibition movement
1920s	Depression affects demands for agricultural production Strong prohibition movement Creation of Australian Wine Board	Depression affects demands for agricultural production Strong prohibition movement
1940s	War creates demands for agricultural produce Large-scale migration from Europe including British but also large movements of Italian, Greek and eastern European populations	War creates demands for agricultural produce Large-scale migration from Europe mainly British with smaller Greek and Dutch populations

Table 11.1 continued

Year	Australia	New Zealand
1950s	Continued large-scale migration The OS (Overseas trip) becomes an important component of the life experience of the intelligentsia post-university Limited licensing laws	Continued British migration The OE (Overseas experience) becomes an important component of the life experience of the intelligentsia post-university Wine not able to be served in restaurants
1960s	Food and wine begin to gain greater coverage in media, e.g. Margaret Fulton Launch of Australian *Gourmet* Magazine Creation of the Australian Wine Bureau under Len Evans First 'boutique' winery established	Food and wine begin to gain greater coverage in media, e.g. Graham Kerr First New Zealand wine exports Wine able to be served in restaurants
1970s	UK joins Common Market leading to a search for new markets Australian wine consumption increases 'Boutique' wineries well established Increase in cellar door sales activity Development of long-haul jet leads to increased inbound and outbound travel Substantial Asian migration begins New product innovation, e.g. avocados	UK joins Common Market leading to a search for new markets 'Boutique' wineries start Development of long-haul jet leads to increased inbound and outbound travel Substantial Asian and Pacific Islander migration begins
1980s	Australia becomes recognized as a significant inbound destination Inbound exceeds outbound travel for first time First media articles focusing on Australian food Australian wines have high impact overseas First wave of boutique cheese and specialist food producers	Dramatic restructuring of New Zealand economy, removal of protection of farmers leads to rapid diversification, including deer, fish and seafish farming First wave of boutique cheese producers Quality New Zealand table wines begin to receive recognition Increased focus on export

Table 11.1 continued

Year	Australia	New Zealand
	Australian seafood exported to Japan Australian *Gourmet* joins with *Traveller* magazine to become Australia's leading food magazine Café culture established in urban areas Growth of wine and food festivals	opportunities leads to product innovation, e.g. kiwifruit *Cuisine*, New Zealand's leading food magazine, launched
1990s	Extensive regional food branding and promotion begins, e.g. Taste of Tasmania Regionalism promoted in Australian food and produce, e.g. Yarra Valley, Barossa Valley, Margaret River Development of first wine and food tourism strategies at state level in New South Wales, Victoria, South Australia Australian national wine strategy seeks to double wine exports Substantial debate over what is 'Australian cuisine' Bush tucker revolution Development of TV programmes which exclusively cover Australian wines and food First Australian wine tourism conference	New Zealand Way branding and promotion begins New Zealand Sauvignon Blanc and Pinot Noir gain international recognition Café culture develops in New Zealand urban areas Substantial growth of small holders in wine and food sectors Substantial growth in wine and food festivals Increased media coverage to New Zealand food and wine
2000	National wine tourism strategy launched Substantial regional promotion linking wine and food Concerns over loss of diversity in produce and GE foods	First New Zealand wine tourism conference First New Zealand food trails First New Zealand regional wine and food brands

In Australia the arrival of large numbers of migrants following the Second World War had an enormous impact on Australian foodways. Indeed, the migration of Italians and Greeks to Australia in the 1950s has been seen as critical for the development of a more cosmopolitan Australian attitude towards food and drinking (Newton 1996). The large Greek and Italian communities in Melbourne for example, led to the establishment of a European style café culture as well as a lifestyle of eating in restaurants. In addition to ways of eating, the new migrants also introduced new products and produce including pasta, salami, real coffee, speciality artisan cheeses, garlic, char-grilled peppers and courgettes into the Australian culinary palette. This position has, however, been challenged by Symons (1993: 12) who argued that multiculturalism 'follows the new cuisine, and not the other way around'. Nevertheless, despite Symons' argument, it is widely perceived that migration has led to the widespread transfer of foodways from the old to the new country, albeit often with changes due to seasonal variation in produce and the availability of produce itself. This change has continued to occur. In the mid- to late-1970s large numbers of migrants from Asia, and from Vietnam in particular, began to arrive in Australia. The arrival of migrant food tastes and cooking styles again went hand-in-hand with the production of Asian vegetables. For many years the nearest most Australians and New Zealanders got to Asian food was the Chinese takeaway or fish and chip shop which sold Chinese food for local tastes. However, the establishment of a sizable domestic ethnic market allowed for restaurants to be established which then attracted Australians and New Zealanders who wanted to investigate new foods, particularly as many of them had also started to travel through Asia.

The importance of changes in policy and institutional arrangements for food and trade should not be underestimated. Most notably the entry of the United Kingdom into the European Common Market was devastating for rural Australia and New Zealand. This event, combined with the first world oil crisis, led to a round of rural economic restructuring which has continued to this day. The loss of preferential treatment meant that both countries had to diversify their range of production as well as find new markets. In New Zealand this led to the development of deer farming, the kiwifruit industry, the development of a horticulture industry growing fruit and vegetables for the Asian market, and the growth of the wine industry.

Combined with political and economic change, revolutions in technology have also impacted on food production. In the nineteenth century the combination of steamships and refrigeration allowed for the export of frozen meat and cheese and butter to the rest of the empire. In the late twentieth century improved air transport not only increased mobility of people, taking their tastebuds with them to and from Australia and New Zealand, but also created opportunities for the export of chilled meats and fish, and fruits and vegetables to Asia and Japan. For example, tuna caught in Australia and New Zealand waters can reach the Tokyo fish market in a little over 24 hours. The diversification of production for export has also gone hand-in-hand with local interest and demand for new foods particular as migrant groups are often involved in the production, export and domestic consumption of some of these items (Wood 1977). Nevertheless, as noted above, the fact that people's experience of taste, flavours and produce is usually broadened while they have been travelling has probably had the greatest impact on Australian and New Zealand foods.

The character of modern Australian and New Zealand food has always been dependent upon overseas travel and trade. However, from the end of the Second World War culinary tastes began to change with the impact of immigration and increased numbers of Australians and New Zealanders travelling overseas as part of their OS (Australian slang for overseas trip) or OE (New Zealand slang for overseas experience). Such travel was usually undertaken by those who had finished further education before embarking on full-time employment. This cultural behaviour is significant not only because it meant that people's culinary experiences were being broadened but also because it was being undertaken precisely by the group of people who would have the level of disposable income to pay for the continued experience of what they tasted overseas when they returned. Furthermore, those who travelled overseas also tended to be those who would and could write about those experiences. Indeed, the travel patterns of Australians and New Zealanders abroad has matched the evolution of food taste. In the early 1950s the OE concentrated on Britain and France as did the domestic restaurant scene. By the early 1960s Italy began to be represented and by the late 1960s wider Mediterranean influences from Spain and Greece were apparent. As Evans (1973: 78–79) noted, 'Increasing travel abroad, especially by young people, helped to develop interest in drinking wine with meals. And after drinking some of the very poor quality ordinary wines of France and Italy they have learnt to appreciate the quality of the ordinary quaffing wines made in Australia.'

As Australians and New Zealanders began to travel to Asia in the 1970s so Asian food influences began to emerge until the 1980s and 1990s when Australian and New Zealand food combined tastes and cooking styles from all over the world in a seemingly post-national cuisine covering everything from Lamingtons (a chocolate and shredded coconut covered square of cake sponge) to lemongrass (Campbell 1997). The tourist exchange of taste is not just one-way though. In the 1990s in particular the Pacific Rim flavours of Australia and New Zealand have become extremely influential in the United Kingdom restaurant scene with Australian and New Zealand chefs highly sought after (Gordon 1999), in much the same way as the flying winemakers of Australia and New Zealand have helped improve old world wine by introducing new world winemaking techniques. As Webb and Whittington (1997: 10) noted, 'Ten years ago, Australian chefs travelled to work in the best restaurants of Europe and the US, honing skills to take back home. Today their talent is being exported and, like Australian wine-makers who have changed wine production and wine styles globally, their informed plurality will impact and influence the way food is cooked and served the world over.'

The combination of migration and travel and the consequent shift from the British food customs of the culturally dominant nineteenth-century European settlers (Simpson 1999) has therefore contributed greatly to what is eaten and produced as well as how it is eaten. Outdoor and sidewalk eating, virtually unknown in the 1960s and the 1970s (it is likely that you would have been arrested!), are now part of local gastronomy. In fact, in New Zealand until the mid-1990s draconian licensing laws and food regulations all but ruled out sidewalk cafés and eating and drinking outdoors (Beckett 1998). However, while New Zealand may be a latecomer to the café scene prevalent throughout Europe for decades, it has wasted no time in catching up. Café and *al fresco* dining is now common in even the most remote parts of New Zealand. In the main centres of Auckland, Wellington, Christchurch and Dunedin this has developed into a wide range of bistros and cafés, offering everything from Thai cuisine to Italian style espresso bars or a unique blend of New Zealand cuisine and popular culture.

As in Australia, cafés and wine bars have been crucial in the development of New Zealand cuisine (Mitchell and Hall 2001a). Beckett (1998: 59) suggests that in the past (even the recent past and in some traditional tearooms) New Zealand food typified by 'solid fare like rock cakes, Anzac biscuits and slabs of bacon and egg pie' were typical. However, she continues, with the advent of the sidewalk café fresh New Zealand ingredients are simply prepared to form a unique cuisine. In 1997 Prime Minister Jenny Shipley (the then Minister of Transport), also, recognized the important role of café society in New Zealand.

> I want to encourage New Zealanders to enjoy the 'café society' trend that is emerging and drink in moderation. People of all ages can now enjoy the company of friends and family over a choice of refreshments. That's much healthier for our society than people drinking simply for the sake of getting drunk.
>
> (Shipley 1997)

It is possible to suggest two (largely circumstantial) reasons for the rapid development of New Zealand café society. As New Zealanders have been exposed to overseas café culture (through international travel and media) they have become increasingly educated and discerning. Increasing numbers of travellers of varying nationality, too, are creating demand for café style dining in New Zealand, particularly as dining is the number one activity of international visitors to New Zealand (Hall and Kearsley 2001). Conversely, local chefs and entrepreneurs have, as a result of their own exposure to other café cultures, developed innovative and experimental café products. It is possible to debate the relative influence of both supply and demand factors. Regardless though, travel and tourism have had a crucial role in changing New Zealand cuisine, a point which can be further illustrated through a discussion of the development of New Zealand fusion cuisine.

Since the 1970s New Zealand cuisine has undergone a rapid and dramatic transformation that has given rise to 'Fusion', 'Pacific Rim' or 'Cross-cultural' cuisine. Fusion has developed as a global culinary phenomenon in the 1990s that 'in the very simplest of terms . . . is the fusion of flavours and techniques from both the West and the East' (Judelson 1997: 7). Chefs who have travelled to new regions of the world (Australians and New Zealanders in Asia or Asian chefs in

America for example) have combined techniques and flavours from their 'home' country with local products and techniques from their adopted country. For Michael Lee-Richards, chef at Michael's, Christchurch, New Zealand 'Fusion food has happened because of the invention of the jet plane and subsequent massive movement of human beings across the planet, and the fact that they brought their taste buds with them' (Judelson 1997: 8).

This cross-pollination of ideas and flavours has been particularly fertile for New Zealand chefs, as 'being from a smaller, more isolated country, the Kiwis went abroad for their "OE" (Overseas experience), picking up ideas magpie-like from around the world. The effect was a bit like a convent girl let out in Soho. Suddenly all the shackles were off' (Beckett 1998: 57). A particularly pertinent example is that of Peter Gordon, Kiwi and chef at the award winning Sugar Club in London.

> In 1985 I went to Bali and spent the next year travelling through Asia on my way to Europe. I was amazed by the food, religions, smells, colours, pace of life and, above all, by the brilliant people I met. Travelling through Indonesia, Malaysia, Singapore, Thailand, Burma, Nepal and India, I developed a great fondness for chillies, coconut, bamboo, spices, vegetables, relishes and anything warm and sunny. It was the most wonderful year of my life.
>
> (Gordon 1997: 8)

In a similar process to the development of the New Zealand café society, it is also possible to suggest that the increasingly well travelled New Zealand culinary palette has began to demand more taste sensations and that this too has allowed chefs to develop fusion dishes. Judelson (1997) expands:

> More people are able to travel further afield, so enjoying the opportunity to experience a wider range of foods. There has been an explosion of food coverage in the media, newspapers, magazines and the television, and the retail industry has responded to the demand created by enlivened interest. An ever-growing range of products is available at supermarkets and other stores, the equipment and utensils are easier to find, and we experience this style of food at more and more restaurants. Which brings us back full circle to the opportunity. As new foods, techniques and styles are absorbed into our culture, so they become the norm.
>
> (Judelson 1997: 8)

While fusion cuisine is not unique to New Zealand the rate at which it has developed is. 'Having thrown off the colonial legacy, New Zealand cooking now represents one of the world's most exciting and innovative cuisines' (Beckett 1998: 56). Beckett went on to argue that the evolution of New Zealand's cooking has been very different from that of neighbouring Australia because there was not the same extent of post Second World War European and Asian migration (also see Simpson 1999). However, such an observation is only partly true, as there have been substantial influxes of Indians and Pacific Islanders since the 1970s as well as a small but significant Vietnamese and Thai immigration. In the case of New Zealand the OE has probably played a slightly more important role than in Australia although, critically, the level of institutional change in New Zealand rural areas from the 1980s on was significantly greater than that of Australia and the need to find new markets and products correspondingly more important (Hall *et al.* 2000a).

A more recent development in Australian and, to a lesser extent, New Zealand food is the promotion of indigenous foods. Possibly as a result of a strengthening national identity an Australian interest in wild and indigenous foods started to occur in the 1970s and found its way into the restaurant scene in the late 1980s and onto the national tables in the 1990s (Bruneteau 1996). The role of restaurants such as Edna's Table (Kersh and Kersh 1998) has proved highly influential in persuading European Australians that indigenous food can be enjoyable (Saunders 1999). However, while restaurant patrons have assisted in promoting indigenous foods, the tourism component has also become important. Kangaroo and emu are animals that are significant not only because they are on the Australian national crest of arms but also because they are good to eat. Moreover, indigenous fruits and greens are also being utilized for cooking. South Australia in particular has utilized indigenous foods as part of their overall gastronomic promotion while a number of resorts and tour companies even offer special packages to harvest and then cook with indigenous foods. In New Zealand bush foods are not as well developed as part of the hospitality and tourism industry although a Wild Foods festival has now been established in Hokotika on the West Coast of the South Island. In addition, there is continued interest in the harvesting of wild game such as boar, deer and goat which is slowly becoming available to both the domestic and the international market.

At the start of the new millennium there have been major changes in the consumption and production of food in Australia and New Zealand compared with fifty years previously. Such changes are not only the result of the industrialization of the food production process and changes in consumption brought about by socio-demographic change, they are also the result of increased mobility which has provided for both migration to these countries and travel which has allowed an awareness of 'foreign' tastes to emerge only for them to be brought back and integrated in the development of 'fusion' cuisine. However, the developing interest in fusion cuisine and local food systems is not just a passive process. The challenge for local economic and gastronomic development is to develop strategies that enable the promotion and expansion of regional and local foods in a manner that improves their positioning in the marketplace and it is to this issue that the chapter will turn.

Strategies for promoting sustainable local food systems

Strategies to integrate tourism and cuisine in order to promote economic development and the creation of sustainable food systems occur at national, regional,

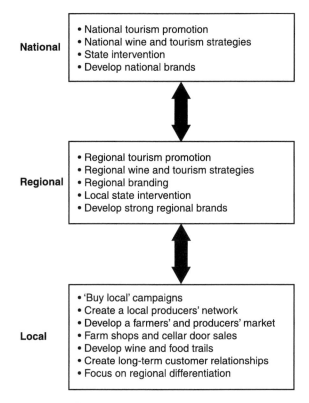

Figure 11.2 Relationship between national, regional and local strategies

and local levels. Ideally, these levels should be integrated in order to maximize the likelihood of policy success. However, often the reality is that different levels of government and industry will undertake their own initiatives without consulting or cooperating with other levels. As Figure 11.2 indicates there are a number of mechanisms for promoting sustainable food systems utilizing the relationship between wine and food each of which operates most effectively at particular levels. Although intervention by the national and local state will occur at all levels it is very common for the policy activities at the higher level to be implemented at the lower level in order to achieve targeted regional and local development goals. This approach has been particularly common within the European Union and in federal states, such as Australia (Hall *et al.* 2000b). The following section provides examples of the different strategies in Australia and New Zealand.

Promoting a country: creating national links between food and tourism

When one product does well overseas there are spin-offs for others. As a country's trade in food and drink develops, it has an effect on tourism.

Similarly, visiting a country and enjoying its products can create a market for those products elsewhere. New Zealand has used this technique to advantage with a number of products, such as wine.

(Bramwell 1994, in Mitchell and Hall 2001b)

The link between tourism and the development of the New Zealand wine and food industries has given rise to opportunities for the co-branding of a number of New Zealand products. In 1994 the New Zealand Tourism Board (NZTB) entered a joint marketing programme with Air New Zealand and Silver Fern Holidays to capitalize on the export success of New Zealand wine to Canada (New Zealand Tourism News [NZTN] 1994). The headline of the article reporting the Canadian venture (NZTN 1994) was 'NZ's wines attract Canadian visitors'. The NZTB combined demographic information with consumer profiles of New Zealand product sales to target key markets in urban centres through the Canadian travel magazine *Latitudes*. The issue featured New Zealand, its wines, wine regions and wine heritage and included a recipe insert called *A Taste of New Zealand*. Readers were offered three 'FIT [free and independent traveller] orientated wine trail tours' (NZTN 1994).

Similar campaigns have also been held in conjunction with food exporters. A 1997 NZTB marketing campaign in four of its key markets involved both tourism wholesalers and two non-tourism partners – Zespri (New Zealand kiwifruit brand) and ENZA (export division of the New Zealand Apple and Pear Marketing Board). The Australian campaign promoted a broader range of products than previously, including 'fine food and wine' (NZTN 1997: 6). One advertisement stated 'We're not ones to brag, but our wines are winning awards, even in France' (NZTN 1997: 6).

Food, export and tourism were regarded as ideal partners for joint marketing activities because they target consumers with a high discretionary income (NZTN 1994), utilize similar brand statements based on New Zealand's 'clean-green image' (Wine Institute of New Zealand n.d.) and reflect and promote the distinctiveness of regions (Mitchell and Hall 2000). Recognizing the importance of the relationship between images of food exports and tourism, the NZTB and *TradeNZ* now jointly market products under the *'New Zealand Way'* brand and *'Fern'* logo. Launched in 1993, *New Zealand Way* is an international branding exercise that identifies, positions and markets quality New Zealand products. It was developed after it was recognized that:

New Zealand is not top of mind internationally and whilst generally positive images exist they lack clarity and consistency. Research showed that while New Zealand was generally regarded as a distant and friendly country, with a strong 'clean and green' association, this was usually a vague understanding and did not translate into competitive advantage. In some developing markets, customers had little or no perception of New Zealand at all.

(New Zealand Way 1998)

The '*Fern*' brand and logo has now been registered in forty-four countries across the globe. New Zealand Way utilize a range of events, advertising, promotional activities and imaginative public relations exercises developed around themes such as '*Fresh The New Zealand Way*', '*Taste The New Zealand Way*' (both associated with food and wine products) and '*Experience The New Zealand Way*' (associated with tourism activities). In 1998 the 170 New Zealand Way 'Brand Partners' jointly accounted for 20 per cent of New Zealand's foreign exchange earnings (NZ$4 billion, €1.8 billion) and represented the top 20 per cent of New Zealand companies (New Zealand Way 1998). Some of the more well known Brand Partners include, amongst others: AJ Hackett Bungy (Queenstown) Ltd, Helicopter Line, Air New Zealand, Quality Hotels Ltd, Corbans Wines, Steinlager (beer), ENZA, Anchor (butter and dairy products), Fernleaf (dairy products) and Cervena (farmed deer) (New Zealand Way 2000). The New Zealand Way and NZTB promotions are examples of national level advancement of the relationships between food and tourism. However, while they may work effectively at the national level and will promote broad level awareness of produce, the costs of participating in these strategies is prohibitive to most small food producers and even local food producers networks may not have the financial resources to be involved. For example, the Australian national wine and food tourism strategy has been substantially criticized for being steered to meet the interests of large export oriented companies even though the majority of visitors to wineries are domestic and the large number of wineries in Australia are only small operations (Macionis and Cambourne 2000).

Regional strategies

At the regional level promotion and branding are extremely common strategies to link food with tourism. In an effort to capitalize on and maximize the tourism potential of the wine industry, several Australian States have instituted specific wine and food tourism bodies to facilitate and coordinate the development of wine tourism. In 1993, the Victorian State Government established (and funded) the Victorian Wineries Tourism Council (VWTC), to develop and implement tourism strategies to promote Victoria's wineries and wine regions. With wine and food experiences becoming one of the main foci of the tourism drive in South Australia, the South Australian government developed a State Wine Tourism strategy and formed the South Australian Wine Tourism Council (SAWTC) in 1996, charged with 'raising the profile of, and championing wine tourism in South Australia' (South Australian Tourism Commission 1996: 8).

The marketing opportunities of wine promotion are also seen as having great potential for increasing the benefits of regional tourism in New South Wales (NSW), with former NSW Tourism Minister, Mr Brian Langton, stating that 'NSW will embrace food and wine as an integral part of the visitor experience, and the focus of food and wine will broaden the destinational appeal of NSW, and encourage more first time visitors to come back for seconds' (Langton 1996). While NSW has yet to establish a formal wine tourism body, it has developed a

Food and Wine in Tourism Plan and established a culinary tourism commit-tee. Interestingly, in all three cases the development of wine and food tourism initiatives occurred because of the financial backing and policy involvement of the relevant state governments and state tourism organizations. The reasons for this are complex but relate primarily to the perceptions by food producers of the tourism industry and the identification of their core business activities.

Hall *et al.* (1997/1998) noted several barriers to creating effective links between wine producers and the tourism industry which can be extended to the majority of primary producers in Australia and New Zealand, including:

- the often secondary or tertiary nature of tourism as an activity in the wine industry;
- a dominant product focus of wine makers and wine marketers;
- a general lack of experience and understanding within the wine industry of tourism, and a subsequent lack of entrepreneurial skills and abilities with respect to marketing and product development; and
- the absence of effective intersectoral linkages, which leads to a lack of inter- and intra-organizational cohesion within the wine industry, and between the wine industry and the tourism industry.

The state food and wine tourism organizations and strategies included a num-ber of marketing, product development, and research activities and initiatives which were designed to overcome these critical developmental issues and facilitate inter-industry integration. Indeed, the formation of specific organizations such as the VWTC, SAWTC and the New South Wales Culinary Tourism Advisory Committee provide the basis for explicitly establishing the wine and food indus-try's profile and position within the tourism sector. They also potentially establish a framework for:

- facilitating the acquisition of tourism and/or wine industry skills and understanding;
- developing an overall wine tourism product; and
- creating and fostering inter- and intra-industry linkages.

In addition, the research activities of organizations such as VWTC and the SAWTC, which aim to quantify the value of tourism and identify the distribution of benefits arising from tourism for producers, may assist in diluting the common producer perception that cooperative arrangements between the wine, food and tourism industries benefit only the tourism sector (Hall *et al.* 1997/1998).

The Australian Bureau of Industry Economics (BIE) (1991a, b) identified four potential roles for government in the development of networks:

- disseminating information on the opportunities created by networks;
- encouraging cooperation within industries through industry associations;
- improving existing networks between the private sector and public sector

agencies involved in research and development, education and training; and
- examining the effects of the existing legislative and regulatory framework on the formation, maintenance and breakup of networks relative to other forms of organization, such as markets and firms.

In the case of wine and food tourism in Australia, government has directly utilized the first three roles in the creation of specific organizations and/or the provision of funding for research, education, cooperative strategies and mechanisms, and information provision. The BIE (1991a,b) considered information gaps to be a major factor in the impairment of network formation. Indeed, there are substantial negative attitudes towards tourism by wineries and some food producers, whereas tourism organizations tend to be far more positive towards the wine and food industry. This situation is reflective of Leiper's (1989) concept of tourism's partial industrialization that suggests that businesses need to perceive that they are part of the tourism industry before they will formally interact with tourism suppliers. Although New Zealand shares numerous similarities with Australia in terms of attitudes of producers towards the tourism industry there has been virtually no government involvement in trying to create networks or producers beyond having large producers participate in cooperative marketing and branding schemes (Hall *et al.* 1997/98). In Australia innovation and the creation of networks has occurred in great part at the regional level because of state involvement; in New Zealand where innovation has occurred it has been because of champions and individual innovators who have been able to generate local interest and involvement.

Creating local networks

Several models of local network development are utilized in food systems (Figure 11.3). The classic industrial model of the food supply chain of producer-wholesaler-retailer-consumer all linked through transport networks has provided for a relatively efficient means of distributing food but it has substantially affected the returns that producers get as well as placing numerous intermediaries between consumers and producers. The industrial model has allowed for the development of larger farm properties, reduced labour costs, and supported export industry, but it has done little to promote sustainable economic development and food systems. In tourism terms this relationship has been utilized in national branding and promotion when multiple supply chains are bundled together to attract the foreign customer.

One alternative is to create a direct relationship between producers and consumers. This can be done by direct marketing and 'box deliveries' (the delivery of a box of seasonal produce direct to the consumer). In relation to tourism, an important direct relationship is the opportunity for the consumer to purchase at the farm or cellar door, allowing the consumer to experience where the produce is from and the people who grow or make it, thereby, creating the potential for the development of long-term relationship marketing. Such direct sales are extremely

Producer   Wholesaler   Retailer   Consumer

A) INDUSTRIAL FOOD SUPPLY CHAIN

Producer

Consumer

B) USING FARM OR CELLAR DOOR SALES OR DIRECT BOX SALES

Producers   Consumer

C) PRODUCERS COOPERATE IN RUNNING A MARKET AND/OR UNDERTAKING
JOINT PROMOTION CAMPAIGNS

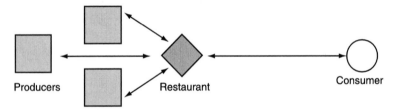

Producers   Restaurant   Consumer

D) PRODUCERS SUPPLY LOCAL RESTAURANT WITH PRODUCE

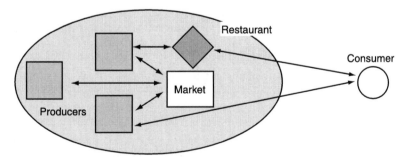

Restaurant

Consumer

Market

Producers

E) MULTIPLE SETS OF RELATIONSHIPS OPERATING WITHIN A NETWORK
PROVIDING A COOPERATIVE BASIS FOR BRANDING AND PROMOTION

Figure 11.3 Creating different supply chains and local food systems

popular with small wineries in Australia and New Zealand and are often utilized by peri-urban and rural producers who are located close to urban centres where they can take advantage of the daytrip market. Nevertheless, such individual developments while useful at the business level and adding to the overall attractiveness and diversity of a location do not constitute a network relationship that can promote a region more effectively.

Cooperative relationships between producers provide the basis for the creation of producer networks that can pool resources to engage in local promotion and branding and undertaking research (Hall *et al.* 1997/1998). In addition, the pooling of resources can also lead to the development of new products such as produce markets. For example, in the case of the Yarra Valley Regional Food group in Victoria, Australia, a group of small producers pooled their resources to run a series of farmers' markets to sell and promote their produce and that of the region. In 1999 they ran four markets. In 2000 they ran eleven and helped generate substantial publicity for the region (Halliday 2000).

Another model of generating local food production is the use of a restaurant to act as the conduit by which local produce is presented to tourists. The development of local purchasing relationships by restaurants can have a substantial impact on local produce as it can assist in developing quality produce and allow producers to gain a clearer understanding of how their produce is being used, as well as providing a guaranteed sales outlet for their produce. In the case of the latter the knowledge of a guaranteed minimum income may allow producers the opportunity to expand production and find other markets for their produce. For example, in the case of both the Barossa Valley in South Australia and the Marlborough region in New Zealand, restaurant local purchasing patterns have significantly assisted the diversification of produce as well as promoting artisan foods and local wines. Similarly, West Auckland restaurants have decided to support their local wine industry by offering only their products (Thompson 2000).

Finally, we arrive at the ideal model of multiple sets of producer and consumer relationships operating within a formal network structure which provides for branding and promotion. In the case of Hawkes Bay in New Zealand, such developments have occurred primarily because of several local champions of the need to promote Hawkes Bay collectively, as they saw that their own individual businesses would be more successful if there was a strong brand and producer network. Indeed, following their formation in July 2000 the Hawkes Bay wine and food group had developed a food and wine trail produced brochures, have improved signage and have engaged in more effective joint promotion strategies. Indeed, such has been the success of the group that local government is having to respond to their initiative. In November 2001 Hawkes Bay also hosted the second New Zealand wine and food tourism conference as part of the development of a national food and wine tourism strategy. However, unlike the Australian examples discussed above, such initiatives have been primarily championed by the private sector rather than having occurred because of government involvement. This bottom-up development of networks contrasts with the Italian experience described by Antonioli Corigliano in Chapter 10 of this volume.

Conclusions: from fusion cuisine to food networks

> It will be interesting to look in on the Australian family in the year 2000. Will we see a highly sophisticated group in an air-conditioned, multi-storey, kitchenless apartment. Eating a pre-cooked frozen meal of prefabricated meat and vegetables, reconstituted in a micro-wave oven and sipping synthetic fruit juice, formulated liquids or perhaps even swallowing a modular pill? Or will we find they have returned to nature and do-it-yourself living, as naked and hirsute they eat their stone-milled, wholemeal, home-baked bread, 'organic' vegetables and home brewed beer?
>
> (Turner 1977: 74)

This chapter has argued that the factors leading to the development of fusion cuisine in Australia and New Zealand are related to the development of strategies to promote local food systems and economic development. Both are a result of globalization. They are interconnected because inasmuch as various facets of globalization have affected the production and consumption of food, those same dimensions can be utilized to promote local foodways, identity, and economic development.

Tourism is integral to contemporary foodways in Australia and New Zealand. Although not the only factor, travel has allowed Australians and New Zealanders to encounter different cuisines of the world as well as identify opportunities to diversify their own rural economies. In addition, the relationship with tourism is being utilized to more effectively brand national and regional foods as well as supply tourists directly in the expectation that this may create further demand when they return to their home countries. At the local level the development of networks is crucial to this task and also allows for the pooling of resources between small enterprises. The quote from Turner above nicely sets the two extremes of Australian and New Zealand foods out for the reader. At one extreme the food reflects much of the industrialization of food as a whole. However, at the other extreme Australia and New Zealand are experiencing a dramatic upsurge of interest in artisan foods, food markets and promoting regions on the basis of their local produce. In the global market long-term competitive advantage will be gained by differentiation on the basis of what is unique to a place, not on the production of low-value undifferentiated product. Promotion of the interrelationships between food and tourism should therefore continue to be an essential component of the place marketing and development mix if rural places in Australia and New Zealand are to thrive in the global food environment of the twenty-first century.

References

Baker, T. (1999) 'Australia's foodways: an overview', *Australian Folklore* 14: 212–221.

Beckett, F. (1998) 'More than mutton', *Decanter*, 23: 56–59.

Bruneteau, J. (1996) *Tukka: Real Australian Food*, Sydney: Angus and Robertson.

BIE, The Australian Bureau of Industry Economics (1991a) *Networks: A Third Form of Organisation*, Discussion Paper 14, Canberra: Bureau of Industry Economics.

BIE, The Australian Bureau of Industry Economics (1991b) 'Networks: a third form of organisation', *Bulletin of Industry Economics* 10: 5–9.

Campbell, J. (1997) *Bloody Delicious! A Life With Food*, Sydney: Allen and Unwin.

Evans, L. (1973) *Wine*, Melbourne: Lothian Publishing.

Gordon, P. (1997) *The Sugar Club Cookbook*, London: Hodder and Stoughton.

—— (1999) *Cook at Home with Peter Gordon*, London: Hodder and Stoughton.

Hall, C.M., Cambourne, B., Macionis, N. and Johnson, G. (1997/1998) 'Wine tourism and network development in Australia and New Zealand: review, establishment and prospects', *International Journal of Wine Marketing* 9(2/3): 5–31.

Hall, C.M. and Kearsley, G.W. (2001) *Tourism in New Zealand: An Introduction*, Melbourne: Oxford University Press.

Hall, C.M., Longo, A.M., Mitchell, R. and Johnson, G. (2000a) 'Wine tourism in New Zealand', in C.M. Hall, E. Sharples, B. Cambourne and N. Macionis (eds) *Wine Tourism Around the World: Development, Management and Markets*, Oxford: Butterworth-Heinemann, pp.150–175.

Hall, C.M., Johnson, G., and Mitchell, R. (2000b) 'Wine tourism and regional development', in C.M. Hall, E. Sharples, B. Cambourne and N. Macionis (eds) *Wine Tourism Around the World: Development, Management and Markets*, Oxford: Butterworth-Heinemann, pp. 196–225.

Halliday, J. (1994) *A History of the Australian Wine Industry 1949–1994*, Adelaide: Winetitles.

Halliday, S. (2000) Food and regional wine tourism: Yarra Valley experience, unpublished presentation at All for One & One For All: A meeting of minds on the development of food & wine in Hawke's Bay, Ormlie Lodge, July.

Hallpike, P. (2000) 'Australia's foodways – Botany Bay to the packaged present: an overview', *Australian Folklore* 15: 166–176.

Judelson, S. (1997) 'Introduction: what is East-West food?' in S. Judelson (ed.) *East West Food: Food from the Pacific Rim and Beyond, with 10 of the World's Hottest Chefs*, London: Hamlyn.

Kersh, J. and Kersh, R. (1998) *Edna's Table*, Sydney: Hodder and Stoughton.

Langton, B. (1996) *News. Tourism New South Wales. Newsletter* Spring: 3.

Leiper, N. (1989) *Tourism and Tourism Systems*, Occasional Paper No.1, Palmerston North: Department of Management Systems, Massey University.

Macionis, N. and Cambourne, B. (2000) 'Towards a national wine tourism plan? Wine tourism organisations and development in Australia', in C.M. Hall, E. Sharples, B. Cambourne and N. Macionis (eds) *Wine Tourism Around the World: Development, Management and Markets*, Oxford: Butterworth-Heinemann, pp. 226–252.

Mitchell, R. and Hall, C.M. (2000) 'Touristic terroir: the importance of region in the wine tourism experience', paper presented at the IGU Conference, Cheju.

—— (2001a) 'New Zealand café society and fusion cuisine', in C.M. Hall and G.W. Kearsley, *Tourism in New Zealand: An Introduction*, Melbourne: Oxford University Press, pp. 120–121.

—— (2001b) 'Taking advantage of the relationship between wine, food and tourism: joint marketing activities', in C.M. Hall and G.W. Kearsley (eds) *Tourism in New Zealand: An Introduction*, Melbourne: Oxford University Press, pp. 193–194.

Newton, J. (1996) *Wogfood: An Oral History with Recipes*, Sydney: Random House Australia.

New Zealand Tourism News (NZTN) (1994) New Zealand's wines attract Canadian visitors, *New Zealand Tourism News* (February): 8.

New Zealand Tourism News (NZTN) (1997) Increasing focus on destination marketing, *New Zealand Tourism News* (December): 6–7.

—— (1998) Tourism marketing networks to play important role, *New Zealand Tourism News* (March): 5.

New Zealand Way (1998) http://www.nzway.co.nz/Media/discover_nzway.html

—— (2000) http://www.nzway.co.nz/brand_partners.html

Saunders, A. (1999) *Australian Food: A Celebration of the New Cuisine*, Sydney: Landsdown Press.

Shipley, J. (1997) Enjoy the cafe society and drink in moderation, says Jenny Shipley, *New Zealand Executive Government News Release Archive* http://www.executive.govt.nz/minister/shipley/jsn2511.htm

Simpson, T. (1999) *A Distant Feast: The Origins of New Zealand's Cuisine*, Auckland: Godwit.

South Australian Tourism Commission (SATC) (1996) *South Australian Tourism Plan 1996–2001*, Adelaide: South Australian Tourism Commission.

Symons, M. (1993) *The Shared Table: Ideas for Australian Cuisine*, Canberra: AGPS.

Thompson, W. (2000) 'West Auckland restaurants to support local wineries', *The New Zealand Herald*, 13 December.

Turner, C. (1977) 'The Australian national food pattern', in B. Wood (ed.) *Tucker in Australia*, Melbourne: Hill of Content.

Webb, M. and Whittington, R. (1997) *Fusions: a New Look at Australian Cooking*, London: Ebury Press.

Wood, B. (ed.) (1977) *Tucker in Australia*, Melbourne: Hill of Content.

12 Regional food cultures: integral to the rural tourism product?

Sean Beer, Jonathan Edwards, Carlos Fernandes and Francisco Sampaio

Introduction

Food culture is an extremely important part of the total cultural product of an area and many regions of many countries have very distinctive food cultures. Equally tourism results from a region or locality satisfying the demands of the tourist, and these demands frequently include the experience of specific landscapes and environments together with the culture, heritage and hospitality of the area. While food culture is embedded in many forms of tourism it may be argued to be particularly relevant to the development of the rural tourism on offer. Rural tourism is frequently portrayed as being in some way 'green' and was one of the first forms of tourism to be promoted as having the potential to approach the elusive goal of being 'sustainable'. This would imply that there is the potential for a viable tourism industry in rural locations to achieve a balance in the use and development of the inherent natural, human and physical capital of these areas without diminishing the natural capital below an acceptable threshold. The contention that local food production systems, if financially viable, can contribute towards maintaining local economies, societies, cultures and environments provides positive encouragement for looking closely at the role of food both in the tourism industry and within local economies. In the UK, for example, the Countryside Agency has recently launched a campaign called 'Eat the View'. This campaign highlights the link between the food that British people buy and the countryside they visit. Ewan Cameron, Chairman of the Countryside Agency, has said that, 'Purchasing decisions made by consumers can have an important influence on how land is managed' (Countryside Agency 2000). 'Some products, because of the way they are produced, their area of origin or other qualities can help maintain the environmental quality and diversity of the countryside, at the same time delivering real benefits to the rural economy and local communities' (WDFLT 2000).

For society as a whole food is central to the political, social, economic, technological and environmental dimensions of sustainability, and it also represents a major industrial/income-generating sector in its own right. Despite this self-obvious truth there is a significant variation in the attitude towards food in different cultures, a fact which has led to aphorisms such as 'the French live to eat and the British eat to live'. This suggests that these countries have food cultures which have developed independently and are valued quite differently.

Food culture in Britain and Portugal

It is difficult to try to rationalize the development of food culture in Britain over the years (see Beer and Redman 1996; Hardyment 1995 and various chapters in Ritson *et al.* 1986). In reality British food culture is multi-dimensional and Britain has undergone a particularly frenzied period of change since the Second World War. Some would say this is because the British are keen to try new things and are never really happy with what they have. Others would say that it is a reflection of the impoverished traditional food culture of Britain. The first point may be true but the second is definitely not. Britain has a rich traditional food culture. One of the perceived problems with the English food culture and with food culture in general, has been the homogenization or 'McDonaldization' of food culture that has led to a decline in regional distinctiveness. These phenomena and the related areas of social differentiation and self-rationalization are discussed by Germov and Williams (1999). (Also see Ritzer 1993 and 1996; Warde 1997; Beardsworth and Keil 1997.) Conversely while Portuguese society has undergone a remarkable evolution and westernization following the 1974 overthrow of a dictatorial regime that rejected western democratic values and practices for fifty years, food and its associated culture is today clearly manifested in its disparate regions, both urban and rural, continental and island. While Britain and Portugal represent two contrasting situations they share an underestimation of the contribution that food makes to regional and national heritage, economy and environment.

Regional food culture in Britain – the regional distinctiveness of west country food

Regional food culture in Britain has long been undervalued with regard to its richness. For example, the south west of England has a diverse and famous culinary history that features products ranging from clotted cream to cider brandy. The west of England is famous for its pasties and pies. It is said 'give a West-countryman a food ingredient and he'll put it in a pasty' (a pasty is a pastry envelope which may be filled with savoury or sweet or both types of filling), but it does not stop there. The glory of west country food is based upon the wealth of raw materials available from its farms, fisheries, gardens and orchards, and the county of Dorset is an example of all that is good in west country farming, food and cooking. Dorset is famous for its livestock farming. Dairying, beef and sheep-meat production are the backbone of its agriculture, producing high quality milk, butter, cream, cheese, beef and lamb. Breeds of livestock were developed which suited the climate, were associated with the region, and led to the development of natural 'brands' and products. The Dorset Down, Dorset Horn and associated Poll Dorset sheep breeds were all natural brands of Dorset and their meat became appreciated in the specialist local areas of production. Local history has it that the

Dorset Horn developed out of a cross between the local Portland breed and Merino sheep that came ashore after the defeat of the Spanish Armada.

Localities in the west of England give their names to foods that are often later developed nation-wide or maybe even internationally. Cheddar cheese is the classic example. Originally the cheese was named after its native area in Somerset but later the term was applied to cheese made by that particular process, hence the term 'cheddaring'. Although one can now buy New Zealand Cheddar, Canadian Cheddar or Cheddar made in Cheshire, there is still a product from the west of England known as west country Farmhouse Cheddar. This has been registered with the European Union as a product with 'Protected Designation of Origin' (PDO) and is produced on a dozen or so farms, mainly in Somerset but also Devon and Dorset. Dorset also has its own cheese – the famous Dorset Blue Vinny, that has a taste that rivals the very best of any blue cheese (this has also acquired a PDO).

As the fields produced the meat and dairy products so the orchards and gardens produced the fruit. Cooking apples, a wide range of dessert apples and, of course, the cider apples, source of the 'scrumpy' cider to quench local thirsts and itself often used in cooking. Then there are sea fish; mackerel, sea bass and sea trout, together with salmon and brown trout fished together with young eels or elvers from the rivers that inspired the novelist and poet Thomas Hardy. At sea we have crabs, lobsters, scallops, mussels, oysters and other shell-fish. From this wealth of ingredients evolved the cookery for which Dorset and the south west is famed, the food which combined with the scenery and the beaches has made the area a major destination for tourists. 'Squab pie, junket and cider brew, richest of cream from the cow' – so said the songwriter Boulton (date unknown); Dorset lamb, Nob biscuits, Apple cake, Stargazy pie, all these are the food of legends.

However, the success of west country food lies not just in these novelties but in its all round quality drawn by skilled cooks from quality ingredients. Devon 'Red Ruby' Beef is an example of such an ingredient. Although originating in Devon there are several great herds elsewhere in the south west. The meat is well marbled allowing it to cook in its own juices, producing its unique characteristic flavour and fine texture giving it the right 'bite'. Well hung, when tender it is ideal for eating hot or cold and as a component of made-up dishes. For a change there is lamb from the downlands and heaths and pork from traditional breeds. Swedes and kale and the widest range of vegetables 'ancient and modern' contribute to the main courses, whilst fruit, heather honey, clotted cream go to make delicious desserts to be followed by those famous cheeses 'real' Cheddar and Blue Vinny.

Regional food culture in northern Portugal

This north west region of Portugal lying between the valleys of the Douro and Minho rivers, the former famous for its port wine vineyards and the Minho which forms the international border with Spain, shares a granitic landscape with the moorlands of south west England. The region's landforms, soils and climate and annual rainfall, on a par with south west England, together with the wealth, ideas and products of Portugal's colonial times and Portugal's geographic position as a bridge between the Celtic gastronomy of north west Europe and the Euro-African Mediterranean culture of semite origin, has resulted in a food culture of which regional society is fiercely proud. While perhaps an over-simplification one might suggest that the foods of the north of Portugal place great emphasis upon high quality locally produced primary products while further south in Iberia foods are more complex mixtures and make greater use of condiments.

One event of considerable significance historically for the food cultures of the northern regions of Portugal was the introduction of maize or 'Indian Corn' from Brazil. This introduction resolved the previous difficulties associated with the low yields of cereals which had resulted in a major nutritional shortfall and had motivated some of the early exploratory and migratory initiatives. Today the region's many, mainly small farms, produce maize, potatoes, root vegetables, various forms of cabbage, olives and their oil and the unique *Vinho Verde* or 'Green wine'. Livestock is both stall fed, milking cows and pigs, while on the higher ground, goats and the endemic beef cattle *Barroso* graze and bees forage.

As with many other subsistence rural societies, a number of cheeses and a highly diverse range of pork products were produced and many of these have come to characterize the region's food culture. Two of these are particularly well known, *Rojões* – a range of cuts of pork meats and offal served with roast potatoes and *Sarrabulho* – a dish of rice cooked in pig's blood and often served as an accompaniment to *Rojões* (*Rojões com Sarrabulho*). Smoking, one of the oldest forms of preserving meat and meat products, is still widely practised and valued and there is a wealth of smoked pork products ranging from *presunto*, smoked pork shoulders, to the many smoked offal/sausage style products. *Chouriças* (smoked sausages) are commonly made with diced pork meat, added spices (salt, white pepper, red pepper), fresh garlic (optional) and the locally produced red *Vinho Verde* wine. The meat is left marinating for three to four days. In mountain communities it is still the practice to smoke the sausages in the kitchen, hanging them over an (open) fireplace. Several restaurants offer this activity as an attraction. Customers enjoy peeking into the smoke house when the sausages and *presuntos* are hanging, just before they go in for their meal.

Fish was for centuries a vital dietary ingredient and while the poor man's staple form of protein was *Bacalhau* (dried cod fish) originally caught off the fishing grounds of Newfoundland, other fish both from coastal waters (*Pescada à Vianense*) and the rivers (trout and savel – sea trout) as well as regional specialities such as the much prized lamprey are characteristic of the gastronomy of the region (Edwards 1998). The importance of codfish is today reflected in the fiestas that characterize the region, many of which frequently include prayers for the safe return of the codfish fleet. While the cultural value of *bacalhau* is reflected in the fiesta, the cultural value of other foods has been recognized recently with their being awarded PDO status. Nineteen products originating in this northern region have been awarded this accolade representing one quarter of those approved for all of mainland Portugal and the Islands. They include six breeds of livestock (three beef, two goat, one sheep), two cheeses, four smoked meats, one olive oil, three honeys and two 'dry stone' fruits – almonds and chestnuts. Traditional desserts are not as conspicuous as the typical entrées and main course dishes and are more likely to be encountered in private homes. However, the shelves of the *pastelarias* (pastry shops) are covered with a wide range of cakes and pastries with particular egg based confections being claimed as 'typical' in many towns and villages.

The value of food as a constituent of the tourist product

The relationship between food and the local economy has often been implicit in the minds of those in authority but all too often the approach has been very reductionist in nature. Thus there have been specific policies relating to agriculture in the European Union and the Member States but in the past these policies have not been followed through to the final consumer. Also the relationship between food production systems and their effect on the landscape and environment have not hitherto been fully considered. Thus at various stages in the past there have been policies which financially supported farmers to plough up moorland, whilst at the same time they could obtain money not to. Increasing recognition that food is highly interlinked within the local economy and specifically within the tourism industry has led to a more holistic approach which is increasingly being used as a model for policy and action and is illustrated in Figure 12.1 with specific examples from south west England and Portugal.

The horizontal axis shown in Figure 12.1 depicts the 'soul' that characterizes good regional/rural food (Pillsbury 1990): good regional foods produced from local ingredients, together with the hospitality and service that all customers – and it is supposed particularly tourists – value as part of the rural tourism product.

The case study areas: south west England and northern Portugal

In both countries we find evidence of a wide range of local initiatives which seek to encourage and promote the production and consumption of local food, and inevitably the tourist is seen as a key market segment although in neither case do the local actors lose sight of the very real importance of the local market.

South west England

Taste of the West and west country cooking

The original 'Food from Britain' campaign in the 1980s was designed to highlight the rich wealth of British food and produced a co-ordinated promotion and development response for an industry that was considered to some extent to be languishing. Recently this promotional role has been taken over more directly by regional food groups such as Taste of the West, which represents the south west of

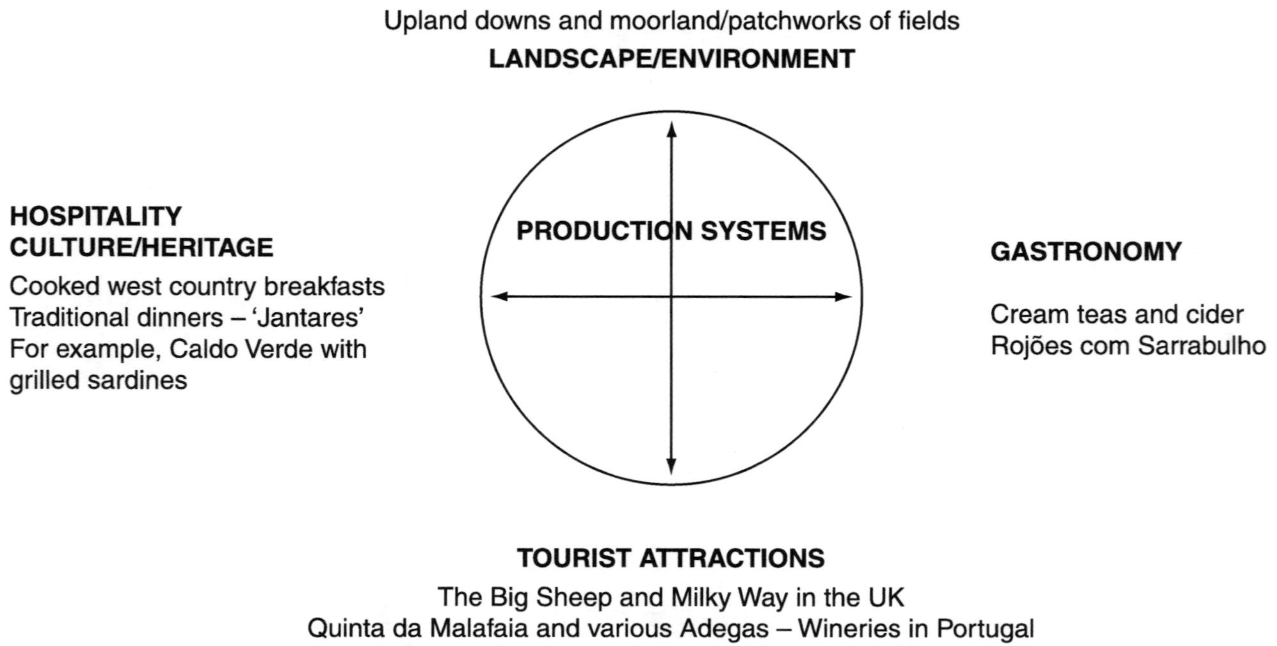

Upland downs and moorland/patchworks of fields

LANDSCAPE/ENVIRONMENT

GASTRONOMY

Cream teas and cider
Rojões com Sarrabulho

PRODUCTION SYSTEMS

TOURIST ATTRACTIONS

The Big Sheep and Milky Way in the UK
Quinta da Malafaia and various Adegas – Wineries in Portugal

**HOSPITALITY
CULTURE/HERITAGE**

Cooked west country breakfasts
Traditional dinners – 'Jantares'
For example, Caldo Verde with
grilled sardines

Figure 12.1 The interrelationship of food production systems, landscape, hospitality, gastronomy and tourist attractions

England. Taste of the West is primarily a group of regional speciality food produ-cers and associated industries. The south west has a high concentration of special-ity food producers with 510 businesses employing 7,200 people giving rise to a turnover in excess of €800 million. In essence it is a limited company led by a board of directors that represent public, industry and community sector interests. It is based in the South West Regional Headquarters of the National Farmers' Union at Exeter. The board is supported by a Chief Executive and a team provid-ing a range of skills relating to food technology, marketing, tourism, catering, hospitality and information technology. Financial support comes from the Minis-try of Agriculture, Fisheries and Food via Food from Britain. In addition money is available for producers via an EU Objective 5(b) Programme. The overall aim of the organization is to work with producers to improve their professionalism and competitiveness. This work is focused in five principal areas. These are:

1   Promotion/marketing.
2   Training.
3   Quality assurance.
4   Food awards.
5   Networking.

The board obviously has a role in promoting the products of its members but it also recognizes a broader role in promoting west country food culture. As part of this it has formed a separate company, Westcountry Cooking, whose principle aim is to develop and promote the food culture of the region. Westcountry Cooking focuses on local food and also the evolving culinary tradition of the area. It is a joint initiative led by the National Farmers' Union and Taste of the West and is grant-aided by the EU and the Ministry of Agriculture, Fisheries and Food, under the Objective 5(b) Programme. Specific projects have included the production of cookery books looking at baking, cream and vegetables, a South West Food Finder and the formation of a supporters' club. Members of the club can obtain publica-tions at a 20 per cent discount, invitations and discounted entry to special events, a newsletter and the chance to participate in the Eateries Guide.

The West Dorset Food and Land Trust

An example of an organization working at a more specific local level is the West Dorset Food and Land Trust. The Trust aims to re-connect people to their food and the land. The Trust has tried to put consumers in touch with producers through developing farmers' markets and a community gardens project (WDFLT 2000). In the longer term the Trust hopes to establish a Community Farm which would act as a resource for schools and local residents and also assist new entrants to farming. The Trust is a voluntary organization and registered charity. The commercial operations, typified by the West Dorset Farmers' markets at Bridport and Dorchester, are run by a trading subsidiary called Local Food Links Ltd. There is a move to try to co-ordinate the markets across the county as a whole under one organization, which will probably be called Dorset Food Links Ltd. Farmers' markets are not a new idea. Traditionally farmers would often sell their products direct to the consumer via local markets. Barnstaple, in the county of Devon, has had an active farmers' market for the last thousand years. Most recently this has been based in the historic Pannier Market, named after the baskets that the farmers used to carry their produce in. The market supplies local people with food but is also a tourist attraction in its own right. In some ways Britain re-discovered farmers markets' from Europe and America. In America these markets are linked to other methods of direct supply such as farm shops and box schemes. Good insights into these recent developments are provided by Aylsworth (1990); Lyson *et al.* (1995); Festing (1994, 1995, 1997); Festing and Hamir (1997); Gale (1997) and Pretty (1998).

Local product guides

One output of many of these initiatives has been local product guides. In Dorset, for example, the West Dorset Food and Land Trust put together their first *Local Food Directory* in 1999, for producers in West Dorset. The aim of the directory is for local people, businesses and visitors to be able to buy local food and other products. This development has been adopted by local councils who, under the aegis of Local Agenda 21 have put together a local products directory which also considers wood and land based crafts. The rationale for the project was that 'buying locally grown food helps the rural economy by keeping money in the community and sustaining much needed local jobs. It also helps the environment by reducing the food miles produce has to travel before being sold' (NDDC 2000). There have also been food trails where maps are used so that individuals can travel round an area sampling the food. Food trails are included in both these directories. The Dorset directory is being distributed through a range of outlets including the Tourist Information Centres, thus helping develop the food dimension of the tourism product.

The Dorset and New Forest Tourism Partnership has taken these ideas further. The Partnership has successfully implemented a new project funded by the European Social Fund under the ADAPT Programme. This project (Online Support, Development and Training for small and medium sized enterprises in the South West Tourism Industry – Information and Communication Technology), focuses on providing training opportunities, consultancy and information, much of it via the Internet. The project has developed a local foods directory, collected background information on the food culture of the area and ideas for menus including detailed recipes. The web-based directory has the ability to be continually updated and to provide direct links to the producers themselves. This resource is directed particularly at the industry itself, as a needs analysis in the area of local food is one facet of the work. Even before the web site went live there were enquires from as far afield as America with regard to some of the producers on the initial list.

Portugal

Specialist producers and processors

The poor economic conditions that prevailed in many of the rural areas of the north of Portugal not only resulted in this region being regarded by sociologists as the most 'rural' of all the countries of the EU at the time of Portugal's accession (Belo Moreira 1986), but also severely restricted enterprise and initiative. The changing attitudes in society in the 1980s and 1990s coupled with access to innovative EU funds supported a range of local enterprise initiatives throughout the region. While many of these related to tourism, widely seen at that time as the panacea to all the economic ills of rural Europe, a number of very successful initiatives concerned themselves with food production and processing. These included breeding programmes to re-vitalize traditional breeds such as *Barroso* cattle, one of the breeds awarded PDO status. In addition to support for primary production a range of initiatives have targeted food processing as a conscious attempt to increase the 'added value' of the products such as the production of high quality smoked meats (Minho Fumeiro at Ponte de Lima), and cheeses (Quinta dos Moinhos Novos at Povoa de Lanhoso). These semi-industrial Small and Medium Enterprises (SMEs) are tapping into the increasing market for traditional products. These products are marketed as being 'artisanal' in that they follow some form of traditional production methods. But the real artisan is the farmer who produces individually or, at times, in cooperation with other farmers.

However, the formation of cooperatives which has typified the renaissance of local food production and processing in south west England has only recently begun to emerge in northern Portugal. In the remote area of Barroso, in the province of Trás-os-Montes, cooperatives are slowly emerging. Products accepted as being traditional/ancestral in terms of the particular method of production, linked to a particular region and which have been determined to possess quality characteristics, seek protective status for the name and traditions. The certification of denomination of origin binds producers to the traditional form of production, predesignated and regulated by specifications (Adere-PG, undated). This protection is limited to local producers; SMEs are not eligible. For example, the *Cooperativa Agrícola dos Produtores de Batata de Semente de Montalegre* promotes the *Alheira de Barroso* (a smoked sausage consisting of various meats) and the *Salpicão de Barroso* (thick sausage, very lean, made from pork loin); the *Cooperativa Agrícola de Boticas*, promotes the *Mel de Barroso* (Honey). The cooperatives produce traditional local products (mostly smoked meats) for up-market clientele, and as with the examples from the south west of England these products become certified as 'denomination of origin' or 'indication of geographic origin'. The attribution of certificates requires that certain standards be met. In the case of *Carne Barrosã* (*barrosã* beef) all animals must be fed, exclusively, from local pastures and natural vegetation. In no situation is it permitted to use any substance that may alter the natural growth of the animals. The maintenance of traditional customs of these mountain communities is essential for continued breeding of these animals.

Farmers interested in certifying their products must meet rigorous standards set by the *Associação Interprofissional para os Produtos Agro-Alimentares de Trás-os-Montes*, in accordance with existing national legislation and regulation. For example, the *Presunto de Barroso* (smoked ham) geographic area for certification is limited to the municipalities of Chaves, Boticas and Montalegre. They are subsistence agricultural communities where pork meat assumes a very important role in the local way of life and household economy. Pork and the transformed products, e.g. smoked meats, are part of the local diet. In fact, pork is the base of the diet of families in this agricultural area of Barroso. In a monograph on Montalegre, Rodrigo (1992) states that 'be it a friend or anyone else, will never leave the home of a barrosã family without eating and drinking'. And the food could be nothing other than what the household produces. And what is produced is the 'blessed *presunto* and smoked *chouriças* that the *barrosã* women do so well and with which such pleasantness offers'. These contributions show how cooperative microenterprise can be very successful. Networks are formed permitting people with common interest and skills to cooperate. Those most involved have tended to be women. They receive further skills training to facilitate the significant effort and funding that is necessary and that may present barriers to such local initiatives.

The recent examples discussed above are beginning to complement the two traditional producer associations, for wine and olive oil. *Adegas Cooperativas* (wineries) are to be found in many of the municipalities of northern Portugal (in the Alto Minho region alone there are five such wine cooperatives) and at an even more local level there are cooperatives that work together for the extraction of olive oil. Olive oil is produced in agreement between the provider of the olives and the owner of the extraction facility. The person bringing the olives agrees to leave half of the olive oil produced from his olives, in exchange for the extraction of the oil. The communal extraction facility is common throughout the north of Portugal. However, in the last two years many of these facilities have closed as a result of European Commission inspired regulation.

Local markets

While we have argued above that the UK is re-discovering local farmers' markets there is the danger that the reverse may happen in Portugal. Both the oldest (Ponte de Lima) and biggest (Barcelos) regular local markets in northern Portugal are being heavily promoted as tourist attractions. In addition, travelling stallholders service markets in most towns and villages and the sale of fresh food products characterize many of these 'local' markets. A significant quantity of fresh and processed food products are sold by individual small 'farmers' and producers who today face the challenge of a rapidly expanding supermarket culture featuring not only aggressive Portuguese chains but also international operators. Anecdotal observation over the last fifteen years suggests that the direct farm sales have declined significantly in some markets (Ponte de Lima) but continue to thrive in other localities (Viana do Castelo). While in most markets one may purchase fish, diverse meats, vegetables, fruits, etc., other markets, usually in smaller towns, are held for specific products, i.e. selling livestock, mainly cattle.

Wine routes

The first documentation relating to *Vinho Verde* dates to the year 1216. It was a wine which only the nobility had the pleasure of drinking. *Vinho Verde* became internationally known during the reign of D. João I (late fourteenth century). There are historical records of English merchants purchasing the *Vinho Verde* directly from the region. A depository was established in Viana at the mouth of the River Lima and between 1599 and 1640 trade flourished. After Portugal's war with Spain the trade ended. In the middle of the seventeenth century the English returned for the wine trade but developed the industry in Porto, replacing the demand for the *Vinho Verde* with a demand for fortified red wine – port.

Along with other wine producing countries of Europe, Portugal has embraced the wine route concept developing this tourism product in the Douro (port wine), the Alentejo and in the green wine region of the Alto Minho. This initiative, organized by the association of green wine viticulturists, seeks to build other dimensions of the tourism product around this 'attraction'. The *Vinho Verde* route takes visitors to *Quintas* (Estates) throughout the region, where you may sample the wine. But if visitors do not want to do the route, they can visit other locations where sampling is also possible, e.g. Solar do Alvarinho in Melgaço. Other tourist routes have also been established, which promote both the local gastronomy and the wines, e.g. pilgrimages to Santiago. It is projects like these that clearly demonstrate the link between tourism provision and the landscape which in the Alto Minho is characterized throughout the river valleys by the vine trellises (approximately 1.5 m high) which border the majority of the small field plots. Clearly a sustainable demand for this young wine will help to ensure the upkeep of these key landscape features which in themselves are a constituent of the appeal of the Alto Minho to visitors.

Gastronomy/weeks and days/Fairs and Congresses/Certification

Over twenty years ago the Casino in Estoril near Lisbon (the largest in Europe) began hosting Gastronomy Weeks promoting Portugal's regional gastronomies. This initiative was welcomed and adopted by a number of the country's Regional Tourist Boards most notably in the Ribatejo and Alto Minho regions. The Ribatejo Regional Tourist Board has subsequently hosted, on an annual basis, the Gastronomy Fair at Santarem which attracts thousands of visitors, while the Alto Minho Regional Tourist Board has hosted an annual Gastronomy Congress since 1987 and in 2001 hosted its first International Gastronomy Congress. In addition to these large annual events, the Alto Minho Regional Tourist Board both publishes illustrated gastronomy texts (Sampaio *et al.* 1997) and actively promotes 'Local Gastronomy Sundays' in selected restaurants of the region during the low season (February–May). This initiative is truly 'local' in that each municipality promotes its own 'local' gastronomy.

A further initiative has been the proposal to award a 'Certificate of the Atlantic Diet' to promote the Atlantic diet of the Celtic culture in contrast with the Mediterranean diet of southern Portugal. Such certification would not only contribute to the tourism product of the area, but would also, it is hoped, defend certain components of the region's gastronomy. Such a defence is thought to be necessary as certain EU food industry directives would effectively forbid the production and sale of a number of classic dishes, for example *Sarrabulho*. Such certification will be supported by recent Portuguese national legislation which states that 'national gastronomy integrates the intangible heritage that warrants safeguarding and promoting' (Diário da República 2000). According to this legislation, 'a series of actions are being taken to inventory, further value, promote and safeguard Portuguese recipes, with the objective of guaranteeing its unique character, as well as promoting its use, in such a way as to also pass on to future generations'. In the municipality of Paredes de Coura, in the Alto Minho region, a Regional Gastronomy Observatory is being proposed specifically for this purpose.

Regional or national (foodstuffs and their preparation) dishes and products certified as 'denomination of origin', are effectively removed from the remit of EU directives targeting the industrialized food industry. Cheese from Serra da Estrela exemplifies how the production of this specific cheese using traditional methods is permitted, although it does not follow contemporary national standards and legislation in terms of modes of production. This certification of 'denomination of origin' safeguards particularities such as these.

Discussion

Hjalager in Chapter 2 of this volume proposes a typology of added value creation in gastronomic tourism, and Table 12.1 adopts her hierarchy as a framework for

Table 12.1 Hjalager's value added hierarchy as applied to current initiatives in south west England and northern Portugal

Region	Indigenous, value added	Horizontal, value added	Vertical, value added	Diagonal, value added
South west England	Local product guides, Activities undertaken by Taste of the West	West Dorset Food and Land Trust, Farmers' markets	Farm shops, Local food trails	Internet-based, Information and training
Northern Portugal	Specialist producers	Certification	Wine routes, Gastronomic events	

describing the range of local food initiatives current in south west England and northern Portugal.

The two examples which have provided the focus for this study have been taken from two countries which have geographical and historical similarities; the western Atlantic seaboard; Atlantic climate, high rainfall and both located in nations that at one time were the major world power and leaders of the age of discoveries. Equally today they are both regions of their respective countries that have a real commitment to developing a sustainable tourism industry in their rural hinterlands.

Hjalager's 'value added hierarchy' demonstrates that in both regions similar initiatives have emerged which attempt to address and support the interrelationships arising from primary production systems of food, hospitality, landscape and tourist attraction as illustrated in Figure 12.1.

An examination of Table 12.1 demonstrates that many of the initiatives are similar; however, an evaluation of their relative success is more complex because while the process may be similar the context differs. For example, there is a much more vibrant tradition and practice of festivals in northern Portugal many of which while having their origin in religious festivals invariably include a significant 'gastronomic' dimension. While this may be partly explained by differences between a predominantly 'Catholic' society as opposed to a predominantly 'Anglican/Presbyterian' one, these differences themselves may well reflect even older traditions and cultures.

Equally, it is far from clear that such cultural differences are paramount or indeed are of any significance to those who choose to visit these rural areas, as the factors that draw visitors to rural areas are not completely understood. However, attractive landscapes, and good food and drink are demonstrably important along with the peace and quiet, lack of commercialization and the opportunity to relax (Edwards 1991). From the point of view of the host community there is also an increasing recognition that it is desirable if not essential to integrate the tourism economy, whatever its basis in the local wider economy. The initiatives described, along with many others, seek to facilitate such integration by developing local gastronomy using local products to increase the attractiveness of the area for visitors. For example, the recent 'Leisure Charter for Historic Villages' initiative in the Serra da Estrela in central Portugal, by INATEL (Instituto Nacional de Aproveitamento dos Tempos Livres – National Leisure Institute) seeks to combine reviving, analysing and recording local gastronomy with the use of this information to underpin the promotion of ten historic villages in this Spanish border region to both domestic and international tourists (Graça *et al.* 2001). Clearly such initiatives should be seen in the context of rural development and this is confirmed by the range of projects supported by the EU under its LEADER I and II programmes (LEADER – Links between Actions for the Development of the Rural Economy). These programmes have supported among others gastronomy initiatives in Denmark, France, Ireland, Italy, Portugal, Spain and the UK. The range of products supported includes meats, mushrooms, onions and other vegetables, apples and other fruits.

If a demand for these gastronomic products can be identified and matched then the opportunities, not only for creating much needed employment but also for ensuring the maintenance of valued traditional landscapes, are considerable. Investigations by Edwards *et al.* (2000) to determine the image of the Alto Minho clearly demonstrated that the gastronomy was perceived as 'distinctive' as opposed to 'international', and earlier studies by Edwards and Fernandes (1998) demonstrated that the gastronomy of the Alto Minho, while highly valued by Portuguese and Spanish visitors, was less appealing to other nationalities. Such a finding suggests that regional gastronomies are likely to be most appreciated by those with a similar cultural background. As such they may be expected to attract visitors from within a country or across those international borders which some-what artificially divide peoples with a common heritage, such as occurs across the River Minho between Galicia (Spain) and the Alto Minho (Portugal). It is perhaps less likely that potential tourists from Normandy will be as anxious to cross La Manche for a meal of Stargazy pie precisely because of the differing cultural heritage implicit within the phrase 'the British eat to live while the French live to eat'.

Having said that, within the UK west country cream teas are famous and people do travel to eat them. Perhaps if Stargazy pie was renamed 'tourte aux pilchard' and was served 'avec beaucoup de cidre de ferme' visitors might cross over from Normandy. In point of fact the cultural divide between areas like Normandy and the south west of England is not as great as it might seem. Both regions are famous for dairy products, cider and cider brandy or Calvados. If we are looking forward with regard to the development of the tourist gastronomic product of an area such as the south west of England or northern Portugal, communication is central along with the areas of quality, authenticity and innovation.

Quality has been defined in many ways but a given specification at a given price is as good a definition as most. To take advantage of the range of opportunities for local food, it needs to be incorporated into the range of tourist food experiences from the local fish and chip shop to the best restaurants. We can already see schemes developing to encourage short local food supply chains. These have cultural, economic, environmental and post 'mad cow' disease (BSE) and foot and mouth, food safety benefits. All this under the heading of consuming the food of the region. At the same time there is ongoing pressure to increase the literal quality of the offering in the food and hospitality industry. These developments have to fight against the ever present consumer pressure for cheaper food as described in Engel's law (Engel's law is a concept widely used in economics that states that 'the proportion of personal expenditure devoted to necessities decreases as income rises' – see Hill 1980). Problems here will start to manifest themselves in changes to the landscape as a result of pressures on food producers to modify and rationalize their systems of production. One thing that foot and mouth disease must have taught the UK is that people value access to and a view of the countryside. Whether campaigns like 'Eat the View' and increasing government environmental support will offset this degradation and keep the rural communities on the land remains to be seen. The alternative will be the vision of the Welsh poet R.S. Thomas in his *A Welsh Testament* of a countryside that has become a 'museum' preserved for the benefit of visitors (Thomas 1996). At the same time authenticity is increasingly important and will be more and more backed up with quality assurance schemes based on geographical areas, systems of production or other aspects of culture.

Communication is the key in all this. Food has been called 'the new rock and roll' and there is extensive interest in food within society as a whole. There are good examples of food stories within all areas of the media. Radio, television, magazines, papers and the Internet are all being used to deliver varying messages on food. Part of this has been the development of the celebrity chef. Using such celebrities to promote regional food might have value (as Fields suggests in Chapter 3), but messages and agendas have to be well defined. Although developing regional food cultures and personal careers are not mutually exclusive, real examples of success in this arena are possibly not as widespread as people think. The secret of success perhaps lies in the message and the way that it is encoded for the target audience. Generic messages have value, but increasingly there is a need to target markets carefully.

Within all this the challenge is innovation. New products adapted to the needs of new consumers are essential. There is ongoing work looking at this in colleges, universities and within industry. The problem is to innovate without destroying the original product. If you consider that all innovation is merely theft from other traditions this is a real challenge. After all, how do we use the concept of 'fusion cuisine' and maintain our cultural integrity?

In reality all these problems represent opportunities, and the secret to building on established successes is to improve quality, maintain authenticity, communicate and innovate.

References

Adere-PG (undated) *Caderno de Especificações da Indicação Geográfica de Proveniência 'Salpicão de Barroso'; 'Presunto de Barroso'; 'Alheira de Barroso'; 'Sangueira de Barroso'; Caderno de Especificações da Denominação de Origem 'Mel de Barroso'; 'Carne Cachena da Peneda'*, Ponte da Barca: Adere-PG.

AEIDL The LEADER Observatory. Chaussee St-Pierre 260, Brussels, Belgium. (http://www.rural-europe.aeidl.be/).

Aylsworth, J.D. (1990) 'Farmers' markets stage a comeback', *Fruit Grower*, June 1990: 8–9.

Belo Moreira M. (1986) 'An outline of Portuguese agriculture', in *Facts and Figures about Portuguese Agriculture*, Thirteenth European Congress of Rural Sociology, Braga: 1–24.

Beardsworth, A. and Keil, T. (1997) *Sociology on the Menu*, London: Routledge.

Beer, S.C. and Redman, M.R. (1996) 'The relationship between post war cultural shift, consumer perspectives and farming policy', in J.S.A. Edwards (ed.) *Culinary Arts and Sciences. Global and National Perspectives*, Southampton, Boston: Computational Mechanics Publications, pp. 351–362.

Countryside Agency (2000) Eat the view – Promoting sustainable local produce, *The Countryside Agency*, p. 2.

Diário da República (2000) 'Gastronomia Portuguesa como bem imaterial integrante do patrimônio cultural de Portugal', *Diário da República*, I Série B, No. 171, 26 July 2000, Portugal.

Direcção Geral do Desenvolvimento Rural (2000) *Guia dos Produtos de Qualidade*, Lisbon: Direcção Geral do Desenvolvimento Rural.

Edwards, J.R. (1991) 'Guest–host perceptions of rural tourism in England and Portugal', in M.T. Sinclair and M.J. Stabler (eds) *The Tourism Industry: an international analysis*, Wallingford: CAB International, pp. 143–164.

—— (1988) 'Voyages of discovery – an exploration of Portugal's regional foods and cultures', in J.S.A. Edwards and D. Lee-Ross (eds) *Culinary Arts and Sciences ll – Global and National Perspectives*. Proceedings of the First International Conference on culinary arts and sciences global and national perspectives, Southampton, Boston: Computational Mechanics Publications, pp. 327–336.

Edwards J.R. and Fernandes, C. (1998) 'Reflections on different approaches to tourism development in mountain villages of the Peneda Gerês National Park', in D.R. Hall (ed.) *Conference Rural Tourism A Global Perspective*, Ayr: Scotland Scottish Agriculture College.

Edwards, J.R., Fernandes, C., Fox, J. and Vaughan D.R. (2000) 'A brand image for the Alto Minho?', in G. Richards and D. Hall (eds) *Tourism and Sustainable Community Development*, London: Routledge, pp. 285–296.

Festing, H. (1994) *Should Farmers Market Direct to Consumers? America says Yes*, Ashford: Wye College Food Industry Perspectives.

—— (1995) 'Direct marketing of fresh produce', unpublished MPhil. thesis, Wye College, Ashford, Kent, UK.

—— (1997) 'The potential for direct marketing by small farms in the UK', *Farm Management*, 9(8): 409–421.

Festing, H. and Hamir, A. (1997) 'Community supported agriculture and vegetable box schemes', paper presented at a Conference on Agricultural Production and Nutrition, School of Nutrition Sciences and Policy, Tufts University, Massachusetts, 19–21 March 1997.

Gale, F. (1997) 'Direct farm marketing as a rural development tool', *Rural Development Perspectives*, 12(2): 19–25.

Germov, J. and Williams, L. (1999) *A Sociology of Food and Nutrition: the social appetite*, Oxford: Oxford University Press.

Graça, P., Joanez, S. and Graça, E. (2001) 'Promoting tourism through historic villages and local food in Portugal', in J.S.A. Edwards and M.N. Hewedi (eds) *Culinary Arts and Sciences lll – Global and National Perspectives*, Proceedings of the Third International Conference on Culinary Arts and Sciences – Global and National Perspectives, Cairo, Poole: Worshipful Company of Cooks – Centre for Culinary Research, Bournemouth University, pp. 372–379.

Hardyment, C. (1995) *A Slice of Life: The British way of eating since 1945*, London: BBC Books.

Hill, B. (1980) *Introduction to Economics for Students of Agriculture*, Oxford: Pergamon Press.

Lyson, T.A., Gillespie, G.W. and Hilchey, D. (1995) 'Farmers' markets and the local community: Bridging the formal and informal economy', *American Journal of Alternative Agriculture*, 10(3): 108–113.

NDDC (2000) *Local Products Directory. Dorset, The Blackmore Vale, Cranborne Chase, East Dorset Heaths and Purbeck*, Blandford, Dorset: North Dorset District Council.

Pillsbury, R. (1990) *From Boarding House to Bistro*, Cambridge, MA: Unwin Hyman.

Pretty, J. (1998) *The Living Land: agriculture, food and community regeneration in rural Europe*, Earthscan.

Ritson, R., Gofton, L. and McKenzie, J. (1986) *The Food Consumers*, Chichester: John Wiley.

Ritzer, G. (1993) 'The McDonaldization of Society', *Journal of American Culture* 6 (1983): 100–107.

Ritzer, G. (1996) *The McDonaldization of Society*, New York: Pine Forge Press.

Rodrigo, João Martins (1992) *O Presunto e o Fumeiro em Barroso*, Montalegre: Câmara Municipal de Montalegre.

Sampaio, F. (1998) *Domingos Gastronômicos (Roteiro)*, Viana do Castelo, RTAM.

Sampaio, F., Gandra da Lima, R. and Costa, A. (1997) *The Good Food Guide of the Upper Minho Portugal*, Viana do Castelo, RTAM.

Taste of the West (2000) *Welcome to Taste of the West*. Promotional material, Bridport: WDFLT.

Thomas, R.S. (1996) *Everyman's Poetry*, London: J.M. Dent.

Warde, A. (1997) *Consumption, Food and Taste*, London: Sage.

Westcountry Cooking (2000) *Westcountry Cooking*. Promotional material, Bridport: West Dorset Food and Land Trust.

WDFLT (2000) *Local Food From Local Land*, West Dorset Food Links Local Foods Directory 2000/2001, Bridport: West Dorset Food and Land Trust.

13 Still undigested: research issues in tourism and gastronomy

Anne-Mette Hjalager and Greg Richards

Introduction

The various chapters in this volume have examined the relationship between tourism and gastronomy from different theoretical, sectoral and geographical perspectives. It is clear from this review that the relationship between tourism and gastronomy is a relatively new field of research, and much work remains to be done to bring this relationship into focus. This concluding chapter tries to bring together some of the major themes and issues identified in the preceding chapters, develops an epistemological framework in which to place the differing analyses of tourism and gastronomy, and presents areas for future research.

One of the things that struck the research team in their deliberations over gastronomy and tourism was the degree of symmetry between these fields. In both tourism and gastronomy there is a simultaneous scale divergence between small-scale, artisanal production and the growing scale of industrialized mass production. McDonaldization is a concern not just for the gastronome, but the growth of the package holiday industry has transferred the rationalization logic of the fast food industry to the realm of holidays (Ritzer and Liska 1997). This symmetry is also reflected by a growing concern for authenticity as industrialized mass production undermines local foods and 'real' holidays.

As well as sharing problems, however, tourism and gastronomy also seem to have found each other as a potential solution. Tourism offers the opportunity for food producers to add value to their products by creating a tourist experience around the raw materials, as Hjalager has shown in Chapter 2. At the same time, gastronomic experiences can add value to tourism by providing the tourist with a link between local culture, landscape and food, and by creating the 'atmosphere' so essential to a memorable holiday experience.

Many of the chapters in this book have also underlined the need to create a sustainable relationship between tourism and gastronomy. As Scarpato (Chapter 8) has argued, gastronomy must be seen as part of a cycle linking the physical, cultural and gastronomic environments, in much the same way as environmental sustainability is dependent on the functioning of eco-cycles (Bramwell *et al.* 1998). In this perspective, there is a need for sustainable gastronomy as well as sustainable tourism. Some integration between these two perspectives might be possible, although Scarpato argues that gastronomers should be the ones to study sustainable gastronomic tourism. For those in the realm of tourism studies, it might be appropriate for 'gastronomic sustainability' to be considered alongside other facets of sustainable tourism, such as environmental sustainability, economic sustainability, cultural sustainability and political sustainability (Bramwell *et al.* 1998). In such a holistic view of gastronomic sustainability, it may be questioned whether one can continue to endlessly add economic value to the gastronomic product. When one reaches the fourth level of added value identified by Hjalager (Chapter 2) for example, the commodification of gastronomic resources implied might damage the cultural sustainability of the gastronomic system.

Having said this, another feeling prevalent in the research group is that one cannot insulate gastronomy from the outside world and ignore the influence of globalization and localization. The approaches taken to globalization in this volume and elsewhere generally tend to polarize in a pessimistic or an optimistic approach, as Scarpato notes in Chapter 8. The conclusion of most of the authors in this volume seems to be that globalization needs to be utilized as a means of strengthening the relationship between tourism and gastronomy. In most cases, this will mean adopting a creative, innovative approach to national, regional and local cusines. The idea that one can preserve traditional foods and cuisines by freezing them in time conflicts with the reality of social, economic and cultural change that is forcing gastronomies to change and develop, just as they always have done. Differing approaches to the challenges of globalization can be seen in the strategies of Portugal and Spain with respect to their cuisines. Portugal has followed a conservative, protectionist path, designating a number of foods and dishes as national heritage and laying down stipulations about the ingredients and preparation of these foods. This may be an effective way of pre-empting moves by the EU to stop certain foods being produced, but at the same time it results in a 'frozen' gastronomy that inhibits development and creativity. In Spain, as Ravenscroft and van Westering (Chapter 9) show, the use of branding to protect the intellectual property content of gastronomic products combined with an emphasis on regionalization gives a much more flexible basis for creative gastronomy. In Spain, just as in New Zealand, the pressure for change has been external and market driven, while in Portugal the stimulus has been largely internal and protectionist. Time will tell which strategy is more effective, but the New Zealand experience indicates that dynamism is essential to a healthy and vital gastronomy.

More than anything, Hall and Mitchell's analysis of New Zealand gastronomy (Chapter 11) shows how important it is to shift from a product orientation to a market orientation. There are signs that this is happening to a degree in most parts of the world, but there is still a tendency to play down the needs of the consumer, as recent scares over food safety have emphasized. Looking at gastronomy from the point of view of the market also provides a strong link between tourism and gastronomy. Tourists are major consumers of gastronomic products, not just when they are on holiday, but also when they return home.

If tourism and gastronomy researchers are to work effectively together, there is a need for a multidisciplinary approach, as Scarpato has pointed out in

Chapter 4. But it is not just a case of gastronomers learning about tourism, but also tourism scholars understanding gastronomy. Scarparto argues for the expansion of gastronomy studies into tourism studies. We could equally argue for a development in the opposite direction.

What do we need to learn more about? That is one question to be discussed in this chapter. Another main question is concerned with the modes of acquiring new knowledge on tourism and gastronomy. The following section provides an epistemological analysis of studies of tourism and gastronomy.

The creation of knowledge

What is knowledge, where does it come from, and how do we share it? Such questions have puzzled humans for centuries (Audi 1998). If we want to reflect on the direction of future research we have to base our analysis in epistemological theories. Epistemological theories can be classified on a continuum between two extremes. One extreme, 'realism', claims that the 'real' world exists out there, independent of any ideas that humans may have. A classical position was taken by Plato, who argued that our perceptions of the world were only poor imitations of reality and that dialogue and reason (not experimentation and interaction with nature) could bring us closer to an understanding of the truth. The opposite extreme is 'idealism' which holds that knowledge exists only in the minds of people and does not necessarily correspond to anything in the real world. Generalizations and laws of nature are not real, they are constructs of the human minds.

It is self-evident that either of these extremes raise problems. Most philosophers take a position somewhat in between, rejecting the absolutes. The positivists lean towards a realist perspective. Those who consider it impossible to divorce science from action tend to lean towards the idealist perspective (Kolb 1984). Obviously, science and economy are research fields that are more likely to work with discovery according to the platonic view of science, while the arts and humanities will tend to object and claim their rights to participate in the construction and conceptualization of the world. But this is still a much too static way of analysing the development of knowledge, that leaves many aspects unexplained.

Such debates in epistemology and the history of science are of major interest in connection with tourism and gastronomy. In the tourism field there is currently much discussion about the status of this relatively new field of inquiry (Tribe 1997), and gastronomy, which Brillat-Savarin tried to establish as a 'true science' in the early nineteenth century has yet to emerge as a recognized scientific discipline. However, one cannot impute to gastronomy and tourism studies that they dwell firmly in very fixed paradigms. Both are, as noted by numerous authors in this volume, places for marriages of scientific approaches, however odd they may seem in the first place.

The kneading together of two research traditions, tourism and gastronomy, has the potential for a widening of perspectives and creating new knowledge. Knowledge creation, according to Nonaka and Takeuchi (1995) proceeds in the form of a spiral, in which implicit knowledge is structured and transformed into explicit knowledge in the form of theories that in turn can be applied in practice. An important part of this spiral is the 'socialization' process, or the bringing together of existing forms of knowledge which are combined in new ways to generate new knowledge. In this light, knowledge creation proceeds in much the same way as the gastronomic developments charted in this volume. New ingredients, new cooking techniques and new forms of presentation and delivery are combined to produce new dishes, new meal experiences and whole cuisines.

However, like cooking, knowledge creation cannot proceed purely on a hit and miss basis – there needs to be a recipe or an approach that guides the research process. In most established disciplines paradigms have been established, challenged and developed over long periods of time. In tourism and gastronomy, however, such structures are still relatively undeveloped. Although Scarpato in Chapter 8 of this volume argues for putting ontology before epistemology, in practice these two tend to develop side by side, with our knowledge of 'what is' informing our understanding of 'what it means to know' (Crotty 1998: 10). As the previous chapters have presented a comprehensive but relatively unstructured analysis of tourism and gastronomy, it now seems appropriate to draw these pieces of knowledge into an epistemological framework, in order to identify the types of knowledge that still need to be developed. This in turn should inform the practice of gastronomy and tourism, as Scarpato suggests.

Perspectives for future research

Many authors represented in this volume emphasize a need for further research. They stumble over questions that cannot be answered immediately and without more substantial, and often empirical, evidence. For example, Antonioli Corigliano (Chapter 10) introduces the concept of industrial districts as a model for the combined efforts of tourism and gastronomy. However, nobody knows whether this model with its many appealing elements will apply well to tourism and gastronomy. Fields (Chapter 3) reveals that the understanding of consumer behaviour concerning food in tourism and leisure situations lags very dramatically behind. Insights from sociology and psychology have only sparsely been applied to this particular issue, and the cognitive impacts of various tourism/gastronomy initiatives are greatly under-researched. On a more operational level, numerous tourism and gastronomy initiatives, like the ones described by Jones and Jenkins (Chapter 7), are performed without genuine and knowledge producing evaluations.

The issue of tourism and gastronomy deserves substantial investigation to understand the dynamics of the development, and to draw conclusions on a more comprehensive basis. In relation to tourism policies this is important not only to create better understanding of tourism as a social phenomenon, but also to direct public and private investments and to meet the expectations of local communities. However, tourism development should not be the only perspective; the chapters in Part II of this volume show that tourism consumption can stimulate local gastronomy and be an instrument to advance and improve agricultural and food production. From an economic point of view this might ultimately be more important than tourism.

It is a major challenge that food can be viewed from the perspective of many academic disciplines. But the quality of the research is endangered if it attempts to take too much into account at once. Boyne *et al.* (Chapter 6) point out that interdisciplinary approaches are required, but the research questions formulated and the theoretical ideas that lie behind the research are crucial. Otherwise there is a risk of heaping up ever more details.

The challenge is not simply to combine and cross-fertilize different disciplines (Echtner and Jamal 1997). These days, inter-disciplinary or trans-disciplinary approaches are required. One way of developing such perspectives is to concentrate on the type of knowledge that needs to be developed, rather than the subject matter itself. In the following sections we describe a number of different types of knowledge that need to be developed in order to construct a holistic view of the field of tourism and gastronomy. These different perspectives are related to the 'realism-idealism' continuum described above (Figure 13.1).

The anecdotal

Case studies are the basis of a number of chapters in this volume, and they are very frequently used in tourism research. Observations, interviews, surveys, content analysis and other techniques are used to collect data about the case and these are presented in the form of a narrative. A case study can identify relevant issues and the various driving forces that are important for the development of tourism or gastronomy in a particular area. Not surprisingly, it is difficult to be very conclusive, although some studies (for example Antonioli Corigliano, Chapter 10, and Beer *et al.*, Chapter 12) tentatively set up recommendations for a development of a prospective tourism based on gastronomy – and gastronomy based on tourism.

Many worthy anecdotal case studies here and elsewhere demonstrate the love or admiration for a region and its people. The studies are guided by a fundamental curiosity, and the efforts can be compared by enthusiasm expressed of

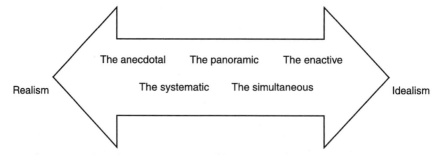

Figure 13.1 An epistemological framework for tourism and gastronomy research

early collectors of antique objects and natural relicts. As if they were fossils, statuettes, bronzes, stones, jewels, fragments of pots or tools, the case studies are stored and displayed in curiosity cabinets. The researchers exhibit their collections in the same way as the collecting emperors presented their rarities – the more special and particular, the better. The organization of the data is guided by aesthetics, not always logic. The explanations are symbolic and labyrinthine, sometimes with a romantic or ideological ingredient that is not necessarily shared by the people of the region.

By comparing case studies with an antiquated mode of knowledge acquisition, we might seem unfair to modern researchers. Don't case studies possess any benefits in contemporary social research? We believe they do.

Case studies can provide valuable insights into specific issues and specific regions. In this sense they are a vital basis for the link between theory and practice pleaded for by Scarpato in the context of modern gastronomy studies. But the time for isolated studies is likely to be over. Case studies should have the added power of comparison, by being integrated into more comprehensive research frameworks. Enhanced benefits of case studies could be created in comparative, possibly transnational, research programmes, where many interlinked studies can influence the establishment of new grounded theory (Strauss and Corbin 1999). This approach has already been developed in embryonic form in some areas of tourism and leisure research (e.g. Bramham *et al.* 1993; Richards 1996), but needs to be applied more widely and in a more structured way.

Tourism and gastronomy could be well-suited to the development of such comparative studies and attempts to construct grounded theory and distinct hypothesis that could be tested more rigorously at later stages (Walle 1997). Examples where such anecdotal approaches would be beneficial, and where a further research effort is particularly needed include:

- The importance of local institutions for the creation of innovative links between gastronomy and tourism.
- The perception of foreign food and adaptive behaviour at home and in the tourist locality.
- The role of tourism in the development of foodways and the development of food traditions in specific localities.
- The invention of new food cultures for tourists: processes, practices and consequences.
- The outcomes, in terms of tourism and tourist satisfaction, of protective, isolationist and innovative food tradition strategies.
- Narratives of landscapes and the influence on the marketing and perception of gastronomy.

The systematic

The systematic approach attempts to grasp a phenomenon, and to organize it into descriptive or analytical categories. Hjalager's chapter in this volume is an example of the systematic approach; Boyne *et al.* (Chapter 6) perhaps another. A systematic approach attempts to map the phenomenon, its background, outcomes, developments, consequences, etc. It constructs classes and sub-classes, a chest-of-drawers in which to place the observed items.

The systematic approach also has its parallels in the history of knowledge. The famous biologist Linné arranged and named plants according to a system that is still in use. He introduced a new scientific methodology that spread quite rapidly to many scientific fields. The analogy to the scientific developments in the eighteenth century and the mode of knowledge creation still has some value today, although we might wish to proceed further than just classification. As tourism and gastronomy are still fairly unresearched subjects, particularly in combination, basic systematization could, however, provide tools and instruments to guide further research. The systematic approach operates with only a few criteria to each object, and it cannot place particular values to the individual items in the classification. The systematic approach does not necessarily tell a story.

Examples where the systematic approach could be useful are in the case of tourism and gastronomy:

- Classes of creolization. The history, the geographical origins, the economic preconditions, the modes of adoption in local eating cultures.
- Types of media influence on regional cuisines and tourism.
- Power relations in the production and supply chains of agriculture/food processing and the tourist industry.
- Regulatory modes for tourism gastronomy at various levels, international, national, regional and private and public.
- Types of gastronomic routes and paths, particularly in relation to their effectiveness and effects on the local economy, society and culture.

The panoramic

Research in the panoramic category is guided by a more or less 'grand' theory or an idea. The researchers want to construct a history or to interpret reality according to a specific point of view, largely to the exclusion of other perspectives.

Chronology is a common organizing principle. Eras of evolution are identified and explained in historical, economic or other contexts. The articles by Scarpato (Chapter 4) and Hall and Mitchell (Chapter 11) utilize this model, Scarpato by analysing gastronomy in a long historical perspective; Hall and Mitchell over a shorter, but crucial, period 'from fusion cuisine to food networks'. Other key words and guiding concepts of the research used in chapters in this book are, for example: professionalization, homogenization and diversity, food safety, reflective eating and meal experiences.

The panoramic view can support – or oppose – any ideology that one can think of. The research takes a perspective that is chosen solely by the researcher, not guided by incidental evidence, as in the anecdotal understanding of knowledge creation, or by the rigidity of system logic, as in the systematic approach.

Most knowledge creation in the social sciences takes place within a panoramic logic. Researchers want to produce explanations of what goes on, how, and why. But panoramic views are highly affected by trends and fashions. Currently, much tourism activity is analysed through the discourses of sustainability, post-modernity and globalization. Planning, on the other hand, seems to have fallen out of favour as a panoramic framework, as have analyses of social classes and the class struggle.

Panoramic research is keen on being useful, but with a veneer of objectivity. Some studies indirectly take sides, for example championing local food producers against McDonald's-style global enterprises, or the preservationist against the change makers. Whether they like it or not, knowledge produced by researchers is transformed into policy recommendations or reworked for guidebooks and interpretation for school classes, tour groups, etc.

There is no doubt that the panoramic approach is the most common. It is applicable to a range of issues that are raised when combining tourism and gastronomy. Examples where this perspective could need further elaboration include:

- Industrial cluster studies, where future research could focus on, for example, identifications of clusters that integrate food and tourism, studies of the driving forces for their establishment and development, the types of networks that link elements together, the innovation processes that ensure a continual renewal, the degree of localization *vis-à-vis* globalization, etc.
- Landscape analysis, the understanding of the beauties of production landscapes, and their co-existence with agro-industrial production and tourism.
- Innovation processes in the agro-tourism and gastronomy tourism product, evaluation of development policies.
- Consumer preferences and behaviour, rituals in eating and drinking during leisure and holidays.
- Consumption of food and drink by mass tourists and independent tourists.
- The stereotyping or protection of food, the impacts of legal instruments.

The simultaneous

The simultaneous approach suspends time and space. In order to surprise and to provoke, it utilizes techniques and interpretation methods that create a 'fake' synchronism. The researchers see themselves as the creators of new views of the world and as questioning established truths.

Tourism and gastronomy are very obvious spheres for dissolution of time and space. Food traditions travel over the globe and, independently of this, the tourists travel to experience food traditions, often with no notion of the dislocations that took place in previous centuries. A number of the contributors to this volume show an analytical interest in such paradoxes. Hall and Mitchell in Chapter 5, for example, point up the difficulties of European nations rejecting 'globalization' or 'Americanization' when European gastronomies owe so much to foodstuffs imported originally from the Americas.

The simultaneous approach supplements the anecdotal, the systematic and panoramic approaches as it transfixes the research and observes the researchers on work. It provides a critical view of the methods and the guiding ideas of research projects.

Challenging aspects for further research include:

- Discourse analysis of research on gastronomy and tourism.
- Reinterpretation of classical writers on gastronomy, such as Brillat-Savarin (1986), in the light of subsequent gastronomic and tourism developments.
- Analysis of media representations of food and travel, such as cook books and TV cookery programmes, and the intertwining of journalism and marketing.
- Analysis of the representation of food and cooking in tourist brochures.
- Analysis of interactive Internet sites featuring gastronomic products for tourists.
- Food and tourism ethics, for example considering the value judgements made about local cuisines by tourists.

The enactive

In this category we include types of research that seek to influence the object of study through action research. We have some examples in this book, where the researchers are closely involved with tourism and gastronomic processes and where they can potentially influence the phenomena they are describing. This is particularly true of Beer *et al.* (Chapter 12) because one of the authors heads the tourist board for one of the study regions. The results of this type of research are often in the form of 'recommendations'. Such studies deal with conceptualizations and strategies, rather than being strictly conclusive in the academic sense, as is expected in the panoramic approach, for example.

It has become far more legitimate for regional universities to involve themselves closely in local development processes, particularly for those located in remote areas. In principle, the networking of industry and universities in the local area is essential to the creation of industrial districts, as mentioned by Antonioli Corigliano (Chapter 10). The existence of the university and its research may even depend directly or indirectly on the prosperity and the demand for qualified labour by the tourist and food industries. These are good reasons to support the industry where possible. The mingling together of vocational and professional training in the universities tends to knit the networks even closer together. The facilities of the universities are crucial for the development of new products, and university staff and students are involving themselves in many other aspects of the development of tourism and gastronomy.

Researchers' participation in local development processes is often met with scepticism from many sides. However, enactive research can be highly beneficial not only for the industry or the regions, but also for the quality of research. Researchers are faced with 'real life problems', which they are obliged to comprehend. Implementation processes of new initiatives deliver most important and up-to-date information for academic research. This may also be one way of answering Scarpato's call to place ontology before epistemology in developing gastronomy and tourism studies.

Examples where an enactive approach could be of interest, also from an academic point of view, are:

- Food safety and quality improvement incentives.
- Branding initiatives.
- Staff qualifications, entrepreneurship and other HRM projects.
- The composition and effects of marketing gimmicks, press and TV promotion, etc.
- Co-operative set-ups, particularly those that are vertical or diagonal in nature (Hjalager, Chapter 2)
- Empowering the tourists: creating new driving forces for food quality.
- Integrating economic, social and cultural values into gastronomy and tourism.

Final remarks

In our view, it is not a case of selecting a single approach to researching tourism and gastronomy: all of the approaches outlined above have merit and can add to our knowledge. Rather we would plead for a more holistic approach to studying tourism and gastronomy, which can take different epistemological positions and disciplinary perspectives into account. As this volume has shown, tourism and gastronomy are complex fields that involve a wide range of resources and actors in their composition. Producing tourism for gastronomers or gastronomy for tourists is like the process of making a meal – a carefully co-ordinated activity that results in a complete and unique experience. Tourism researchers, just like Scarpato's chefs, have often felt themselves to be ignored by mainstream academia. The basic problem for both tourism and gastronomy studies is a relatively isolated position at the edge of established disciplines. Only by integrating different disciplinary perspectives into a creative and innovative view of the world can tourism or gastronomy scholars begin to claim any centrality for their work.

As Bell and Valentine (1997: 11) argue, 'different ways of thinking (through food) can elaborate different theoretical perspectives – and, most fruitfully of all, the *spaces between* different perspectives can open up still newer ways of thinking' (emphasis in original).

We should not succumb to the idea that by adapting or combining all the different approaches noted here the challenge is over. There are clearly many gaps in our knowledge, but simply filling all the gaps is not enough. To become gastronomers we must do more than prepare and eat the meal, we must do so in a reflexive manner. We must ensure not only that all the elements of a good meal are there, but that they work effectively together. In research terms, we should resist the idea that particular forms of research are somehow 'better' than others (e.g. Dann *et al.* 1988) and try to value different research efforts in terms of their contribution to our holistic understanding of the relationship between tourism and gastronomy.

Our experience in writing this book has already crystallized many of our own ideas about future research directions, some which will doubtless be pursued in the context of ATLAS and other tourism and gastronomy networks. Although open networks such as ATLAS are a good way of launching research pro-grammes, ultimately there is a need for structures to support the research effort. The plea by Hjalager in Chapter 2 for combined tourism and food research units seems on the face of it to be a good idea. Practical experience indicates, however, that integration may be difficult, with increasingly social science or management orientated tourism departments diverging from increasingly biological science based food studies. This illustrates the practical problems involved in creating the holistic approach espoused here. A high degree of difficulty, however, does not mean it is not worth trying.

References

Audi, Robert (1998) *Epistemology: A Contemporary Introduction to the Theory of Knowledge*, London: Routledge.

Bell, D. and Valentine, G. (1997) *Consuming Geographies: We are Where We Eat*, London: Routledge.

Bramham, P., Henry, I.P., van der Poel, H. and Mommaas, H. (eds) (1993) *Leisure Policy in Europe*, Wallingford: CAB International.

Bramwell, B., Henry, I., Jackson, G., Prat, A.G., Richards, G. and van der Straaten, J. (eds) (1998) *Sustainable Tourism Management: Principles and Practice* (2nd edn), Tilburg: Tilburg University Press.

Brillat-Savarin, J.-A. (1986 [1826]) *Smagens Fysiologi*, København: Gyldendal.

Crotty, M (1998), *The Foundations of Social Research: Meaning and Perspective in the Research Process*, London: Sage.

Dann, G., Nash, D. and Pearce, P. (1988) 'Methodology in tourism research', *Annals of Tourism Research*, 15: 1–28.

Echtner, Charlotte M. and Jamal, Tazim B. (1997) 'The disciplinary dilemma of tourism studies', *Annals of Tourism Research*, 24, 4: 868–883.

Kolb, David A. (1984) *Experiential Learning. Experience as a source of learning and development*, Englewood Cliffs: Prentice-Hall.

Nonaka, Ikujiro and Takeuchi, Hirotaka (1995) *The Knowledge-creating Company: How Japanese Companies Create the Dynamics of Innovation*, New York: Oxford University Press.

Richards, G. (ed.) (1996) *Cultural Tourism in Europe*, Wallingford: CAB International.

Ritzer, G. and Liska, A. (1997) ' "McDisneyization" and "post-tourism": complementary perspectives on contemporary tourism', in Rojek, C. and Urry, J. (eds) *Touring Cultures: Transformations of Travel and Theory*, London: Routledge, pp. 96–109.

Strauss, Anselm and Corbin, Juliet (1999) *Basics of Qualitative Research: Techniques and Procedures for Developing Grounded Theory*, Thousand Oaks: Sage.

Tribe, J. (1997) 'The indiscipline of tourism', *Annals of Tourism Research*, 24: 638–657.

Walle, Alf H. (1997) 'Quantitative versus qualitative tourism research', *Annals of Tourism Research*, 24, 3: 524–536.

Index